The
Dictionary
of
Unfamiliar
Words

D0963331

The Dictionary of Unfamiliar Words

By The Diagram Group

Skyhorse Publishing

Copyright © 2008 by Diagram Visual Information Limited

All Rights Reserved. No part of this book may be reproduced in any manner without the express written consent of the publisher, except in the case of brief excerpts in critical reviews or articles. All inquiries should be addressed to Skyhorse Publishing, 555 Eighth Avenue, Suite 903, New York, NY 10018.

Skyhorse Publishing books may be purchased in bulk at special discounts for sales promotion, corporate gifts, fund raising, or educational purposes. Special editions can also be created to specifications. For details, contact the Special Sales Department, Skyhorse Publishing, 555 Eighth Avenue, Suite 903, New York, NY 10018 or info@skyhorsepublishing.com.

www.skyhorsepublishing.com

10 9 8 7 6 5 4 3 2 1

Library of Congress Cataloging-in-Publication Data

The dictionary of unfamiliar words : over 10,000 common and confusing words explained / by The Diagram Group.
     p. cm.
  Includes index.
  ISBN 978-1-60239-339-4 (alk. paper)
  1. English language--Dictionaries. 2. Vocabulary. I. Diagram Group.
  PE1628.D53 2008
  423--dc22

                              2008025863

Produced by The Diagram Group

Editors: Nancy Bailey, Paul Copperwaite, Michael Munro

Art Director: Richard Hummerstone

Designer: Philip Patenall

Art: Pavel Kostal, Kyri Kyriacou, Lee Lawrence

Contributors: Carole Dease, Peter Dease, Jonathan Edwards, Michael Munro, Catherine Riches

Printed in China

Foreword

The Dictionary of Unfamiliar Words is different from the standard dictionaries in that it does not waste space on defining simple everyday words that speakers of English will never need to look up, such as dog, eat, rain, purple, quickly, etc. Instead it concentrates on identifying for definition those words that the average person will often encounter but which will not be immediately familiar or understandable, helpfully organizing these into subject areas.

In doing this it follows the tradition of the very beginnings of dictionary-making, when scholars drew up lists of "difficult" words that most people would need to have defined. This book applies that selection to the current subjects with such fields as Computing, Communications, Surgical procedures, and Politics, which are often only covered by highly specialized or technical dictionaries.

The alphabetical listing of a traditional dictionary means that if you don't know a word or how to spell it you can't find it. *UNFAMILIAR WORDS* offers a solution.

UNFAMILIAR WORDS has **eight major sections** containing collections of the most frequently used words in **52 subject areas**.

1) If you know the word, but not its spelling and definition, simply consult the WORD FINDER. This listing directs you to the section containing the word, its spelling, definition, and words used in this subject.

2) If you do not know the word, but know there is a name for the object or subject you are considering, then consult the section in which the word is used and search for the definition. For example, you know there is a word defining the removal of the breast. Consult the Surgical procedures section and very quickly you will find mastectomy.

3) If you partly remember a word, but cannot recall it—for example, you know there is a word for the study of fossils and that it ends in "ology"—then look in the section of Fields of Study and you will find paleontology.

4) If you do not know the difference between similar words, then you can consult a section in which these words are used. For example, in the Law section you will learn to distinguish between *habeas corpus* and *corpus delicti*.

5) If you know some words in a subject area, but would like to know more, then consult the appropriate section.

UNFAMILIAR WORDS is a book to help **expand your vocabulary**. By using this system you will never be "lost for words" again. You will discover and be able to use words you never knew existed.

Contents

Word
Finder

word finder

Autocrat 246
Autodidact 234
Autogenic 434
Autogenic training 434
Autograft 422
Autoimmune disorder 398
Automatic writing 288
Automobilist 118
Autonomic nervous system 370
Autopsy 240
Auto-responder 446
Autosuggestion 254, 434
Autotroph 328
Auxiliary verb 63
Auxins 508
Avalanche 302
Avant-garde 86
Avatar 455
Ave atque vale 86
Ave Maria 86
Avoirdupois system 361
Awareness through movement 434
Axilla 371
Axis 211
Axon 371
Ayatollah 262
Ayurveda 434
Ayurvedic medicine 434
Azania 218
Azeotrope 342
Azilian 276
Aztec 196, 276

B

B 270
B4N 466
Babalawo 290
Babushka 86
Babylonians 197
Baccalaureate 234
Bach Flower Essences/Remedies 434
Bachata 138
Bachelor 234
Bachelor's degree 234
Back end 455
Back hack 455
Back to the drawing board 75
Backboard 474
Backbone 371
Back-checking 484
Backcourt 474

Backfill 508
Back-formation 63
Backhoe day 456
Backing 316
Backing store 450
Backronym 456
Backs 488
Backstroke 494
Backup 450
Bacteriophage 328
Bacterium 328
Badge 106
Badlands 302
Badminton 473
Bailiff 240
Bails 478
Bain-marie 496
Bake 496
Bake blind 496
Baker's dozen 75, 361
Baking tray 106
Bakor 290
Balance of payments 222
Balance routine 482
Balance sheet 222
Balanced budget 222
Balk 276, 473
Balk line 476, 491
Balkanization 246
Ball 473
Ballad 123, 149
Ballerina 135
Ballet 132
Balletomane 118
Balloon angioplasty 422
Ballot 246
Ballpoint pen 446
Balneology 434
Balsamic vinegar 501
Bamboo shoots 501
Banana problem 456
Banana republic 246
Bandanna 188
Bandeau 188
Bandwidth hog 456
Bank of England 222
Banker 159
Banner blindness 456
Banshee 87
Baptistery 184
Bar 240, 302
Bar mitzvah 262
Barbarism 63
Barbecue 496

Barbican 184
Barbiturates 416
Bard 496
Bare-root 508
Barfogenesis 456
Baritone 152
Barium enema 422
Barium meal 422
Barking up the wrong tree 75
Bark-ringing 508
Barney page 456
Barometer 353
Baroque 138, 174
Baroque art 164
Baroque pop 138
Barracks 184
Barre 135
Barrier island 302
Barriers to entry 222
Barrister 240
Barrow 276
Barter 222
Bartholin's glands 371
Bas relief 163
Basal ganglia 371
Basal metabolic rate 371
Basalt 308
Basaltware 170
Base 342
Base dressing 508
Baseball 473
Bases 473
BASIC 450
Basilar membrane 371
Basilica 184
Basket 474
Basketball 474
Basmati rice 501
Basophil 371
Basque 188
Bass 152
Bass music 138
Basso profundo 152
Baste 496
Bastille 206
Bastion 184
Bat out 496
Bateau neck 188
Bates method 434
Batholith 308
Bathos 120
Batik 188
Baton 472
Battement 135

Language

1

grammar and linguistics

ablative A grammatical noun case that indicates movement away or a cause of something.

ablaut A change in the vowel in different forms of a verb, such as tenses, for example "hang" and "hung."

accidence The part of grammar that deals with inflections of words.

accusative A grammatical noun case that indicates a direct object of a verb or preposition.

acronym A word made up of initials or parts of other words, for example, NATO.

active Used to describe a form of verb in which the grammatical subject performs the action, for example, "The government took steps." *Compare* **passive**.

acute accent A mark (´) placed above a vowel in some languages to indicate pronunciation or stress.

adjective A word that modifies or describes a noun, for example, "green" or "happy."

adverb A word that modifies a verb, adjective, or another adverb, for example, "brightly."

affix A word element that only occurs as an attachment to another word or part of a word, such as a prefix or suffix.

agential Used to describe a case of nouns that identify the person peforming the action of a verb, for example, "singer."

amelioration A process by which the meaning of a word changes to something more favorable.

ampersand A character (&) used in printing and writing to represent "and."

antonym A word that means the opposite of a given word.

aorist A simple past tense, especially in ancient Greek, that does not imply continuance or momentariness.

apostrophe A punctuation mark (') used to show that a letter has been omitted or to indicate possession, such as in "David's house."

apposition A grammatical construction in which one noun or noun phrase explains another immediately next to it, for example, in "Picasso, the painter."

argot A special language used only among members of a particular group.

article A word used to identify the noun that it precedes.

aspect A form of a verb that relates it to the passage of time, such as repetition, beginning, or duration.

attributive A word or group of words that modifies a noun to which it is immediately adjacent.

auxiliary verb A verb that accompanies and augments the meaning of a main verb, for example, "can" in "can do."

back-formation The formation of a word by assuming it must be the root of an existing word, for example the verb "babysit" derived from the noun "babysitter."

barbarism An expression or use of words that is considered unacceptable or incorrect.

brackets A pair of punctuation marks, [ ], used to enclose words added to a text. *Compare* **parentheses**.

buzzword A word used in a particular jargon that gains a wider, fashionable, currency.

calque *See* **loan translation**.

cant A specialized vocabulary used among a particular group of people.

case The relationship that a word has to the other words in a sentence, often shown by the form the word takes.

cedilla A mark placed under a letter "c" in French to show that it is pronounced as "s," for example, "façade."

circumflex A mark (^) placed over a vowel in some languages, such as French, to show a change in pronunciation.

clause A group of words that forms part of a sentence, usually containing a subject and a predicate.

coinage A new word or expression.

colloquial Used to describe words or expressions that are found in everyday speech.

colon A punctuation mark (:) that introduces another phrase such as a quotation or a list.

comma A punctuation mark (,) used to separate items in a list or indicate a brief pause.

comparative Used to describe an adjective or adverb comparing two things, for example, "brighter" or "more brightly."

complement A word or group of words that follows a verb and completes a predicate.

compound A word formed from two or more other words or word parts.

conjugation A verb inflection or a complete set of the inflections of a verb.

conjunction A word used to connect other words, phrases, or sentences, for example, "but."

consonant A speech sound or letter representing one that is not a vowel and is pronounced by constriction, for example, "t."

copula A verb that identifies or links the subject with the predicate in a sentence, for example, "looks" in "She looks very happy today."

copulative Used to describe a verb that acts as a copula.

dangling participle A participle that is not correctly related to the word it is supposed to modify, for example "flying" in "Flying home that night, the weather broke."

dash A punctuation mark like a long hyphen, used, for example, to indicate a change of the subject or introduce a further statement.

dative A noun case that indicates the indirect object of a verb.

declension An inflection or set of inflections for a noun, pronoun, or adjective.

deep structure A term used in linguistics to mean the underlying structure of relationships between the elements that make up a sentence.

definite article An article that specifies a noun; in English "the" is the definite article.

demonstrative pronoun A pronoun that specifies a particular person or thing, such as "this, that, or those."

descriptive linguistics The study of a language at a particular stage in its development without relating it to other stages or other languages.

desiderative Used to describe a sentence, clause, or verb form that expresses a desire.

deterioration *See* **pejoration.**

determiner A word that qualifies a noun or noun phrase, for example "my."

diachronic Used to describe the study of the development of a language over time.

diacritic A mark attached to a letter to show a modification of sound or stress.

dialect A form of a language used in a particular region or by a particular group of people.

diction A person's choice and use of words and expressions in speaking or writing.

dieresis A punctuation mark (¨) placed over a vowel to show that it is pronounced (as in Brontë) or is pronounced separately (as in naïve).

diphthong A speech sound that, within one syllable, changes from one vowel sound to another.

disjunctive Used to describe a word that indicates opposition or contrast.

elevation Another word for amelioration.

ellipsis A punctuation mark consisting of a series of periods (...) used to show that something has been omitted.

elliptical clause A clause in which something is omitted, usually because it is understood. In the sentence "If in doubt, check the manual." "If in doubt" is an elliptical clause, with words such as "you are" omitted.

eponym A person's name from which the name of a place or thing is derived.

ergative Used to describe a case of verbs that take the same noun as either subject or object, for example "broke" in "She broke the glass" and "The glass broke."

etymologist A person who studies the origins of words.

etymon A form of a word from which another word has been derived.

exclamation point A punctuation mark (!) used to show that something is being exclaimed. Also called exclamation mark.

finite verb A verb that is inflected in some way, such as to indicate person, tense, or number.

frequentative Used to describe verbs that express an action that is repeated.

genitive A noun case that indicates possession, measurement, or source.

gerund A verb form that ends in "-ing" and can be used as a noun, for example, "swimming."

glossary An alphabetical list of specialized words and phrases, given their explanations.

gradation Another word for ablaut.

grammar The way in which elements of a language are put together to make sentences, or the study of the structure of a language.

grave A mark (`) placed above a vowel in some languages to indicate pronunciation or stress; used in English poetry to show that a final syllable–ed is pronounced, as in "slakèd."

historical linguistics The study of the changes in a language over a period of time.

homograph A word with the same spelling as another word but a different meaning.

homonym A word with the same sound (and sometimes the same spelling) as another word but with a different meaning.

homophone A word with the same sound as another word but with a different meaning and spelling.

hybrid A word made up of elements from different languages, for example, "television" from "tele" (Greek, meaning "far") and "visio" (Latin, meaning "see").

hyphen A punctuation mark (-) used to link parts of a compound term or show that a word at the end of a line continues on the next line.

idiolect The variety of a language that is used by an individual.

idiom A group of words with a meaning that cannot be deduced

from its constituent parts, such as "at the end of my tether;" also used to mean the vocabulary of a particular group.

idiomatic Used to describe use of language that is natural to native speakers or employing many idioms.

imperative A form of a verb or a construction that is used to express a command.

imperfect Used to describe a verb form that expresses an uncompleted or ongoing action, as in "We were walking."

imperfective aspect An aspect of verbs that expresses action without reference to its completion or beginning.

inchoative Used to describe a verb form that expresses a beginning.

indefinite article An article such as "a" or "an" that does not specify the noun that it modifies.

indicative A form of a verb that is used mainly to make statements.

infinitive The basic uninflected form of a verb, usually accompanied by "to" as in "to be."

inflection A change in the form of a word that indicates a different tense or number.

instrumental Used to describe a case of nouns that indicate the means by which something is done.

interjection A part of speech or expression that can make sense when uttered alone, for example, "Hello."

interrogation point *See* **question mark**.

interrogative A form of a verb or a construction that is used to express a question.

intransitive Used to describe a verb that does not have a direct object. *Compare* **transitive**.

iterative Another word for frequentative.

jargon A language that is special to a profession, culture, or subject, often technical, and is not easily understood by outsiders; also used to mean any apparently nonsensical language .

langue Any language considered in the abstract as belonging to a community.

lexeme A fundamental meaningful unit of a language.

lexical Relating to the vocabulary of a language.

lexicographer A person who compiles or writes dictionaries.

lexicography The art or practice of compiling or writing dictionaries.

lexicology The study of the history and structure of the vocabulary of a language.

lexicon A dictionary or glossary.

lexis The total set of words used in a language.

lingua franca A language used for communication between speakers of different languages, often containing elements of several languages.

linguistics The study of the structure and uses of language.

loan translation A word or phrase created in a language by translating a word or phrase in another language, for example "superman" from the German "übermensch."

loan word A word that has been borrowed from one language and become naturalized in another language.

localism A word or expression that is only used in a particular place.

locative Used to describe a case of nouns that indicate the place where something is done.

locution An individual word, phrase, or expression, or a particular person's way of speaking.

modifier A word, clause, or phrase that in some way qualifies or limits another word or group of words, for example "army" in "an army vehicle."

monosyllable A word with only one syllable.

mood A category of a verb indicating a semantic or grammatical difference.

morpheme A word or part of a word that cannot be further divided into smaller elements.

morphology The structure and form of words, especially the different forms such as inflections that can be classified.

neologism A word or expression that is newly created.

nominative A grammatical noun case that indicates the subject of a verb.

nonce word A word invented by someone for a specific occasion, not likely to become established in the language.

noun A word that gives a name to a thing or person and can be the subject or object of a verb.

object The part of a sentence that denotes the person or thing affected by the action, usually a noun or substantive.

objective A grammatical noun case that indicates the object of a verb.

oblique Used to describe any case of nouns other than the nominative or vocative.

onomastics The study of the history, forms, and origins of proper nouns.

paragraph A distinct part of a text, usually marked by beginning on a new, indented, line.

parentheses A pair of punctuation marks, ( ), used to enclose explanatory or qualifying words. *Compare* **brackets**.

parlance A particular way of speaking, or the specialized idiom of a particular group of people.

parole A term used to mean a language as it is actually spoken by individual speakers.

paronym A word that shares the same derivation as another word.

parse To analyze a sentence by breaking it down into its constituent parts and explaining the function of each and their relationships.

participle A form of a verb that can also function as an adjective, such as "cooked" or "pressing."

particle A short uninflected word used in conjunction with another word, such as "up" in "turn up."

passive Used to describe a form of verb in which the grammatical subject is the object of the action, for example, the sentence "The government took steps." in the passive would be "Steps were taken by the government." *Compare* **active.**

past participle A verb form that expresses a completed action, such as "tasted."

patois A regional dialect, or a jargon belonging to a particular group of people.

pejoration A process by which the meaning of a word changes to something less favorable.

pejorative Used to describe an expression that means something unpleasant or derogatory.

perfective aspect An aspect of verbs that expresses completed action.

perfect participle Another word for past participle.

period A punctuation mark (.) that shows the end of a sentence or follows an abbreviation.

phoneme Any of the speech sounds in a language that convey a difference in meaning.

phonetics The sounds used in speech, or the scientific study of these.

phrasal verb A verb made up of a verb plus one or more particles, for example "clean up."

phrase A group of words forming a unit that is not a complete sentence.

pluperfect Used to describe a verb form that expresses an action, that has been completed before the time of speaking, as in "We had walked."

polysyllable A word that contains many syllables.

portmanteau word A word formed by combining the sounds and meanings of two other words.

possessive A case of nouns or pronouns that expresses ownership, often shown by an apostrophe followed by "s" as in "Jane's car."

predicate The part of a sentence that asserts or denies something, often containing a verb and the object of the sentence.

prefix A word or word part that is added to the beginning of another word, such as "dis-" in "dislike."

preposition A word used before a noun or pronoun to mark its relation to the rest of the sentence, such as "to" in "I went to the beach."

present Used to describe a verb form that expresses a current action, as in "We walk."

present participle A verb form that expresses current action, such as "speaking."

preterit A form of a verb that expresses a completed action, for example, "We slept."

progressive Used to describe a verb form that expresses an action that is prolonged or continuous, as in "We are walking."

pronoun A word used in the place of a noun to avoid it having to be named twice, such as "it" in "She called the dog and it came to her."

proper noun A noun that is the name of a person, thing, place, or event, such as "Anna" or "France."

question mark A punctuation mark used to show that something is being asked.

reflexive A form of a verb in which the subject and the object are the same, for example, "He washed himself."

semantics The study of meaning in language.

semicolon A punctuation mark (;) used to mark a pause longer than a comma but shorter than a period.

sentence A group of words forming an independent grammatical unit, usually made up of a subject and a predicate that contains a finite verb.

sesquipedalian Used to describe words that are long and have many syllables.

slang Language that is not appropriate in formal contexts, often deliberately used in place of formal terms by a particular group of people .

solecism A usage that constitutes a breach of the standard rules of grammar or syntax.

structuralism An approach to the study of language that concentrates on its internal structure as opposed to the history of its development or its relationships with other languages.

subject The part of a sentence that denotes the person or thing performing the action, usually a noun, pronoun, or noun phrase.

subjective Used to describe a case of nouns and pronouns that identify the subject of a finite verb.

subjunctive A form of a verb that expresses a doubt, condition, supposition, or contingency, for example, "were" in "If I were you I'd wait a while."

substantive A word or group of words that acts as a noun.

suffix A word or word part that is added to the end of another word, such as "-ness" in "dampness."

superlative Used to describe an adjective or adverb expressing the highest degree of comparison, for example, "brightest" or "most brightly."

swung dash A printing character (~) used to take the place of a word or part of a word that is deliberately omitted.

syllable A single unit of sound made in the pronunciation of a word.

synchronic linguistics Another term for descriptive linguistics.

synonym A word that mean the same as another word.

syntax The way in which sentences are grammatically constructed, or the branch of linguistics that studies this.

tense The form of a verb that indicates the time of an action, such as present, past, or future.

thesaurus A book that lists synonyms for words.

tilde A mark (~) placed over a letter in some languages to indicate pronunciation, such as over the "n" in the Spanish "Señor."

transformational grammar Grammar that studies ways in which grammatical elements are rearranged to change meaning.

transitive Used to describe a verb that has a direct object. *Compare* **intransitive**.

umlaut A punctuation mark (¨) used in German over a vowel to show that its pronunciation is modified.

usage The way in which expressions are actually used by people, or a particular expression that is used.

verb A word used to express existence or an action, or to assert something.

vernacular Used to describe the everyday language used by ordinary people.

vocabulary All of the words and phrases used in a language or by a person, or a listing of some of these.

vowel A speech sound or letter representing one that is not pronounced using constriction, for example, "a, e, i, o, u."

figures of speech and rhetoric

alliteration The use of the same consonant at the beginning of several successive words, especially in a line of verse.

allusion Reference, especially when this is indirect or passing, to something else.

anacoluthia The lack of syntactical sequence, as when the latter part of a sentence does not fit grammatically with the former part.

anadiplosis Repetition at the beginning of a sentence, line, or phrase of the last words of the preceding one.

analogy Comparison made between two or more things in order to show their similarity.

anaphora Repetition of a word or words at the beginnings of successive clauses.

anastrophe Another word for inversion.

antiphrasis The use of a word to mean the opposite of its usual meaning, especially for ironic effect.

antithesis The balancing and contrasting of two words, phrases, or ideas by placing them side by side.

antonomasia The use of a person's title instead of his or her name, or the use of a name to stand for an idea.

apophasis The deliberate mentioning of a subject by saying that it will not be mentioned.

aporia The expression of doubt about what to say or do.

aposiopesis The act of breaking off midway through a sentence as if unwilling or unable to continue .

apostrophe The act of addressing a person or object, whether present or not, while in the middle of a discourse.

catachresis Incorrect use of words.

chiasmus The reversal in a second parallel phrase of the order of words in an initial phrase.

circumlocution An indirect way of saying something, or the use of indirect modes of expression.

climax The arrangement of sentences or clauses in such a way as to build in intensity.

emphasis Particular intensity or force placed on a word, part of a word, clause, or sentence to underline its importance.

epanalepsis Repetition of a word or clause previously used after a long passage or digression.

epanophora Another word for anaphora.

epanorthosis The immediate replacement, in order to achieve an effect of stress, of one word or phrase by another that is considered more correct.

exclamation A sudden cry or statement.

gemination Immediate repetition of a word or phrase for rhetorical effect.

hendiadys The use of two nouns joined by a conjunction instead of one noun and an adjective, such as in "in spite and hatred" rather than "in spiteful hatred."

hypallage The reversal of the usual relationship between two words.

hyperbaton The transposition of the usual order of words, as in "came the Spring."

hyperbole The deliberate use of exaggeration in order to create an effect.

hysteron proteron A rhetorical device in which the natural order of words is inverted.

inversion The reversal of the order in which words would normally be used.

irony The use of words to mean or imply the opposite of what they usually mean.

kenning The use of a conventional metaphoric name for something or someone, especially in Old Norse poetry.

laconism Extreme economy of expression, saying things in very few words.

litotes Deliberate understatement or negation of the contrary in order to achieve an effect, such as in "not a little tired" instead of "very tired."

malapropism Unintentional use of a wrong word for one that it sounds like.

meiosis *See* litotes.

metaphor A comparison of one person or thing with another by saying that the first is the second, as in "He was a tiger in combat."

metonymy An expression in which the name of something is used to mean something that is related to it, as in "die by the sword" to mean "die by violence."

onomatopoeia The use or formation of words whose sound is intended to imitate the action or sound they mean, such as 'bang" or "splash."

oxymoron The use of contradictory terms together to create an effect, such as in "sweet conqueror."

paral(e)ipsis The emphasizing of something by pretending that it does not have to be mentioned.

parenthesis An expression in which something is inserted into a phrase or sentence that would be complete without it.

periphrasis An indirect way of expressing something.

personification The representation of something as if it were a person or had human qualities, such as in "Death came and took her."

pleonasm A superfluous word or phrase, or the use of more words than necessary.

polysyndeton The use of several conjunctions one after another to create an effect, as "smiling and waving and dancing up and down."

prolepsis The anticipation and answering of possible objections before they can be raised.

prosopop(o)eia Another word for personification.

rhetorical question A question asked for effect, to which no answer is expected, such as "Whatever happened to good manners?."

sarcasm Mocking language used to insult someone or something or express contempt.

simile A comparison of one person or thing with another by saying that the first is like the second, as in "She sang like an angel."

spoonerism The unintentional, often ludicrous, transposition of the opening sounds of two or more words, as in "tons of soil" instead of "sons of toil;" named for W.A. Spooner (1844–1930), an English clergyman renowned for doing this.

syllepsis A construction in which a word applied to two other words really only matches one of them or matches each in different ways, such as in "She lost her umbrella and her way."

synecdoche An expression in which part of something is used to stand for the whole (as in "a sail" to mean "a ship"), or the whole is used to mean a part (as in "The navy arrived." to mean "A sailor arrived.").

tmesis The insertion of a word or part of a word in another word.

zeugma *See* **syllepsis**.

idiomatic expressions

according to Hoyle In a way that adheres to the rules relating to a particular activity. Edmond Hoyle (1672–1769) was an English authority on games.

ace in the hole A secret advantage, or some kind of resource kept until needed. It refers to a high-value card in stud poker which is kept face down while bets are made.

Achilles' heel A weakness that may not seem important but is actually mortal. The ancient Greek hero Achilles was made invulnerable by being dipped in the river Styx as a child. His mother held him by the heel, which was not dipped, and it was a wound there that killed him.

acid test Any decisive test or ordeal; from the former use of nitric acid to test a metal for its gold content.

act of God A potentially destructive event that happens in nature, such as a flood or earthquake, that cannot be controlled by human action.

albatross around one's neck A constant burden or source of concern; from the poem *The Rime of the Ancient Mariner*, by Samuel Taylor Coleridge (1772–1834), in which a sailor who killed an albatross was made to wear the dead bird around his neck as a penance.

all at sea In a state of confusion or perplexity; from the idea that sailors who went out of sight of land in the time before navigational aids were invented would be completely lost.

all over but (or bar) the shouting Essentially finished or decided although still going on; from old English elections in which the voters expressed their preference by shouting for the candidate they wanted.

all things to all men Trying to please everybody, especially when being overly accommodating; from a Bible reference in which St Paul used this phrase of himself, meaning that he was adaptible in trying to spread the Christian message.

all thumbs Very clumsy with one's hands. The idea is that the person's fingers do not work properly, as if each was a thumb instead.

alpha and omega The beginning and the end of something, or its most important part; from these words meaning the first and last letters in the Greek alphabet.

and thereby hangs a tale Often used to introduce a story about something that is seen or mentioned. The phrase come from Shakespeare's *As You Like It*.

apple of one's eye A particularly beloved person or thing; from biblical references to the human eye appearing like a round apple.

as the crow flies By a direct, straight route; from the idea that a crow always flies in a straight line.

at a loose end With nothing to do and somewhat bored; from crew members on old sailing ships being told to tidy up loose ends of ropes and rigging if they had nothing better to occupy them.

at loggerheads Involved in a dispute.

at sixes and sevens In a confused or disordered state.

at the end of one's rope (or tether) So harassed or troubled that you are at the limit of your ability to cope; from a tethered horse being unable to reach more grass to eat because its rope is fully stretched.

back to the drawing board Said when a project or undertaking has ended in failure and something new must be tried; from the idea of a designer drawing up a plan or diagram of something.

baker's dozen Thirteen items; from a former practice by bakers of giving a free thirteenth roll or loaf to a customer who bought a dozen.

barking up the wrong tree Taking a wrong direction in an activity; from the idea of a hunting dog being mistaken over which tree a hunted animal has climbed.

beat around the bush To fail to come to the important point about something; from the idea of a hunted animal hiding in a bush while the hunter is too timorous to follow it in there.

bee in one's bonnet A preoccupation or obsession, especially one seen as odd; from the idea of a bee buzzing around inside the hat on someone's head, unable to get out or be at peace.

beg the question To assume erroneously that something that was to be proved has been proved.

behind the eight ball In an unfavorable or uncomfortable position; from the ball in the game of pool that is numbered eight.

behind the scenes Out of the public view; from the theater, in which events in a play were sometimes intended to have taken place without being shown to the audience.

be left holding the bag To be blamed or made responsible for something illegal or wrong.

between the devil and the deep blue sea In a position between two undesirable alternatives; from the old nautical use of the word devil to mean a ship's gunwale. Someone suspended, eg for painting the ship, over the gunwale would have only the sea below him.

beyond the pale Utterly intolerable or unacceptable; from the pale being used to mean the boundary between the part of Ireland controlled by the English and the rest of the island which was considered uncivilized.

birthday suit A state of nakedness; from the idea of being born naked.

bit between one's teeth Someone who takes this has thrown off any control or restraint and is doing something energetically; from the idea of a horse grasping the bit in its mouth so that the rider cannot use this to control it.

bite the bullet To face up to something unpleasant with resolution; from the practice of surgeons amputating the limb of a wounded soldier without anesthetic giving the patient a bullet to bite on to combat the pain.

bite the dust To be defeated, ended, or be killed; from the idea of a wounded person falling face down on the ground.

bitter end The last extremity; from the end of a rope on a sailing ship being tied around a bitt (post for securing ropes).

blacklist A list, often imaginary, of defaulters or people who have otherwise earned disapproval; from the black-bound books in which town clerks recorded the names of criminals.

black sheep Someone who brings disgrace, especially to a family; from the idea that most sheep are white and a black one would be both conspicuous and undesirable.

blow one's own horn To boast about yourself or your achievements; from the street vendors' practice of blowing a horn to attract customers.

bolt from the blue A sudden, unexpected occurrence; from being compared to a bolt of lightning.

bone to pick A grievance or complaint; from the idea of picking all of the meat from a bone until none is left.

born with a silver spoon in one's mouth Born into a rich and privileged family.

break the ice To take the tension or reserve out of a meeting or social occasion among people who don't know one another; from the idea of having to break the ice in a frozen river before being able to get a boat moving.

burn one's bridges To make any going back impossible; from the idea of an army commander trying to encourage his men to fight by showing them there can be no retreat.

burn the candle at both ends To exhaust yourself by doing too much, especially by staying up late when you have to get up early.

burn the midnight oil To stay up late working or studying; from the idea of using an oil lamp.

bury the hatchet To agree to stop fighting or quarreling; from a

Native American custom of physically burying a hatchet to symbolize the end of a dispute.

busman's holiday A vacation spent doing what you do for a living; from the idea of a bus driver spending vacation time driving around.

butter someone up To ingratiate yourself with someone by flattery.

buy a pig in a poke To buy or take on something without having seen it properly first; from the idea of buying a pig that is concealed by the poke (bag) it is in.

by hook or by crook By any means necessary; from the idea of using any tool that comes to hand.

by the book In a way that strictly adheres to the established rules (as recorded in writing).

call a spade a spade To speak frankly without euphemism.

call the tune To decide what is to happen or be done; from the proverbial phrase "He that pays the piper calls the tune."

carry coals to Newcastle To do something unnecessary or superfluous; from the city of Newcastle, England, being a center of the coal industry.

caught red-handed Discovered in the act of committing a crime or doing something wrong; from the idea of a murderer's hands being stained red with blood.

chip on one's shoulder To have one of these is to have a grievance or be overly touchy; from the idea of a belligerent man putting a wood chip on his shoulder and daring anyone to knock it off.

climb on the bandwagon To join others in supporting a cause or a political party, or to follow a trend; from the idea of climbing aboard a wagon in a parade on which a band was playing.

cock-and-bull story A story, especially an excuse, that is obviously false; from the idea of old morality tales that often featured talking animals.

come clean To confess fully that you have done something wrong.

cool one's heels To be obliged to wait for something or be kept hanging around.

cotton (up) to someone or something To take a liking to, or be pleased by, a person or thing; from the pieces of cotton fluff that clung tenaciously to the clothing and hair of workers in cotton mills.

crocodile tears An insincere display of grief or sympathy; from the old idea that a crocodile wept to lure victims.

cross the Rubicon To commit yourself irrevocably to a course of action; from Julius Caesar's act of crossing the river Rubicon, which meant he was committing his forces to civil war.

cry over spilt milk To pointlessly lament a misfortune that cannot be undone.

cry wolf To raise a false alarm; from the old tale of a boy who played tricks on his neighbors by crying out that a wolf was near.

dark horse A candidate or entrant in a race who achieves unexpected support or success; apparently from a well-known Tennessee horse trader who owned a fast black stallion and would ride it like an ordinary horse to fool others into racing against it for money.

Davy Jones's Locker The bottom of the sea, where sunken ships go.

dog in the manger A person who will not allow someone else to use something that he or she has but is not using; from one of Aesop's fables in which a dog lying in a manger of hay would not let other animals eat the hay.

dose of your own medicine Punishment in the same form as that you have previously given to someone else.

dyed-in-the-wool Out-and-out or thoroughgoing; from the dyeing of wool before it is made into cloth, thus fixing the color more firmly and uniformly.

eat humble pie To be forced to admit, humiliatingly, that you were wrong; from the medieval "umble pie," a pie made from the umbles (internal organs of deer).

elbow grease Great physical effort put into doing something.

face the music To face up to a punishment or ordeal; from military punishments in which defaulters were punished on a parade during which drums were beating.

fair-weather friend Someone who stops being supportive or loyal when you run into difficulties and need help.

feather in one's cap An honor or accomplishment to be proud of; from the old use of feathers as military decorations awarded for valor.

feet of clay An unsuspected weakness; from the idea of a marble or bronze statue being imperfect or cheaply finished.

fish in troubled waters To try to obtain personal benefits by exploiting a disturbed situation.

flash in the pan Something that is initially successful or promising but quickly fails; from old flintlock muskets that were fired when the flint struck a spark to ignite a small amount of gunpowder in the weapon's "pan" that would then ignite the main charge. Often it would be only the powder in the pan that ignited and the gun failed to fire.

fly in the ointment Something that spoils or hinders a

proceeding, especially when not anticipated.

fly off the handle To suddenly become very angry; from a frontiersman's anger when the head of a poorly-made ax came off while he was attempting to swing it.

for the birds Of no value whatsoever.

get cold feet To lose your nerve, or be too fearful to go ahead with something.

get down to brass tacks To address the essential facts, or get down to serious business; from the brass tacks in the counter of a dry-goods store, where a piece of cloth would be laid when a price was being agreed.

get someone's goat To annoy or anger a person.

get something off one's chest To confess, or speak about something that has been bothering you, especially when this comes as a relief.

get up on the wrong side of the bed To start the day in an irritable mood for no apparent reason.

gilded cage A life that is luxurious but involves a lack of freedom.

gild the lily To try to beautify something that is already beautiful and needs no further adornment.

give someone the cold shoulder To deliberately ignore or snub someone.

go Dutch To share the cost of something, especially on a date where each person pays his or her own way.

go haywire To break down, especially in a spectacular way; from the use of wire to bind hay, which often got caught in machinery or on people's clothing.

go the whole hog To do something thoroughly and without holding back.

go to pot To deteriorate or decline; from the use of inferior cuts of meat to make a pot of stew rather than being eaten as dishes.

grasping (or clutching) at straws In such a desperate situation that you will try even the most unhopeful way of solving it; from the idea of a drowning person trying to gain a hold on anything at all, however flimsy.

gravy train An occupation that yields great profits for little or no labor.

hail-fellow-well-met Used to describe a person or attitude that is overly, often falsely, friendly.

hair of the dog (that bit you) An alcoholic drink taken in the hope of countering the effects of a recent overindulgence in alcohol.

have one's nose out of joint To be disgruntled through having been annoyed by something.

have the last laugh To triumph in the end, especially after having suffered reverses.

hit below the belt To unfairly do or say something that hurts someone else, especially a personal attack; from boxing, where punches that land below an opponent's belt are illegal.

hold water To be convincing or seem logically sound; from the idea of a container that has no unwanted holes in it.

hook, line, and sinker Completely and utterly; often used when someone has been deceived; from the idea of a fish swallowing an angler's hook then pulling the rest of the tackle under the water.

Indian summer A spell of mild weather in the late fall, or period of calmness or prosperity toward the end of something.

in hot water In trouble, and likely to be reprimanded.

in someone's hair In a situation of annoying or inconveniencing a person.

in the doghouse In disgrace or disfavor; from a type of sleeping shelter on an old sailing ship that was notoriously uncomfortable.

in the pink In a state of robust good health.

ivory tower A place or way of life that is cut off from the unpleasant realities.

John Hancock A person's signature; from the prominent signature made by John Hancock on the Declaration of Independence.

keep one's fingers crossed To keep wishing and hoping that all will go well; from the physical act of superstitiously crossing the fingers.

keep one's nose to the grindstone To work extremely hard.

kick the bucket Die.

kill two birds with one stone To accomplish two aims by a single action.

knock on wood A phrase spoken by someone who has just claimed to have avoided a misfortune so far and wants this to continue; from the superstitious touching of wood to avoid ill luck.

knock someone's socks off To completely astonish or overwhelm someone.

know the ropes To know how to do something properly; from novice crew members on sailing ships having to learn what all the ropes were for and how to handle them.

land of Nod A state of being asleep.

last straw A setback that comes on top of several others and leads to final collapse or defeat.

laughing up one's sleeve Secretly amused about something, especially something that another person does not know about.

lay an egg To do something that fails in its aim, such as telling a joke that no one finds funny.

lead someone down the garden path To mislead or deceive someone.

let the cat out of the bag To give away a secret; from the idea of selling someone what they think is a pig inside a bag that actually contains only a cat.

life of Riley A carefree and luxurious existence.

lock, stock, and barrel In its entirety.

looking out for number one Considering your own interests to the exclusion of anyone else.

mad as a hatter Completely insane; from the former use of mercury in processing furs or hides to make hats. Hatters absorbed large amounts of this over the years which gradually poisoned them, often leading to mental disturbance.

make a clean breast of it To confess in full to having done something wrong.

make a mountain out of a molehill To greatly exaggerate the importance of an incident or difficulty.

make a virtue of necessity To do something you have been obliged to do as if it was your choice to do so.

make (both) ends meet To earn enough money to meet your basic needs; from the splicing of old ropes on sailing ships to avoid having to obtain a new one.

make no bones To be frank about something; from the idea of eating meat or fish without making a fuss about the bones that might be found in the dish.

meet one's Waterloo To be finally and totally defeated; from the final defeat of Napoleon Bonaparte at the battle of Waterloo in 1815.

Murphy's Law An imaginary rule that states "if something can go wrong, it will;" perhaps from an Irish engineer who first formulated it.

nine days' wonder Something or someone that achieves great fame but only for a short while.

nip and tuck In a state of close competition, with no way of predicting the eventual winner.

Old Glory A nickname for the flag of the United States of America.

old hat Old-fashioned, behind the times, or having been used too often.

on tenterhooks In a state of suspense or anxiety about something; from the idea of cloth being suspended on a tenter (frame for stretching cloth while it is drying).

on the horns of a dilemma In a situation in which a difficult choice must be made, often between two equally unpleasant options.

on the level Honest, and with no intent to deceive.

on the loose At liberty, especially when you consider yourself free to act as you please.

paint the town red To take part in a wild celebration or drinking spree.

pass the buck To refuse to accept responsibility for something that has gone wrong and blame someone else.

pay lip service To agree to or go along with something insincerely.

pay the piper To face up to the consequences of what you have done; from the idea of enjoying a dance to piper's music and then having to pay the musician.

pay through the nose To be charged an extremely high price for something.

pie in the sky A wish or promise that is extremely unlikely to be fulfilled.

play fast and loose To behave in a dishonest or inconsistent manner.

play possum To pretend to be dead or sleeping; from the use of this tactic against predators by the opossum.

play safe To act in a way that involves no risks.

play second fiddle To be in a supporting or subservient role to someone else; from an orchestra in which the first violinist holds the most important position.

play to the gallery To try to appeal to the least cultured of tastes, or to use crude methods of gaining support.

pop the question To ask someone to marry you.

pot calling the kettle black A situation in which someone accusing another person of a fault is also guilty of the same fault.

pour oil on troubled waters To attempt to calm a dispute or disturbed situation.

primrose path A life of pleasure and ease.

pull someone's leg To make a playful attempt to fool or deceive someone.

pull strings To use personal influence to make something happen.

pull the wool over someone's eyes To deceive or fool someone; from the woolen wigs formerly worn by judges. Someone who had succeeded in fooling a judge likened this to physically pulling his wig down until he could not see properly.

put your foot in your mouth To make a verbal blunder, especially in saying something that embarrasses others.

raise Cain To make an angry commotion.

read between the lines To understand something that is not explicit but implied.

red herring Something intended to mislead or divert attention from something else; from the old practice of dragging a herring across a track to confuse tracking dogs.

ring true To seem to be genuine or convincing; from the old method of testing for a counterfeit coin by listening to the sound it made when it struck stone.

see eye to eye To be able to come to an agreement.

shot in the arm Something that gives a person more energy or encouragement; from the idea of an intravenous shot boosting someone's health.

skeleton in the closet A secret, especially one that would cause embarrassment if known; from the use of real human skeletons by anatomists who often obtained these illegally.

sow one's wild oats To indulge in wild behavior, especially sexual promiscuity, while young; from inexperienced farmers using the seed of wild oats (that would not produce a crop) and having to learn not to do this by experience.

spill the beans To let out a secret; from a method of voting in secret societies in ancient Greece using white or black beans. To upset the container and let everyone see how many black beans (negative votes) it contained would be potentially embarrassing.

steal someone's thunder To spoil the effect of someone's plans by doing the same thing first; from the old theater use of a machine to simulate thunder, which could be stolen.

stool pigeon A person who betrays others, especially a criminal who informs on other criminals; from the old method of hunting pigeons by decoying them with another bird tethered to a stool.

straw in the wind A sign or indication of what might be about to happen.

take something with a grain of salt To treat something skeptically or with reservations.

take the bull by the horns To confront difficulties, or begin an action resolutely; from the cowboy sport of bulldogging, ie grabbing a steer by the horns and wrestling it to the ground.

talk turkey To discuss something in a direct way; from turkey hunters imitating the birds' sounds in order to lure them.

the devil to pay Great trouble to be faced as a consequence of something you have done; from the old nautical use of pay to mean "smear with tar" and the devil being the gunwale, hence the idea of a difficult job to do.

the real McCoy The real or genuine article; apparently from a famous boxer who had many imitators claiming to be the real individual.

throw down the gauntlet To issue a challenge to someone; from the medieval practice of knights throwing down a metal gauntlet as a sign that they wished to do single combat.

tie the knot To marry; from the old custom of physically tying together sleeves or corners of the garments of a bride and groom as part of the ceremony.

under the weather Feeling slightly unwell, especially after a night of indulgence; from seasick people going below decks on a ship.

warm the cockles of one's heart To touch someone, or make someone feel happy and affectionate.

win hands down To win easily or convincingly; from the idea of a jockey in a horserace who, seeing that he cannot lose, relaxes his grip on the reins.

worth one's salt Tending to merit what you are paid; from the ancient Roman practice of paying soldiers a salt allowance.

worth one's weight in gold Extremely valuable.

Foreign terms used in English

abbé A French word meaning a priest.

ab initio A Latin phrase meaning from the beginning.

ab ovo A Latin phrase meaning from the beginning (literally, from the egg).

absit omen A Latin phrase meaning may there be no ill omen, used to express a wish that something bad that has been mentioned will not actually happen.

acte gratuit A French word meaning an action taken without a motive.

acushla An Irish word meaning darling (literally, pulse of my heart).

à deux A French phrase meaning between or of two, especially two people.

ad hoc A Latin phrase meaning for this purpose, often used to describe something that is improvised.

ad hominem A Latin phrase meaning to the man, often used to describe attacks made on an opponent's character as opposed to his arguments.

adieu A French word for farewell. The literal meaning is (I commend you) to God.

ad infinitum A Latin phrase meaning to infinity.

adios A Spanish word for farewell. The literal meaning is (I commend you) to God.

ad lib Shortened from *ad libitum*, a Latin phrase meaning at your pleasure, used to mean spontaneous or improvised.

ad nauseam A Latin phrase meaning to the point of nausea, used to mean to a point where someone is disgusted.

ad valorem A Latin phrase meaning in proportion to the value of something.

aegrotat A Latin word meaning he is ill, used to mean a sickness certificate.

a fortiori A Latin phrase meaning for a stronger reason.

aga A Turkish word meaning a leader or commander.

agent provocateur A French phrase meaning provoking agent, used to mean a person who deliberately encourages another to commit an illegal act for which they can be prosecuted.

agnus dei A Latin phrase meaning lamb of God, the opening words of a prayer to Jesus.

à la mode A French phrase meaning according to the fashion, used to mean in fashion.

al fresco An Italian phrase meaning in the cool, used to mean done in the open air.

alma mater A Latin phrase meaning bountiful mother, used by people to refer to the school or university from which they graduated.

aloha A Hawaiian word meaning love, used as both a greeting and a farewell.

alter ego A Latin phrase meaning other self, used to mean a very close friend or associate.

amicus curiae A Latin phrase meaning friend of the court, used to mean a person who advises a court but is not involved in the particular litigation.

amour-propre A French phrase meaning self-love, used to mean self-respect.

angst A German word meaning fear, used to mean a general feeling of anxiety.

annus horribilis A Latin phrase meaning year of horrors, used to mean a year in which many horrible things happened.

annus mirabilis A Latin phrase meaning year of wonders, used to mean a year in which many wonderful things happened.

apartheid An Afrikaans word meaning the state of being apart, used to mean the government policy of racial segregation formerly practiced by South Africa.

apparatchik A Russian word meaning a bureaucrat.

a priori A Latin phrase meaning from the previous, used to mean deduced or known to be true.

arrière-pensée A French word meaning an unspoken thought or mental reservation.

arrivederci An Italian word meaning farewell or until we meet again.

ars longa, vita brevis A Latin phrase meaning art is long, life is short.

au contraire A French phrase meaning on the contrary.

au courant A French phrase meaning in the current, used to mean fully informed.

au fait A French phrase meaning to the point, used to mean up to date or fully informed.

auf wiedersehen A German phrase meaning until we meet again, used as a farewell.

au revoir A French phrase meaning until we meet again, used as a farewell.

avant-garde A French phrase meaning a vanguard, used to describe artists or ideas that are ahead of their time.

ave atque vale A Latin phrase meaning hail and farewell.

ave Maria A Latin phrase meaning hail Mary, the opening words of a prayer to the Virgin Mary.

babushka A Russian word meaning grandmother, used to mean an old woman or a type of headscarf.

banshee An Irish word meaning woman of the fairies, used to mean a female spirit whose wail is a portent of death.

beaux-arts A French phrase meaning the fine arts.

belles lettres A French phrase meaning fine letters, used to mean works of literature.

bête noire A French phrase meaning black beast, used to mean a person or thing that someone particularly dislikes or fears.

bildungsroman A German word meaning education novel, used to mean a novel about a person's formative experiences.

billet-doux A French phrase meaning sweet letter, used to mean a love letter.

blitzkrieg A German word meaning lightning attack, used to mean a sudden intensive military offensive.

bodega A Spanish word meaning wineshop, used to mean a grocery store that sells wine.

bona fide A Latin phrase meaning good faith, used to describe anything that is genuine or honest.

bonjour A French word meaning good day, used as a greeting.

bon mot A French phrase meaning good word, used to mean a witticism.

bonsai A Japanese word meaning plant grown in a pot, used to mean the growing of dwarf trees or shrubs in containers.

bon vivant A French phrase meaning good living, used to mean someone who enjoys the best in food and drink.

bravura An Italian word meaning spirit, used to mean boldness or brilliance in doing something.

burn A Scottish word for a stream.

cantina A Spanish word for a bar that serves liquor.

carte blanche A French phrase literally meaning blank card, used to mean a free hand to do as you wish.

casus belli A Latin phrase meaning occasion of war, used to mean a reason or excuse for going to war or beginning a dispute.

cause célèbre A French phrase meaning famous case, used to refer to any matter or issue that arouses great public interest or controversy.

cave A Latin word meaning beware.

caveat emptor A Latin phrase meaning let the buyer beware, used to mean the idea that a buyer must not assume that the quality of a purchase is guaranteed .

ceilidh A Scottish Gaelic word meaning a visit, used to mean a social gathering with music, singing, and often dancing .

c'est la guerre A French phrase meaning that's war, used to imply that people must accept disappointments or reverses in any field of competition.

c'est la vie A French phrase meaning that's life, used to comment philosophically on a reverse or disappointment.

chef-d'oeuvre A French phrase meaning head of the work, used to mean a masterpiece.

che sarà sarà An Italian phrase meaning what will be, will be.

chutzpah A Yiddish term meaning audacity, courage, or nerve.

ciao An Italian word used as a greeting or farewell.

cognoscenti An Italian word meaning those who know, used to mean connoisseurs.

colleen An Irish word for a young girl.

comme il faut A French phrase meaning how it should be, used to describe something that is done in the correct or fashionable way.

compos mentis A Latin phrase meaning of sound mind.

connoisseur A French word meaning one who knows, used to mean a person with great knowledge and appreciation of something, especially one of the arts.

contretemps A French word meaning against time, used to mean an embarrassing incident or a minor disagreement.

cordon sanitaire A French phrase meaning quarantine line, used to mean a buffer zone.

coup de grâce A French phrase meaning blow of mercy, that is, a final killing blow that puts a fatally wounded person out of his misery; used to mean the action or event that finally destroys or ends something.

coup d'état A French phrase meaning blow of state, used to mean a sudden overthrow of a government.

crème de la crème A French phrase meaning the cream of the cream, used to mean the very best.

cri de coeur A French phrase meaning cry from the heart, used to mean a heartfelt or impassioned cry or appeal.

cui bono A Latin phrase meaning for whose good.

dacha A Russian word meaning a gift, used to mean a house or cottage in the country.

danke schoen A German phrase meaning thank you very much.

de facto A Latin phrase meaning in fact, used to describe something that exists in fact but not necessarily by right or agreement.

Dei gratia A Latin phrase meaning by the grace of God.

de jure A Latin phrase meaning in law or by right, used to describe something that exists according to law or right but is not necessarily recognised in fact.

déja vu A French phrase meaning already seen, used to mean the feeling that you have already experienced something that is happening now.

de luxe A French phrase meaning of luxury, used to describe something that is of the most luxurious or rich quality.

démodé A French word meaning outdated or no longer fashionable.

Deo volente A Latin phrase meaning God willing.

de rigeur A French phrase literally meaning of strictness, used to describe something that is required by custom or fashion.

dernier cri A French phrase meaning latest cry, used to mean the latest fashion.

de trop A French phrase literally meaning of too much, used to describe anything that is superfluous or unwanted.

deus ex machina A Latin phrase meaning god out of a machine, used to mean a contrived, unlikely solution to a problem.

diaspora A Greek word meaning scattering, used to mean the dispersion of a people to other parts of the world, or the worldwide communities of a people, especially of the Jews.

Dies Irae A Latin phrase meaning day of wrath, used to mean a Latin hymn that describes the Day of Judgment.

dolce vita An Italian phrase meaning sweet life, used to mean a life of luxury and ease.

ecce homo A Latin phrase meaning behold the man, used to mean a representation of Christ crowned with thorns.

echt A German word meaning real or authentic.

éminence grise A French phrase meaning gray eminence, used to refer to someone who wields considerable power behind the scenes. It was originally applied to a French monk who was the private secretary of Cardinal Richelieu, virtual ruler of France under Louis XIII.

en famille A French phrase meaning with the family, used to describe something done, for example a meal, in an informal way at home, among the family.

enfant terrible A French phrase meaning terrible child, used to mean someone who behaves in an embarrassing, disruptive, or unconventional way.

en fête A French phrase meaning in festival, used to describe a place that is holding a festivity or a person that is dressed for festivities.

en garde A French phrase meaning on guard, used especially in fencing to warn fencers to be ready to begin a bout.

en masse A French phrase meaning in a mass, used to mean in a group or all at once.

en passant A French phrase meaning in passing, usually referring to remarks made.

entente cordiale A French phrase meaning cordial understanding, especially between countries.

entre nous A French phrase meaning between ourselves, used to describe something that is in confidence.

entrepreneur A French word meaning someone who undertakes something, used to mean someone who owns or runs a business.

ergo A Latin word meaning therefore or hence.

ersatz A German word meaning substitute, used to describe something artificial or imitation.

esprit de corps A French phrase meaning spirit of the group, used to mean a feeling of belonging to a group and having pride in sharing its aims.

esprit de l'escalier A French phrase meaning wit of the staircase, used to mean a witty remark that only comes to mind too late, after you are on your way out of a place.

estaminet A French word meaning a small bar, cafe, or bistro.

et al. Short for et alia, a Latin phrase meaning and the others.

et cetera A Latin phrase meaning and the rest, used to mean that other things which are not named should be included.

eureka A word exclaimed when someone discovers something, from an ancient Greek word meaning I have found it.

ex cathedra A Latin phrase meaning from the chair, used to describe an official pronouncement, especially by the Roman Catholic Pope, that is considered authoritative.

exempli gratia A Latin phrase meaning for the sake of example, the full form of the abbreviation eg.

ex gratia A Latin phrase meaning out of kindness, used to mean done as a favor and without legal obligation.

ex libris A Latin phrase meaning from the library of, used to mean a bookplate.

ex officio A Latin phrase meaning from the office, used to describe something said or done officially or by right of office or position.

ex post facto A Latin phrase meaning after the deed, used to describe something that is retrospective in effect.

ex voto A Latin phrase meaning from a vow, used to describe something done in accordance with a vow, or to mean a votive object.

fait accompli A French phrase meaning an accomplished fact, used to mean something that has already been done and cannot be altered.

faites vos jeux A French phrase meaning place your bets, used by croupiers in roulette.

faute de mieux A French phrase meaning for the lack of anything better, used to refer to something that is only accepted as good enough because nothing superior is available.

faux-naïf A French word meaning false naïve, used to describe someone or something with a false appearance of unsophistication.

faux pas A French phrase meaning a false step, used to mean any mistake or blunder.

favela A Portuguese word meaning shantytown, used especially in Brazil.

felo de se A Latin phrase meaning felon of yourself, used to mean a person who commits suicide.

femme fatale A French phrase meaning fatal woman, used to mean a woman who is very attractive to men and who often leads them into trouble.

festina lente A Latin phrase meaning hasten slowly.

festschrift A German word meaning festival writing, used to mean a collection of essays written by various authors in honor of another author or scholar.

fête champêtre A French phrase meaning country festival, used to mean an outdoor entertainment such as a picnic or lawn party.

fiesta A Spanish word meaning feast, used to mean a religious festival or any kind of celebration.

fille de joie A French phrase meaning girl of pleasure, used to mean a prostitute.

film noir A French phrase meaning black film, used to mean the type of moody gangster movies made in the 1940s.

fin de siècle A French phrase meaning end of the century, used to describe anything typical, especially in being decadent, of the period around the end of a century, especially the 19th.

flagrante delicto A Latin phrase meaning while the crime is blazing, used to mean red-handed or in the act.

flânerie A French word meaning dawdling, used to mean aimless or idle behavior.

flâneur A French word meaning dawdler, used to mean someone who engages in aimless or idle behavior.

floruit A Latin word meaning he (or she) flourished, used to state when a person in history was most active, especially when the person's dates of birth and death are not recorded.

force majeure A French phrase meaning greater force, used to mean an irresistible force or an event that cannot be controlled.

frisson A French word meaning a shiver, used to mean a thrill or sensation of excitement or fear.

führer A German word for leader, often used to mean a tyrant.

futon A Japanese word meaning a padded quilt laid on the floor as a bed, often folded into a couch when not in use.

garda An Irish word for a police officer, a member of the Garda Siochána (guard of the peace).

geisha A Japanese word meaning art person, used to mean a young woman trained in the arts of music, dancing, and conversation to act as a professional companion for men.

gemütlich A German word meaning pleasant, friendly, or promoting a sense of wellbeing.

genius loci A Latin phrase meaning the spirit of a place, used to mean the typical atmosphere or ambience of a place.

gesundheit A German word meaning good health, said conventionally when some one sneezes.

glasnost A Russian word meaning openness, used especially to mean the policy of increased openness in government introduced under Gorbachev in the former Soviet Union.

gloria A Latin word meaning glory, used to mean a hymn in praise of God that begins with this word.

gombeen-man An Irish word for a storekeeper who practises usury.

Götterdämmerung A German word meaning twilight of the gods, a time when the gods of German mythology perish in combat with the forces of evil.

goy A Yiddish word meaning person, used to mean someone who is not a Jew.

gracias A Spanish word meaning thank you.

grande dame A French term meaning great lady, used to describe a woman who is highly respected in her field.

Grand Guignol A French term for a play that is intended to horrify the audience, from the name of a theater in Paris that specialized in plays of this kind.

Grand Prix A French phrase meaning great prize, used to mean any of several road races for sports cars held in various countries around the world.

gringo A Spanish word meaning foreigner, used disparagingly in Latin America for a North American or Englishman.

gulag A Russian word, originally an acronym, meaning a forced-labor camp.

gung ho A phrase adapted from a Chinese term meaning work together, used to describe a dedicated and enthusiastic person or attitude.

habitué A French word meaning frequented, used to mean someone who often goes to a particular place.

hacienda A Spanish word for a large ranch or ranch-house.

hafiz A Persian word for a person who has memorized the Koran.

haiku A Japanese word meaning amusement verse, used for a form of poem which has exactly 17 syllables.

haji An Arabic word for a Muslim who has made a pilgrimage to Mecca.

haka A Maori word meaning a war chant and dance.

hakenkreuz A German word meaning hooked cross, used to mean the swastika.

hakim An Arabic word for a physician.

halal An Arabic word meaning lawful, used to describe meat from animals that have been slaughtered in accordance with Islamic law.

hara-kiri A Japanese term meaning belly cut, used for the practice of ritual suicide by disembowelment.

hausfrau A German word meaning a housewife.

haute cuisine A French phrase meaning high cooking, used to mean cookery of a high degree of skill or elaborateness.

hejira An Arabic word meaning emigration or flight, used to refer to any flight from danger but especially the flight of Muhammad from Mecca to Medina in 622.

herrenvolk A German word meaning master race.

hibachi A Japanese word meaning fire bowl, used for a portable brazier used in cooking.

hic jacet A Latin phrase meaning here lies, used on gravestones.

hoi polloi An ancient Greek term meaning the many, used to refer to the common people or masses.

Homo sapiens A Latin phrase meaning wise man, used to refer to human beings as a species.

honi soit qui mal y pense A French phrase meaning let him be ashamed who thinks evil of it, used as the motto of the British Order of the Garter.

honoris causa A Latin phrase meaning for the sake of honor.

hors de combat A French phrase meaning out of the fighting, used to mean put out of action by being injured or damaged.

hors d'oeuvre A French phrase meaning out of the work, used to mean food served as an appetizer before a meal.

howdah A Hindi word for a seat for passengers carried on an elephant's back.

hubris An ancient Greek word meaning pride or arrogance, used particularly to mean the kind of excessive pride or conceit that often brings about someone's downfall.

idée fixe A French phrase meaning fixed idea, used to mean an obsession.

id est A Latin phrase meaning that is, the full form of the abbreviation i.e.

ignis fatuus A Latin phrase meaning foolish fire, used to mean a naturally produced phosphorescent light sometimes seen over swampy land at night.

ikebana A Japanese word used for the art of flower arranging.

impresario An Italian word meaning someone who undertakes some action, used to mean a theatrical producer.

in absentia A Latin phrase meaning in someone's absence.

in esse A Latin phrase meaning in existence.

in extenso A Latin phrase meaning at full length.

in extremis A Latin phrase meaning in the furthest extreme, used to mean on the point of dying.

infra dig (or dignitatem) A Latin phrase meaning beneath someone's dignity.

ingénue A French word meaning ingenuous person, used to mean someone who is innocent or inexperienced.

in loco parentis A Latin phrase meaning in the place of a parent, used to describe someone who takes on the responsibilities of a parent.

in memoriam A Latin phrase meaning in memory of, often used on gravestones.

in perpetuum A Latin phrase meaning forever.

in posse A Latin phrase meaning possible or potential.

in propria persona A Latin phrase meaning in person.

in re A Latin phrase meaning in the matter of.

in situ A Latin phrase meaning in position, used to mean in the original or proper place.

inter alia A Latin phrase meaning among other things.

intifada An Arabic word meaning uprising, used to mean the Palestinian uprising against Israel beginning in 1987.

in toto A Latin phrase meaning in all, used to mean completely or wholly.

in utero A Latin phrase meaning in the womb.

in vino veritas A Latin phrase meaning in wine there is truth, used to mean that people will say what they really feel when they have been drinking alcohol.

in vitro A Latin phrase meaning in glass, used to describe a biological process that is artificially made to happen outside the body, especially fertilization.

ipse dixit A Latin phrase meaning he himself said it, used to mean an unsupported assertion.

ipsissima verba A Latin phrase meaning the very words, used to mean verbatim.

ipso facto A Latin phrase meaning by that very fact.

ipso jure A Latin phrase meaning by the law itself.

j'adoube A French phrase meaning I adjust, used by a chess player who touches a piece only to adjust its position and not to make a move.

jai alai A Basque phrase meaning joyous game, used to mean a court game in which players propel and catch a ball using a special basket strapped to the hand.

jalapeño A Mexican Spanish word for a type of hot green or red chili pepper (from *chile jalapeño*, a chili from Jalapa, Mexico).

je ne sais quoi A French phrase meaning I don't know what, used to mean something that you find hard to define or specify.

jeu d'esprit A French phrase meaning play of spirit, used to mean something done wittily or cleverly, especially a piece of writing.

jeunesse dorée A French phrase meaning gilded youth, used to mean the wealthy and fashionable young people of a society.

jihad An Arabic word meaning conflict, used especially to mean a holy war waged by Muslims against infidels.

joie de vivre A French phrase meaning joy of living, used to mean enjoyment or love of life.

judo A Japanese word meaning art of gentleness, used to mean a type of martial art.

kabuki A Japanese word meaning singing dancing art, used to mean a type of traditional Japanese drama.

kalashnikov A type of Russian submachine gun, from the name of its makers.

kamikaze A Japanese word meaning divine wind, used to mean a suicidal action, especially that of Japanese pilots in World War II who deliberately crashed their airplanes onto enemy ships.

Kanaka A Hawaiian word meaning human being, used to mean a Hawaiian of Polynesian descent.

kaput A German word meaning done for, used to mean broken, destroyed, or out of order.

karaoke A Japanese word meaning empty orchestra, used to mean the pastime of singing a popular song to a prerecorded backing tape.

karate A Japanese word meaning empty hand, used to mean a type of unarmed martial art.

kibbutz A Hebrew word meaning gathering, used to mean a collective agricultural community in Israel.

kimono A Japanese word meaning garment, used to mean a traditional long Japanese robe or a garment in this style.

kitsch A German word meaning art or writing that is oversentimental or vulgar.

kosher A Yiddish word meaning proper, used to describe something that is correct, especially food prepared according to Jewish dietary restrictions.

kyle A Scottish word meaning a narrow channel or strait.

Kyrie eleison A Greek phrase meaning Lord have mercy, used as an invocation in the Roman Catholic, Anglican, and Greek Orthodox churches.

laird A Scottish word for lord, used to mean a landowner.

laissez faire A French phrase meaning allow to do, used to mean noninteference in something, especially by a government in the commerce of a country.

laissez-passer A French term meaning allow to pass, used to mean a document allowing its holder to come and go freely.

lambada A Portuguese word meaning the snapping of a whip, used to mean a type of dance originating in Brazil.

lapsus linguae A Latin phrase meaning a slip of the tongue.

lei A Hawaiian word for a garland of flowers worn around the neck.

leitmotif A German word meaning leading motif, used to mean the main or recurring theme in something.

leprechaun An Irish word meaning small body, used to mean a mischievous elf.

lignum vitae A Latin phrase meaning wood of life, used to mean either of two types of tropical American tree.

literati A Latin word meaning literate people, used to mean literary or scholarly people.

littérateur A French word meaning literary person, used for a professional writer.

loch A word used for a lake in Scotland, from Gaelic.

loco A Mexican Spanish word meaning crazy.

loco citato A Latin phrase meaning in the cited place, the full form of the abbreviation loc. cit.

locum tenens A Latin phrase meaning place-holding, used to mean a person who acts as a temporary substitute for someone else, especially a physician.

locus classicus A Latin phrase meaning classical place, used to mean a passage from a classic work that is often cited.

Luftwaffe A German word meaning air weapon, used for the German airforce.

machismo A Mexican Spanish word meaning maleness, used to describe the quality of exaggerated maleness.

macho A Mexican Spanish word meaning male, used to describe a person or thing that shows exaggerated maleness.

mademoiselle A French word meaning my damsel, used to mean a young unmarried woman.

magnum opus A Latin phrase meaning great work, used to mean the greatest individual work that someone creates, especially in the arts.

maharajah A Hindi word meaning great king, used to mean a ruler in India, especially one of the princes in the past.

maharishi A Hindi word meaning great sage, used to mean a teacher of spiritual knowledge.

maître d'hôtel A French phrase meaning master of the hotel, used to mean a headwaiter or major-domo.

mal de mer A French phrase meaning seasickness.

mañana A Spanish word meaning tomorrow, often used to indicate an unspecified time in the future.

maquillage A French word for makeup (cosmetic).

matinée A French word meaning in the daytime, used to mean a daytime peformance of a play or a daytime showing of a movie.

mauvais quart d'heure A French phrase meaning bad quarter of an hour, used to mean any short period during which something unpleasant happens.

mavourneen An Irish term meaning my love.

mea culpa A Latin phrase meaning my fault, used to acknowledge guilt, especially in Roman Catholic ritual.

memento mori A Latin phrase meaning remember you must die, used to mean an object that reminds you of your mortality, such as a skull.

ménage à trois A French phrase meaning household of three people, used to mean a situation in which a lover of one member of a couple lives in the same house as the couple.

mens sana in corpore sano A Latin phrase meaning a sound mind in a sound body.

merci A French word meaning thank you.

Messrs An abbreviation of the French word messieurs, used as the plural of Mr.

métier A French word for profession or trade, used to mean something that a person is particularly good at.

mirabile dictu A Latin phrase meaning wonderful to relate, used to refer to something surprising.

moccasin An Algonquian word used to mean a soft leather shoe.

modus operandi A Latin phrase meaning method of operation, used to mean the way someone usually does something, for example a criminal. Often abbreviated to m.o.

modus vivendi A Latin phrase meaning method of living, used to mean a compromise that allows two conflicting people or attitudes to exist in relative harmony.

Monsignor An Italian word meaning my lord, used as a title for some members of the Roman Catholic clergy.

mot juste A French phrase meaning right word, used to mean the most appropriate expression.

mullah A Turkish word meaning master, used to mean a Muslim teacher, scholar, or religious leader.

mutatis mutandis A Latin phrase meaning the necessary changes having been made.

ne plus ultra A Latin phrase meaning no more beyond, used to mean the most perfect example of something.

nil desperandum A Latin phrase meaning never despair.

noblesse oblige A French phrase meaning nobility obliges, used to mean the type of honorable behavior that is supposed to be incumbent on people of rank or privilege.

noli-me-tangere A Latin phrase meaning do not touch me, used to mean a picture showing Jesus appearing to Mary Magdelene after his resurrection.

non sequitur A Latin phrase meaning it does not follow, used to mean something that does not follow logically from what has already been stated .

nostalgie de la boue A French phrase meaning nostalgia for the mud, used to mean a longing for the degraded circumstances that someone sprang from but has risen above.

nota bene A Latin phrase meaning note well, the full form of the abbreviation n.b., used to draw attention to something important .

nouveau riche A French phrase meaning new rich, used to mean someone who has only recently become wealthy and is inclined to be ostentatious in spending.

nulli secundus A Latin phrase meaning second to none.

Nunc Dimittis A Latin phrase meaning now let depart, used to mean the canticle of Simeon in the Bible.

obiter dictum A Latin phrase meaning something said in passing.

objet d'art A French phrase meaning object of art, used to mean something, especially something small, that is considered to be a work of art .

oeuvre A French word meaning work, used to mean a work of art or all of the works created by a particular artist.

opere citato A Latin phrase meaning the work cited, the full form of the abbrviation op. cit., used to refer a reader to another text that has already been cited.

opus A Latin word meaning a work, used to mean a particular piece of music by a composer.

ora pro nobis A Latin phrase meaning pray for us.

origami A Japanese word meaning paper folding, used to mean the art of creating ornamental objects by folding paper.

O tempora! O mores! A Latin phrase meaning oh the times! oh the customs!, used to exclaim that these are bad in some way.

outré A French word meaning having gone beyond, used to describe something that has exceeded what is customary or proper.

pace A Latin word meaning peace, used to express polite disagreement with someone else's opinions.

pachuco An American-Spanish word meaning a youth,

especially one who belongs to a street gang.

papier-mâché A French term meaning chewed paper, used to mean a mixture of paper pulp and paste that hardens as it dries.

papoose An Algonquian word for a baby or young child.

par avion A French phrase meaning by airplane, used to label air mail.

par excellence A French phrase meaning by excellence, used to mean done or being to the highest degree or standard.

pari-mutuel A French term meaning mutual bet, used to mean a system of betting in which the total stake is divided among the winners.

pari passu A Latin phrase meaning equal step, used to mean with equal speed.

parti pris A French phrase meaning side taken, used to mean a prejudice or preconceived opinion.

paseo A Spanish word meaning stroll, used to mean a stroll or a place where people stroll.

passim A Latin word meaning scattered, used to mean that something referred to occurs frequently in a text.

pâté A French word meaning paste, used to mean a savory paste.

pax vobiscum A Latin phrase meaning peace be with you, used in the Roman Catholic church.

pension A French word meaning grant, used in Europe to mean a relatively cheap boarding house.

per capita A Latin phrase meaning according to heads, used to mean for or of each person.

per pro A Latin phrase, short for per procurationem, meaning through the agency of; the full form of the abbreviation p.p. used by someone signing a letter on behalf of someone else.

per se A Latin phrase meaning by itself, used to mean intrinsically.

persona non grata A Latin phrase meaning an unacceptable person, used to mean someone who is not welcome or acceptable.

pétillant A French word meaning effervescent, used to describe wine that is slightly effervescent.

pibroch A Scottish word for a piece of bagpipe music.

pièce de résistance A French phrase meaning piece of strength, used to mean the best item in a group of creative works.

pied-à-terre A French term meaning foot on the ground, used to mean a house that the owner uses as a secondary home, such as an apartment in town.

piña colada A Spanish phrase meaning strained pineapple, used to mean a mixed drink made with rum, pineapple juice, and coconut cream.

pinxit A Latin word meaning he painted it, used as an inscription on a painting.

pis aller A French term meaning worst going, used to mean a final recourse.

plat du jour A French phrase meaning dish of the day, used to mean a dish that a restaurant is featuring on a particular day.

playa A Spanish word meaning shore, used to mean a flat area at the bottom of a desert basin.

plus ça change A French phrase, shortened from plus ça change, plus c'est la même chose, meaning the more it changes the more it remains the same, used to imply that apparent change to something is merely superficial and does not affect its essence.

post hoc A Latin phrase meaning after this, used to describe the fallacy of assuming a later event is caused by an earlier one.

post meridian A Latin phrase meaning after noon, the full form of the abbreviation p.m.

post mortem A Latin term meaning after death, used to describe something happening after someone's death or to mean a medical examination carried out on a dead body.

poteen An Irish word meaning little pot, used to mean Irish whiskey distilled illegally.

pourboire A French term meaning for drinking, used to mean a gratuity.

pourparler A French term meaning for speaking, used to mean a preliminary discussion before a main one.

pousse-café A French term meaning coffee pusher, used to mean a drink of spirits taken with coffee after a meal, or a drink made up of liqueurs that do not mix but form separate layers.

powwow An Algonquian word meaning talk, used to mean a conference or conversation.

presidio A Spanish term meaning guard, used to mean a fortress such as one established by the Spanish in the southwestern United States.

prima donna An Italian phrase meaning first lady, used to mean a female opera star or a person who is temperamental and hard to work with.

primus inter pares A Latin phrase meaning first among equals.

pro bono publico A Latin phrase meaning for the good of the public.

pro forma A Latin phrase meaning for the sake of form, used to describe something that is done perfunctorily or automatically.

pro patria A Latin phrase meaning for your country.

pro rata A Latin phrase meaning in proportion.

prosit A German word meaning may it be beneficial, used as a drinking toast.

pro tem A shortening of the Latin phrase pro tempore, meaning for the time being, used to mean temporarily or temporary.

putsch A German word meaning push, used to mean an attempt to overthrow a government by force.

que pasa? A Spanish phrase meaning what is happening?, often used as a greeting.

quid pro quo A Latin phrase meaning something for something, used to mean a fair exchange or something given in exchange for something else.

quis custodiet ipsos custodes? A Latin phrase meaning who will guard the guards?

qui vive A French phrase meaning long live who? (a sentry's challenge), used to mean a state of alertness or watchfulness.

quod erat demonstrandum A Latin phrase meaning which was to be demonstrated, the full form of the abbreviation Q.E.D., used to show that something has been proved.

quondam A Latin term meaning that once was.

quo vadis? A Latin phrase meaning whither goest thou?

raison d'être A French phrase meaning reason for being, used to mean a reason or justification for the existence of something or someone.

rara avis A Latin phrase meaning rare bird, used to mean an unusual thing or person.

re A Latin word meaning being the thing, used to mean about or concerning.

realpolitik A German word meaning politics of realism, used to mean a cynical policy of pursuing a state's own interests.

recherché A French word meaning searched out, used to describe something rare, refined, or affected.

reductio ad absurdum A Latin phrase meaning reduction to absurdity, used to mean carrying an argument to the point at which it becomes absurd.

rentier A French word meaning someone who rents, used to mean a person whose income comes from regular unearned amounts such as from rent payments.

répondez s'il vous plaît A French phrase meaning please reply, the full form of the abbreviation R.S.V.P., used on invitations to show that an answer is expected.

requiescat in pace A Latin phrase meaning may he rest in peace, the full form of the abbreviation R.I.P., often used on tombstones.

res publica A Latin phrase meaning public thing, used to mean the state.

retroussé A French word meaning tucked up, used to describe a nose that turns up at the end.

risqué A French word meaning risked, used to mean suggestive or bordeing on the indecent.

roman à clef A French phrase meaning novel with a key, used to mean a novel in which real people are described but under false names.

roman-fleuve A French term meaning stream novel, used to mean a series of novels involving a family over several generations.

roué A French word someone broken on the wheel, used to mean someone leading a debauched life.

salsa An American Spanish word meaning sauce, used to mean a spicy cooking sauce and also a type of Latin-American dance music.

samizdat A Russian word meaning self-published, used to describe texts that are published clandestinely.

sanctum sanctorum A Latin phrase meaning holy of holies, used to mean a place regarded as private or sacred.

Sanctus A Latin word meaning holy, used to mean a Roman Catholic hymn that begins with this word.

sang-froid A French term meaning cold blood, used to mean calmness in a testing or dangerous situation.

Sassenach A Scottish word for an English person or a Highlander's word for a Lowland Scot.

sauve qui peut A French phrase meaning save himself who can, used to describe a situation of panic or disorder.

savoir-faire A French term meaning knowing what to do, used to mean the ability to do the right thing.

savoir-vivre A French term meaning knowing how to live, used to mean the quality of being at ease in society.

sayonara A Japanese word meaning farewell.

schadenfreude A German word meaning harm joy, used to mean pleasure taken at the misfortunes of someone else.

schlemiel A Yiddish word used to mean an unlucky, clumsy, or long-suffering person.

schmalz A German word meaning melted fat, used to mean excessive sentimentality.

schmuck A Yiddish word meaning penis, used to mean a foolish or contemptible person.

schnook A Yiddish word used to mean a gullible or stupid person.

semper fidelis A Latin phrase meaning always faithful, used as the motto of the United States Marine corps.

shalom A Hebrew word meaning peace, used as a greeting and a farewell.

shebeen An Irish word meaning poor quality beer, used to mean an illegal drinking den.

shieling A Scottish word meaning a shepherd's hut.

shikse A Yiddish word meaning a non-Jewish girl.

shillelagh An Irish word meaning cudgel.

sic A Latin word meaning thus, used in texts to show that something is quoted exactly from the original.

sic transit gloria mundi A Latin phrase meaning thus passes the glory of the world.

Sieg Heil A German phrase meaning hail to victory, used as a Nazi salute.

siesta A Spanish word meaning sixth (hour), used to mean a sleep taken in the afternoon, especially after the midday meal.

s'il vous plaît A French phrase meaning if it pleases you, used to mean please.

sine die A Latin phrase meaning without a day, used to mean with no set time limit.

sine qua non A Latin phrase meaning without which nothing, used to mean something that is absolutely essential.

Sinn Féin An Irish phrase meaning ourselves alone, used as the name of an Irish republican political movement.

soi-disant A French term meaning calling yourself, used to mean self-styled.

son et lumière A French phrase meaning sound and light, used to mean a sound and light display staged at a historical site to portray the site's history.

sotto voce An Italian phrase meaning below the voice, used to mean in an undertone, or something said in an undertone.

soupçon A French word for suspicion, used to mean a small amount.

sporran A Scottish word for a large pouch worn with the kilt as part of Scottish Highland dress.

squaw An Algonquian word meaning woman, used, offensively, to mean a Native American woman.

Stabat Mater A Latin phrase meaning the mother was standing, used to mean a Roman Catholic hymn that begins with these words.

status quo A Latin phrase meaning the state in which, used to mean the existing state of affairs.

Sturm und Drang A German phrase meaning storm and stress, used as the name of a German literary movement of the 18th century.

sub judice A Latin phrase meaning under judgment, used to describe a matter that is being considered by a court.

succès de scandale A French phrase meaning success of scandal, used to mean something that is successful because of its notoriety.

succès d'estime A French phrase meaning success of esteem, used to mean something that pleases the critics but not the general public.

sui generis A Latin phrase meaning of its own kind, used to describe something considered unique.

summum bonum A Latin phrase meaning the greatest good.

tableau vivant A French phrase meaning living picture, used to mean a silent and motionless group of people posed to portray a famous scene or event.

tant mieux A French phrase meaning so much the better.

tant pis A French phrase meaning so much the worse, used to mean never mind.

Taoiseach An Irish word meaning leader, used as the title of the prime minister of the Republic of Ireland.

tapas A Spanish word meaning covers, used to mean appetizers or snacks.

Te Deum A Latin phrase meaning Thee, God, used to mean a Roman Catholic hymn that begins with these words.

te igitur A Latin phrase meaning thee therefore, used to mean a Roman Catholic prayer that begins with these words.

tempus fugit A Latin phrase meaning time flies.

terra firma A Latin phrase meaning firm ground, used to mean the land as opposed to the sea.

terra incognita A Latin phrase meaning unknown ground, used to mean an unexplored or unfamiliar territory.

tête-à-tête A French phrase meaning head to head, used to mean an intimate conversation or meeting between two people.

thé dansant A French phrase meaning dancing tea, used to mean a dance held in the afternoon at which tea is served.

tour de force A French phrase meaning feat of strength, used to mean something that is done with great skill.

tout de suite A French phrase meaning at once.

tout le monde A French phrase meaning everyone.

trompe l'oeil A French phrase meaning deceive the eye, used to mean a painting that is made to give an illusion of reality.

tu quoque A Latin phrase meaning you also, used by someone being accused to accuse the accuser of the same crime.

vade mecum A Latin phrase meaning go with me, used to mean a guidebook that someone carries around.

vendetta An Italian word meaning vengeance, used to mean a prolonged feud or campaign of vengeance.

verboten A German word meaning forbidden.

verbum sapienti sat est A Latin phrase meaning a word is sufficient to the wise.

vers libre A French phrase meaning free verse.

via media A Latin phrase meaning middle way, used to mean a compromise.

vice versa A Latin phrase meaning relations being reversed, used to mean in reversed order or the other way round.

victor ludorum A Latin phrase meaning the winner of the games, used to mean a sports champion.

vide A Latin word meaning see, used to refer a reader to another place in a text or to another text.

vieux jeu A French phrase meaning old game, used to mean something that is old-fashioned.

vingt-et-un A French phrase meaning twenty-one, used to mean the card game of blackjack

vin ordinaire A French phrase meaning ordinary wine, used to mean cheap table wine.

vis-à-vis A French phrase meaning face to face, used to mean in relation to.

voilà A French word meaning see there, used to draw attention to something.

volte-face A French term meaning turn face, used to mean a reversal of opinion or policy.

vox populi A Latin phrase meaning voice of the people, used to mean public opinion.

weltanschauung A German word meaning world view, used to mean someone's philosophy of life.

weltschmertz A German word meaning world pain, used to mean sadness at the evils of the world.

wigwam An Abnaki word meaning abode, used to mean a Native American tent-like dwelling.

wunderkind A German word meaning wonder child, used to mean someone who accomplishes great things while still young.

zeitgeist A German word meaning time spirit, used to mean the spirit of the age.

English words and American equivalents

abseil rappel
accelerator gas pedal
action replay instant replay
adjustable spanner monkey wrench
aerial antenna
aerodrome airdrome
aeroplane airplane
air gun BB gun
Allen key allen wrench
aluminium aluminum
articulated lorry semitrailer
assault course obstacle course
athletics track and field
aubergine eggplant
badge pin
baking tray cookie sheet
beach buggy dune buggy
bellboy bellhop
bill (restaurant) check
biscuit cookie
blind shade
blue-eyed boy fair-haired boy
boiled sweets hard candy
bonnet (car) hood
boot (car) trunk
bottom drawer hope chest
bowler hat derby
braces suspenders
breeze block cinder block
brooch pin
building society savings and loan
bumper fender
bunker (golf) sandtrap
cadger moocher
call box phone booth
called up (for military service) drafted
candyfloss cotton candy
caravan trailer
caretaker janitor
car park parking lot
cash card ATM card
casualty ward emergency room

catapult slingshot
central reservation (road) median strip
changing room locker room
chartered accountant CPA
chemist's shop drugstore
chips french fries
chiropodist podiatrist
cider hard cider
city centre downtown
classified advertisements want ads
clingfilm plastic wrap
clock in/out punch in/out
coleslaw slaw
condom rubber
cornflour cornstarch
cot crib
courgette zucchini
court shoe pump
crazy golf miniature golf
crèche daycare center
crisps potato chips
curriculum vitae (CV) resumé
curtains drapes
cutlery flatware
dinner jacket tuxedo
docker longshoreman
dosshouse flophouse
drainpipe downspout
drapery dry goods
draughts checkers
drawing pin thumbtack
dual carriageway divided highway
dummy pacifier
dungarees overalls
dustbin garbage can
dustman garbage collector
duvet comforter
elastic band rubber band
engaged (phone line) busy
estate agent realtor
estate car station wagon
ex-directory (phone number) unlisted
exhaust pipe tailpipe
ex-serviceman veteran
extra time (in game) overtime

facecloth washcloth
fair carnival
fanlight transom
fete fair
fire engine fire truck
fire hydrant fire plug
firefly lightning bug
flapjack pancake
flat apartment
flatmate roommate
flick knife switchblade
Friesian (cow) holstein
fringe bangs
fruit machine slot machine
frying pan skillet
full stop period
funfair carnival
galoshes overshoes
garden yard
gents (toilet) men's room
gobstopper jawbreaker
grill (food) broil
gritter salt truck
guard's van (train) caboose
hairgrip bobby pin
hair slide barrette
hall of residence dormitory
handbag purse
hessian burlap
hire purchase installment plan
hoarding billboard
hockey field hockey
holiday vacation
holidaymaker vacationer
horsebox horse trailer
houseman (hospital) intern
housetrained housebroken
housewife homemaker
ice hockey hockey
icing frosting
icing sugar confectioners' sugar
indicator (automobile) blinker
ironmonger hardware store
jam jelly
jemmy jimmy

jumble sale rummage sale
knickers panties
ladder (in pantyhose) run
ladybird ladybug
leave (of absence) furlough
lectern podium
letterbox mailbox
level crossing grade crossing
lift elevator
lift (in an automobile) ride
litter bin trashcan
litter lout litterbug
lodger roomer
lodging house rooming house
lollipop sucker
lorry truck
lost property lost-and-found
lounge suit business suit
lovebite hickey
maintenance (payments) child support
mangetout snow pea
market gardening truck farming
maths math
mileometer odometer
mince ground beef or hamburger
mincer meat grinder
mobile phone cellphone
mortise lock dead bolt
muffin English muffin
music hall vaudeville
nappy diaper
night safe night depository
note (money) bill
noticeboard bulletin board
noughts and crosses tick-tack-toe
numberplate (automobile) license plate
off-licence liquor store
off-the-peg off-the-rack
own brand store brand
pack (of cards) deck
packed lunch bag lunch
paper fastener brad
paper round paper route
paraffin kerosene
patience (card game) solitaire

pavement sidewalk
pedestrian crossing crosswalk
pelmet valance
period pains cramps
petrol gasoline
petrol station gas station
pharmacy drugstore
phone box phone booth
piebald pinto
pigsty pigpen
pigtail braid
pinafore jumper
pitch (sports) field
plait braid
plimsoll sneaker
plough plow
plughole drain
pneumatic drill jackhammer
pontoon (card game) blackjack
porridge oatmeal
postcode zip code
poste restante general delivery
pouffe hassock
pram baby carriage
presenter (TV) announcer
press stud snap fastener
press-up push-up
propelling pencil mechanical pencil
provisional licence learner's permit
puncture flat
Queen's evidence state's evidence
queue line
rag-and-bone man junkman
recorded delivery certified mail
refectory cafeteria
removal van moving van
return ticket roundtrip ticket
reverse the charges (phone call) call collect
ring road beltway
ring spanner box end wrench
rise (pay) raise
roundabout traffic circle
rubbish garbage
runner bean string bean
saloon (automobile) sedan

salt cellar salt shaker
sandpit sandbox
sandshoes sneakers
scrap paper scratch paper
secateurs clippers
seesaw teeter-totter
sell-by date expiration date
setsquare triangle
shareholder stockholder
shop store
shopping trolley shopping cart
shorthand typist stenographer
sidelight (automobile) parking light
silencer (automobile) muffler
single ticket one-way ticket
skirting board baseboard
sleeper (railroad track) tie
sleeping partner silent partner
slip road on-ramp or exit ramp
smear test pap smear
soda water club soda
spanner wrench
sports day field day
spring onion scallion or green onion
spring roll egg roll
stag night bachelor party
standard lamp floor lamp
starter appetizer
stock cube bouillon cube
stone (in fruit) pit
subeditor copy editor
sump oil pan
supply teacher substitute teacher
surgical spirit rubbing alcohol
suspender belt garter belt
swede rutabaga
sweetcorn corn
sweets candy
swiss roll jelly roll
swotting cramming
takeaway takeout
tallboy highboy
tap faucet
taxi rank cabstand
telegram Wire

telltale tattletale
tenpin bowling bowling
term (academic) trimester or semester
terraced house row house
ticket tout scalp
tights pantyhose
till cash register
tin opener can opener
toffee apple candy apple
torch flashlight
tote (betting) pari-mutuel
town hall city hall
trade union labor union
trainers sneakers
tram streetcar
transport cafe truck stop
treacle molasses
trimmings fixings
trousers pants
trouser suit pants suit
truant play hooky
truncheon nightstick
turn-ups cuffs
underpants shorts
undertaker mortician
unit trust mutual fund
valve (electronic) vacuum tube
vest undershirt
visiting card calling card
waistcoat vest
wallet billfold
wardrobe closet
water pistol squirt gun
watershed divide
weatherboard clapboard
wellingtons rubber boots
Welsh dresser hutch
wendy house play house
wheel clamp denver boot
white spirit turpentine
wholemeal wholewheat
windscreen windshield
zebra crossing crosswalk
zed zee
zip zipper

fields of study or practice

acarology The study of mites and ticks.

anemology The study of winds.

angiology A branch of medicine that deals with the blood vessels and lymphatic system.

anthropology The study of humankind, including origins, behavior, and institutions.

astrology The study of the movements of celestial bodies with regard to their supposed influence on human characteristics and actions.

bryology A branch of botany that deals with bryophytes, ie mosses and other plants that reproduce by spores.

calligraphy The art or practice of ornamental handwriting.

campanology The art or practice of ringing bells to create music.

cardiology A branch of medicine that deals with the heart and diseases of the heart.

carpology A branch of botany that deals with the study of fruits and seeds.

cartography The art or practice of drawing maps of regions.

cetology A branch of zoology that deals with the study of whales and other cetaceans.

choreography The art or practice of composing dance steps.

chorography The art or practice of drawing maps.

chorology The study of geographical relationships within a region or the distribution of plants and animals.

chromatography The technique of analyzing the composition of a liquid or gas by adsorption in a medium.

chronology The study of time or the sequence of dates.

conchology The collection and study of seashells and mollusk shells.

cosmology The study of the origin, nature, structure, or evolution of the universe.

craniology The study of the shapes and sizes of human skulls.

criminology The study of crime and the behavior of criminals.

cryptology The study of codes and ciphers and their analysis.

cytology The study of the cells of animals and plants, including their formation and structure.

dactylography The study of human fingerprints, especially as a means of identification.

dactylology The practice of using manual sign language, as in communicating with people with hearing impairment.

demography The study of human populations, especially statistics on their size, distribution, and structure.

dendrochronology The study of the annual rings of trees and the use of these in dating past events.

dendrology The branch of botany that deals with trees and shrubs.

deontology The branch of ethics that deals with moral responsibility.

dermatology The branch of medicine that deals with the skin and diseases of the skin.

ecology The study of the relationships between living organisms and their environment.

endocrinology The branch of medicine that deals with the endocrine glands.

enology The study of wine.

entomology The study of insects.

epidemiology The branch of medicine that deals with epidemics, including their transmission and control.

epigraphy The study of ancient inscriptions.

epistemology The study of the nature of knowledge.

eschatology The branch of theology that deals with the end of the world.

ethnology The study of the origins and characteristics of peoples and races.

ethology The branch of zoology that deals with animals in their normal environment.

etiology A branch of medicine that deals with the causes of diseases.

etymology The study of the origins and development of words.

futurology The study of the future of humankind.

genealogy The study of the ancestry of a person or group.

geology The study of the origins, structure, and composition of the earth.

geomorphology The study of the origins and development of the earth's topographical features.

gerontology The study of human aging and the elderly.

glottochronology The study of the historical relationships between languages.

gynecology The branch of medicine that deals with diseases of women.

helminthology The study of parasitic worms.

hematology The branch of medicine that deals with diseases of the blood.

herpetology The branch of zoology that deals with reptiles and amphibians.

histology The study of the tissues of animals or plants.

horology The art or practice of making clocks and watches, or the study of time.

hydrography The study and mapping of rivers, seas, and oceans.

hydrology The study of the water on the earth and in its atmosphere.

hypnology The study of sleep and hypnosis.

ichthyology The study of fish.

lexicography The art or practice of writing or compiling dictionaries.

lexicology The study of the history and structure of the vocabulary of a language.

limnology The study of life in bodies of fresh water.

lithology The study of rocks, especially their composition and texture.

malacology The branch of zoology that deals with the study of mollusks.

meteorology The study of the earth's atmosphere and the weather.

metrology The study or science of weights and measures.

mycology The branch of botany that deals with the study of fungi.

myology The branch of medicine that deals with muscles and muscle diseases.

myrmecology The branch of zoology that deals with the study of ants.

nomology The study of laws and lawmaking.

nosology The branch of medicine that deals with the classification of diseases.

odontology The study of teeth and diseases of teeth.

oncology The branch of medicine that deals with the study and treatment of tumors.

ontology The branch of philosophy that deals with the nature of being.

oology The study of birds' eggs.

ophiology The branch of zoology that deals with the study of snakes.

ophthalmology The branch of medicine that deals with the eye and eye diseases.

ornithology The branch of zoology that deals with the study of birds.

orography The study of relief features such as mountains or the mapping of these.

orthography The study of spelling or systems of writing, or the correct way of spelling.

osteology The study of bones.

otology The branch of medicine that deals with the ear and ear diseases.

paleethnology The branch of ethnology that deals with early human beings.

paleography The study of ancient manuscripts.

paleontology The study of ancient organisms through their fossilized remains.

palynology The study of pollen and spores.

pathology The branch of medicine that deals with the nature and causes of diseases.

pediatrics The branch of the medicine that deals with the development, care, and diseases of children.

pedology The study of soil.

penology The study of the punishment of crime and prisons.

petrology The study of the origin and composition of rocks.

pharmacology The science of drugs and their uses.

philology The study of language.

phrenology The study of the shape of the human skull, especially with a view to determining character.

physiology The study of the functioning of organisms.

phytology The study of plants.

phytopathology The branch of botany that deals with the diseases of plants.

pomology The study of fruits and their cultivation.

potamology The study of rivers.

psephology The study of elections from a sociological or statistical viewpoint.

pteridology The branch of botany that deals with the study of ferns.

radiology The branch of medicine that deals with the use of X-rays and radioactive substances in the diagnosis and treatment of disease.

reflexology A form of therapy used in alternative medicine, in which the soles of the feet are massaged .

rhinology The branch of medicine that deals with the nose and diseases of the nose.

scatology The study of excrement, for example in medical diagnosis; also used to mean obscene language.

seismology The study of earthquakes.

selenography The study and mapping of the surface of the moon.

selenology The astronomical study of the moon.

semiology The study of signs, symbols, and signals.

Sinology The study of the history, culture, and language of China.

speleology The study or exploration of caves.

stomatology The branch of medicine that deals with the mouth and its diseases and disorders.

stratigraphy The study of the composition and relative positions of rock strata.

teleology The philosophical doctrine of final causes, or the interpretation of things in terms of purpose.

teratology The branch of biology that deals with the study of monsters or congenital abnormalities.

topography The study of the surface features of a region or the mapping of these.

topology The branch of mathematics that deals with the properties of shapes and surfaces.

toxicology The study of poisons, especially their effects and antidotes.

tribology The study of friction and lubrication between moving surfaces.

trichology The branch of medicine that deals with the hair and diseases of the hair.

ufology The study of unidentified flying objects.

uranography The astronomical study and mapping of the stars and galaxies.

vexillology The study of flags.

zoology The study and classification of animals.

zymology The study of the chemistry involved in fermentation.

enthusiasts

ailurophile Someone who loves cats.

Anglophile Someone who admires England, its culture, or its people.

arctophile Someone who loves and collects teddy bears.

audiophile Someone who is enthusiastic about stereo or high-fidelity sound reproduction.

automobilist Someone who loves and collects automobiles.

balletomane Someone who loves ballet.

bibliophile Someone who loves and collects books.

campanologist Someone who is enthusiastic about bell-ringing.

cartophilist Someone who collects trading cards.

cruciverbalist Someone who compiles or enjoys completing crossword puzzles.

deltiologist Someone who collects and studies postcards.

discophile Someone who collects phonograph records.

enophile Someone who loves and collects wines.

Francophile Someone who admires France, its culture, or its people.

Hellenophile Someone who admires Greece, its culture, or its people.

herbalist Someone who grows or collects herbs, especially those with medicinal uses.

Hispanophile Someone who admires Spain, its culture, or its people, or that of another Spanish-speaking country.

Italophile Someone who admires Italy, its culture, its language, or its people.

lepidopterist Someone who collects specimens of butterflies and moths.

numismatist Someone who collects coins.

philatelist Someone who collects stamps.

phillumenist Someone who collects matchbooks, matchboxes, or matchbox labels.

Russophile Someone who admires Russia, its culture, or its people.

Sinophile Someone who admires China, its culture, or its people.

spelunker Someone who explores caves as a hobby or pastime.

toxophilite Someone who enjoys archery.

twitcher A dedicated bird watcher.

vexillologist Someone who collects flags.

xenophile Someone who loves foreign peoples, cultures, or customs.

zoophile Someone who loves animals.

The Arts

literature

allegory A form in which the action and other elements stand for something else in real life.

alliteration Use of a sequence of words beginning with the same initial letter.

antithesis Placing ideas together to stress a contrast.

aphorism A brief, witty statement of a general truth.

assonance Use of words which repeat similar vowel sounds.

bathos Sudden change from the exalted to the ridiculous or banal.

deconstruction Critical interpretation of a text by studying linguistic signs in isolation from other elements such as knowledge of its author and cultural background.

epigram A brief but memorable statement making a pithy observation.

epilogue A postscript outlining what happens to characters after the ending of the main story, or a final passage to point a moral or offer an explanation to the reader.

episode An incident or group of incidents forming a section of a story; one installment of a serialized story.

euphemism An inoffensive substitute for a distasteful word or phrase.

euphony A combination of pleasant sounding words.

euphuism A high-flown rhetorical literary style.

foreword An introduction, in which the author sets out his intentions, or written by another person giving an endorsement of the book or its author.

hyperbole Use of exaggeration for emphasis.

innuendo Subtle or indirect implication, usually of something discreditable.

irony Using expressions of which the opposite to the literal meaning is intended.

litotes Assertion of a positive by denying its negative, often in the form of a deliberate understatement for effect.

metaphor Use of an object or action to represent another. Mixed metaphor is the joining together of unmatched metaphors with ridiculous results.

metonymy Use of a suggestive or related word instead of naming the thing meant.

neologism A newly coined word or expression.

onomatopoeia Use of words which sound like the thing

described.

oxymoron A statement combining two conflicting terms for effect.

palindrome A word or phrase that reads the same backwards.

parody Imitating another work or style with intention to ridicule.

pastiche An imitation of another's style.

periphrasis A roundabout way of expressing a point.

personification Giving objects or concepts a personal living form.

preface An introduction, often explaining the structure or purpose of what follows.

prologue An introductory section explaining what happens before the main action.

pun Comic play on words which sound similar but differ in meaning.

simile Likening one thing to another.

stream-of-consciousness Narrative using an uninterrupted sequence of thoughts, perceptions, and feelings.

structuralism A critical discipline which studies a text in relation to other known elements, including knowledge of the author, contemporaneous culture, literary convention, and facts not mentioned in the text but known to intended readers in addition to the text itself.

syllepsis Use of one word linked in different senses to two statements, usually used for its comic effect.

synecdoche A figure of speech where use of a part stands for the whole.

tautology unnecessary repetition

zeugma Another expression for syllepsis.

Literary styles, periods and genres

autobiography An account of the writer's own life.

biography The story of a person's life, recounted by someone else.

chronicle A chronological account of events.

crime story A story built around criminal activity where the identity of the criminal is known or unimportant.

detective story A story hinging on the solving of a crime, how it was committed, and the identification of a murderer, thief, or other criminal.

epistle A letter or a literary work imitating letter form.

epitaph A eulogy commemorating the dead.

essay A prose composition on a particular subject.

fable A short, allegorical story to point a moral, especially using animal characters.

faction A retelling of a story concerning real people and events, but which imaginatively constructs dialogue and incident where no factual record exists.

fantasy A story involving things or happenings not known in real life.

fiction Literature, especially stories, based on invented character and incidents—though fiction may often be set against a background of real events and draw on real-life experience.

gothic A style characterized by gloom, the grotesque and supernatural, popular in the late eighteenth century and revived in the twentieth; often set in ruined castles, abbeys, or old houses.

graphic novel An extended, self-contained story told in picture strip form.

historical Set in a period earlier than the present.

horror story A tale intended to frighten, often involving the supernatural.

lampoon A satire ridiculing a person.

legend An unverifiable story handed down from earlier times, or a modern story that presents similar characteristics; used in medieval times when telling the life story of a saint.

magic realism Originally used in the 1920s to describe paintings which combined surreal fantasy with matter-of-fact representation; adapted for more recent literary work which combines documentary realism with imaginative fantasies.

memoir A biography or historical account based on personal knowledge; stylistically, memoirs usually indicate fragments of autobiography rather than a complete retelling.

myth A fictitious story, frequently intended to explain a phenomenon and generally concerning gods or beings from before written history; a story in which a theme or character embodies an idea in a similar way.

novel A fictitious narrative in which characters and action are usually a reflection of real life.

novelette A short novel, usually light and often sentimental in tone.

novella A short narrative tale that is longer than a short story, often one with a moral or satirical point.

picaresque A genre in which a roguish hero or heroine goes through a series of adventures.

roman à clef A story based on real characters and events known to the author, but presented under fictitious names.

romance Originally a tale of chivalry or of characters remote from ordinary life (and written in one of the Romance languages), popularly a story of love, usually somewhat idealized, and with a happy ending.

satire A genre using irony or ridicule to hold contentious issues, folly, or evil in scorn.

science fiction (SF) A genre that makes imaginative use of scientific knowledge or conjecture of future scientific development. When this is pseudo-scientific with no grounding in real science, it is often known as science fantasy.

short story A short but complete piece of prose fiction concentrating on a single theme.

thriller A tale of mystery, espionage, or crime of which the main purpose is to entertain with suspense and shock.

western A tale set in the western states of the US, especially in the period of settlement and early development, usually involving gunmen, outlaws, or settlers in conflict with Native Americans.

Poetry terms and forms

acrostic A verse in which the initial letters of each line form a word or phrase reading downwards.

alexandrine A line of verse in iambic hexameter.

anapest A metrical foot with three syllables, two unstressed and one stressed.

antistrophe The second of two metrical systems used alternately within a poem.

aubade A poem that greets or evokes the dawn.

ballad A narrative poem in short stanzas, often of folk origin and intended to be sung.

blank verse Unrhymed verse, often (especially in Shakespeare) in iambic pentameters.

caesura A pause in a line, usually for sense, but forming part of the metrical foot.

couplet Two lines of rhymed verse in the same meter. In a closed couplet the meaning is complete.

dactyl A metrical foot of one stressed syllable followed by two unstressed ones.

elegy A serious reflective poem, especially one lamenting a death.

envoi A brief postscript in verse or prose.

epic A long narrative poem usually concerning a central character of heroic stature, or incidents of national or tribal importance.

foot A metrical unit of a group of syllables, a unit of rhythm.

free verse Verse that is unrhymed and follows no strict metrical pattern, cadence often providing form.

haiku A form of epigrammatic Japanese verse with exactly 17 syllables.

hexameter A metrical line of six feet.

iambic A metrical foot of two syllables with the second accented.

lay A short narrative poem, usually meant to be sung.

limerick A five-line comic verse, the third and fourth lines shorter and rhyming, the other lines sharing a different rhyme.

meter The rythmical structure of a line of verse.

octave A group of eight lines of verse.

ode A lyric poem, usually in elaborate form, typically addressed to and eulogizing a particular subject.

ottava rima An eight-line stanza form in iambic pentameter, the rhyme pattern abababcc.

pentameter A meter of five feet to the line.

prosody The principles and elements of versification: meter, rhyme, etc.

quatrain A group of four lines, usually rhymed.

refrain A phrase, line, or group of lines repeated through a poem, usually at the end of each stanza.

rhyme Similarity in the sound of endings of different words, especially vowels of the last stressed syllables (and any which follow them). Masculine rhymes stress the last syllable, feminine do not; imperfect rhymes have vowels which do not quite match; identical use the same word, often with different meaning; eye rhymes look but do not sound the same (though in old poems this may be due to a change in pronunciation); internal rhymes are when a word within a line rhymes with its last word.

rhythm The pattern of stress through verse. Sprung rhythm has one stressed and several unstressed syllables to each foot.

scansion The metrical pattern of a line.

sestet A group of six lines.

sonnet A poem of 14 lines in iambic pentameter rhymed to a fixed scheme: Petrarchan—divided in both form and sense as an octave and a sestet (the rhyme scheme usually abbaabba, cdecde or cdcdcd); Miltonic—similar but without the break; English or Shakespearean—three quatrains and a couplet (abab, cdcd, efef, gg); Spencerian—three quatrains and a couplet (abab, bcbc, cdcd, ee).

spondee A metrical foot of two syllables, both accented.

stanza A group of lines forming a regular metrical division within a poem.

strophe The first of a set of metrical systems (usually repeated) in a poem.

tercet A group of three lines, often connected by rhyme.

terza rima A series of tercets rhyming aba, bcb, cdc, and so on.

tetrameter A meter of four feet to the line.

threnody A funeral song or dirge.

trimeter A meter of three feet to the line.

trochee A metrical foot of two syllables, the first accented the second not.

verse Technically, one metrical line of a poem, but more commonly used to mean a stanza and as a general description of poetry as distinct from prose.

verse libre (French) Free verse.

weak ending One that is unaccented.

theater and drama

Drama styles, genres and forms

Broadway The fashionable theater area of New York City.

burlesque A coarse form of dramatic parody that seeks to entertain through distortion or ridicule, for example in the comic treatment of serious and well-known works.

burletta A variation on burlesque, the burletta developed along more musical lines. The sense of parody slowly disappeared, to be replaced by a popular formula of songs and stage effects.

cabaret Musical entertainment offered in a nightclub or restaurant usually inolving singing and dancing.

commedia dell'arte Italian comedy characterized by the use of improvisation and masks.

farce A humorous play whose structure consists of character stereotypes, mishaps, coinincidences, innuendo and embarrassing disclosures.

grand guignol A French total horror genre.

interlude A medieval morality play.

kabuki Highly stylized traditional Japanese theater with music and dance.

legitimate theater Professional, high-quality theater, as opposed to vaudeville or burlesque.

masque A typical European Renaissance dramatic form, with actors using masks and costumes.

melodrama A sensational romantic drama.

minstrel show A nineteenth-century farcical US show consisting of impersonations of blacks by white musicians using blackface make-up.

miracle play A medieval religious drama that re-enacted miraculous incidents from the lives of saints on the day dedicated to them.

morality play A medieval allegorical drama examining how ordinary people deal with temptation.

music hall A British equivalent of vaudeville.

musical A drama interspersed with numerous songs and dance set-pieces.

Noh Theater Classic Japanese theater. These slow-moving plays can take up to eight hours to perform.

off-Broadway Presented at a theater that is outside the Broadway district, often being experimental in nature.

pantomime Originally all mime, it is based on children's fairy tales and traditionally features transvestite performances from the male romantic and female comic lead roles.

passion play A type of mystery play that originated in the Middle Ages and sought to represent the suffering and death of Christ.

repertory theater A theater company that presents a succession of different plays as opposed to one single play.

Restoration comedy A witty, bawdy seventeenth-century comedy of the type popular in England after the restoration of Charles II to the throne.

showboat A kind of floating theater that plied US inland waterways at the turn of the twentieth century stopping to give performances at various settlements.

soliloquy A speech supposedly unheard by the other actors in which the character confides their innermost thoughts to the audience.

stock company A theater company that presents a repertory of plays at a single theater.

straw hat Used to describe the type of performance staged in resort areas in summer.

summer stock The plays performed by a stock company in a summer program.

theater-in-the-round A theater or performance where the audience is on all sides of the stage.

theater of the absurd A type of drama that tries to portray the absurdity of human life using illogical, meaningless, and deliberately confusing action and dialogue.

tragedy A serious drama where the protagonist is overcome by social or psychological circumstances or personal failure.

vaudeville A variety review of contemporary song and dance. It enjoyed its heyday before the advent of cinema.

Technical theater terms

apron An extension of stage in front of the proscenium arch.

auditorium The area where the audience sits.

batten A wooden bar or metal pipe from which scenery or lights are suspended.

border A horizontal scenic cloth or curtain masking lights and space above stage.

box A separate compartment in an auditorium, seating a small group of people; usually on the sides near the stage but in some old theaters a whole tier may be divided.

box office The place where tickets are bought. At one time, only boxes were reserved.

box set A stage scene that is made up of enclosing walls, like a room.

brace A support set at an angle to hold scenery upright and secured by a weight on a projecting foot.

circle A balcony or tier in the auditorium. The dress circle, usually the most expensive seats where spectators used to dress formally, is the first tier.

cloth A piece of canvas scenery suspended from above: a backcloth at the rear of the stage, or a cloth with shapes cut from it so that the audience can see beyond.

cyclorama A curved and stretched cloth around the rear of the stage which gives the impression of sky or extensive space.

dimmer A rheostat, or electrical apparatus to lower the intensity of lamps.

dips Sockets in the stage for plugging in lamps or electrical effects.

downstage The front part of a stage, toward the audience.

flat A scenic unit of canvas stretched on a frame.

flies The space above the stage where scenery and lighting can hang out of audience view.

floats Footlights, because thy were originally wicks floating in bowls of oil.

flood A lamp that gives a broad spread of light but is not focusable.

foh Front-of-House, the audience part of the theater, including foyers, bars, etc.

follow spot A spot which can be moved to keep an actor lit as he or she moves about the stage.

footlights A row of lights at the front of the stage, necessary in the past to counter the heavy shadows cast by overhead lighting on actors' faces.

forestage The area of stage in front of the curtain in proscenium theaters.

gallery The highest of the tiers of audience seating.

gauze A fine mesh cloth, often painted, visible when lit from the front but disappearing when only lit from behind.

greenroom A room or area in a theater where actors can relax while not on stage.

op (opposite prompt) The left hand side of the stage when facing the audience (right in UK).

pit The seating area on the lower level of the auditorium (now more frequently called the stalls). An orchestra pit is a lowered area in front of a proscenium for musicians.

prompter A person who, unseen by the audience, reminds an onstage actor of his or her lines by whispering them.

proscenium The wall dividing the auditorium from the stage where the proscenium arch is located.

spot A directional lamp.

stalls Separate seats, usually with arm rests, originally at the front of the lower level of the auditorium, now usually all that level.

tabs Tableau curtains, originally used to disclose a tableau, now usually as house tabs for a front curtain.

thrust stage A stage projecting into the audience area.

trap An opening in the stage, covered by hinged or sliding panels, as in a grave trap, a rectangular opening for obvious purposes. A star trap has triangular hinged panels filling a circular hole through which an actor can pop up suddenly.

traverse Curtains which are drawn across the stage.

upstage The rear area of a stage, away from the audience.

wings Areas beyond the acting area to the side of the stage.

cinema

Cinema styles and genres

animation Still paintings, drawings, or puppets filmed to give illusion of movement (cartoons). Walt Disney (1901–66), produced the first full-length feature.

documentary Structured, factual film, sometimes part-dramatized with actors.

film noir Moody style of gangster or thriller film, often shot in dark contrasting images.

New Wave A movement of French 1950s directors whose films revitalized techniques and subject matter.

western A story of the white settlers in America and their conflicts with the Native Americans and each other. At first simplistic "cowboy and Indian" tales, they developed allegorical, mythical, and epic dimensions, rarely historically accurate. Usually made in the US, e.g. *Stagecoach*, *High Noon*. Spaghetti Westerns were 1960s westerns made in Europe by Italian companies.

Cinematic terms and technical words

close-up A technique of holding the camera near the subject and taking the picture at close range.

cut A rapid movement between scenes, to add pace and excitement to the narrative

dissolve Movement from one scene to another by fading the first out and the second in so that the two merge imperceptibly.

dubbing Either replacing the soundtrack with a foreign language one, combining several soundtracks on a single one, or adding sounds such as music to the film.

fade in An effect in which the image appears on screen gradually out of darkness.

fade out The opposite of fade in, in which the image gradually fades away into darkness.

frames The individual still pictures which make up a film.

long shot A shot in which the camera seems to be a long way from the subject, which appears in the distance.

montage French for editing; often used to mean an image developed by rapid cuts instead of in one shot.

panning Moving the camera to follow a moving object or person, or to create a panoramic view of a scene.

reel A film spool, usually containing about 1000 feet of film, approximate running times of 15 mins (silent) and 11 mins (sound). Early cinemas with one projector had to stop to change reels, thus a reel was a convenient production (or part) length and movies were hired as One- or Two-Reelers.

rough cut Footage that has had a preliminary edit, but not a final one.

rushes Unedited footage, usually screened at the end of a day's filming.

scene A series of shots that make up one single unit of the film's action; also, the stage-setting and backcloths for a film.

sequence A single episode in a film which is uninterrupted.

shot A series of frames concerned with a single event.

star system The use of actors to attract and keep audiences, depends on actors constantly playing similar parts.

studio system The application of assembly-line manufacturing and cost control principles to film production. It emphasizes planning and management over creative process.

take Any of several shootings of a scene in a film, producing different versions for the director to choose from.

technicolor Three films, each sensitive to different colors, run simultaneously in a special camera. Superseded by Eastmancolor, which uses a single film run in a standard camera.

tracking Moving along with a camera to follow the action

widescreen A projection screen wider than the standard aspect ratio (proportion) of 4 ft high by 5 ft wide, usually 3 ft x 7 ft. Several patented systems: Cinemascope uses a standard proportion frame on 35mm film but uses an anamorphic lens to squeeze the picture onto the negative and again to correct it when projected from the print; Panavision uses double width (70mm) film, either in the camera and projection or for camera only, and then squeezes the image onto a 35mm print for projection; Todd A-O uses 65mm film; Vistavision uses 35mm film, but run sideways through the camera.

dance

Dance forms and styles

ballet A form of dance with unique traditions and techniques. It has been defined as a synthesis of arts: dancing, drama, music and decor.

belly dance A solo dance performed by a woman with sinuous, provocative movements of the belly and hips.

bharata natyam An ancient Indian dance that combines graceful, flowing movement with the more assertive gestures of the pantomime.

big apple Based on the Charleston, this 1930s dance is orchestrated by a caller who gives instructions to couples arranged in a large circle.

black bottom A 1920s ballroom craze, it was characterized by slide and hobble steps, Charleston rhythm and a slap on the backside.

bolero A lively Spanish dance characterized by aerial action.

bugaku Originating in China, this classical Japanese court dance is performed exclusively by men, elegantly robed and often wearing masks. The dancers move slowly in unison, using their hands to create geometric patterns.

cakewalk A dance in which couples walk in a square formation and take exaggerated high steps and turn corners precisely in mimicry of the white man's artificial manners.

cancan An energetic dance performed by women, involving high kicks and the lifting of frothy skirts.

cha cha A Latin American ballroom dance.

chaconne An old Spanish dance.

Charleston A lively dance with sidekicks from the knees.

clog dance A kind of solo step dance performed with clogs to accentuate the rhythm. Originally a French peasant dance.

Dance of death Originated in the Middle Ages when it was believed that the dead rose up at night to dance over their graves, and lured people into the dance and then death. Also known as the "danse macabre."

disco A dance poupular in the 1970s and set within a structure of certain moves and steps designed to give the impression of "cool."

fandango An eighteenth-century Spanish couples dance. An exuberant, erotic dance in triple time, the dancers enticingly advance and retreat without touching, and at certain sudden halts in the music hold seductive poses.

flamenco Often accompanied by strident guitar brushstrokes, rhythmic hand-clapping and singing, flamenco, a gypsy dance from the south of Spain, is characterized by a high-arched back and rhythmic footwork. The dancers, who should be completely masculine if men and ultrafeminine if female, should epitomize poise, pride and controlled sensuality.

folk dance The traditional dance of the common people and a reflection of their culture. They are communal dances done for pleasure by rural people.

fox-trot A twentieth-century American ballroom dance that consists of easy walking steps to syncopated rhythms.

gavotte A kind of folk dance originating from Gap, in the Haute-Alpes region fo France.

hasapikos A Greek butcher's dance, it is a slow chain dance using small steps and frequent knee bends. It is accompanied by the bouzouki.

hula An essential feature of Hawaian culture, the hula is accompanied by chanting and the actual style of each performance is determined by the chant.

hustle A form of dance to Latin-influenced disco music, originating in the 1970s, in which two partners perform elaborate stylized turns.

jig A lively sixteenth-century solo-step dance native to the British Isles.

jitterbug A variation on the two-step, it was the link between swing and rock'n'roll. Its distinct style is marked by strenuous movements and occasional acrobatics.

limbo A West Indian dance in which the dancer, bending backwards, passes under a horizontally supported stick, without touching it, to rhythmic accompaniment.

line dance An Irish dance involving lines of people linking arms and dancing as one with highly rhythmic footwork.

line dancing A country and western style of group dance in which people dance as individuals, following the same steps, but in lines rather than as couples.

mambo A Cuban dance, the mambo is fast, syncopated and the partners move fairly independently from each other.

Maypole dance Takes place around a flower-decked pole hung with ribbons on May day. A symbolic fertility rite, the dancers holding a length of ribbon, circle the pole in opposite directions weaving in and out of each other, creating a unified ribbon pattern.

merengue A sideways Latin American two-step for couples.

minuet An elegant 17th century French court dance, it began as a folk dance and gradually became a slower, more dignified and complex dance that graced many an aristocratic ballroom.

morris dance A traditional English folk dance accompanied by tambourines, bells, etc., involving much handkerchief waving.

polka A vigorous nineteenth-century Bohemian dance, that became refined in the ballrooms of Europe and the US, but faded in the twentieth century.

polonaise A Polish national dance, it became a stately court dance for couples and featured in ballets.

rumba A social and sexually suggestive dance of Afro-Cuban origin. Highly syncopated in 4/4 time, it became popular in New York and London in the 1930s.

samba A Brazilian dance with African influence, samba is fast, violently danced by a soloist in the middle of a group of dancers. Especially popular at Carnival in Rio and Sao Paulo.

square dance An American folk dance for an even number of couples arranged in sets to form a square. The dance consists of a number of figures whose description is called out by a non-dancing caller.

sword dance An ancient Mediterranean folk dance for men. Two groups, representing darkness and light make high leaps and move in rings and interweaving lines. The climactic figure is often a network of swords held aloft.

tango A slow, graceful ballroom dance, characterized by frequent deep bending of the knees and quick changes of direction. A most complex and subtle dance from nineteenth-century Argentina.

tap dance An indigenous American step dance form usually in complex, syncopated rhythms and executed audibly with the toes and heels of the feet in specially designed shoes.

tarantella Believed to have originated in the Italian town of Taranto in southern Italy, it is a swift. whirling dance executed by two people to music in 6/8 time.

waltz A round dance in triple measure. Originally an Austrian and Bavarian peasant dance, its wide, gliding steps and rapid turning movement caught everyone's imagination the world over. It remains the most popular dance ever.

yang ko Accompanied by chanting, dancers represent the exploits of mythical and heroic Chinese figures.

Classical dance terms

Because classical ballet had its origins in France, its technical vocabulary is in French.

air, en l' (in the air) A succession of movements is executed in the air. The opposite is par terre.

arabesque A pose as though poised for flight, supported on one leg, the other extended backward and the arms disposed harmoniously, usually with the greatest reach.

attitude A pose on one leg with corresponding arm open to side or back, other leg extended to back at 90° with knee bent, corresponding arm raised above head. The raised leg has heel touching supporting leg and the same arm as the supporting leg raised above head.

ballerina A female dancer of the chief classical roles in a company; also called prima ballerina.

barre A wooden bar just above hip height to give hand support for ballet class exercises.

battement (beating) Leg exercises of various kinds executed with a beating motion.

batterie (succession of beats) Movements in which the feet beat together during jumps, *grand batterie* when the jump is high, *petite batterie* when the elevation is slight.

battu A beaten step

bourrée A series of small even staccato steps; the pas de bourrée involves three transfers of weight from foot to foot and has over 20 different variations.

brisé (broken) A leap with the legs lightly beaten before landing on both feet.

chassé A step from a plié in fifth, sliding one foot out, heel down, before transferring weight to it; also done as a jumping step.

choreograper Someone who composes dance steps.

choreography The art of composing dance, or the steps composed.

ciseaux (scissors) A jump from and ending in fifth with legs apart like open scissors.

closed position A position with the feet in first, third or fifth.

corps de ballet Usually the dancers in the company not classed as soloists who dance together. In the Paris Opera, the whole company are known as the corps, lower ranks being called *les quadrilles*.

coryphée A leading member of the corps de ballet. In classical French and Russian ballet, it is a term used for a minor soloist.

coupe A step with the weight on the right foot, with the left drawn up in front in fifth, cutting away the right foot which is raised, or similar executed as a jump. *Coupe dessou* is with the foot behind.

couru A running step. *See* **bourrée**.

dégagé Freeing the working foot in preparation for a step, or shifting weight from one foot to the other.

demi Half, as in *demi plié* (half bent knees), *demi-pointe* (half on toes)

divertissement Originally a danced interlude in an opera, a self-contained series of dances inserted in the main ballet, such as when the main characters sit to watch an entertainment, usually designed to show off technique.

elevation A term applied to all aerial movements.

enchainement (linking) A sequence of steps making a continuous phrase.

entrechat A jump in fifth in which the legs are crossed and uncrossed at the lower calf. Entrechats are numbered not by the beats but by the number of positions taken by the legs, even numbers land in fifth, odd on one foot. Nijinsky reportedly reached entrechat dix (ten).

étoile Star. *Premier Danseur Etoile*, is the highest title given to leading dancers of the Paris Opera.

fermé (closed) In positions first, third and fifth.

fish dive A position in which a dancer is caught and supported by a partner with head and shoulders just clear of the floor.

fouetté (a whipped movement). A step executed on pointe, the working leg whipped out to the side and in to the knee with a slight circular movement, frequently combined with turns as *fouetté en tournant*, to which it gives momentum.

jeté (thrown step). A spring forward, backward or sideways; *grand jeté* is a leap from one foot to the other.

ouverte Open position of the feet.

pas (step) A complete leg movement walking or dancing, also a solo or a dance for a certain number as *pas de seul* (one), *de deux* (two), *de trois* (three), *de quatre* (four).

petit tours (little turns) Short fast turns progressing in a line.

piqué Stepping directly onto pointe without bending knee.

pirouette A turn on one foot propelled by swing of the arm.

plié (bend). Bending of the knees while erect with the feet turned out, heels on the ground; *demi plié* becomes so low that the heels must be raised; *grand plié* lower with the buttocks as near the heels (still kept as close to the ground as possible).

pointe The extremity of the toe, or a point on the toe.

pointe shoes Shoes with reinforced toes, originally padded with cotton but since 1860s stiffened with glue and darned to give support when dancing on toe tips.

premier danseur (male), **danseuse** (female). The leading dancer or, for women, the rank below *étoile*.

prima ballerina *See* **ballerina**.

prima ballerina assoluta A title bestowed on only a few occasions on the outstanding leading dancer of the Russian

Imperial Ballet.

promenade A slow turn on one foot with the body held in a set pose.

régisseur A stage manager responsible for mounting and rehearsing ballets in repertoire.

relevé (lifted step) Raising on full or part point.

repetition rehearsal

révérence A bow or curtsy.

rivoltade A jump and turn with one leg passing in front of the other landing in reverse direction.

sur les pointes (on the pointes). *See* **pointe.**

terre à terre (ground to ground). Steps which leave the ground only sufficiently to be pointed

toe shoes Another term for pointe shoes.

tour a turn

tutu Originally a short petticoat sewn together between the legs at each performance for concealment; now short classical ballet skirt made of underpants trimmed with several layers of superimposed frills.

variation A solo dance, especially a solo section of a pas de deux.

music

Musical styles, genres and movements

absolute music Music free of all reference to anything outside the essential nature of the music. The listener's attention is not distracted by lyric or association, and can therefore focus entirely on the beauty of the music itself.

aleatory music Any form of music that involves elements chosen at random by the performer, usually by such methods as the throwing of dice or the splashing of ink onto music paper. The term "aleatory" comes from the Latin word alea, meaning dice or game of chance.

alternative rap Rap or hip hop music that does not conform to any of the established forms or genres.

bachata The traditional style of folk music of the Dominican Republic.

baroque A style of music characterized by ornamentation and use of counterpoint. The baroque era lasted for about 150 years, beginning in 1600 with the first attempts at opera, and ending in 1750 with the death of its great master, Johann Sebastian Bach.

baroque pop A fusion of Pop music with elements from orchestral classical music such as large string sections and massed horns.

bass music Rap or hip hop music from the mid 1980s in which electronic drum machines replaced drum breaks sampled from recordings.

bebop A form of jazz invented by black jazz artists in the United States in the 1940s who were determined to break free from the constraints of the big dance bands. Small groups of musicians were typical, playing at fast tempos, often extemporizing, and displaying great instrumental virtuosity. Also known as bop or rebop.

beguine A broad term referring to the traditional music of a large part of the West Indies including Cuba, Jamaica, Hispaniola, and Puerto Rico. Characterized by the almost universal use of the clarinet and the trombone.

belair The drumming style of the island of Martinique. Named for the very large traditional drum used on the island.

bhangra A musical style that developed among Britain's large Asian population and has its roots in the traditional music of the Punjab region of India.

bikutsi A traditional Cameroonian musical style based on the rhythmic music of the Beti people.

blaxploitation Music soundtracks from movies of the blaxploitation genre popular during the 1970s. Blaxploitation movies were among the first in the United States to feature black characters in leading roles and to be made by black directors.

blue-eyed soul Soul music produced or performed by white musicians.

bluegrass Country music evolving from the Scots-Irish traditional music of the southern Appalachian Mountains. Bluegrass uses traditional mountain dance-group instrumentation, usually featuring unamplified mandolin, banjo, and fiddle.

blues The blues is a distinctive, indigenous black-American song form, important not only in its own right, but also because it was a major element in the evolution of jazz and, later, rock'n'roll.

boogie-woogie A jazz piano style based on blues guitar, with a strong, repetitive left-hand bass line and usually having eight beats to the bar. An early boogie-woogie hit was "Honky Tonk Train Blues" released in the 1930s by Meade "Lux" Lewis.

Brill Building pop Pop music produced by professional songwriters and to be performed by musicians under contract. Named for the Brill Building in New York City, which was home to the offices of several music publishing houses.

British rap Rap music performed by British musicians and often featuring the influences of traditional Caribbean music such as reggae.

Britpop A form of rock music produced by British bands in the 1990s and characterized by memorable guitar-driven tunes, a brash outgoing attitude, and a pre-occupation with British as opposed to American cultural experience.

brown-eyed soul Soul music produced or performed by Latino musicians.

bubblegum pop Optimistic, lightweight, pop music of the late 1960s and early 1970s often written by professional songwriters working for music publishing houses and performed by session musicians.

chamber music A style of music that first appeared in the fifteenth century, written for performance in a chamber, or room, rather than in a church or theater. Although chamber music has long been a staple of the concert hall, it retains an air of intimacy, with the number of musicians usually limited to eight.

chimurenga Zimbabwean political protest music of the 1970s.

Christian rap Rap or hip hop music with a Christian message.

church music Music that forms an integral part of organized Christian worship. Over the centuries, this has mainly taken the form of music performed by choirs, but it is not unusual to find it being provided nowadays by folk musicians or even rock groups.

classical music In technical musical usage this means music composed during the late eighteenth and early nineteenth centuries, characterized by the development of the sonata by such composers as Mozart. In popular use, however, the term is used to mean any serious art music as distinct from jazz, pop, or folk.

cocktail Music produced in the early 1990s that imitated the popular easy listening styles of the 1950s and 1960s.

comedy rap Rap music with a comedic theme, usually in the lyrics but sometimes also in the music.

consort music A form of chamber music for a "consort," a small group of instruments such as viols or recorders. When the instruments are all of the same family the group is called a whole consort; when instruments belonging to more than one family are used together this is called a broken consort or a mixed consort.

contemporary R&B The modern, commercially focused, version of R&B that developed from the urban R&B movement of the 1980s and 1990s.

country and western A style of twentieth-century popular music that developed in the United States out of the folk music of the rural southeast, with its Scottish and Irish folk music influences, and western, cowboy-style music. The form was also influenced by black musical styles such as the blues, and has become widely popular outside the United States. Also known as country music or C & W.

country-soul A fusion of Soul and Country music in which established Country songs are reinterpreted by Soul musicians.

cowpunk A fusion of punk and country music that emerged in the early 1980s.

deep funk Little known and rare funk music from the 1960s that is highly sought after by modern Rap and Hip Hop musicians.

deep funk revival Modern music produced in imitation of the style of deep funk.

deep soul An early form of soul music usually performed by vocalists and musicians strongly influenced by the gospel music of the American South.

dirty rap Rap or hip hop music characterized by sexual themes.

dirty south A form of rap from the second half of the 1990s in which profanity and sexual themes are dominant.

disco A form of R&B music that developed from funk in the early 1970s. Disco abandoned many of the vocal and improvised elements of funk in favor of a strong beat.

dixieland A New Orleans jazz style played in duple time by small groups and marked by ensemble and solo performances.

djadbong A traditional Senegalese musical style with many similarities to reggae used in ritual ceremonies.

doo-wop A form of R&B and rock music popular in the 1950s and performed by groups of harmonized singers usually unaccompanied by instruments.

East Coast rap Rap music originating from the East Coast of the United States; particularly from New York City. East Coast Rap was the original form of Rap music and dominated the genre until the 1990s.

electronic music Any form of music that involves sounds produced electronically, such as by manipulating an oscillating current, or electronic instruments, especially keyboards. Sythesizers are typical instruments, and prerecorded sounds, sometimes on repeating loops of magnetic tape, are often used in performance.

emo A variant of punk music in which the lyrics are highly personal to the performer and address emotional issues.

folk music Essentially this means any type of music that springs from the common people and is passed down from one generation to the next, largely by oral means, often being closely bound up with a particular culture or group of people. The music is usually performed on traditional acoustic instruments, and the term is also used to mean music or song composed in this idiom by contemporary musicians.

foreign language rap Rap music performed in languages other than English or Spanish.

fuji A Nigerian musical style that developed in the second half of the 20th century.

funk A form of R&B music that became popular in the 1970s and which is often said to have originated with the 1970 James Brown single *Get Up (I Feel Like Being A) Sex Machine*. Funk is characterized by primordial emotions and extended improvisations around a simple musical theme.

gabba An extreme form of techno music characterized by backbeats that exceed 200 beats per minute.

gangsta rap A form of rap or hip hop music that developed in the late 1980s and featuring the frequent use of profanity and stories of urban crime in the lyrics.

G-funk A slow and understated form of gangsta rap invented in the early 1990s by rap artist Dr Dre.

go-go A variant of hip hop and R&B music that evolved in the city of Washington DC in the mid 1980s. Characterized by an emphasis on beat rather than lyrics.

golden age hip hop Hip hop music from the period between 1986, when hip hop music first became commercially successful, and 1993 when gangsta rap and other hardcore rap styles started to dominate.

gospel music A form of religious music that originated in the evangelical churches of black populations in the southern United States. Containing elements of jazz and blues, it often takes the form of a call and response between the preacher, who sings or declaims a line, and the congregation, which sings an affirmatory reply.

goth rock A variant of rock music popular in the late 1980s and characterized by gloomy, introspective, and highly personal lyrics.

grunge A fusion of rock and punk music that became popular in the 1990s.

gwo ka A drum-based musical style from the island of Guadeloupe in the Caribbean.

hair metal Rock or heavy metal music of the late 1980s performed by highly commercialized bands characterized by elaborate hairstyles, grotesque makeup, and highly theatrical costumes and stage sets.

hardcore rap A form of rap music in which confrontational lyrics and aggressive backing tracks predominate. Gangsta rap is the most widely known form of hardcore rap, but not all hardcore rap concentrates on criminal themes.

highlife A West African style of music that combines African dance music with Western guitar sounds and jazz influences.

Hi-NRG A highly energetic form of dance music from the late 1980s that relied heavily on the use of synthesizers and drum machines.

hip hop A musical style originating in New York City in the 1970s and featuring a spoken voice track (rap) backed by a musical track usually constructed from fragments of recorded songs.

house A broad category of music that emerged from the dance club culture of the early 1980s. House music is predominantly instrumental, involves the use of music and sounds sampled from a wide range of sources, and has a simple but very dominant beat.

impressionism A musical technique or movement that shared the aim of impressionism in painting, that is, to capture and convey an impression of changing reality or fleeting mood. The main exponent of this style was the French composer, Claude Debussy (1862–1918).

industrial A fusion of rock and electronic music characterized by the use of sounds sampled from real-world sources (such as machinery or street noises) and by its rapid and aggressive rhythms.

jaipongan A modern Javanese musical style that evolved from the traditional Javanese dance music known as ketuk tilu and featuring the inclusion of Western instruments and dance movements.

jangle pop A popular form of rock music that evolved in the United States in the mid-1980s. Characterized by a revival of the folk guitar and pop sounds of the 1960s.

jazz An improvised Afro-American musical idiom. Although its melodies and harmonies are influenced by European music, its rhythms are fundamentally African. Jazz is marked by evolutionary changes that represent more than simple fashion or responses to social change. Its unusual rhythms and complex harmony arrangements combined with a mix of technique and improvisation have influenced everything in its wake.

jazz rap A fusion of jazz and rap music that features the rhythms of rap and the tonal qualities of traditional jazz.

jit A Zimbabwean musical style featuring percussion and vocals.

juju A Nigerian musical style with roots in the traditional drum-based music of the Yoruba people.

junkanoo A Bahamian style of dance music that evolved from the traditional music of West Africa.

kraut rock Rock music from 1970s Germany characterized by an increasing emphasis on the use of sampled sounds and electronic music.

Latin rap Rap music performed by Latino musicians either in English or Spanish.

Latin soul A variant of soul music performed by Latino musicians and popular in the 1960s in New York City. Latin Soul included elements of mambo, pop, and jazz music.

left-field hip hop A fusion of rap and electronic music styles characterized by the use of highly sophisticated sampling and editing equipment. Vocals tend to be less significant than the backing track in left-field hip hop.

lo-fi Rock music from the 1980s recorded on low quality recording equipment by amateur musicians.

madchester A form of rock music performed by British musicians from the city of Manchester in the late 1980s and early 1990s. Characterized by a fusion of house music dance rhythms and pop melodies.

makossa A Cameroonian style of dance music.

marabi A South African musical style that emerged in the 1920s from a fusion of Western jazz and the traditional music of the Zulu, Xhosa, and Soto peoples.

march A piece of music, usually in duple meter and with a second part known as a trio, suitable for soldiers to march to, or one composed in this style. A notable composer of marches is the American bandmaster John Philip Sousa (1854–1932), who wrote such pieces as "Stars and Stripes Forever." Marches, particularly in the late nineteenth and early twentieth centuries, have often been adapted for dances.

math rock A style of rock music characterized by complex and technically-demanding instrumentation.

mbalax A Senegalese musical style that developed in the 1970s from the traditional drum music of the Wolof people.

mbaqanga A South African musical style that evolved in the Black Townships in the late 1950s and early 1960s.

mbira A traditional Zimbabwean musical style originating with the Shona people and named for the mbira hand piano which is the style's primary instrument.

mbube A South African musical style that emerged from a fusion of church singing and the traditional choral music of the Zulu people.

mento A Jamaican style of dance music.

Midwest rap Rap music originating from the Midwest of the United States; particularly from Chicago, Detroit, Cleveland, and Mineapolis.

minimalist music A musical movement based on extremely simplified, prolonged, rhythms and patterns with great use of repetition of individual phrases and avoidance of embellishment. It often makes use of the instruments and techniques of electronic music. A notable exponent of this type of music is the American composer Philip Glass (1937–), with such compositions as "Akhnaten."

mod Music produced by British bands of the 1960s in the style of American R&B.

Motown A record company set up in the 1960s in Detroit (the "Motor Town" from which the name is derived) by Berry Gordy, Jr. The name became associated with a characteristic style of black music that combined rhythm and blues with the rhythms and ballad style of pop music, often with orchestral backing. The company featured a stable of songwriters and composers that scored many hits in the 1960s and 70s, including Smokey Robinson and The Supremes.

neo-soul Soul music produced since the late 1990s that closely imitates the style of soul music from the 1970s.

New Age music New Age music is a term applied to the works of composers and musicians who strive to create soothing audio environments rather than follow song structures. Born of an interest in spirituality and healing in the late 1970s, it is often used as an aid in meditation.

new jack swing A musical style that developed in the 1980s as soul musicians began incorporating elements of rap and hip hop into their music.

New Orleans R&B A form of R&B music popular in the city of New Orleans. Characterized by an optimistic tone, the use of piano and horn accompaniment, and Caribbean rhythms.

nyahbinghi A form of reggae music characterized by dominant drum rhythms.

Oi! A form of punk music that developed in the late 1970s in Britain that attempted to return to the populist non-commercial origins of punk. Characterized by extremely simple tunes and lyrics.

old-school rap Rap music produced by the first generation of rap artists in New York City in the 1970s and 1980s.

omutibo A Kenyan musical style developed in the 1960s and 1970s and characterized by the use of two guitars and empty soda bottles for percussion.

opera Drama set to music with the texts wholly or largely sung. Its seriousness or elevation of purpose and intention usually distinguishes it from other forms of musical theater with text.

operetta A form of musical theater also known as comic opera or light opera. Operetta (the Italian word for "little opera") occupies a position in the theater somewhere between opera and musical comedy.

party rap Rap or hip hop music that emphasizes strong rhythms rather than inventive vocals.

Philly soul Soul music originating from the city of Philadelphia in the early 1970s. Characterized by a lush tonal quality and highly distinctive vocalists.

political rap Rap or hip hop music with overtly political or sociopolitical themes.

pop-rap Rap music that combines traditional elements of rap with some melodic forms from pop music.

post disco A transitional musical style that emerged from disco music in the late 1970s and eventually evolved into modern house music in the early 1980s.

program music A type of music, usually instrumental in form, that is intended to evoke a scene, communicate an idea, or tell a story. Typical subjects for program music are poems, extracts from plays, well-known paintings, or particular sections of landscape.

punk A type of rock music that originated in the mid–1970s, characterized by fast and aggressive playing, often deliberately unpolished, and confrontational lyrics and performance styles. Also known as punk rock.

quiet storm A relaxed, sensuous, and romantic form of R&B popular in the 1980s and early 1990s. Named for the 1975 Smokey Robinson album *A Quiet Storm*.

ragtime A style of jazz piano playing with a highly syncopated melody, very popular in the late nineteenth and early twentieth centuries. It developed out of black minstrel music and was popularized by the pianist and composer Scott Joplin (1868–1917).

rap A type of pop music in which performers declaim or chant over a prerecorded musical accompaniment, often using short extracts (called samples) from other well-known recordings. The form is characterized by the street language of black culture and boastful, often confrontational, words.

reggae A style of pop music that originated among black people in the West Indies, with a strongly accented upbeat. Popularized by such performers as Bob Marley (1945–81), reggae is often political in content, and is associated particularly with Rastafarianism.

retro-soul Soul music produced after the peak popularity of soul in the first half of the 1970s.

rhythm and blues (R&B) A very popular and wide-ranging style of music that emerged from traditional blues in the 1940s. R&B can be characterized by its use of blues chords played over a strong and consistent backbeat and by its emphasis on composition rather than the improvisation common in traditional blues. Hip hop, rap, soul, and disco are all categories of R&B and R&B also formed the foundation of rock and roll.

riot grrrl A form of feminist punk music that developed in the United States in the 1990s.

rock music A type of pop music that developed out of rock'n'roll in the 1960s and 1970s. It is based around amplified instruments, especially the electric guitar and electric bass, and is characterized by a strong bass line and driving rhythms. It is typically performed by rock groups, and while fast dance music is the staple form, slower ballad-style songs are also a popular part of the repertoire.

rococo A light and harmonic style of music that came to prominence in the early and mid eighteenth century in Europe, chiefly in France and Germany, following the baroque period. It is similar to baroque music in being characterized by ornamentation, but it is distinguished from baroque especially in featuring reduced use of counterpoint and less formality and complexity.

romanticism A movement in European music of the late eighteenth and early nineteenth centuries, based on a revolt against classicism in favor of more imaginative, free, and picturesque modes and subject matter. It is characterized by the expression of emotions and interest in the sublime, as often represented by nature, and the exotic. It paralleled the Romantic movement in literature, from which it often borrowed themes and subjects.

salsa A type of Latin American dance music that originated in the mid–1970s. It developed initially among the Hispanic community of New York City and its influences include the Latin American big band dance music of the 1940s as well as modern jazz, Afro-Caribbean rhythms, and rock music. The name is also used for the style of dancing to this music and is derived from a Spanish word for a hot sauce typically served with Mexican food.

screamo A variant of punk and emo music characterized by vocalists who alternate between lyrically sung verses and guttural screamed choruses.

séga A Madagascan style of dance music characterized by a variation of the waltz rhythm.

serial music A form of music based on repetition or the use of series in composition, such as repeated rhythms, timbres, or pitches.

Shibuya kei A style of Japanese Pop music that originated in the Shibuya district of Tokyo and characterized by an extremely eclectic mix of musical influences from the West.

shoegaze A form of late 1980s and early 1990s British rock characterized by the motionless "shoe-gazing" performances of its practitioners.

singspiel A form of German comic opera of the late eighteenth and early nineteenth centuries in which there is spoken dialogue as well as self-contained musical set-pieces. The term is a German word meaning "song-play," and its exponents included Mozart, whose "Magic Flute" is often considered as its apotheosis.

sonero A traditional Cuban musical style that forms the foundations for a wide range of modern Latin music.

soukous A popular form of African dance music that originated in the Democratic Republic of the Congo (then called Zaire) in the 1970s.

soul A commercialized form of R&B that became popular in the 1960s and 1970s. A large range of musical styles are categorized under soul.

southern rap Rap music originating from the southern states of the United States; particularly from Miami, New Orleans, and Atlanta. Southern rap has never been as popular as East Coast rap or West Coast rap but has produced many individual popular tracks.

spiritual A religious folk song, generally associated with

American blacks. Spirituals became an aspect of culture in the deep South, and many used biblical themes in their texts to express symbolically the plight of the slaves, their longing for freedom, and their faith in God and a meaningful afterlife.

spouge A Barbadian musical style that was popular throughout the Caribbean in the late 1960s and early 1970s. Characterized by reggae, calypso, and soca influenced melodies and rhythms performed at a highly accelerated tempo.

swing A 1940s bridge between orchestras and rock'n'roll, swing featured big bands with strong brass sections and a swinging, rolling rhythm, often provided by a double bass.

taarab A musical style popular among the Swahili-speaking peoples of East Africa that emerged from a fusion of Egyptian and Indian melodies with African rhythms.

thrash A form of rock or heavy metal music that developed in the 1980s. Characterized by a very rapid tempo, aggressive atonal guitar playing, and visceral subject matter.

turntablism A distinct form of hip hop music in which the music that forms the backing track for the vocalist (rapper) in traditional hip hop music becomes the central element of the performance. Turntablists manipulate vinyl records on multiple turntables to create their music.

underground rap Rap or hip hop music with either a much greater emphasis on linguistic inventiveness than mainstream forms or a greater emphasis on the use of extreme profanity and disturbing criminal themes.

urban R&B A form of R&B popular in the 1980s and 1990s and characterized by romantic ballads, melodic dance tracks, and professional production standards.

West Coast rap Rap music originating from the West Coast of the United States; particularly from Los Angeles. West Coast rap was the most popular form of rap music throughout the mid 1990s.

zouk A modern Caribbean style of dance music that utilizes both traditional musical styles and contemporary electronic music as inspiration.

Zydeco A type of popular music that developed from the Cajun and black populations of Louisiana bayou country. It combines traditional Cajun dance melodies and rhythms and French lyrics along with blues and rock influences. It is usually played by small groups in which the accordion and fiddle are prominent.

Musical forms

anthem A choral piece for use in church services.

arabesque An ornate musical passage.

ballad A narrative song, or piece in similar style.

cancan A composition in 2/4 time in which one part is repeated by and overlaps another. In vogue in Paris in the 1830s.

cantata A sung work, now usually accompanied by an orchestra, shorter than an oratorio.

capriccio A short, lively instrumental piece, often humorous.

chamber music Music for a small group of musicians, suitable for playing in small halls.

chorale A stately hymn, especially of the Lutheran Church.

coda A passage bringing a work or movement to a conclusion.

concerto A work for a solo instrument, with orchestral accompaniment.

contrapuntal Typical of or using counterpoint.

counterpoint Two or more melodic lines combined harmoniously.

divertimento An entertaining chamber suite or miniature symphony.

divertissement A fantasia on well-known tunes.

étude A study, or exercise, to display technique.

fugue A composition of many parts on a short theme and using counterpoint.

Gregorian chant Unaccompanied church vocal music without definite rhythm.

impromptu An improvised composition or a piece suggesting spontaneity.

intermezzo A play with music between acts of an opera, later any interlude or a short movement in a symphony.

lieder A German song style (*lied* = song), especially as used by Romantic composers.

madrigal An unaccompanied song for several voices.

Mass A musical setting of the Liturgy of the Eucharist.

minuet A graceful seventeenth-century court dance in triple time, used as third movement in many classical symphonies.

motet A piece of polyphonic sacred music for unaccompanied voices.

movement A section of a large work, especially a symphony, usually complete in itself.

music theater Theatrical work with music and drama integrated, as opposed to opera where music tends to be the most important component.

nocturne A lyrical serenade, especially in Chopin's works for piano.

opera Extended drama, its text sung, often with bravura solo and multiple voice passages.

operetta Light opera, often with spoken dialogue.
oratorio A work for solo voices, chorus, and orchestra, usually of a religious or contemplative nature.
overture An orchestral introduction to an opera or ballet, sometimes to a symphony, or an independent and usually programmatic concert work.
plainsong A nonmetrical church chant.
polyphony Music with independent melodies interwoven.
program music A piece depicting elements of a story, scene, or philosophical ideas.
recitative A singing style like declaimed speech, used for essential narration in some operas and oratorios.
requiem A funeral mass and a musical setting of it.
rhapsody An instrumental fantasia, often based on folk song.
rondo A piece of instrumental music with a recurring main theme.
scherzo A lively piece, often humorous, in triplet time and used for the third movement of symphonies and sonatas.
serenade or **serenata** A piece appropriate for evening; a composition in several movements for a small group.
sinfonietta A short, light form of symphony.
sonata An instrumental work in three or four movements for soloist or with piano accompaniment.
suite A group of dances, or a set of instrumental pieces drawn from a longer opera, ballet, or similar work.
symphonic poem A narrative orchestral piece, usually in one movement.
symphony An extended orchestral work, usually in four movements.
toccata Keyboard work to display virtuosity.
variations Development of a single theme through a variety of forms.

Musical instructions

accelerando getting gradually faster
adagio slower pace
ad libitum at the performer's discretion
affettuoso with warmt
agitato restlessly
alla breve twice the speed notes show
allegretto moderately fast
allegro fast pac
andante gently, flowing
animato animatedly

apassionato passionately
arpeggio with notes in rapid succession
calando getting gradually slower and quieter
coll'arco with the bow
col legno striking the strings with the stick of the bow
con bravura boldly
con sordino with a mute attached to the instrument
crescendo increase volume gradually
da capo repeat from beginning
dal segno repeat from the place marked
decrescendo decrease volume
diminuendo getting softer
dolce sweetly
dolente sadly
doppio movimento twice as fast
estinto so soft you can hardly hear
falsetto singing above normal range
fine end
forte loudly
forte-piano loudly, then immediately softly
fortissimo very loudly
fortississimo as loudly as possible
forzando with strong accents
giocoso merrily
glissando sliding through notes
grave slowly and heavily
grazioso gracefully
largo broadly, and slower than adagio and lento
legato smoothly
lento slower than adagio
maestoso grandly
marcato with each note emphasized distinctly
mezzo forte moderately loud
mezzo piano moderately soft
obbligato essential
ossia or (used when suggesting an easier alternative)
pianissimo very softly
pianississimo as softly as possible
piano softly
pizzicato plucked not bowed
poco a poco little by little
preciso precisely
rallentando slowing down
rinforzando reinforcing
segue following without a break

sempre always
sforzando strongly accented
smorzando gradually getting slower and softer
sostenuto sustained
sotto voce in a low voice
spiritoso spiritedly
staccato sharp and separated, not flowing
sul ponticello with the bow close to the bridge
sul tasto with the bow close to the fingerboard
tempo primo at the original tempo
tenuto with the full note value or slightly longer
tremolo rapidly repeating one note
tutti all, the whole orchestra or chorus
unison all singing the same notes
vivace lively
volte subito turn the page quickly

Types of singing voice

alto High in Italian. The lower type of female voice, but originally in church music the male high voice above the melody sung by tenors. Now mainly used to describe boys and female voices in choirs.

baritone A man's voice of intermediate range, the usual range in which most men speak and sing.

bass The lowest male voice, a true bass not only reaches low notes, but also has a deep quality. Although often given long low notes, the bass can be as vocally agile as any other singer.

basso profundo A bass voice of unusually low range.

boy soprano A boy with an undeepened voice in the soprano range.

castrato An adult male voice in soprano or contralto range achieved by castration to prevent voice deepening. Found in European church choirs in seventeenth and eighteenth century and a popular voice for operatic composers such as Handel.

coloratura soprano A soprano with an agile, florid style.

contralto The lowest range of any female voice.

counter tenor The term now more usually used for an adult male alto soloist.

falsetto A male voice pushed above the normal range, as in the adult alto, now usually used for a tone lacking the fullness of the counter tenor.

heldentenor Hero tenor in German. A tenor with the power to sing above the sound of a large orchestra.

lyric soprano A light and sweet soprano.

mezzo-soprano A female vocal range almost as high as a soprano and almost as low as an alto, usually rich and ideal for dramatic roles in opera which are frequently written for this range, for example, Carmen.

soprano The highest type of female voice, approximately from middle C upward for two octaves, or the same range for a boy or castrato. They may be either light and sweet, or richly dramatic.

spinto soprano A lyric soprano with some elements of the dramatic.

tenor The highest natural adult male voice which may be either light and agile, or rich and sonorous.

treble Another term for boy soprano.

arts terms and techniques

Painting and drawing

abstract art An art form that represents ideas (by means of geometric and other designs) instead of natural forms. *Compare* **representational art**.

brush drawing Generally an Oriental technique of painting that relies on varieties of brushwork, usually executed over a wash of diluted watercolor.

caricature A picture ludicrously exaggerating the qualities, defects, or peculiarities of a person or idea.

cartoon (**1**) A humorous sketch or drawing usually telling a story or caricaturing some person or action. (**2**) In fine arts, a preparatory sketch or design for a picture or ornamental motif to be transferred to a fresco or tapestry.

chiaroscuro (Italian, "light-dark") (**1**) The rendering of light and shade in a painting. (**2**) The subtle gradations and marked variations of light and shade for dramatic effect. (**3**) A woodcut print produced from two blocks.

colors, complementary Two colors at opposite points on the color scale, for example, orange and blue, green and red.

colors, primary Red, yellow, and blue, the mixture of which will yield all other colors in the spectrum, but which themselves cannot be produced through a mixture of other colors.

colors, secondary Orange, green, and purple, colors produced by mixing two primary colors.

composition The organization of the parts of a work into a unified whole.

coulisse Objects and figures arranged at the sides of a painting in order to focus the eye onto the central piece of the work.

diptych A work of art with two panels, as in a two-panelled altarpiece.

distemper A cheap and impermanent method of painting in which powdered colors are mixed with glue.

dragging A technique of applying paint lightly over a textured surface to gain the effect of both light and dark "broken" color.

easel picture (or cabinet picture) (in the Renaissance) A small painting meant to be displayed on an easel rather than hung.

egg and dart (in classical art) A decorative technique that alternated arrowlike shapes with oval forms.

etching A process in which a special needle is used to draw a design on a metal plate overlaid with wax. The plate is then treated with acid, inked, and finally used to print reproductions of the design.

figurative Representing a human or an animal form.

finger painting A Chinese watercolor technique using a finger instead of a brush.

foreshortening Reducing or distorting in order to represent three-dimensional space as perceived by the eye, according to the rules of perspective.

foxing A brown spotting that discolors prints, caused by dampness.

fresco The technique of painting on moist lime plaster with colors ground in water or a limewater mixture. The paint and plaster bond chemically to become permanent.

fugitive pigments Inferior pigments that tend to fade when exposed to the sun or disintegrate in a polluted atmosphere.

genre painting A realistic style of painting in which everyday life forms the subject matter, as distinguished from religious or historical painting.

hard-edge painting A painting executed in long and thick flat color areas, all of which have sharply defined edges.

highlight The lightest point or tone in a painting.

icon A religious painting (usually on wood or ivory) associated with Eastern churches.

impasto (1) In painting, the thick application of paint. (2) In ceramics, the application of enamel or slip to a ceramic object to form a decoration in low relief.

isocephaly (in classical Greek art) A technique which poses groups of figures at the same height, regardless of the action or purpose of each figure.

landscape A painting whose main subject is pure landscape without human figures; rare in western art before the seventeenth century.

lay figure A wooden model of the human body that is jointed so that it can be posed and arranged in clothing; used by artists and sculptors.

letterism Letters, symbols, and words placed in artistic juxtaposition; an art form popular in the 1950s.

macalature A "thin" or partially obscured print made from a plate that needs re-inking.

makemono A painting (generally Oriental) on a long scroll.

middle distance (or middle ground) The represented space in a picture between background and foreground.

miniature A tiny painting (less than 6 in across), usually a portrait.

mural A painting or decoration applied to a wall, usually executed in oil, fresco, or tempera.

narrative painting One that tells a story; very popular in Victorian England.

oiling out A process of rubbing oil into a painting to brighten up colors. Although a luster is restored for a while, the ultimate effect is to further darken the shades.

optical mixing The visual mixing of colors performed by the eye from a distance, e.g. dabs of blue and yellow paint combine to give the sensation of green.

palette (1) A flat surface used by a painter to mix colors, traditionally oblong with a hole for the thumb. (2) The range of colors available to a painter.

papiers collés (French: "pasted papers") Pictures made from bits of paper, tissue, cardboard, etc., that have been glued together in artistic color or form.

passage (1) A particular part of a painting. (2) The transition from one shade to another. (3) A special technique. (4) An area in a painting that has been painted over by someone other than the artist.

paste (1) A soft, subdued color. (2) A dry paste made up of ground pigments, chalk and gum water formed into a stick. (3) A drawing made with such a stick.

pellicle The fine "skin" that forms when oil paint dries.

perspective A method of representing three-dimensional volumes and spatial relationships on a flat surface.

petard An artwork produced to draw attention to itself through unusual composition, subject matter, etc.

pigments Dry paints or dyes that are mixed with oil, water, or other material.

plastic (in a painting) Conveying a three-dimensional impression through the modeling and movement of the figures.

polychrome Of many or various colors.

polyptych A work of art involving two or more panels, most frequently more than three panels, since diptych (two panels) and triptych (three panels) are more commonly used.

portrait painting A representation of a human being. The first portraits were usually of kings or leaders.

primary colors *See* **colors, primary.**

priming The application of a coat of white paint (usually zinc or lead) to a sized canvas in order to prepare it for painting.

psychedelic art Pseudo-visionary works created by artists under (or claiming to be under) the influence of drugs.

quadratura Painting on a ceiling or a wall to create the illusion of limitless space.

relief (1) The projection of an image from its background.

(2) (painting and drawing) The apparent projection of parts conveying the illusion of three dimensions. (3) (printing) Any process in which ink impressions are produced from the high areas of prepared printing blocks.

representational art An art form that endeavors to show figures and objects exactly as they appear to the eye. *Compare* **abstract art**.

retreating color Shades of green or blue used to suggest distance.

scumbling A painting technique in which parts are overlayed with opaque or semi-opaque color applied lightly with an almost dry brush.

secondary colors *See* **colors, secondary**.

squaring The transferral of a small sketch to a larger space by dividing the sketch into numbered squares and copying the design in each square onto the larger surface.

stenciling A method of producing images or letters from sheets of cardboard, metal, or other materials from which images or letters have been cut away.

still life A study of an arrangement of inanimate objects, such as fruit or flowers; a favorite form of the Dutch School.

tactile values Those elements in art that convey an illusion of the tangible, so that the viewer's senses react to temperature, motion, texture, etc.

texture (1) The visual and tactile quality of a work effected through the particular way the materials are worked. (2) The distribution of tones or shades of a partcicular color.

tinsel painting (or oriental or crystal painting) A painting on glass that has been backed by tinfoil; a popular fad in the nineteenth century.

tone The quality or value of color, e.g. warm or cold tones.

triptych A series of three painted panels or doors that are hinged or folded.

trompe l'oeil (in painting) The fine, detailed rendering of objects to convey the illusion of spatial and tactile qualities.

underpainting The initial painting of a picture in one color to lay out the composition.

values (in painting) The degree of lightness or darkness in a color.

vanitas A still life art form developed in the seventeenth century to reflect the transience of life. Usually depictions of such objects as dead flowers, skulls, hourglasses, etc.

veduta A painting of a city or town lucid and faithful enough that the location is easily identified.

Painting and drawing media

acrylic paint A synthetic, quick-drying paint that can be used in thick, heavy layers or thin washes on most surfaces. Additives can be used to provide matt or gloss finishes.

airbrush A compressed-air powered atomizer which is used to spray paint. Shaped like a large fountain pen, it produces a fine mist of color giving a smooth finish with subtle tonal gradations. The instrument is commonly used in advertising and graphic design.

chalk A soft stone, similar to a very soft limestone, used for drawing. Crayon is powdered chalk mixed with wax or oil.

encaustic The process of burning-in colors, particularly through inlaying colored clays, and by fusing or burning wax colors into the surface of ceramics.

gouache (or poster paint) An opaque mixture of watercolor paint and white pigment, as opposed to pure watercolor which employs transparent colors.

inks Liquids for drawing or painting; generally the colors are a suspension or present as a dye. Sometimes, as with Indian ink or white ink, there may be opaque pigments in suspension. Inks may be applied with different types of pen or soft hairbrushes.

oil paint A paint made by mixing color pigments with oil (usually linseed oil) to produce a malleable, slow-drying substance. The technique evolved gradually during the latter Middle Ages. The van Eyck brothers did much to perfect the medium.

pastel A paint medium of powdered color mixed with gum arabic to form a hard stick. When applied to paper, the color adheres to the surface and can be made permanent by fixing with spray varnish.

pencil A mixture of graphite and clay in stick form covered by a hard casing. The greater the clay element, the harder the pencil.

tempera A paint medium made by mixing color pigments with substances such as egg white, egg yolk, glue, gelatine, or casein. True tempera is when the colors are ground with egg yolk only. The medium was largely supplanted in the fifteenth century by oil paint.

watercolor A paint medium of color pigments mixed with water-soluble gum arabic. When moistened with water, a watercolor paint produces a transparent color that is applied to paper, usually white, the paper showing through the paint.

Sculpture: terms and techniques

alabaster Marble-like stone, usually white.

anaglyph A carving or ornament in bas-relief.

armature A metal or wood framework used to support a sculptor's clay, plaster, or wax model.

assemblage Sculpture creation by constructing the work from diverse objects. *Compare* **carving**.

atlas (or Telemon) A male statue used as a column, as in an ancient Greek temple.

banker A sculptor's workbench.

bronze An alloy of copper or tin used by sculptors in ancient Greece, Rome, China, and Africa; revived in modern times.

bust A sculpture of the upper part of the human body.

calvary A representation of the crucifixion.

cameo A small bas-relief carving in stone, glass, or shell, the design in relief being a different color from the background.

candlemaking Now regarded as a skilled decorative sculptural process. Liquid candle wax can be colored, perfumed, and whipped to make it frothy; when set it can be carved like clay.

carving Sculpture creation by "subtracting" or removing extraneous material to create the finished work. *Compare* **assemblage**.

caryatid A female statue used as a column, as in an ancient Greek temple.

cast A figure made from the mold of original model. *See* **cire perdue, plaster cast, sand cast**.

chryselephantine Made or decorated with gold and ivory, in the manner of ancient Greek statues.

cire perdue (French: "lost wax") A traditional method for casting bronze sculptures. The model with a waxed surface is enclosed in the mold. The wax is melted and runs through holes at the bottom. Molten metal is then poured through holes at the top, filling up the space left by the wax.

corbeil A sculpture of a basket of fruit or flowers, used as an architectural ornament.

diaglyph A carving or ornament in intaglio.

figurine A miniature figure.

free-stone An easily worked fine-grained limestone or sandstone.

genre sculpture A style that reflects everyday or rustic life; hallmark of Etruscan art, and of Biblical subjects in the Middle Ages.

gesso A mixture of plaster of Paris or gypsum and glue, used as a base for bas relief or to prepare a painting surface.

gisant A figure that is recumbent on the stone lid of a tomb.

heroic sculpture A figure or group of figures carved larger than life.

intaglio Carving in which the design is cut into the surface. *Compare* **relief**.

kore A female draped statue found in Archaic Greek art as a votive offering or placed on a grave. Similar male statues are called kouros.

kouros An ancient Greek male statue, usually nude, placed on graves or as votive offerings.

light sculpture A form of sculpture that utilizes light bulbs, the sun, and laser beams as the primary medium of expression.

mantle A clay mold around a wax model.

maquette (French: "small model") A small wax or clay model made by a sculptor in preparation for larger work.

marble A stone popular for sculpture because of its extreme durability, found in all colors ranging from nearly pure white to nearly pure black.

mobile A movable sculpture of shapes cut out of wood or sheet metal, linked by wires or rods in order to revolve easily or move up and down; invented by American sculptor, Alexander Calder (1932). *Compare* **stabile**.

modeling Building up of forms in three dimensions by means of plastic material such as clay or wax.

origami The art (originating in Japan) of folding paper.

papier mâché (French: "chewed paper"). A fine paper pulp that can be cast and moulded into strong structures. Easily absorbent paper, such as newsprint, is best.

pietà A representation of Mary with the body of Jesus.

plaster cast An intermediate stage in bronze sculpture from which the final mold is made.

polychromatic sculpture Sculpture painted in naturalistic colors to make it more lifelike; mostly pre–1500s.

putto (or amorino) A figure of a small child or cherub.

relief Sculpture that is not free-standing from its background; various degrees, from bas-relief (low relief) to alto-relievo (high relief). *Compare* **intaglio.**

restrike An impression taken from a sculptor's mold at some time after the original edition.

sand cast A mold of special sand made from a plaster model and from which a bronze cast is produced.

sculpture-in-the-round Sculpture that can be seen from all sides.

spall A chip broken from a stone carving.

stabile A sculpture resembling a mobile, but which does not move. *Compare* **mobile.**

synthetic sculpture Sculptures made from man-made materials. Expanded polystyrene blocks or sheets are excellent for ephemeral sculptures. Fiberglass sculpture is generally a mixture of polyester resin and shredded glass fibers.

Printmaking: terms and techniques

aquatint An engraving method producing fine-grain tonal areas rather than lines. invented mid eighteenth century and popular in the next century for reproducing watercolors. The tone ground is first etched on the plate, then acid-resistant designs are drawn on before further etching.

burin A short steel engraving tool, usually lozenge-shaped in section, cut obliquely to a point. The round handle is pushed by the palm while the fingers guide the point.

burr A rough, upturned edge made by an engraver's burin or needle. It gives a soft, rich line to drypoint, but is removed when sharp line is required as in line engraving.

drypoint An engraving technique dating from the fifteenth century. The design is scratched directly onto a copper plate with a sharp tool held like a pen, often producing a "burred" edge, giving a soft, rich texture, but this only survives for small editions.

edition The number of copies printed at one time.

engraving Any method of cutting into metal or wood to make a surface to receive ink for printmaking, but frequently used for what is technically called line engraving.

etching Developed in the sixteenth century, engraving on a wax-covered metal plate which is scratched with a needle to expose the surface then placed in acid, which cuts into the plate where scratched. Longer exposure to acid makes a darker print line.

intaglio Carving in small scale, as on a gemstone, the design being cut into the surface. Hence any such form of printmaking process such as etching (as opposed to a cameo gem or relief etching, and a woodcut in which the ground is cut away leaving a projecting design).

limited edition A fixed number of copies printed, usually individually numbered and signed by the artist, e.g. 3/25, indicating that this is the third impression from an edition of 25 copies. Plates are often defaced or destroyed when the edition is complete to prevent later printing. The size of the edition affects market value.

line engraving Engraving directly onto a metal plate with cutting tools, producing precise lines and shading added by hatching dots. Probably began in fifteenth-century Italy, flowering in the work of Dürer.

linocut A form of relief printing in which a design is cut into linoleum, a twentieth-century technique used by Matisse and Picasso.

lithography Printing from a design drawn in greasy crayon directly on a slab of stone or other smooth surface. Ink rolled over the stone adheres only to the drawing to create the printed image.

mezzotint Engraving using tonal areas. A rocking tool creates a burred surface on the plate, which is smoothed away to leave the desired strength of image. Invented in the seventeenth century but rarely used since photographic ways of reproduction were invented.

monotype Printmaking from an image printed (usually in oils) on a sheet of glass or metal. Only one sheet can be printed, though the color can then be reinforced and a few successive differing images made.

print Strictly, any picture or design made from an inked surface, but also used for art images made by stencil and other processes. Loosely used for all kinds of mechanically produced reproductions of paintings.

proof A trial image taken of a print.

relief etching A process in which the design is drawn in acid-resistant varnish and the non-printing surface etched away with acid, so that the printing surface stands out in relief (the opposite of the intaglio process).

serigraphy A form of silk screening.

silkscreen printing The use of fine silk mesh mounted on a frame to support a stencil, so that "island" parts of the stencil (like the center of an "o") do not fall out. Alternatively, the use of a similar screen in which the cut stencil is replaced by painting the design directly on the screen with a glue or varnish. Ink is forced through unmasked parts of the screen by a squeegee. Andy Warhol was well known for his silkscreen pictures.

state Any of the images through which a print may pass as the artist alters the design, as frequently occurs in the work of Rembrandt. If no changes are made, this may be described as the "only state." Art historians may dispute whether differences are deliberate or merely caused by wear on the plate.

stencil A sheet of paper, metal or other material perforated with a design through which color can be applied to a surface beneath.

woodcut A form of relief printing in which a design is cut or gouged out of the surface of a block of hardwood. Ink or paint is then applied to the surface to print out the design. Separate blocks can be used for multicolored images or, especially in eighteenth- and nineteenth-century Japan where the technique was perfected, different areas of a single block may also be inked differently.

wood engraving A technique like woodcut but using hardwood sawn across the grain and with a finer design, cut more shallowly using burins and similar engraving tools. Thomas Bewick excelled in this technique.

Photography: terms and processes

bas relief An effect of dimensional depth created by making a light-positive image on film and exposing this sandwiched with the negative, but not quite in alignment when making a print.

chemical toning Converting a black and white image to color by the use of chemicals or dyes.

collage The combining of images from several photographs, usually rephotographing to provide a finished print.

combination printing Abutting images from more than one negative to create one image, as in creating a panoramic scene, usually by joining prints and rephotographing, or combining the same image repeated to form repetitive or kaleidoscopic effects.

contre jour Photographed into the sun or light source.

cropping Cutting or framing an image to improve the composition of the image.

daguerreotype An early type of photographic process using a light-sensitive silver-coated metallic plate.

fixing The process of washing a photographic image with a preservative solution to prevent it from becoming discolored.

image distortion Changing the spacial relationship between parts of the image, usually by printing with paper at an angle to the enlarger beam.

lith processing Making intermediate negatives exposed to different tonal values, used in posterization.

montage printing Combining two images so that they appear as one.

negative A photographic image, plate, or film in which the actual light areas appear dark and vice versa.

posterization (or tone separation) Producing an image in which certain levels of grey tone are eliminated, using lith processing. This limits the range of tones for more graphic boldness.

Sabbatier effect (or pseudo-solarization) Tonal reversal of parts of the image by exposing a negative to light half way through its development.

transparency (or slide) A photographic image on a transparent base.

arts styles and movements

abstract expressionism (c. 1940–) A movement that developed in New York in the 1940s which broke away from the realism hitherto dominant in American art, and which became the first American movement to have a significant influence on European art. Notable pracitioners included Jackson Pollock (the main exponent of action painting) and De Kooning.

Art Nouveau (c. 1890–1915) A development of the Arts and Crafts movement, with two main strands: one of fluid symmetry and flowing linear rhythms, one of geometrical austerity.

Arts and Crafts movement (c 1870–1900) Based on the revival of interest in the medieval craft system and led by William Morris, its aims were to fuse the functional and the decorative, and to restore the values of handmade crafts in the face of the growing mass-produced wares of the late nineteenth century.

baroque art (c 1600–1720) Drawing on the exuberance of mannerism and on the resurgence of Roman Catholic doctrine, the aim of baroque art was to unite the main parts of building, sculpture, and painting into an overall dramatic effect that is mainly "frontal," i.e. it is best seen from one, rather than many viewpoints. Its exuberance and monumentality make it one of the most robust movements in art history.

Bauhaus School (c. 1919–33) A German school of architecture and applied arts founded by the architect Walter Gropius. The aim was to integrate the disparate arts and crafts under the principle of function dictating form. The influence of the bauhaus masters on modern architecture has been deep and long-lasting.

cubism (c 1907–23) The style developed by Picasso and Braque in response to Cézanne's late works, and to African tribal art. The first major painting in this style was Picasso's *Les Demoiselles d'Avignon* (1906), and the term itself was coined by a critic after seeing Braque's 1908 work. "Analytic" (early) cubism presented the work from a variety of viewpoints. "Synthetic" (late) cubism introduced decorative elements such as lettering and applied materials such as newspaper (collage) to achieve a balance between the depiction of reality and the picture as an object of reality in its own right. Cubism has been enormously influential on modern art.

Dada (c. 1915–23) An art movement originating in Zurich 1915, Dada (the name chosen at random) rejected accepted aesthetic values and advocated an irrational form of non-art or anti-art.

Leading figures included the poet Tristan Tzara and the sculptor Jean Arp.

Der Blaue Reiter "The Blue Rider" (c. 1911–14) A loose-knit group of expressionist painters including Kandinsky, Klee, and Marc, united by Kandinsky's dictum that "the creative spirit is hidden within matter."

Die Brücke (The Bridge) (c. 1905–13) A group of German expressionists, including Kirchner, whose manifesto was to overthrow the concept of art as an end in itself, and to integrate art and life by using art as a means of communication. Influenced by tribal art and van Gogh, the founders lived and worked communally, using clashing colors and aggressive distortions in their intense works.

expressionism (c. 1905–25) An emphasis on pictorial distortion or chromatic exaggeration within any art of any period. The movement emphasizing heightened emotion and the artist's subjective vision, and was characterized by bold brushwork and stylized forms. Influenced by Gauguin, van Gogh, Munch, and Fauvism, the movement includes the more specific groups of Die Brücke and Der Blaue Reiter.

fauvism (c. 1905–07) A shortlived but influential movement of artists surrounding Matisse, characterized by daring, spontaneous handling of paint in bold, brilliant, often non-representational color. "Fauve" means "wild beast," a critic's response to a 1905 exhibition of works by Matisse and others.

futurism (c. 1909–19) A movement of writers and artists founded by the poet Filippo Marinetti (who described speed as "a new form of beauty.") Its manifesto advocated incorporating the thrust of modern technology into art in order to express the movement and dynamism of modern life.

impressionism (1874–1886) Centering on a diverse group of eight artists, including Cézanne, Renoir, Manet, and Monet, who held eight exhibitions between 1874 and 1886, the movement derives its name from a painting by Monet, *Impression: Sunrise*. Impressionists were concerned with light and its effects, and the use of "broken" color.

kinetic art (c. 1930–) An art form in which light and balance create a work that moves, or appears to move. Air currents, electric motors, artificial lighting, etc., are used to create such effects.

mannerism (c. 1520–1700) A mainly Italian style deriving from the all-pervasive influence of Michelangelo and Raphael (i.e. in their "manner") that exaggerated their styles into extravagant contortions for an emotional effect.

minimal art (c. 1960–) A rejection of the aesthetic qualities of art in favor of the physical reality of the art object. Materials used are usually non-traditional and often in geometrically arranged units, as in the sculptor Carl Andre's notorious *Equivalent VIII* (1966), which consisted of 120 fired bricks arranged in a solid rectangle on London's Tate Gallery floor.

naive art (20th century and earlier) Works by self-taught artists whose fresh, untutored style is noted for its simplicity and innocence. Notable naive artists include Grandma Moses and "Douanier" Rousseau.

neo-classicism (c 1750–1850) A movement that developed in revolutionary France, expressing the qualities of harmony, order and clarity associated with Greek and Roman art. Classical subjects were used as allegories for the present political situation. The antithesis of romanticism, it espoused accepted notions of beauty and tended to reject individual inspiration.

New York School (c. 1945–60) A loosely associated group of mainly abstract expressionist painters, such as Pollock and De Kooning, who attempted to build a uniquely American non-representational mode of artistic expression.

op art (c. 1950–) A form of abstract art that bases itself on creating static two-dimensional objects which appear to move on a flat surface.

pointillism (or divisionism)(c. 1880–1915) Based on the color theories of Chevreul, its aim was to achieve greater pictorial luminosity by placing small marks of pure primary color on the surface, allowing them to merge at a viewing distance to create an optical mixture.

pop art (c. 1955–) A reaction against abstract expressionism, the movement started almost simultaneously in the US and UK, and used the images of mass media, advertising, and pop culture, presenting common, everyday objects as art.

post–impressionism (c. 1880–1910) A term loosely applied to a diverse group of artists whose paintings developed from Impressionism and who worked in widely divergent styles, e.g. Gauguin and Matisse.

Pre-Raphaelite Brotherhood (1848–56) Founded by William Holman Hunt, John Everett Millais, and Dante Gabriel Rossetti, this group sought to recapture the innocence and beauty of Italian forms before Raphael, in protest against what they saw as the prevailing "frivolity" of art of their day.

realism (c 1830–80) A largely French movement that developed in reaction to idealized and mythical/historical subjects. Courbet is by far the most notable practitioner of the form.

Renaissance (c. 1300–1545) Meaning "rebirth," the term

describes the revival of classical learning and art. Centered at first in Florence, it marked the end of the Middle Ages and was the outstanding creative period in western art. Architecture, painting, and sculpture, deriving from Greek and Roman models, developed with an unparalleled vigor and prominence, and the artist gained a role in society hitherto unknown, mainly due to the rival city states that employed them. Artistic innovation included perspective and painting with oil.

rococo art (c 1735–65) A mainly French style, rococo is characterized by elaborate and superficial decoration. Elegance was the keynote and the style mirrored the extravagance and brilliance of court life.

romanticism (c 1780–1850) A mainly literary movement, romanticism was a reaction against neo-classical principles and the Industrial Revolution. Deriving inspiration from untamed nature, romanticism centered on the importance of individual feeling towards the natural world.

School of Paris (c 1910–50) The large international group of Paris-based artists which made the city the center of the art world until the emergence of the New York School.

surrealism (c. 1924–) A French avant-garde movement which drew on dadaist principles in art and on the psychoanalytic theories of Freud. Irrational association, spontaneous techniques and an elimination of premeditation to free the workings of the unconscious mind, and an interest in dreams, inspired its practitioners.

symbolism (c 1880–1905) Influenced by the Pre-Raphaelites and by romanticism, Symbolism originated in France as an intellectual alternative to the straight visual work of the Impressionists. There were two main strands: those, e.g. Redon, influenced by literature, and those, e.g. van Gogh, who explored the symbolic use of color and line to express emotion.

decorative arts

decorative arts techniques

brass rubbing

appliqué An alien material applied to the surface of an art object or painting for ornamentation.

brass rubbing An impression made of a brass engraving by covering it with paper and rubbing the paper with graphite or chalk.

cameo A gem on which a design has been engraved in relief.

chasing Ornamentation on metal by embossing (carving or stamping a design) or engraving (cutting lines into wood, metal, etc.).

collage A work of art created by attaching paper, wood, fabric, etc., onto a flat surface.

découpage The decoration of a surface with shapes cut from paper or cardboard.

enamel Glass that has been heated to form a base of porcelain, which is then decorated with scenes or designs. Popular in the fifteenth and sixteenth centuries.

faceting A process of cutting regular planes on stone in a predetermined pattern that is related to the stone's crystalline structure. The first precious stones used for decorating jewelry were not faceted at all, but smoothed and rounded into the cabochon style (a cabochon is a stone with a flat back and a domed face). It was discovered, however, that some stones reflect more light if they are cut into facets, and so the face was cut into regular panes as in the rose cut. The backs of these

Faceting
1 Cabochon cut
2 Baguette cut
3 Rose cut,
4 Trap cut
5 Antique cushion
6 Brilliant cut
7 Fancy cut

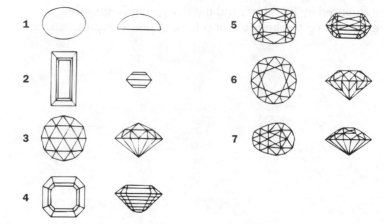

early cut stones were still flat, but through experiment lapidaries learned to shape the bottom of a stone into a point (known as a pavilion) that further increased the gem's "fire."

gilding Covering an object with gold.

inlaying The decoration of an object with fine materials set into its surface.

macramé Ornamental work created by weaving and knotting coarse thread into patterns.

marquetry Colored or varnished woods, ivory, or other materials that are inlaid flush with the surface of an object.

millefiori A glassmaking technique in which flowerlike sections appear from sticks of colored glass that have been cut on the transverse. Sometimes used for beads in jewelry; also embedded in shapes of clear glass to form paperweights.

macramé

netsuke Small Japanese figures (predominantly animals) usually carved from ivory and used to decorate belts, purses, tobacco pouches, etc. Highly collectable, these miniature works of sixteenth-century art are said to acquire an "aura" the more they are handled.

ormolu Gilded bronze used to decorate furniture.

paper cuts Pictures cut into paper.

repoussé Decorative art worked in metal with the design hammered into relief from the reverse side.

rosemaling Carved or painted decoration with floral motifs.

setting A method of mounting gemstones, holding them in place. Some settings are designed to be as unobtrusive as possible, but others are developed so that they become design elements in their own right.

sgraffito Ceramic decoration in which the topmost layer (glaze,

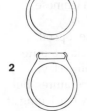
1

2

3

4

5

6

7

8

Setting
1 Bezel
2 Clawg
3 Riveting
4 Graining
5 Flush
6 Invisible (for pearls)
7,8 Modern (for unusual shapes)

plaster, etc) is carved with a design to reveal selected areas of the ground.

silhouettes Pictures made by reproducing in one color, usually black, the outline of the model. The traditional outline for the silhouette is a profile likeness, although in the nineteenth century, the clothing was often included so that the artist's skill could be shown in depicting the frill and flounces of contemporary fashion.

silhouette

stenciling A method of transfering a design by painting through shapes cut in a thin sheet of metal, paper or similar material. Stencils can be used for tiny designs, such as initials or small sunflower motifs, or for giant designs suitable for decorating an entire room.

tole An object made of tin and decorated with colorful designs.

stencilling

Pottery and porcelain

argil Clay used by potters.

basaltware Black, unglazed pottery.

biscuit ware Pottery fired but not glazed.

blunger A vessel in which pottery ingredients are mixed.

bone china Porcelain containing bone ash made in twentieth-century UK, for high-qu ality tableware.

cameo ware Pottery with raised white designs on a contrasting background.

celadon ware Pottery originating in China, with a pale gray-green glaze.

ceramics (1) Anything made of baked clay. (2) The potter's art.

china (originally "Chinaware") Chinese porcelain of the sixteenth century; now any Chinese porcelain or western version.

chinoiserie Decoration on eighteenth-century European porcelain, depicting Chinese scenes.

clair de lune Pale gray-blue glaze applied to certain Chinese porcelain.

clay The potter's basic material, found just below the topsoil, formed by decomposition of rock: kaolin or china clay, a pure white, coarse clay; ball clay, a highly plastic, fine pure clay; fireclay, a dark rough clay, able to stand high temperatures, but not plastic; buff or stoneware, a smooth plastic clay hardening at high temperatures.

coiling

coiling A simple method of producing clay pots. Cylindrical strips of clay are formed from the clay body and then and then coiled on top of one another.

crackleware Pottery or porcelain with a network of fine cracks in the glaze.

creamware High-quality earthenware perfected by Josiah Wedgwood in eighteenth-century Staffordshire, England.

delftware Tin-enameled earthenware, mostly blue and white, originally made in Delft (Holland) in the seventeenth and eighteenth centuries.

earthenware Pottery fired to a relatively low temperature (2012°F), easy to work, and having a dull finish.

enamel Colored glaze used to decorate pottery already glazed; popular in the fifteenth and sixteenth centuries.

faience Fine pottery with a colorful glaze, named after Faenza, Italy, one of its sources.

fairing Pottery of a type sold or given as a prize at traveling fairs.

firing The process of hardening shaped clay by heating it. *See* pottery.

glazing A process for producing a finish to pottery. Glaze is a coating of glass that gives the pottery a smooth surface color, and makes it waterproof.

glost firing A second firing for the purpose of fusing the glaze after the initial biscuit firing.

imari Japanese porcelain with a decorated blue underglaze over which the colors of red and gold are laid.

ironstone Hard, white pottery introduced by C J Mason in the nineteenth century.

jasperware Colored stoneware with raised designs in white, invented by Josiah Wedgwood.

kiln A chamber in which clay is fired.

lambrequin Scalloped edging decorating an item of porcelain.

majolica (or maiolica) Brightly decorated pottery in sixteenth-century Italian style.

molded ware Pottery formed by pressing the clay against or into some kind of mold.

muffle A kiln in which pottery is fired without direct exposure to the flames.

Nanking ware Chinese-style porcelain with a blue and white pattern, originally imported into Europe from Nanking.

pallet A spatula or paddlelike implement used for mixing or shaping clay.

Parian ware Fine white porcelain resembling marble, produced in Britain and the US.

paste The mixture from which porcelain is made.

porcelain The finest pottery, white all through and translucent. *See* paste.

potter's wheel A device with a flat rotating disk on a platform, usually powered by a treadle, on which clay is molded by hand.

pottery Strictly, all baked-clay ware except stoneware and porcelain. More generally, the art of shaping and molding all clays while soft and malleable and firing them in a kiln to render the created shapes firm and stable. Firing drives off the water combined with the constituent materials within clay and binds them together. Glazes are often added to make the ware waterproof.

saggar A casing made of fine clay in which delicate ceramic ware is fired.

slab ware Pottery made from slabs of clay that have been rolled out to an even thickness and cut into flat shapes.

slip Clay in liquid form, used for casting, joining, or decoration.

stoneware Hard, strong type of pottery fired at about 2282°F, and able to hold liquid without glazing; used for items such as pots and heavy dishes.

terracotta Brownish-red burnt-clay pottery, baked in molds and used for architectural molding, sculpture, and decorative vessels.

throwing The process of shaping wet clay by hand on a potter's wheel.

turning Final trimming of partially dried pottery on potter's wheel or lathe.

underglaze A pigment or decoration applied to pottery before it is glazed.

furniture and furnishings

Furniture styles

Abbotsford period/baronial style/monastic style Weighty Regency Gothic revival furniture of the 1820s and 1830s originally made for Sir Walter Scott's Abbotsford home (Scotland).

Adam A delicate eighteenth-century English neoclassical style developed by Robert Adam.

Adirondack

Adirondack furniture A simple American rural wood style produced from the 1890s to the early 1940s. Named after the mountains in New York State.

American Chippendale A plainer and more Palladian version of the late eighteenth-century British domestic style. It used local woods, not just mahogany, and rural versions persisted beyond 1800. *See* **country Chippendale**.

American Chippendale

American empire style An early nineteenth-century blending of French Empire and British Regency features in which mahogany was followed by rosewood and black walnut (1820s on). C H Lannuier and Duncan Phyfe were the outstanding makers.

American Jacobean furniture The predominant seventeenth-century colonial English form, also known as pilgrim due to most existing examples, especially oak chests, coming from New England. Rectangular, simply decorated, and a few basic types.

American moderne A loose description of a 1930s US style, derived from Art Deco and international modern, that often incorporated materials such as bakelite and chrome.

American moderne

American Queen Anne style A colonial style that started later and lasted longer than in Britain with more solid rather than veneered walnut being used.

American William and Mary style A longer lasting colonial version of the British style. Walnut and maple wood, together with new tables, desks, and cupboards, began to replace oak pieces in wealthy homes.

Art Deco A decorative arts and architectural style emanating from Paris in 1925 and common in both Europe and America. Stylized and modernist, it reconciled methods of mass-production and manufactured materials (such as bakelite) as well as using luxury items. Furniture included metalwork designs.

American William and Mary style

art furniture movement A British 1860s and 1870s design

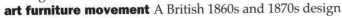

movement led by Eastlake and Godwin that favored simplicity but wanted fine design for mass production as well.

Art Nouveau A dominant style of decoration and of avant-garde design in Europe from the 1880s to World War I. Called "Le Modern Style" in France, "Jugendstil" in Germany, and "stile Liberty" in Italy. Art Nouveau creatively adapted sinuous natural forms in an attempt to avoid architectural and design styles based on archeological recreations of the past. Also influenced by Japanese art.

Art Nouveau

Arts and Crafts movement British late nineteenth-century crafts revival inspired by William Morris to return to individual craftsmanship in the tradition of medieval guilds, and thus non-industrial quality that included deliberately priming cottage furniture.

auricular style A Dutch-devised sinuous early seventeenth-century variant on late mannerist ornamentation, originally developed in silverwork. The German description "Knorpelwerk" means "cartilage work."

auricular style

baroque Seventeenth- and early eighteenth-century European furniture of elaborate ornamental character with sweeping S-curves an important feature.

Bauhaus A German school of architecture and design 1919–33. Founded by the architect Walter Gropius, it epitomized the marriage of modern design, mass production, industrial design, and a Teutonic romantic approach to abstract art. Alfred Arndt (b. 1898) led the furniture workshop.

Biedermeier sofa style A conventional nineteenth-century style developed in Germany and based on French Empire and English Regency neoclassical styles. Popular with the middle class, it spread to Scandinavia and Russia. Furniture came in light-colored woods with ebony ornamentation and horsehair upholstery. Named after a journal's figure of fun.

Biedermeier

Boston Chippendale A local American style produced c. 1755–90 featuring slender cabriole legs, sober ornamentation, and bombé chests.

Buhl (or Boule or Boulle) A style developed by the French cabinetmaker André C Boulle (1642–1732) using inlays of metal and tortoiseshell.

Byzantine chair furniture An East Roman Empire furniture style based in Constantinople from the fifth to fifteenth centuries. It inherited and elaborated early Christian and Hellenistic forms, blending them with Persian, Islamic, and even Chinese influences. It featured elaborate turnings, metal X-frame chairs, foot stools, lecterns, round or semicircular dining tables, canopy beds, open and closed cupboards, separate bookcases in the late

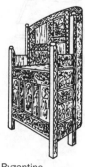
Byzantine

period, and elaborately decorated chests.

Chinese Chippendale A modern term for British 1750s and 1760s rococo fashion and oriental ornament, as popularized by Thomas Chippendale, that featured pagodas and geometrical fretwork.

Chippendale An elegant and ornate mid eighteenth-century English style developed by Thomas Chippendale.

Churrigueresque A lavishly exuberant Spanish baroque style named after three prolific architect brothers. Its chairs were usually leather upholstered and the decoration's abundant inlaid features influenced Spanish colonial patterns.

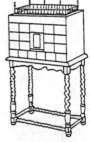

Churrigueresque

consulate style A brief French transitional period named after Napoleon's term as First Consul. More formal and rectangular than the preceding directoire pieces, it introduced many of the military and Egyptian motifs that became common under the Empire.

country Chippendale A late eighteenth-century rural English and American simplified version of the main style using local woods rather than mahogany .

desornamentado style A Spanish late sixteenth-century reaction against excessive Renaissance decoration in architecture and furniture. The sparse furniture was allowed plain molding, turned legs, and panels. Lasted until the nineteenth century in Mexico and provincial Spain.

De Stijl A Dutch purist modernist movement that published a magazine of this title 1917–31. At least four members, especially Gerrit Rietveld, designed furniture on a rigorous application of an ideology based on the right angle and use of primary colors.

directoire Revolutionary furniture that reduced in scale and simplified the preceding Louis XVI style, especially in its late Etruscan phase. The fasces and cape of liberty were important additions to the traditional classical ornaments.

directory/American regency A very early nineteenth-century transitional phase between early US federal and empire styles that drew on Sheraton's later output. It brought in paw feet, the federal eagle, and classical flutings.

Egyptian style/Egyptiennerie A late eighteenth- and early nineteenth-century style in France and the US, much influenced by ancient Egypt, emphasizing martial glory, the letter N (for Napoleon), the swan (Josephine's favorite), gilt bronze, and mahogany. It was revived in the US in the 1860s and 1870s.

directoire

Etruscan furniture Inventive pieces by this ancient Greek-influenced people included the woven basket chair, the unique cista (round chest or casket), a solid tub-shaped armchair in bronze, bronze tripods and candelabra, and the placing of foot

Federal style

François I style

Georgian style

and head rests on the Greek couch.

Federal style An American neoclassical style coinciding with the first generation of the new republic. It blended Anglo-French influences in mainly mahogany or fruitwood pieces. The American eagle was the outstanding decorative feature.

Fernandino style A Spanish Napoleonic Empire-derived style named after King Ferdinand VII (1820–33). Its somewhat clumsy products boasted bronze mounts, giltwood appliqué, and many classical symbols.

François I style A French Italianate style that made furniture more colorful and elaborately carved. It incorporated architectural elements, arabesque, and mannerist motifs. Walnut was the most common wood employed.

Georgian style A term used in furniture for a variety of styles popular in England under the reigns of George I, II, and III. Its use reflects the fact that Britain's most famous designers (Chippendales, Adam brothers, Hepplewhite, and Sheraton) flourished in the greater part of this regal era.

Glasgow school A group of designers centered around the Glasgow School of Art, and led by Charles Rennie Mackintosh, his wife Margaret Macdonald, her sister Frances, and her husband Herbert MacNair. They were a major force in Art Nouveau handicrafts and architecture. The furniture was light, simple, and open, with Celtic motifs, and was marketed in London from 1898.

Gothic style European furniture from the twelfth to sixteenth centuries revived in the nineteenth century. Massive oak pieces centered on the chest, stonemasonry-style carving, arcading, and vivid painting. Introduced the cupboard, wainscot chair, slab-ended stool/bench (fifteenth century), and the linefold motif.

Greek ancient furniture Almost none survives, but there are artwork depictions from the ninth century BC to the Roman end of the Hellenistic era. The couch (kline) was the outstanding item. Tables were small three- or four-legged designs kept under the kline. The cupboard first appeared in Hellenistic times and the kibotos chest followed Egyptian precedent.

Hepplewhite style Furniture produced to or similar to the designs of the London shop-owner George Hepplewhite (active c. 1760–86), whose posthumous *Cabinet-maker and Upholster's Guide* (1788; revised editions 1789, 1794) contained almost 300 unsigned examples. Ten in a catalog of the same year are his only signed work. Hepplewhite reinterpreted Adam's neoclassical style into a simpler, gentler-curved elegance. Serpentine and bow fronts, the shield-back chair, window seats, and Prince of Wales feathers are all characteristic.

high-tech/industrial style International functional furniture design propagated in 1970s America that strives for novelty and ergonomic efficiency.

high Victorian style Another term for rococo revival in Britain and America.

Hispano-Moresque style Mudéjar ("Moorish inspiration") geometrically inlaid Spanish furniture of the late Gothic and Renaissance periods.

international style European interwar style, so-called in 1932, that spread to America and the rest of the world. Its functional, often standardized furniture is made today.

international style

Isabellino style A neo-Gothic revival in mid nineteenth-century Spain named after Queen Isabella (1833–68) that surpassed others in both color and ornamentation.

Jacobean style A general term for seventeenth-century English furniture. It initially differed little from Tudor work until continental-style arabesque carving and mannerist decorations grew in popularity. Upholstery and lightness became more general, as did the gateleg table. The Commonwealth (1649–60) reduced decorating to a minimum, typified by the Cromwell chair. From 1660, England rejoined the European baroque mainstream and began the Age of Walnut.

Jacobean style

Japanese style (Japonism/Japonaiserie) A late nineteenth-century taste for Japanese art after trade resumed in 1853. Many major British designers, such as Godwin, adapted furniture to Japan's asymmetrical lightness and simplicity. Continental Art Nouveau makers took up the fashion in the 1890s, and America was influenced from the late 1870s, especially in bamboo work.

Liberty style *See* **Art Nouveau**.

Louis XIII style Early seventeenth-century French furniture in showy mannerist fashion and made of ebony or walnut wood, decorated with lavish semi-precious stones and veneering. Flemish-imported geometric panels are its most distinctive feature. The cabinet, the most important piece, sometimes had a fall front added. Mainly oblong-shaped tables abounded and dining tables first had extensions. Upholstery included leather and became fixed for the first time.

Louis XIV style France's baroque period centered on the glorious reign of the Sun King, of which the vast new Palace of Versailles (1688 on) was the apotheosis. Furniture formed part of an integrated royal program of the decoration, in which magnificent but disciplined design enveloped the 20,000-member hierarchical court, where even the size of foot stools was graduated. New and enduring furniture forms were the canapé sofa, the confessional

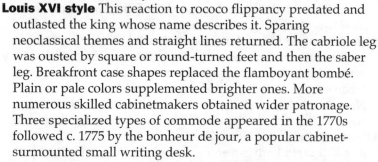

Louis XV style

armchair, the fauteuil armchair, the console table, often marble topped, and the commode, which ousted the traditional chest. Chinoiserie joined the decorative repertoire from the 1670s.

Louis XV style The true Louis XV rococo style occupies the middle years of that king's reign and is arguably furniture's richest period. The finest aristocratic homes had winter and summer sets of curving furniture, elegantly made from up to 50 types of wood that were carved and ornamented to the highest standards with metalwork, chinoiserie, gilt, mirrors, porcelain plaques, and bright colors. The bergère easy chair, first made c. 1725, proliferated as did the cabriole chair, the duchesse-type rolltop model made for the king himself, and the mechanically ingenious dual-purpose "secretaire à Capuchin" or "à la Bourgogne."

Louis XVI revival A mid nineteenth-century style that crossed the Atlantic from the court of Napoleon III and Empress Eugènie's Second Empire to Civil War-era America. More ostentatious than the original, especially in deep-button, coil-sprung upholstery. Widespread and prolonged use in burgeoning grand hotels across the world led to its description as "Louis the Hotel" style.

Louis XVI style

Louis XVI style This reaction to rococo flippancy predated and outlasted the king whose name describes it. Sparing neoclassical themes and straight lines returned. The cabriole leg was ousted by square or round-turned feet and then the saber leg. Breakfront case shapes replaced the flamboyant bombé. Plain or pale colors supplemented brighter ones. More numerous skilled cabinetmakers obtained wider patronage. Three specialized types of commode appeared in the 1770s followed c. 1775 by the bonheur de jour, a popular cabinet-surmounted small writing desk.

mannerist style A European fashion of Italian origin in the late sixteenth and early seventeenth centuries that emphasized arabesque and grotesque ornament. The even more serpentine auricular phase prevailed until the coming of baroque.

mission furniture An American style arising from the British Arts and Crafts movement, which inspired Gustav Stickley (1854–1942) to found his own *The New York Firm* (1898–1915). It made simple, massive oak pieces with cloth, canvas, or leather upholstery, as did the Royston Community (1895–1938). Stickley's magazine *The Craftsmen* (1901–15) spread the gospel of utility of design to the west coast.

Moorish style A long-lasting Islamic Iberian style created by the ruling Moors who invaded from North Africa and were brilliant woodcarvers and leatherworkers. Little furniture was used or survives from this era, in which richly covered cushions were important, but it was part of the Muslim world inspiration for a 1856–1907 revival. *See* **Hispano-Moresque**.

neoclassical style Furniture of Greco-Roman inspiration (archeological discoveries from the 1740s) from the 1760s to the 1830s embracing many different national styles.

neo-Gothic style/Gothic revival Historicist, romantic, and catholic attempts to revive Gothic medieval art from the late eighteenth to the end of the nineteenth centuries. The first furniture designs were published in 1742, influenced Chippendale, and produced the Gothic Windsor chair, popular for two decades. Regency Gothic preceded the stronger nineteenth-century revival, which swept the continent during the 1830s, and dominated American work 1830–80 ending with the Eastlake phase.

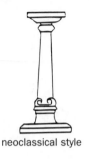

neoclassical style

Palladian style The first distinctive British Georgian style designed by the architect William Kent, who drew inspiration from the work of Andrea Palladio. His furniture combined lavishly sculpted Italian baroque models with symmetrical ornament to match the interior designs. Kent's work was published in 1744.

Pennsylvania German/Dutch An eighteenth- and nineteenth-century softwood local style retaining European baroque features, especially the Schrank wardrobe and the softwood chest with their folk decoration.

Philadelphia Chippendale Pennsylvania's capital style of c. 1755–90, rich in rococo carving and fluted coronets on cabinets.

neoclassical style

pillar and scroll/American restoration style A brief imitation of France's post-Napoleonic fashion, emphasizing pillar feet, scroll brackets, and arms. Documented by John Hall's 1840 pattern book.

plateresque style An early sixteenth-century Spanish Renaissance style derived from silversmith work decorating simple furniture shapes with geometric intricacy.

Queen Anne An early eighteenth-century English baroque style characterized by fine upholstery and wood inlays. Key elements included the cabriole leg; the drop handle; figured walnut veneering; fiddleback chair backs; and minimal carved decoration. Better joinery eliminated stretchers. New forms introduced were the china (display) cabinet, the spoonback chair for more comfort, and the card table, the tea table, and the kneehole desk.

Régence style An important transitional style between the main Louis XIV and XV periods. Cultural life returned from Versailles to Paris and this lighter atmosphere was reflected in more curvaceous furniture, the cabriole leg, and the removal of stretchers. Forms included new commodes and the bergère armchair. Ornamentation followed the lozenge shape, foliate scrolling, espagnolettes, and ormolu mounts. Slipcovers were an innovation for those not able to afford separate seasonal suites of furniture.

Regency Gothic A brief British fashion in the late eighteenth and early nineteenth centuries, inspired by Pugin's father, for Gothic church ornamentation that predated the fuller Gothic revival.

Regency style

Regency style A decorative early nineteenth-century English style that drew on Greco-Roman, Egyptian, Chinese, and French Empire themes and hence at the time was called English Empire. Named after George IV's Regency and reign (1811–30), it extended either side through the pattern books of Sheraton, Hope, and George Smith (active 1804–28). "Grecian" arch-backed chairs with scroll arms and saber legs best exemplify the style's elegance. The sofa table was a Regency innovation. Decoration included the acanthus, dolphin, and brass inlay.

Renaissance revival A mid and late nineteenth-century European and American style initiated in Italy, massive and rectangular with a veritable orgy of nationalistic decoration from many sources. Remained particularly popular with the Italian and German public until 1914.

Renaissance style

Renaissance style European classical and architecturally inspired furniture of the fifteenth to seventeenth centuries with many phases and national variations. Walnut began to replace oak. New forms included the cassone, the mule chest, and the chest of drawers. Cupboards proliferated into the wardrobe, armoire and cabinet.

Restoration style (**1**) Post-Waterloo French Bourbon taste that continued Empire work wholesale except that it removed Napoleonic devices and rejected mahogany for lighter-colored woods. (**2**) Spirited English furniture from the restoration of Charles II to the close of James II's reign in 1688. The first to adapt continental baroque. Walnut supplanted oak. Fertile ornamentation brought in spiral turning, scrollwork, deep carving, gesso decoration, and floral marquetry. Caning, lacquering, and japanning were all new techniques. Numerous new forms appeared, such as the wing chair, the daybed, the slant-front bureau, in c. 1670, the scritoire writing cabinet, and small occasional tables.

rococo A style of French asymmetrical furniture, originating in the eighteenth century, emphasizing the S-shaped curve and comfort in reaction to baroque formality. It was characterized by improved plush upholstery, chinoiserie, bright colors, swirling carving, and extravagant marquetry. The style was widely exported and represents the zenith of restless frivolity of Louis XV furniture.

rococo revival A European and American middle-class reenactment of rococo, beginning only 60 years after its eclipse, but this often symmetrical version offered the added comfort of coil-sprung, button-backed upholstery, in new French seating forms. It dominated 1840s–70s US fashion despite other revivals.

rococo style

Romanesque style Early medieval work that rarely survives. An exception is the famous and so-called Dagobert bronze throne, a monumental eighth-century Frankish continuation of the Roman X-frame folding chair. Chip carving on brightly painted oak timber predominated in pieces resembling the era's Romanesque architecture.

Romanesque style

Roman style Marble, iron, bronze, silver, wooden, and wicker furniture of Rome and its Empire that reinterpreted Etruscan, Greek, Hellenistic, and Egyptian precedents. The most common chair was the curule, derived from the Greek "diphros okladias." The first console tables for sideboard use against a wall appeared, as did four-legged tables with stretchers. The cupboard was developed with "armaria" for weapons and the open buffet display board.

Scandinavian furniture A vanguard post–World War I modern furniture movement marrying fine design to industrial production and materials. Alvar Aalto in Finland spearheaded the movement, followed by Kaare Klint in Denmark. After 1945, Scandinavian designers, though still often home-based, were working for an appreciative and growing US-led world market.

Second Empire An ornate nineteenth-century French style.

Sheraton A late eighteenth-century English style developed by Thomas Sheraton, characterized by graceful proportions.

Spanish colonial style Spanish overseas imperial furniture of the seventeenth and eighteenth centuries made chiefly in Mexico City, Lima, Bogotá, and Quito though Cuba and the Philippines were also major producer colonies. European in form, but often with Indian carving and a more lavish use of silver, mother-of-pearl, and other ornament than at home. Mexico continued the desornamentado style, while Peru remained faithful to baroque.

transition style Two periods of French furniture a century apart. The first coincides with Louis XIV's first years on the throne: baroque features began to appear. The second, more significant, occupies Louis XV's final years: rococo furniture began to receive neoclassical ornamentation and more restrained curves.

Tudor style English, predominantly sixteenth-century furniture in a Renaissance, increasingly mannerist-influenced provincial style. It developed the draw-leaf table by 1550, the decorative nonesuch chest, and the Farthingale chair (the latter two being nineteenth-century names). Holly and ebony were new woods. The reign of Elizabeth I is sometimes separated from the four earlier Tudors, but, in fact, the ornate Italianate trend only became more pronounced.

William and Mary style Late seventeenth-century English baroque furniture much influenced by the Dutch and Huguenot designers in the royal couple's household. Made of walnut and with Dutch marquetry and oyster veneer. New forms were the 1690s bureau, the bookcase, the card table, and the tea table. Carved scroll supports and the baluster were popular details.

Furniture terms

armoire A large ornate cabinet or wardrobe.

chaise longue A reclining chair with a long padded seat resembling a settee.

chesterfield A large padded sofa, often with button upholstery, with no woodwork showing.

cheval glass A long mirror mounted on swivels in a frame.

chiffonier An ornamental cabinet with drawers or shelves, or a high and narrow chest of drawers.

club chair A deep, thickly upholstered easy chair with heavy arms and sides, and often a low back.

commode An ornate, low cabinet or chest of drawers, usually on legs or short feet.

console table A table supported by decorative brackets fixed to a wall.

credenza A cupboard or sideboard, typically without legs.

davenport

davenport A small writing desk with side drawers and sloping top.

dos-à-dos A sofa that accommodates two people seated back to back.

escritoire A portable writing desk, typically with a hinged top closing over small drawers.

farthingale chair An armless chair with a high seat and low straight back.

fauteuil An upholstered armchair.

love seat A large chair or small sofa that seats two people.

morris chair A large easy chair with an adjustable back and big loose cushions.

farthingale chair

ottoman A long upholstered seat, with or without a back.

pier table A table designed to stand against a wall between two windows.

pouffe A large firm cushion used as a seat, or a low, soft, backless couch.

secrétaire A drop-front desk, sometimes with drawers below and a bookcase above.

tabouret A low stool or cabinet.

tallboy A double chest of drawers, with one section standing on top of the other.

teapoy A small tea table, typically with three legs.

tête-à-tête An S-shaped sofa allowing two people to face each other when seated.

tete-à-tete

torchière A slender decorative candlestand, often with a tripod base.

triclinium A couch or set of couches surrounding three sides of a table.

whatnot or **étagère** A lightweight stand with three or more open shelves.

Windsor chair A comfortable wooden chair with arms, a spoked back, and splayed legs.

Windsor chair

architecture

acropolis

adobe

acropolis A hilltop citadel, especially in ancient Greece, and most notably in Athens, containing the most splendid temples and treasuries.

adobe A Spanish word for a sun-dried brick, common in ancient cultures and especially in arid lands. Particularly associated with the house building of the Pueblo Indians in the southwest USA and Mexico.

aedicule A small shrine or tabernacle of wood or stone, framed by columns and surmounted by an entablature and pediment.

almshouse Housing endowed by a public or private charity for use by the poor.

amphiprostyle A temple with columns and a portico at each end.

amphitheater An open-air, round or oval theater with rising rows of seating.

apartment house A building containing multiple dwelling units with a common entrance and services.

aqueduct An elevated masonry or brick channel for carrying water, widely used by the Romans.

arsenal A building for manufacturing and storing armaments. Two historic examples are in Venice and Piraeus.

baptistery Either a separate building or the part of a church reserved for the performance of the rite of baptism.

barbican Fortifications protecting a draw-bridge, castle entrance, or fortified town gate.

barracks Block accommodation for the military since Roman times.

basilica In classical architecture, a large rectangular Roman hall with colonnades and a semi-circular apse, used primarily as a court of law. By the fourth century, it was adapted as one of the basic plans for Christian churches in western architecture, as opposed to the cruciform plan adopted in Constantinople for the east.

bastion A pentagonal work projecting from the main rampart. Dominant feature of European military architecture from the sixteenth to nineteenth centuries.

belvedere

belvedere An open-sided roofed terrace, usually at the top of a building, with a commanding or interesting view of a town square, formal garden, or landscape.

bunker An underground military installation for protection against air attack.

campanile Italian for a bell tower detached from the main body of a church.

castle A fortified building, set of buildings, or place.

catacomb A subterranean burial ground, best known as used by the early Christians outside the walls of Rome.

cathedral A Christian church which is also the seat of a bishop and hence the center of a diocese.

cenotaph A monument to those buried elsewhere.

chalet A Swiss mountain hut.

chantry A small self-contained chapel, usually inside but sometimes outside a medieval church, financially endowed by the founder so that regular masses could be said for the repose of his or her soul.

chapel (1) A small church which is not a parish church. (2) A Nonconformist church.

chapter house The administrative meeting place of a monastery or cathedral.

cenotaph

circus (1) A hippodrome for horse and chariot racing. (2) A circular arrangement of terraced houses, as in Bath, England.

citadel A fortified place attached to, or within, a city.

conservatory A glass greenhouse which can combine the function of growing and protecting plants and domestic use.

cottage A small country dwelling place usually originally built for a farm laborer and his family.

crescent A crescent-shaped row of terraced houses.

duplex apartment A maisonette, or a flat or apartment on more than one floor.

flat/apartment A single-story unit of habitation in a multi-story building.

folly A sham building, sometimes a ruin, built to enhance a vista or a landscape.

fort A small stronghold with all-round defenses such as an Iron Age fort, American West log fort, or Roman garrison.

fortress A large, complex military stronghold with defense in depth and considerable perimeter. In the nineteenth century, a whole city defended by a ring of forts might be so designated.

forum In Roman architecture an open space surrounded by public buildings and colonnades. In ancient Rome the forum was the centre of civic and commercial life.

forum

gatehouse The rooms or apartments above a fortified medieval gateway.

gazebo A small summerhouse or pavilion with a view, or a belvedere on the roof of a house.

hall church A type of church common in Germany in which the aisles are the same height as the nave, which is therefore lit from the aisle windows.

hôtel A large French town house.

gazebo

hunting lodge Buildings usually located in forests to accommodate hunters.

hypostyle A thickly pillared hall, especially in ancient Egypt, in which the roof rests directly on the columns.

kiosk (1) A small pavilion or summer-house. (2) A small shop building on the street or inside a bigger building.

lighthouse Tall structure containing a light to warn approaching ships of coastal dangers.

loggia An open-sided gallery, usually with pillars, common in Renaissance Italy.

lych gate A covered wooden gate at the entrance to a churchyard.

manor house A medium-sized medieval house in the country or a village, the center of a manor.

manse A house attached to a church, and provided for the minister in Scotland and northern England.

mansion house A grand residence.

martello tower An English artillery coastal fortification copied from a tower captured in Corsica 1794; 74 were built on the east and south coasts of England against the French invasion threat 1805–12.

martyrium A Christian church sited over the grave of a martyr or martyrs.

mausoleum A large, grand tomb comprising a separate structure or building.

mews A small terrace of stables and staff accommodation in a cobbled street behind a row of rich town (especially London) houses.

minaret A tower usually attached to a mosque from which the Muslim faithful are called to prayer.

minster A loose term given to a number of medieval English cathedrals and major churches. It originally implied a monastery and monastic church.

mausoleum

monastery A building complex, including a church or abbey, inhabited by monks or nuns.

mosque Islamic place of worship.

motte-and-bailey A mound or motte surmounted by a wooden (later stone) tower (bailey) and enclosed by a ditch and palisade. The earliest example of this primitive castle form is on the River Loire (France) and is dated 1010.

museum Building for the presentation of valuable or historical artifacts.

obelisk A monument of Ancient Egyptian origins, consisting of a tall tapering shaft of stone with a pyramidal top.

observatory A building housing a telescope.

odeion A small classical building for musical contests.

orangery A conservatory for growing oranges, glazed on the south side.

oratory A small private chapel.

outhouse A small building detached from a house, such as a garden shed or sometimes a toilet.

pagoda A Buddhist Indian, Southeast Asian or Chinese temple in the form of a tower, copied as a decorative building in Europe from the eighteenth century P'ai Lou, a highly decorated Chinese gateway.

palace, palazzo A major royal or episcopal residence.

penthouse (1) An outhouse with a lean-to roof. (2) A separate structure on the roof of a high rise building.

refectory A communal dining hall.

skyscraper A very tall building of steel skeletal construction, developed in the USA from the 1880s.

stadium A sports ground for athletics.

stave church A Scandinavian timber-framed and timber-walled church built from the eleventh century onward.

pagoda

stoa In Greek architecture, a covered colonnade or hall (often with shops) open on the colonnaded side and sometimes two-storied.

synagogue A Jewish place of worship.

tabernacle The portable sanctuary in which the ancient Israelites carried the Ark of the Covenant.

temple A place of worship particularly associated with classical Greek architecture.

theater A building designed for the performance of plays.

thermae Roman public baths.

tower A very tall structure, usually square or circular, designed for observation, communication, and defense.

tower block A high rise apartment block.

tabernacle

town hall Municipal buildings for the council and local administration.

triumphal arch A Roman monumental gateway, much imitated in the Renaissance and since, to celebrate military victory or prowess.

triumphal column A decorated column to celebrate a military victory.

viaduct A series of arches which carry a road, canal or railway over a valley, water, or low ground.

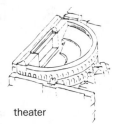

villa (1) A Roman or Renaissance country house. (2) A modern detached house.

watchtower A tall tower for military observation, often part of a castle.

theater

fashion and clothing

accessories Things that are made to match and be worn with a garment, such as gloves or bags.

angora The long soft hair of the angora goat or the fur of the angora rabbit, or a fabric made from these.

appliqué A decoration stitched to a garment or piece of material, or the technique of doing this.

arctic A type of waterproof overshoe.

argyles Socks with diamond-shaped patterns in various colors on a background of a single color.

bandanna A large, colorful handkerchief often worn around the neck.

bandeau A narrow band of material worn around the head by women and girls.

basque A tight-fitting bodice worn by women.

bateau neck A neckline that is slightly curved, like the shape of a boat.

batik Fabric that is printed by covering some areas with a removable wax that repels dye, so that only unwaxed areas are colored, or the technique of doing this.

batwing sleeve A sleeve that has a very deep armhole but is tight at the wrist.

black tie A black bow tie worn with a dinner jacket by men on formal occasions.

boater An old-fashioned stiff straw hat with a flat crown and a straight brim.

bobby socks Ankle-length socks worn by girls.

bolero A short jacket, originally from Spain, ending above the waist and worn open.

bomber jacket A waistlength jacket, usually made of leather, with a zippered front, elasticated waistband, and cuffed sleeves; modeled on jackets worn by military pilots and crew.

boot-cut jeans Jeans with legs that flare slightly at the bottom to fit over the ankles of boots.

brocade A heavy fabric with a raised design.

broderie anglaise Openwork embroidery sewn onto white cotton, especially on lingerie.

burnoose A long hooded cloak worn by men in some Arab countries.

bustier A tight-fitting, strapless, women's top worn as an undergarment or outer garment.

camisole A bodice with shoulder straps, cut straight at the top and worn as an undergarment.

cap sleeve A very short sleeve that covers only the top part of the arm.

capri pants Tight-fitting women's pants with legs that end at the calf.

cashmere A soft fabric made from the hair of goats that live in the Kashmir region.

catwalk A raised platform along which models walk to display new clothes designs.

chador A loose robe of dark material worn by some Muslim women, covering the body from head to foot as well as most of the face.

chambray Light fabric woven with white thread on a colored warp.

Chantilly lace Ornamental bobbin lace with designs made using silk thread.

chenille A fabric with a tufted pile, woven from silk, cotton, or rayon.

cheongsam A Chinese women's dress with a slit skirt and a high, stiff collar.

chiffon A sheer fabric, woven from silk, nylon, or cotton.

chignon A roll of hair gathered at the back of a woman's head.

chinos Pants made from coarse, twilled cotton.

choker A necklace or neckband that fits tightly around a woman's throat.

cloche A women's hat shaped like a bell.

cocktail dress A woman's short dress designed for wearing at semiformal occasions such as cocktail parties.

codpiece A baggy pouch worn over the genitals with hose or breeches by men in the fifteenth and sixteenth centuries.

coiffeur A male hairdresser.

coiffeuse A female hairdresser.

coiffure A hairstyle, especially an elaborate one.

corsage A small bouquet of flowers worn by a woman at her wrist, shoulder, or breast.

costume jewelry Jewelry that is highly decorative but is made from inexpensive rather than precious materials.

couture The fashionable and expensive part of the dressmaking and clothes-designing business.

couturier A person who designs fashionable clothes and oversees the making and selling of them.

crinoline A stiff linen fabric used in the past to line and stiffen clothes, or a petticoat made of this.

cruiserwear Light, casual clothes suitable for wearing in hot weather or on vacation, especially on a pleasure cruise.

crushed velvet Velvet that has been treated with heat and pressure to produce a permanently crinkled surface.

Cuban heel A broad, moderately high, tapering heel on a boot or shoe.

culottes Women's or girls' pants cut with a wide flare to look like a skirt.

dashiki A large, loose garment for the upper body, originally from Africa.

décolleté Cut with a very low neckline to expose the upper part of the breasts.

derby A men's felt hat with a stiff, curved brim and a rounded crown.

dirndl A full skirt gathered tightly at the waist, or a dress with this kind of skirt.

djellaba A long, loose, hooded cloak with wide sleeves, worn in many Muslim countries.

dolman sleeve A tapering sleeve that is very wide at the top of the arm and narrow at the wrist.

Empire line A high-waisted style of women's dresses, popular in France in the reign of the Emperor Napoleon.

ensemble A full outfit of clothes worn at the same time, especially of matching clothes.

espadrilles Light shoes with canvas uppers and soles made from rope or other flexible material.

Eton collar A high, stiff, white collar, especially one turned down onto the lapels of a jacket.

Fair Isle A multicolored pattern used in knitwear made with Shetland wool.

fedora A soft felt hat with a brim that can be turned up and a crown with a crease running from front to back.

fleece A sleeved garment for the upper body, made of lightweight but warm material.

foulard A scarf or necktie made of lightweight, usually printed, silk or rayon.

gladrags Fancy clothes, especially the best clothes that somebody keeps for special occasions.

godet A triangular piece of material inserted in a skirt or sleeve to make it fuller or give it a flare.

gusset A piece of material inserted in a garment to strengthen a part or enlarge it.

haberdasher A person who deals in men's clothing and accessories.

halter A type of women's top that ties behind the neck and leaves the back bare.

harem pants Women's baggy pants that are fitted closely at the ankle.

haute couture The most fashionable and expensive part of the business of women's fashions.

hobble skirt A long skirt cut so narrow at the ankle that the wearer's walking is restricted.

hosiery Socks and stockings.

houndstooth check A pattern of small broken checks woven or printed on cloth.

huaraches Sandals with low heels and uppers made of interwoven strips of leather.

jabot A ruffle or frill worn at the front of the neck of a shirt or blouse.

jodhpurs Riding pants that are very wide at the thighs but fitted closely from the knees down.

jumper A sleeveless, one-piece dress usually worn over a blouse or sweater.

kaffiyeh A headdress worn by Arab men, consisting of a square of cloth held on by a band.

khaki A hard-wearing, light yellowish brown cloth, often used for uniforms.

kilt A knee-length, skirtlike garment worn by men as part of traditional Scottish Highland dress.

kimono A long, wide-sleeved Japanese robe fastened by a sash, or a women's dress in similar style.

knee-highs Stockings or socks that reach up to just below the knee.

knickerbockers Full pants that are gathered at the knees.

knife pleat A very narrow, often permanent, flat pleat in a garment, especially a skirt.

lamé A fabric with metallic threads, usually gold or silver, woven into it.

legwarmers Knitted footless stockings worn over over tights or pants, especially by dancers.

leotard A tight one-piece garment for the torso, with or without sleeves, worn particularly for dancing or exercise.

mannequin A person who models clothes at fashion shows or for photographs.

modiste A person who designs, makes, or sells fashonable clothes for women.

moleskin A heavy cotton fabric brushed to give it a suedelike appearance.

Mother Hubbard A loose, baggy dress for women.

muumuu A type of long, loose, brightly colored dress originally worn by Hawaiian women.

needlecord A type of corduroy material with very narrow ribs.

negligee A women's loose, light dressing gown.

Oxfords Men's low-heeled shoes that lace at the front.

paisley Woolen material woven or printed with a swirling pattern of rounded abstract shapes.

Panama hat A lightweight South American hat made of hand-plaited straw.

panne A type of velvet with a very smooth and shiny finish.

parka A hooded jacket or coat with a warm lining, designed for cold weather.

pedal pushers Women's or girls' calf-length pants, originally designed for cycling.

pencil skirt A very narrow straight skirt.

peplum A short ruffle extending from the waist of a jacket, dress, or blouse to the hips.

Peter Pan collar A soft collar with turned-down, rounded ends.

picture hat A wide-brimmed women's hat elaborately decorated with flowers or ribbons.

plus fours Baggy knickers gathered below the knee, worn in the past for sports.

polo neck A tubular collar for a sweater or shirt, worn rolled down.

polo shirt A short-sleeved, pullover sport shirt made of knitted jersey.

prêt-à-porter Ready-to-wear, or clothing that is ready to wear.

raglan sleeve A sleeve that extends from the neckline of a garment in one piece.

raw silk A type of rough, untreated silk fabric made from the cocoons of silkworms.

rayon A synthetic fabric made from cellulose.

rebozo A Mexican women's scarf worn over the head and shoulders.

rollneck A rolled-down collar similar to but wider than a polo neck.

salopettes A skiing garment consisting of quilted pants reaching to the chest and held up by shoulder straps.

sari An Indian or Pakistani women's garment consisting of a length of cloth wrapped around the waist like a skirt then draped over the shoulder and sometimes the head.

sarong A length of cotton worn wrapped around the waist to make a long skirt.

seersucker A light cotton or rayon material with a crinkled surface.

separates Garments that can be bought individually and worn along with other garments.

serape A colorful Mexican woolen shawl worn by men over the shoulders.

shantung A heavy silk fabric that has a rough, uneven finish.

shell suit A lightweight tracksuit made of waterproof material lined with cotton, often used as leisurewear.

shirtwaist A women's dress with a bodice tailored like a man's shirt.

slicker A long waterproof raincoat made of plastic, rubber, or oilskin.

slingbacks Women's shoes that are open at the back and held on with a strap over the heel.

sloppy joe A large, loose sweater.

sombrero A wide-brimmed Mexican straw hat with a high crown.

spandex A synthetic fabric made from polyurethane, used in making stretch clothing.

stiletto heel A very high, thin, pointed heel on a women's shoe.

supermodel A woman who models clothes and has become very successful and famous.

sweatshirt A long-sleeved heavy cotton pullover worn for sports or leisure.

terry A cotton fabric with an uncut pile on both sides, used for bathrobes and towels.

thong A garment worn for swimming or sunbathing, consisting of thin strips of material that cover the genitals but leave the buttocks bare.

turtleneck A tubular, closefitting, high collar on a sweater or pullover.

tuxedo A men's dinner jacket.

twinset A matching short-sleeved sweater and cardigan, worn together by women.

velour A fabric with a thick pile like velvet.

wasp waist A very narrow waist on a woman, especially when this is achieved using a tight corset.

watered silk Silk that has been given a wavy shiny finish by being damped and pressed.

wedgies Shoes in which the sole and heel are formed into a solid wedge shape.

Wellington boots (1) boots reaching above the knee in front but lower in back. (2) waterproof rubber boots reaching almost to the knee.

white tie A white bow tie worn by men as part of formal evening dress.

wild silk Silk from silkworms that are wild rather than farmed, or a fabric made from this.

windbreaker A warm jacket that fits closely at the cuffs and waistband.

wingtips A type of shoe made with a cap that extends from the toe back along the sides.

yarmulke A skullcap worn by Jewish men and boys.

yashmak A veil worn by Muslim women to cover the face when in public.

yoke A part of a garment that is fitted around the neck or shoulders and to which the rest of the garment is attached.

zoot suit A type of men's suit with wide, tapering pants and a long, wide-shouldered coat that was fashionable in the 1940s.

History

3

history terms

Ancient Eastern civilizations

Buddhism A religious and philosophical system founded c. 520–530 BC.

burning of the books (255–210 BC) The Qin dynasty attempt to destroy all literature in private hands except official records and some practical works.

caste system A system of social stratification in India, deriving from the Aryan hereditary division of the population into priests (Brahmins), warriors and rulers (Kshatriya), farmers and merchants (Vaisya), and laborers, artisans, and domestic servants (Sudra).

Hindu beliefs These grew from a post–2000 BC fusion of Aryan, Dravadian, and Munda cultures. Probably the world's oldest surviving faith.

Sanskrit The oldest member of the Indo-European family of languages. Its grammar was fixed before c. 400 BC.

Veda The oldest Hindu writings, dating from c. 1000 BC incorporated in four collections.

warlord A military commander wielding civil power. Sometimes in nominal allegiance to the king or emperor, usually defying such control.

Central and South American cultures

Aztec AD 1325–1521 Invading Aztec tribes ended the ruling Toltec power and in 1325 founded Tenochtitlán (now Mexico City). Aztecs were Indians rich with gold and silver, and medicinal skills. They composed poetry and music. Their state was militaristic, with a large, well-equipped army. Human sacrifice was the basis for faith according to Aztec religion. Between 1519 and 1521 Hernando Cortés and 400 Spanish troops invaded and defeated this Central American civilization.

Chibcha Advanced Indian civilization AD 1200–1538, conquered by the Spanish in the 1500s. They used gold, emeralds, and made textiles, baskets, and pots. They lived in small villages and farmed the lowlands of the high plains of the central Colombian Andes where they lived.

Incas AD 1200–1535 The Incas built an extensive empire, the hub of which was the city of Cuzco. Their ruler was known as the "Only Inca," and was regarded as a god. The Inca were sun-worshippers, and practiced human sacrifice. Their last king,

Atahualpa, was captured by the Spanish expedition led by Pizzaro.

Mayan AD 100–1542 An Indian civilization based on agriculture. Mayans built their homes and pyramidal temples from limestone. They carved important dates on stone using picture writing which has recently been deciphered. Cities were centered around royal houses and religious structures. Mayan culture is noted for its advances in architecture, the arts, astronomy, and mathematics.

Olmecs The Olmecs flourished between 800 BC and AD 200. They developed a counting system and a calendar, carved stone statues, and wrote using hieroglyphics. La Venta, the site ruins in Tabasco, was a major Olmec settlement.

Olmecs

Teotihuacán 100 BC–AD 750 The Teotihuacáns built an enormous city inhabited from about AD 400 and organized as a metropolis from about the beginning of the Christian era. The city included two outstanding temoles-pyramids, dedicated to the Sun and the Moon respectively. Little is known about Teotihuacán culture. They farmed and irrigated the land, and set up trading posts with Mayans. The city was sacked and burned by invading Toltecs in about AD 650.

Teotihuacan

Toltec AD 900–1200 During the 900s Toltec Indians established an empire, making Tula (north of Mexico City) their capital. They controlled the Valley of Mexico until 1200. A fierce people, they invaded the Yucatán Peninsula then rebuilt an old Mayan religious center, Chichén Itzá. They worshipped the feathered serpent Quetzalcoatl and also believed in human sacrifice.

Toltec

Zapotec and Mixtec AD 300–1524 Indians who built their religious center of Monte Alban 1000–500 BC on a mountain top which they flattened themselves. They farmed, used a calendar, and wrote using hieroglyphics. Elaborate Zapotec tombs suggest that they believed in an afterlife. Mixtec Indians from western Oaxaca occupied the Zapotec "city" of Monte Alban before AD 1 and after 900.

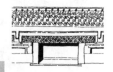

Zapotec

Middle east empires and civilizations

Assyrians A people who lived in Mesopotamia. Their state was a dependency of Babylon which emerged as major independent state. Assyrian rulers were renowned for their buildings, and their troops for fighting prowess.

Babylonians Rulers of a succession of kingdoms and empires in Mesopotamia. Noted for culture and architectural splendor.

Carthaginians A people who lived in what is modern Tunisia, based on the city of Carthage, reputedly founded by the Tyrian princess Dido. A center for trade and exploration, Carthage was destroyed by Rome in 146 BC.

Fertile crescent An area bordering the Mediterranean and including the Nile valley where western civilization and its derivations began. It was farmed with settled communities from c. 8000 BC.

Hittites An Indo-European people dominating an area west of Euphrates river between 2000 and 1000 BC. They were frequently at war with Egypt.

Phoenicians A people who lived in a region settled from 3000 BC corresponding to modern Lebanon. Sea traders and colonizers, the Phoenicians extended their empire to Carthage and Cyprus. First Persia, then Alexander the Great conquered the eastern part.

Ancient Greece

Achaeans A Greek people whom Homer identifies as the besiegers of Troy. Their capital was Mycenae.

acropolis The central, fortified administrative and religious district in Greek cities. The best-known is that of Athens, which was also a sanctuary.

agora An open meeting-place in Greek cities. The Roman forum was based on it.

Delian League A confederacy of Greek city-states led by Athens against Persia.

demos A Greek word denoting common people who held citizenship and therefore had rights.

Epicureanism A Greek philosophy identifying good with pleasure but advocating a withdrawn and quiet life.

hoplite A Greek heavily armed foot soldier who largely replaced the more aristocratic cavalry and chariot fighter.

oligarchy Government by a small faction or group of families, from Greek words meaning "a few" and "chief" or "principal."

phalanx A Greek military formation of ranked armored hoplites.

polis The Greek term for a city-state—an area dominated by and administered from a central fortifiable town.

pyrrhic victory One which proves more costly than defeat. Named for the Greek ruler who defeated a Roman army in 280 BC.

stoicism A Greek philosophy adopted by Rome stressing private rectitude and involvement in public affairs.

tyrant A Greek synonym for king or ruler, not necessarily denoting one who has seized power unconstitutionally or who rules oppressively.

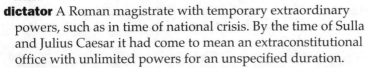

Ancient Rome

Augustus A Roman title of honor awarded to Octavian and subsequently adopted as a name as well as a title.

Caesar An aristocratic Roman family name which became an imperial title.

Capitol The triple religious shrine on Rome's Capitoline Hill.

Celts A people dominating western and central Europe from the Bronze Age to the middle of the first century BC.

centurion A Roman officer commanding an army unit of 100 men.

Caesar

dictator A Roman magistrate with temporary extraordinary powers, such as in time of national crisis. By the time of Sulla and Julius Caesar it had come to mean an extraconstitutional office with unlimited powers for an unspecified duration.

Etruscans Italic people who invaded from Asia Minor and settled between the Arno and Tiber rivers. By the 6th century BC they had achieved a high cultural level. By the 5th century BC they had been absorbed by Rome, who took over many aspects of their art and religious practices.

forum A Roman central open area surrounded by temples and other public buildings and suitable for public meetings. It was derived from the Greek "agora."

Gauls A Celtic people who inhabited a Western European area corresponding to modern France, Belgium, western Germany, and northern Italy. They sacked Rome in 390 BC, and were conquered primarily by Julius Caesar 58–50 BC.

gladiator An armed fighter for arena contests. Up to 5000 pairs could perform in one spectacle.

Goths A Germanic people who constantly attacked the Roman empire from the 3rd–5th century AD.

Huns A nomadic people invading south-eastern Europe in the 4th century AD and building up an empire won through cavalry and archery tactics. They conquered the Visigoths, but their power disintegrated after the death of Attila.

legion A Roman military unit, originally a citizen army, later comprising 4000 to 6000 heavy infantry soldiers with cavalry support.

Ostrogoths An Eastern Gothic people who established an empire bordering the Black Sea. They were conquered by the Huns c. AD 370.

patricians A Roman privileged citizen class for whom certain high state and priestly offices were reserved.

plebians A Roman central citizen class with self-administrative rights.

Punic Wars A series of conflicts between Carthage and Rome 264–146 BC.

Sabines An Italic tribe who lived east of the Tiber river and were conquered by Rome. Legend recounts that Roman settlers kidnapped their young women to provide brides.

Samnite Wars Conflicts between southern Italian mountain tribes, possibly of Sabine descent, and Rome between 343 and 290 BC.

senate The Roman assembly of heads of patrician families. It held the supreme administrative authority, even under the empire.

Visigoths A Gothic people who spread from Spain through Gaul then drove south to Rome, which they sacked in AD 410.

Dark Ages

Anglo-Saxon Chronicle AD 891–1154. Historical account begun during the reign of Alfred the Great.

Anglo-Saxons West Germanic peoples who settled in Britain and dominated from AD 500 until the Norman Conquest.

Danegeld A tax levied on the Anglo-Saxon population of England to buy off Danish invaders.

Franks A Germanic tribe of the Rhine region conquering Gaul from c. AD 500 and establishing an empire.

Goths An East Germanic people from Scandinavia who invaded parts of the Roman empire from the 3rd to the 5th centuries AD.

Moors Muslims of mixed Berber and Arab descent conquering Spain 711–1492.

Norsemen Western Scandinavian people raiding, exploring, and colonizing south to France, west to Britain, north to Labrador and Greenland.

Picts A warlike people who lived in what is now Scotland with an independent kingdom AD 297–843.

Saxons Germanic peoples from the Baltic coast raiding and settling through Germany to Gaul and Britain. Their European lands were eventually incorporated into the Frankish empire.

Scots A Celtic people from northern Ireland colonizing Argyll in the 5th century and giving their name to Scotland.

Vandals A Germanic people invading Gaul and Spain c. AD 400. They sacked Rome AD 455, and ruled a North African kingdom AD 429–534.

Vikings Another name for Norsemen.

Crusades and conquests 1050–1400

Albigenses A Cathar sect in southern France professing Manichaean dualism (good and evil of equal power, therefore denying God's supremacy over Satan). They were savagely suppressed 1209–44.

Almoravids Berber Islamic tribesmen conquering Morocco and Algeria 1054–1147 and southern Spain 1085–1118. They succumbed to Christian reconquest.

Assassins Politico-religious Islamic sect sponsoring murder of opponents c.1094–c. 1256.

Black Death The name given to the form of bubonic plague that caused widespread death throughout Europe in the 14th century.

Cathars *See* **Albigenses**.

Dance of death Also called "danse macabre," an allegorical concept of the power of death over all mankind, even the most powerful. Probably inspired by the carnage of the Black Death 1346–52 and the Hundred Years' War 1337–1453.

Domesday Book A 1086 survey of land holdings in England initiated by William the Conqueror.

Holy Sepulchre A tomb in Jerusalem reputed to be that of Jesus Christ. The crusades sought to recover it from Muslim rule.

Hundred Years' War 1337–1453 Fought over the English Plantagenet kings' claim to the French throne. It ended in the expulsion of the English from most of France.

Jacquerie 1358 A French peasant revolt against the nobility.

Knights of St John A military religious order originally responsible for the welfare of pilgrims to the Holy Land. Installed at Rhodes 1310, they were forced by Turkish conquest to move to Malta 1522–30.

Knights Templar A military religious order, 1119–1314, founded to protect pilgrims to the Holy Land and to gain territorial and political influence.

Knights, Teutonic *See* **Teutonic Knights**.

Lombard League An alliance of city-states resisting attempts at domination by the Holy Roman Empire 1167–1250.

Magna Carta A 1215 charter of English liberties granted by King John under threat of baronial civil war.

Manichaeism *See* **Albigenses**.

Model Parliament 1295, the first full English parliament.

Mongols A nomadic central Asian people whose empire under Genghis Khan stretched from China to the Danube.

Saracens Arab peoples adopting Islam and opposing crusaders.

Schism 1054, the formal separation between the Orthodox

(eastern) and the Roman Catholic (western) Churches.

Seljuks Turkoman tribes invading western Asia and dominating Palestine and Persia from the 10th to 13th centuries.

Sicilian Vespers A 1282 massacre of Angevins in and around Palermo precipitating a Spanish-aided revolt against French rule.

Templars *See* **Knights Templar.**

Teutonic Knights A religious and military order 1190–1525 establishing a feudal state covering Prussia and the eastern Baltic.

The Renaissance

Great Schism 1378–1417, a period in which rival popes claimed office. It led to calls for church reform.

neo-Platonism The revival of a philosophical system developed in the third century.

new learning Study of biblical and classical texts in the original languages.

Ottoman empire 1300–1922 The Turkish empire that replaced the Byzantine empire and dominated the eastern Mediterranean throughout the 16th and 17th centuries.

Tudor, House of 1485–1603 Kings of England of Lancastrian and Welsh descent.

Universal Man A renaissance concept of the individual respected for skills in many fields of knowledge rather than for high birth.

Wars of the Roses 1455–85 A dynastic conflict for the English throne between the Lancastrian and Yorkist branches of the House of Plantagenet.

Reformation/Religious wars 1515–1688

Anabaptists A radical Protestant movement founded in 1525 and first based in Zurich. They established a communistic, polygamous theocracy in Munster in 1534 which was suppressed in 1535.

Anglican Church The reformed church of England, first established in 1534 but retaining elements of Roman Catholic dogma and ritual.

Cavaliers *See* **Royalists.**

Commonwealth 1649–60 A republican state in England between the execution of Charles I and the restoration of Charles II.

Council of Blood (Council of Troubles) 1567–74 A Spanish instrument for suppression of religious and political revolt.

Covenanters Scottish Presbyterians opposed to Catholicism, episcopacy, and monarchical absolutism.

Diet of Worms 1521 A Holy Roman Empire assembly attended by Luther under safe-conduct from Charles V. Its edict subsequently outlawed Luther.

Dissenters Those who disassociated themselves from the Church of England.

divine right (of kings to be absolute rulers) A doctrine adhered to by James I that caused the downfall of Charles I.

Fronde 1648–53 French civil disturbances led by royal princes and members of the aristocracy during the minority of Louis XIV. Its failure paved the way for the king's subsequent absolutism.

Glorious Revolution 1688 An almost bloodless coup d'état which replaced the Catholic authoritarian James II with the Protestant William III and Mary II.

Gunpowder Plot 1605 A Catholic conspiracy to blow up James I at the opening of Parliament.

Holy Office *See* **Inquisition.**

Huguenots French Protestants, mainly Calvinist. They were powerful political and military challengers of royal power. Their military base at La Rochelle was captured after a siege by Richelieu (1628).

indulgences The Catholic doctrine of remission of temporal punishment for confessed sins through penance, good works or almsgiving. Abuse of plenary (full) indulgences led to Luther's repudiation of the doctrine. The pecuniary aspect was abolished in 1562.

Inquisition (Holy Office) A Roman Catholic tribunal concerned with investigating and punishing heresy.

Jesuits *See* **Society of Jesus.**

Levellers 1645–9 An English radical republican party.

Lollards An English reforming sect following the teachings of John Wycliffe.

Nonconformists Dissenters from the Church of England.

Nonjurors Anglican clergymen refusing to take the oath of allegiance to William III and Mary II.

Parliamentarians Supporters of Parliament rather than the king during the English Civil War.

Pilgrim Fathers English Puritans who founded the colony of Plymouth in New England 1620.

Pilgrimage of Grace 1536 A northern English rebellion against the dissolution of the monasteries. It was savagely suppressed.

Popish Plot 1678 Fictitious allegations against English Catholics fabricated by Titus Oates and others. At least 35 innocent people were executed.

predestination The doctrine of Calvinist and other beliefs that God has determined from eternity those to be saved or damned regardless of merit or actions.

Presbyterians Reformers advocating elected church government without bishops or interference by secular rulers.

Puritanism A Church of England reform movement in the late 16th and 17th centuries seeking to exterminate all remnants of Catholic doctrine and ritual.

Quakers *See* **Society of Friends**.

Restoration 1660 The return of the Stuart dynasty after the Commonwealth. Also refers to the social and artistic fashions introduced during the period 1660–1714.

Roundheads *See* **Parliamentarians**.

Royalists Supporters of Charles I and II during the English Civil War.

Rump 1648–60 The English Parliament after it was purged of members unacceptable to the army.

Society of Friends (Quakers) A Christian sect without ritual, creed or priesthood, founded in 1650 by George Fox.

Society of Jesus (Jesuits) A Catholic missionary and teaching order founded in 1534 by Ignatius Loyola, a Spanish soldier. Military in discipline and often controversial.

Thirty Years' War 1618–48 A central and western European conflict originally fought on Catholic versus Protestant issues but becoming increasingly secularized. France and Sweden both entered on the Protestant side.

Age of Reason 1688–1709

East India Company A trading company which effectively ruled British India from 1708–1857.

Encyclopédie 1751–80 A 35-volume showcase for radical views on science, politics, religion, and economics.

enlightened despotism Rule by an absolute monarch intended to ensure the economic, intellectual and social comfort of subjects.

Home Rule Irish agitation for complete self-government from the 1770s to 1920s.

Jacobites Supporters of the Stuart pretenders to the British crown. They mounted unsuccessful rebellions in 1715 and 1745.

Jansenism A Catholic sect, latterly centered on the Port Royal lay convent in Paris, which denied free will and promoted austerity and church reform. Condemned by Pope in 1713, the ensuing controversy split the French church.

penal laws Anti-Catholic legislation in England, Ireland and

Scotland denying land inheritance and voting rights, and restricting access to legal, military, political, and scholastic professions. Pressure for their repeal lasted from the 1700s to 1920s.

philosophes French intellectuals advocating changes in political and social structure as well as in religion and philosophy.

Pragmatic Sanction 1713 An attempt to guarantee succession to the Austro-Hungarian throne of Maria Theresa.

South Sea Bubble A financial crash in Britain caused by the failure of a company formed in 1711 to trade with the Spanish American colonies.

Whigs British landed gentry and merchants who were against aristocracy and represented mercantile and dissenting interests. The word originally denoted a Scottish horse thief.

The Americas 1491–1763

House of Burgesses The first elected colonial legislature, in Virginia in 1619.

Iroquois A native North American people originally living between the Hudson and St Lawrence rivers.

Mayflower Compact A self-government agreement with equality under law made by the Pilgrim Fathers while still at sea.

Mohawks A native North American people, a tribe of the Iroquois, originally living along the Mohawk River.

Orders of Connecticut 1639, the first written constitution providing for male franchise and self-government.

Sioux A native North American people originally ranging across the Great Plains from Lake Michigan to the Rocky Mountains.

Zenger Case 1735 A New York libel action which established freedom of the Press.

American War of Independence 1763–89

Articles of Confederation The constitution which created the United States of America by a meeting of Congress in 1777. Effective 1781.

colonists Americans born in and living on the American continent.

Conventions Constitutional assemblies.

Declaration of Independence A document asserting that "these united colonies are and of right ought to be free and independent states" 1775–76.

Hessians German mercenary soldiers hired by the British.

Loyalists Americans loyal to the British Crown.

Patriots Americans demanding independence from Britain.
Tory a loyalist

French Revolution

Ancien régime The name given to the social system in force in
France before 1789.
assignats Paper currency issued during the Revolution which
depreciated rapidly.
Bastille A royal prison in Paris used exclusively for state
prisoners.
citoyen/ne (French: citizen/citizenness) The abolition of titles
required all French men and women to be addressed simply as
"citizen."
Emigré/e A noble fleeing the revolution; they forfeited their
estates and were liable to summary execution if they returned.
Girondins A left-of-center political group that opposed the
Jacobin National Assembly.
guillotine An execution machine named for its inventor and first
used in April 1792. Also called "the national razor."
Jacobins A club patronised by radicals, hence a catch-all term for
extreme Revolutionaries. They opposed the Girondins in the
National Assembly and gained control.

guiillotine

Montagne An extreme left grouping in the National Convention.
National Assembly The legislative body which succeeded the
Estates-General, and which was dominated by the Third Estate,
representing the people.
parlements Pre-revolutionary judicial assemblies with no
legislative powers.
Quatorze Juillet The day on which the Bastille fell, July 14, 1789.
Reign of Terror The period after Louis XVI's execution from
October 1793 to July 1794 when the Jacobins ruled and during
which thousands of people were executed for political reasons.
sans-culottes A name for republicans, originally meant as an
insult, referring to the trousers worn by common people rather
than courtly breeches.
tricolor A cockade or flag adding revolutionary blue and red (to
signify willingness to die) to the Bourbon dynasty's white.
tumbril A two-wheeled cart used to take condemned prisoners to
the guillotine.

North America 1780–1860

Democratic-Republicans A post-Revolutionary political
grouping mainly of small farmers and workers advocating

states' rights (led by Jefferson). It became the Democratic Party in 1828.

Federalists A post-Revolutionary political grouping mainly of propertied and commercial classes advocating central government (led by Hamilton).

Forty-Niners 77,000 men who rushed to California in 1849 at news of gold discovery.

Gadsden Purchase 1853. Territory acquired from Mexico permitting easy rail connections to be built between Texas and California.

gerrymandering Redrawing election district boundaries for political purposes (possibly because of Massachusetts governor Elbridge Gerry, 1812).

"Jim Crow" A blackface song and dance act based on a deformed livery stable slave (c. 1833) which came to symbolize racial prejudice.

Lynch's Law Summary justice meted out by Virginia planter Charles Lynch in 1780 as head of an extralegal court.

Monroe Doctrine 1823 A declaration closing the Western hemisphere to European colonization and interference while accepting existing European colonies.

Republicans A party formed originally in 1854 by disaffected Democrats opposed to the extension of slavery and remnants of the old Whig party.

Scott (Dred) Decision 1857 A legal ruling that the fugitive slave Scott could not claim freedom by living in free territory nor had he the right to bring a law suit in a federal court.

sectionalism The tendency to favor or oppose territorial expansion, tariffs, and other economic measures according to state rather than national interests.

Trail of Tears 1838–39, the six-month journey undertaken by 14,000 Cherokee Indians who were being forcibly relocated. 4000 died on the journey.

Underground Railroad An escape route for southern slaves to Canada frequently opposed by white workers fearful for their own jobs.

American Civil War

butternut A light brown dye used for Confederate uniforms, obtained from a solution of acorns or walnut hulls.

carbet-bagger A Northern adventurer in the South during the Reconstruction period, seeking pecuniary or political gains.

emancipation The abolition of slavery.

free state One where slaves have been freed or where slavery has not been permitted.

Ku Klux Klan A postwar secret society dedicated to re-assert white supremacy through violence.

Reb Contraction of Rebel, that is, a Confederate supporter.

Rebel yell The shrill and chilling shout given by Confederate troops as they advanced.

Reconstruction The political process by which the southern states were restored to the Union.

Secession The act of leaving the Union by any state.

state An internally autonomous territorial and political unit.

Territory A part of the US with its own legislature but a governor appointed by the president and not admitted as a full state.

United States of America 1860–1927

Emancipation Proclamation Lincoln's statement affirming the abolition of slavery as a war aim (1862). 4 million slaves were automatically freed (1863).

IWW Industrial Workers of the World, a cross-industry grouping of workers set up in 1905.

Jim Crow laws Legislation enacted in southern states after emancipation to restrict Black rights and enforce segregation.

Molly Maguires 1860s to 1880s A secret Irish-American society especially active in mining areas.

NAACP Crusading National Association for the Advancement of Colored People, founded 1909.

Scallywags (alternatively "scalawags") White Southerners who supported Black emancipation and the Republican Party.

Wobblies A nickname for the IWW.

19thC Europe

Chartism 1838–48 An English popular movement demanding male suffrage, annual Parliaments, reform of electoral boundaries, and voting by secret ballot.

Commune 1871 A radical Paris government opposed to the peace terms for the end of the Franco-Prussian war and the right-wing composition of the newly elected National Assembly. It was suppressed with atrocities on both sides.

Conservative Party A British right-of-center political party that developed from the 1832 electoral reforms and is the heir to the Tory Party. It was originally pragmatic rather than ideological in motivation.

Corn Laws 1815–46 British legislation regulating grain imports. They were beneficial to farmers but caused staple food shortages in larger, particularly industrial, towns and in impoverished rural areas.

Duma The Russian elected legislative assembly unwillingly convened by Nicholas II in 1905 and finally overthrown in the 1917 Bolshevik revolution.

Entente cordiale An alliance between Britain and France in 1904 largely due to the behind-the-scenes diplomacy of Edward VII.

Fenians Agitators for Irish independence, members of a secret organization prepared to use violence if constitutional means failed.

Janissaries A corps of elite but turbulent Turkish troops eventually suppressed with the loss of between 6000 and 10,000 lives in 1826 by Sultan Mahmud II.

Jingoism Excessively chauvinistic patriotism, derived from the music-hall lyrics "we don't want to fight but by jingo if we do…the Russians shall not have Constantinople."

Labour Party A British left-of-center political party evolving from the 1893 socialist Independent Labour Party and incorporating trade unions and socialist organizations.

Liberal Party A British centrist political party evolving from the 1830s and containing radical elements as well as remnants of the old Whig Party.

pogrom A deliberate organized persecution of an ethnic group, especially Jews in Russia. The name comes from Russian and Yiddish words for thunder and destruction.

Protocol of Elders of Zion A faked memorandum of alleged agreement at the 1897 Zionist Congress for world domination. Classic anti-Semitic propaganda.

Social Democratic Party A Russian political group agitating for parliamentary government. Founded in 1898, it split into Bolsheviks (meaning majority, the more radical wing) and Mensheviks (meaning minority, the more moderate wing) in 1903.

Tolpuddle Martyrs 1834 English farm workers sentenced to transportation to Australia for seven years for forming a trade union. Public outcry led to their return in 1836.

The world 1814–1914

Boxers A Chinese nationalist secret society which unsuccessfully attempted rebellion to overthrow foreign interests 1900–1.

Great Trek 1834–38 The migration with ox wagons by Boer farmers from Cape Colony to the north and east of the Orange River after Britain abolished slavery.

Kuomintang A Chinese political party founded in 1912,

dominant from 1928 to 1949.

privateering Activities by armed but privately owned vessels commissioned for war service by a government. Really a species of legalized piracy.

sepoys Native Indian soldiers recruited into British service.

shogunate 1192–1867 Japanese rule by a sequence of hereditary military dictators paying only nominal allegiance to the emperor.

suttee A Hindu practice by which a widow immolated herself on her husband's funeral pyre. The British tried to stamp out the custom from 1829 with limited success.

T'ai Ping Rebellion 1850–64 A Southern China revolt against Manchu rule led by Christian convert Hung Hsiu-ch'uan (1812–64) in which probably between 20 and 30 million died.

United States of America 1918–1941

bootlegging The making, carrying, and selling of illegal goods, notably alcohol during Prohibition.

Committee to Investigate un-American Activities Set up in 1938 to enquire into Nazi activities but then changed to devote itself almost entirely to exposing alleged Communist subversion.

Depression, The The worldwide economic crisis of the early 1930s characterized by mass unemployment and galloping inflation.

Dust Bowl, The Farming areas impoverished between 1934 and 1936 by topsoil erosion caused by drought, winds, and unsuitable crop selection.

Monkey Trial 1925 A trial in which the Tennessee schoolteacher John Scopes was fined for teaching Darwin's theory of evolution.

Moral Rearmament A Christian revival movement founded in 1938 by the German-American evangelist, Frank Buchman.

New Deal Roosevelt's 1932 pledge for the people while accepting the Democratic presidential nomination; also the legislative program of his administration.

Prohibition 1920–33 legislation prohibiting the sale of alcohol which led to illicit sales and gangsterism.

St Valentine's Day Massacre A 1929 incident in Chicago in which seven gangsters were killed by members of a rival gang, probably ordered by Al Capone.

Scottsboro Boys 1931–37 An Alabama case involving nine black youths accused of raping two young white women.

Europe 1918–1940

appeasement A policy of agreeing to the demands of a potentially hostile nation in order to maintain peace, specifically the British government's attitude to Hitler's Germany 1937–38.

axis A national alliance to co-ordinate foreign policy, specifically the pact between Hitler and Mussolini in 1937.

Black and Tans 1919–21, A British force sent to Ireland to combat Sinn Fein and using very similar terror tactics. Nicknamed for the color of their uniforms.

Comintern 1919–43, an international Communist organization to promote revolutionary Marxism, also called Communist International and Third International. It was founded by Lenin and used by Stalin as a political instrument.

Communist Party A party formally constituted in Russia in March 1918 from the Bolshevik Party that became the ruling party. Similar, minority parties were created elsewhere. In all countries within the Soviet sphere of influence, the Communist Party was the ruling party, usually the only one permitted, until the 1990s.

concentration camps Centers for the detention of political and other opponents, first set up by the British in South Africa during the Boer War 1899–1902. German camps were established in Nazi Germany first in 1933 at Dachau and Oranienburg to use Jews, other ethnic minorities, and political or religious opponents as forced labor. Later camps, such as Auschwitz and Belsen, were just extermination centers claiming millions of lives.

Communist Party
Lenin

Falange A right-wing Spanish political party founded by José Primo de Rivera (1903–36) in 1933 and taken over by Franco as the ruling and legislative body.

fascism A right-wing militarist, nationalist and authoritarian regime, such as that founded by Mussolini 1919 and inspiring, among others, the German Nazi Party.

Five-Year Plans 1928, 1933, 1938, The Soviet system of economic planning aimed at development of heavy industry (latterly armaments) and collectivization of agriculture. They never really fulfilled their targets and were usually either quietly abandoned or run into the next in sequence.

General Strike 1926, a week-long 3-million strong strike by most sectors of British labor, triggered by private coal-mine owners attempting to cut pay rates and increase the working day. Essential services during the strike were run by volunteers, including students.

Gestapo "Geheime Staatspolizei" The German secret state police, established by Goering in 1933 to arrest and murder opponents of the Nazi Party. Enlarged under Himmler 1934, it became part of the SS 1936.

gulag The Russian administration of forced labor camps (acronym for State, or Main, Administration of Corrective Labor Camps) from the 1930s. Used for detention of political opponents, especially intellectuals.

Kristalnacht 9–10 Nov 1938, Nazi-led riots, triggered by the assassination of a Nazi diplomat in Paris by a Polish Jew, in which German Jewish shops, homes, and synagogues were looted and demolished, and up to 30,000 Jews were deported to concentration camps.

kulak A Russian term meaning a tight-fisted person; used of peasant farmers who gained land after 1906. After 1917 they opposed collectivization of agricultural land, and in 1929 Stalin began their liquidation.

Maginot Line 1929–34, A line of French defensive fortifications south of Belgium to the Swiss border. The Belgians refused to extend the line along their German frontier, so the strategy was useless, as proved by the German advance in 1940.

Marxism-Leninism Karl Marx 1818–83, promulgated that human actions and institutions are economically determined, that class struggle is the basic agency of historical change, and that communism will eventually supersede capitalism. Lenin adopted the ideological basis but modified and interpreted it to stress that capitalism survived through imperialism. He developed the idea of the Communist Party as a professional elite leading the struggle against capitalism, and thereby eventually exercising a post-revolutionary dictatorship of proletariat.

Nazi Party "Nationalsozialistische deutsche Arbeiterpartei" A right-wing, authoritarian, and nationalist German party founded in 1919 and led from 1921 by Hitler. It took power when Hitler was offered the post of chancellor in 1933 and dominated German life until its collapse at the end of World War II.

putsch A German word for thrust, meaning an attempt to overthrow a government, such as that led by Hitler from a Munich beer-hall in 1923, which failed ignominiously.

Reichstag The parliament building of the German empire in Berlin. It was burned down in February 1933 almost certainly with Nazi assistance though the Communists were blamed.

SA "Sturmabteilung" An organization of Nazi brownshirted storm-troopers founded in 1921, led by Ernst Roehm and eliminated as a power force in 1934.

SS "Schutzstaffel" The Nazi blackshirted bodyguard for Hitler founded in 1923 and commanded by Himmler from 1929. It acquired executive and military functions including elite "Waffen-SS" regiments who were exempt from normal army control and "SS-Totenkopfverbande" who provided concentration camp guards.

Sinn Féin Gaelic for "Ourselves Alone" An Irish nationalist party founded 1902 and absorbing other groups 1907–8. It was prominent in the 1913–14 Irish home rule crisis and the 1916 Easter Rising. Now the political wing of the Irish Republican Army (IRA).

Soviet A Russian term for a local, regional or national elected government council which grew out of the pre-Revolutionary workers' councils. These initially democratic bodies were dominated by Bolsheviks (later Communists) after 1917.

Spartacists "Spartakusbund" 1916–19 A German revolutionary socialist group led by Rosa Luxemburg and Karl Liebknecht 1871–1919, and named for Spartacus, the leader of the 73 BC slave revolt against Rome. It formed the nucleus of the German Communist Party and was bloodily suppressed in 1919 with its leaders being killed.

swastika A hooked cross; an ancient religious symbol associated in the late 19th century with the revival of interest in German legends and mythology. It was adopted as a symbol by extreme right-wing groups in Germany from 1919 and was made Germany's national emblem in 1935.

World 1918–1949

Afrikaans A South African language closely related to Dutch and Flemish. Afrikaners are descendants of original Dutch and French Huguenot settlers.

aliyah A Hebrew word meaning migration of Jews to Palestine, mainly from eastern Europe but eventually from throughout the Diaspora.

apartheid An Afrikaans word, meaning state of being apart, used for the Afrikaner doctrine of racial segregation which made people of mixed race or African descent into second-class citizens, restricted geographically, educationally, socially, and professionally.

civil disobedience A policy of non-violent non-cooperation initially propagated in India by Mahatma Gandhi in 1920 as a means to independence.

Congress Abbreviated name of the Indian National Congress

civil disobedience
Mahatma Gandhi

Party. Formed in 1885 as an educational association to encourage political development, it became the principal vehicle for opposition to British rule. It was led by Gandhi from 1920.

Haganah A secret society formed by Jews in Palestine in 1920 to defend themselves against attacks by Arabs. It formed the nucleus of the eventual Israeli army.

Long March 1934–35, the 6000 mile (9700 km) journey to northern China by 100,000 Communist forces and civilians fleeing from the Kuomintang in the south. Only 4000 survived.

mahatma A Sanskrit word meaning "great of soul," given as a title to Gandhi by his Hindu followers.

Mapai "Miphlegeth Poalei Israel" A workers' party formed by Jewish immigrants in Palestine in 1930 and serving in Israeli coalition governments 1948–77. In 1968 it combined with smaller socialist parties to form the modern Israeli Labor Party.

Muslim League An Indian political movement active from 1906 and prominent from 1934, aiming at an independent state. This was achieved in 1947 with partition and the creation of Pakistan.

warlords Chinese generals commanding private armies who dominated various provinces politically as well as militarily between 1916 and 1928.

World War II

Anschluss Germany's annexation of Austria in 1938.

blitz/blitzkrieg An aerial campaign with heavy bombardment. Applied particularly to German bombings of Warsaw and London.

final solution The German attempt to exterminate all Jews through deportation to forced labor concentration camps, mass gassings, and other executions.

kamikaze Japanese planes loaded with explosives flown by pilots trained to make suicidal crash attacks on targets.

Luftwaffe The German air force.

Panzer A German armored vehicle, especially a tank.

partisans French, Italian, Greek, Yugoslav, and other resistance fighters against German occupation.

Phony war The period from September 1939 to April 1940 during which Britain was officially at war with Germany but no actual fighting took place.

U-boat or "Unterseeboot" A German submarine.

V-1 and V-2 "Vergeltungswaffe eins/zwei" German flying bombs with rocket engines used principally in raids against

British towns and cities.

Vichy The French town which was the center for the puppet regime installed during the German occupation 1940–45.

war bonds Government debt certificates, guaranteeing payment with interest, sold to help the war effort.

Wehrmacht The German armed forces.

United States of America 1945–1990s

Black Muslims A political movement of black people adapting Islamic religious practices and seeking to establish a black nation.

CIA Central Intelligence Agency. It was set up in 1947 to counter Communist activities outside the USA but increasingly after 1967 undertook internal surveillance activities.

Cold War A phrase coined by Bernard Baruch to describe the ideological conflict between western countries and the Soviet bloc.

Gray Panthers An organization fighting for the rights of older and retired people, founded in 1972.

Hot Line An emergency communications link between the US and USSR presidents from 1963 to reduce the risk of accidental war, especially nuclear strikes.

Iran-Contra Affair A scandal from 1986 over secret deals to sell arms to Iran and divert the proceeds to fund Contra rebel forces in Nicaragua.

Pentagon Papers Classified documents detailing US involvement in Vietnam from 1945 to 1968, "leaked" to the press in 1971.

Watergate The scandal over the bugging of Democratic headquarters during the 1972 election campaign, exposed by campaigning journalists. President Nixon was forced to resign in 1974 after admitting false denial of knowledge (1974).

Europe 1945–1990s

Berlin Wall 1961–89. A concrete barrier built by East Germany across the border between East and West Berlin to stem the flood of over 2 million refugees fleeing west. Over 200 people were killed by border guards while attempting to cross the mine-strewn and barbed-wire hedged area.

Brezhnev Doctrine 1968–89 Justification for intervention by Warsaw Pact countries in the affairs of member states. Promulgated by Soviet Communist leader Leonid Brezhnev (1906–82) to explain why five countries under Soviet control invaded Czechoslovakia in 1968 to quash the Prague Spring.

Bundestag One of two houses of the West German federal parliament, 1949–90, which was based in Bonn.

CAP (Common Agricultural Policy) Subsidies from a central fund to farmers of countries belonging to the EC. Controversial, it led to so-called butter mountains and wine lakes through over-production in these areas.

Cod War 1972–76 A fishing dispute between Britain and Iceland.

COMECON 1949 An association of Soviet-dominated nations, originally those of East Europe but later including Mongolia (1962), Cuba (1972), and Vietnam (1978) intended to co-ordinate economic development. Used by Stalin to put pressure on Yugoslavia and to counter growing western economic interdependence.

Common Market: *See* EC.

Council of Europe An organization established in 1949 to achieve greater European unity, matters of national defense being excluded. Belgium, Denmark, France, Ireland, Italy, the Netherlands, Norway and Sweden were original members. Greece, Iceland and Turkey joined later in 1949, then West Germany (1951), Austria (1956), Cyprus (1961), Switzerland (1963), and Malta (1965). (Greece withdrew in 1969.)

détente A French diplomatic term meaning reduction of tension between two countries with opposing policies; used especially in reference to US—USSR relations from 1968 onward.

dissidents A term applied to those individuals, particularly in eastern Europe and the USSR, refusing to conform with the politics and beliefs of the society in which they live. Often persecuted, imprisoned, exiled or executed.

EC (European Community) A European grouping from 1958, consisting of the European coal and steel community (ECSC), the European Economic Community (EEC), and the European Atomic Energy Commission (Euratom). The aim of the original member countries (Belgium, France, Italy, Luxembourg, the Netherlands, and West Germany) was to work together for economic and political union. Now also includes Denmark (1973), Greece (1981), Ireland (1973), Portugal (1986), Spain (1986), and UK (1973), and reunited Germany (1990).

EFTA (European Free Trade Area) A European economic grouping from 1960, originally of Austria, Denmark, Norway, Portugal, Sweden, Switzerland, and UK. Finland joined 1961, Iceland 1970. Denmark, Portugal, and UK subsequently left to join the EC .

EOKA An anti-British Greek Cypriot terrorist group led by Colonel Grivas and designed to obtain independence for

Cyprus from direct British rule 1955–59. It staged a coup in 1974 which led to Turkish invasion and forced partition.

ETA Initials of a militant Basque terrorist group seeking to create an independent republic; responsible for many acts of sabotage, murder, and intimidation.

Eastern Bloc The Communist states of eastern Europe, including those of the Balkans. Its strength through cohesion has been weakened politically and economically since 1989.

enosis A Greek term meaning unity, describing the Greek Cypriot movement for political union with Greece. The Turkish Cypriot minority was bitterly opposed this and it led directly to 1974 invasion and partition.

glasnost A Russian word meaning openness. Set in motion in 1985 by Gorbachev, this policy meant that the intellectual atmosphere lightened and that contemporary social matters, politics, and the history of Stalinist era could be discussed.

Greens Ecology parties which first contested West German elections 1979. While in most European countries, few parliamentary seats have been gained, successful grass roots lobbying and use of media have forced other parties to acknowledge and promote environmental issues.

IRA (Irish Republican Army) A militant nationalist organization striving for a united independent Ireland through increasingly terrorist means; responsible for many civilian deaths both in Britain and Northern Ireland. Considered the military wing of *Sinn Fein*, it is also called Provisional IRA.

Iron Curtain The barrier, political and military, that was considered to separate the Soviet bloc from western Europe after World War II.

Marshall Plan 1948 The crucial financing by the US of European postwar economic recovery, conceived by Secretary of State George Marshall (1880–1959). USSR rejection meant that $17,000 million mainly went to West European countries.

NATO (North Atlantic Treaty Organization) An organization created in 1949 committing the US to peacetime European defense. Initial signatory states were Belgium, Canada, Denmark, France (withdrew 1966), Iceland, Italy, Luxembourg, the Netherlands, Norway, Portugal, UK, US. Greece and Turkey signed 1952 and West Germany 1955.

ostpolitik A German term for the policy of improving relations with East Europe begun in 1969 by West German Chancellor, Willy Brandt.

perestroika A Russian word meaning restructuring, used to describe the attempt by Gorbachev to regenerate the Soviet economy by encouraging market forces, decentralizing factory management, and generally democratizing the Communist Party and government.

Politburo (contraction of "Politicheskoe Buro") The Russian name for the supreme executive and policy-making Communist Party committee.

Prague Spring 1968–69 An attempt to present "socialism with a human face" in Czechoslovakia as initiated by Dubcek. It was suppressed by Soviet invasion.

Solidarity A Polish trade union and reform movement formed in the late 1970s in the Gdansk shipyards and officially registered in 1980. It demanded liberalization of the Communist regime and formation of free trade unions. It won short-lived concessions before it was banned and its leader Lech Walesa detained. Clandestine throughout the rest of the decade, it formed part of the first non-Communist government since 1948 in 1989.

Truman Doctrine 1947 The provision by president Harry Truman (1884–1972) of US aid to Greece and Turkey as part of the anti-Communist foreign policy which signaled the start of the Cold War containment policy.

Velvet Revolution 1989–90 The peaceful end to Communist rule in Czechoslovakia. So named for the quiet resignation of the Communist government following massive but peaceful demonstrations.

Truman

Warsaw Pact 1955 An East European defense treaty under Soviet leadership as a response to NATO. Signatory states were Albania (ceased to participate 1961, withdrew 1968), Bulgaria, Czechoslovakia, East Germany, Hungary, Poland, Romania, and USSR.

World 1948–1990s

ANC African National Congress. A political pressure group, especially in South Africa. It was banned and its leaders imprisoned 1964–90.

ANZUS Australia, New Zealand, and US Pacific security treaty signed 1951. New Zealand withdrew 1985.

Arab League An organization of independent Arab states formed in 1945 to promote military, economic, political, and cultural cooperation.

Azania A black nationalist name for South Africa.

Contras Nicaraguan right-wing exiles conducting a guerrilla campaign against the Sandinista government 1979–90 with covert arms supplies from US.

Cultural Revolution 1965–68 A Chinese youth-led mass

movement inspired by Mao Zedong to change popular ideology. It wrecked many lives and cultural institutions.

Dirty War An Argentine military campaign against left-wing guerrilla groups and other opponents of the regime 1976–82.

Eisenhower Doctrine 1957 A US initiative to limit USSR influence in the Middle East by economic and military aid.

FLN Front de Liberation Nationale, an Algerian nationalist political and military movement 1954–62.

Fatah, al- The Syrian branch of the PLO, increasingly powerful after 1967.

Eisenhower

Fatwa 1989 The death sentence pronounced by a fundamentalist Iranian leader on the British writer Salman Rushdie for his novel *The Satanic Verses*, deemed blasphemous by devout Muslims.

Gang of Four A group of radical Chinese Communist leaders, including the widow of Mao Zedong, advocating revolutionary rather than economically pragmatic policies in power 1974–76. They were tried and condemned in 1980.

Great Leap Forward The Chinese Communist attempt to accelerate agricultural collectivization 1958–61.

Intifada The Arab name for the uprising against Israeli occupation in the Gaza Strip and West Bank.

Irgun A Jewish terrorist organization 1931–48 active against the British Mandate.

Khmer Rouge A Cambodian Communist guerrilla force 1970–89 led by Pol Pot.

Likud An Israeli right-wing political alliance winning elections in 1977, 1988.

Maoism Marxist ideology emphasizing the peasantry rather than the proletariat as the main force for revolutionary change, propounded by Mao Zedong (1893–1976).

Mau Mau A Kenyan black militant and terrorist movement 1952–60.

Mujaheddin Afghan Islamic guerrillas 1979–90 fighting the USSR invasion in support of the Marxist government.

PLO Palestine Liberation Organization, founded 1964 in Jordan and dominated by Syria. Led by Yasser Arafat, it has mounted attacks on Israeli-occupied territory and has been involved in international terrorism.

PLO
Yasser Arafat

Pathet Lao A Laotian rebel movement established 1949. It aided the Viet Minh in 1953 and fought against government forces 1959–75. It has been the effective government since 1975.

Red Guards Chinese young people prominent in the 1965–69 Cultural Revolution.

SEATO South-East Asia Treaty Organization, set up in 1954 by

Australia, Britain, France, New Zealand, Pakistan, Philippines, Thailand, and US to combat Communism. Dissolved 1977.

SWAPO South West Africa People's Organization. A black independence movement founded in 1959. Banned in 1978, it continued guerrilla activities to 1989.

Sandinistas A Nicaraguan opposition group waging guerrilla war against the Somoza regime and achieving political power in 1979. Defeated in 1990 elections.

Shining Path A Maoist guerrilla group in Peru 1980–82.

Tamil Tigers Sri Lankan separatist guerrillas, leading terrorist raids and opposing intervention by Indian troops.

Third World Under-developed and poorer nations of Africa, Asia and Latin America neither part of the capitalist west nor the communist east but often regarded as a proving ground and sphere of influence by both.

UDI The unilateral declaration of independence by the white Southern Rhodesian government in 1965 to avoid moves towards black majority rule.

Vietcong Communist guerrilla forces in South Vietnam 1954–73, 1975–76.

Viet Minh A North Vietnam Communist political group formed in 1941 by Ho Chi-minh. Its forces entered Hanoi to to form a government in1945. It became part of the Vietnam Workers' Party in 1951.

Society

4

economics and finance

antitrust laws A group of laws intended to prevent practices that tend to restrict competition such as price fixing and the formation of monopolies.

appreciation Increase in the value of assets. *Compare* depreciation.

arbitrage A situation in which it is possible to buy an asset in one market and then sell it immediately in another market at a higher price.

arbitration The appointment of an impartial individual to settle a dispute, for example between unions and management.

asset stripping The practice of buying a large company with the intention of breaking up its component businesses and selling them individually.

assets Property, goods or money owned by an individual or firm.

balance of payments A country's balance of payments is the difference between the amount it receives for its exports and the amount it pays to other countries for its imports. The balance of payments is divided into: visible items, which are goods, e.g. cars, coffee, oil; and invisible items which are services, e.g. banking, insurance, shipping.

balance sheet A statement showing the assets and liabilities of a business enterprise at a particular point in time.

balanced budget When the government's spending equals its revenue from, for example, taxation. *Compare* **budget deficit; budget surplus.**

Bank of England The UK's central bank, which acts as the government's banker and implements its monetary policies, as well as regulating the banking industry.

barriers to entry Anything that makes it difficult for a company to establish itself in a new market. Barriers to entry may range from high initial investment costs to illegal restrictive practices.

barter To trade in exchange for other goods or services instead of in exchange for money.

bear A speculator on a stock exchange who buys expecting prices to decrease. *Compare* **bull.**

bear market A market in which prices are falling.

bear raid A form of market manipulation in which traders attempt to artificially drive down the price of a security by large scale short selling.

big bang The day in 1986 when, in the course of one day, the London Stock Exchange was deregulated and new computing technology brought in.

big ugly A slang term for a large, long-established, primarily industrial company.

bilateral trade Trading between two countries where each attempts to balance its trade with that of the other.

black economy Economic activities which take place without the paying of taxes.

black market Economic activity (e.g. trading and currency exchange) that is not taxed and is not recorded as part of National Income.

blue chip company A stock market quoted company considered reliable in terms of both dividend income and capital value.

BOE An acronym for Barrels of Oil Equivalent used to measure quantities of both crude oil and natural gas. One boe is equivalent to the energy contained in one barrel of crude oil.

bond A certificate of debt issued to raise funds and carrying with it a fixed rate of interest until a specified future date.

bonus issue When a company offers its existing shareholders newly issued shares at no charge in proportion to their existing holdings. Also known as a scrip issue.

Brent crude A blend of crude oil from the North Sea the price of which is a benchmark against which the majority of oil traded in the world is compared.

bubble A situation in which a particular investment or class of investments is producing such good returns that they attract an increasing amount of investment until prices are far higher than can be justified by a rational analysis of likely future returns from those investments.

budget An estimate of government spending and government revenue for the coming year. If government spending is higher than government revenue, there is a budget deficit. If government spending is lower than government revenue, there is a budget surplus.

budget deficit When the government's spending exceeds revenue from taxation. *Compare* **balanced budget; budget surplus**.

budget surplus When the government's revenue exceeds its spending. *Compare* **balanced budget, budget deficit**.

bull A speculator on the Stock Exchange who buys expecting prices to rise. *Compare* **bear**.

bull market A market in which prices are rising.

business cycle The tendencies of some economies to fluctuate regularly between boom and depression.

callable stock Stock that the issuer reserves the right to buy back on demand at a previously agreed price. Loans and bonds may also be "callable."

capital Consists of all goods and services which are used in the production of other goods and services, e.g. machinery, factories, education, and training. Capital can also mean the money value of a company's assets.

capital expenditure Spending on fixed assets (such as equipment).

capital goods Goods that are used to produce other goods rather than to be sold to consumers.

capital market Financial institutions that deal with medium- and long-term capital and loans.

capitalism An economic system essentially based on the private ownership of the means of production, distribution, and exchange.

cartel A group of firms within an industry who collude against competition to regulate prices and/or output to their own advantage.

cash flow The movement of money into and out of a business entity.

central bank A bank for banks, the central bank can lend other banks money in the last resort; it can also exercise some control over their activities. Central banks tend to work closely with the government. The US central banking system is the Federal Reserve.

clearing banks The main British commercial banks that make use of the Central Clearing House in London for the transfer of credits and checks between banks.

closed shop A firm which allows only union members to be employed operates a closed shop.

closing price The price of a security at the moment a market closes at the end of the day.

collective bargaining Negotiations over pay and conditions between people representing the employers and trade union officials.

command economy An economic system in which resources are allocated by central government rather than by market forces.

commercial bank A bank which is used by the general public, for private and business transactions.

commodity 1 A general name which covers both goods (e.g. bananas, televisions), and services (e.g. hairdressing, banking). **2** A raw material or primary product (e.g. tea, rubber, tin).

commodity market A market in which commodities (raw materials) are bought and sold. It is not necessary for the commodities to actually be exchanged; pieces of paper carrying the rights of ownership are sufficient.

common stock Any kind of share where the owners receive their dividend of company profit only after payments have been made to other shareholders with priority such as those with preferred stocks. Preferred stocks have a stated rate of dividend payment.

consumer price index A measurement of how much money can buy in terms of a selection of goods and services typically consumed by the average household. If there has been inflation a dollar will buy less than it did previously.

cooling off period A period of time in which a party to a contract may decide not to continue with the contract, usually without penalty.

cost-of-living index A numerical scale representing the costs necessary to maintain a minimal standard of living.

credit crunch An economic situation in which there is a shortage of cash to lend to businesses and individuals, and interest rates are high.

creditor Any entity (including a person, company, or government) that provides credit. A debtor owes payments, financial or otherwise, to a creditor.

current account The part of the balance of payments composed of the balance of trade and the invisible balance.

cyclical unemployment Unemployment resulting from downward fluctuations in economic activity within trade cycles.

dawn raid The practice of buying a large proportion of a company's stock as soon as the listing stock market opens. The intention is to acquire a significant holding in a company at everyday market prices as a prelude to a formal takeover bid, the announcement of which is likely to cause the market price to rise substantially.

day trading The practice of trading in such a way that all transactions are finished in one trading day and all holdings are liquefied by the end of that day.

debtor Any entity (including a person, company, or government) that owes payments, financial or otherwise, to creditor.

debt-equity swap A method used by companies to reduce debt by swapping existing bonds (a form of debt) for newly issued stock (a form of equity).

deer market A market with little trading activity in which prices are neither rising nor falling dramatically.

deflation 1 A policy pursued by a government aimed at reducing inflation. **2** A fall in the general level of prices.

demerger The separation of an existing company into two or more completely separate businesses.

depreciation The fall in value of capital, such as machinery, due to wear and tear, old age, obsolescence, or a fall in the market price.

depression A severe downturn in the trade cycle characterized by high levels of unemployment, low output and investment.

deregulation The abolition or reduction of state controls and supervision over private economic activities.

devaluation Reducing the value of a currency against other currencies.

disposable income The money an individual has left to spend after all direct taxes have been deducted.

dividend A portion of the profits of a company made to its shareholders.

division of labor The division of production into separate processes each of which is performed by different people. Under the division of labor, work becomes more and more specialized, and this allows a higher level of skill to develop.

Dow Jones averages A set of well-known and indices of the performance of shares on the United States stock exchange.

dumping Selling goods in foreign markets at artificially low prices.

durable goods Goods—usually consumer items, such as large appliances—that are consumed over time and require infrequent replacement.

econometrics The use of mathematical and statistical methods to test economic theories.

economic growth A rise in the National Income which implies a rise in living standards.

economics The study of the arrangements that societies make concerning the use and development of the limited resources on our planet.

economy of scale Any saving in costs that results from an increase in the scale of an operation. For example, a larger factory may be able to produce each unit of product more cheaply than a smaller factory.

ECU Acronym for European Currency Unit, based on the composite value of a number of European Union currencies and functioning as the reserve asset and accounting unit of the European Monetary System.

elasticity The measure of the sensitivity of demand for goods and services to changes of price or other product variables.

emerging markets Investment opportunities in developing countries.

entrepreneur Someone who risks their own capital in a business enterprise.

equity The investment made by the owners and shareholders of a company in that company.

ethical investment The practice of making investment decisions based on ethical criterion. For example, an ethical investor may refuse to invest in enterprises that trade in or manufacture armaments.

European Monetary System A financial system used to stabilize exchange rates between currencies of member states.

exchange The price at which one currency can be exchanged for another currency, or for gold. To prevent fluctuations in the rate of exchange, exchange rates can be fixed or controlled. Exchange rates which are left free to market forces are known as floating exchange rates.

financial year Any annual period at the end of which accounts are made up.

first lien position A lender or creditor in a first lien position has priority in case a debtor defaults and collateral has to be liquefied to settle the debt. For example mortgage lenders are usually in a first lien position; if a borrower defaults on his payments the mortgage lender is the first creditor to receive remuneration from the sale of the property.

fiscal policy The government's plan for taxation and government spending. Fiscal policy is one way in which a government can attempt to control the economy. Another way is through monetary policy which attempts to guide the economy by controlling the money supply.

fixed costs Those costs a firm has which do not vary with every change in output, e.g. the cost of machinery or buildings. These contrast with variable costs which do vary with output, e.g. the amount spent on materials used in the production process.

flexible labor market A labor market in which employees are willing to work flexible hours, to retrain for new skills, to relocate geographically in order to find work, and to accept performance-related pay. A flexible labor market usually also requires employment laws that allow for the easy hiring and firing of employees.

foreign exchange market The market in which one foreign currency is exchanged for another.

foreign position The amount of foreign currency liabilities held by an individual, institution, or country.

forward price The price for a physical commodity to be delivered at some agreed time in the future. Forward prices are used in futures trading.

free market Trade which flows freely between countries without barriers such as tariffs and quotas.

full employment When all those who desire a job are employed and only frictional unemployment remains.

futures An agreement to buy goods at a fixed date in the future at a fixed price. Futures are sold where the price of goods fluctuates, for example, there are futures for commodities such as fruit, and also it is possible to buy futures in foreign currencies. If the price fluctuates, above the amount agreed the buyer gains; if the price fluctuates below, the buyer loses. Futures are a hedge against uncertainty.

Giffen good Any good that is purchased in greater quantities as its price increases.

gilts Government securities on which interest payments will be met and will be repaid at par on the due date.

gold standard A system in which the value of a currency is legally fixed in terms of how much gold it is worth.

greenwashing The practice of encouraging potential investors or customers to believe that a company has environmentally friendly practices, especially when these are seemingly contradictory to that company's core business. An example might be environmental programs or initiatives launched by an oil company.

gross domestic product Total value of all goods and services produced domestically annually by a country and is equal to gross national product less receipts from investment incomes from abroad.

gross national product The money value of all goods and services produced in a country during a period of one year.

hedge fund A form of private unregulated investment fund that typically employs trading strategies that have greater risk than are permitted in other investment funds. Using money from wealthy individuals and institutions a hedge fund typically seeks to make profits by engaging in high risk, short-term speculation on bonds, currencies, stock options, and derivatives. Hedge funds often use the selling short technique.

illiquid asset An asset that cannot easily be converted into cash and, therefore, has low liquidity.

incomes policy A government policy of keeping wage increases under control in order to reduce or prevent inflation.

indexation The adjustment of wages, interest rates and other forms of income to compensate with changes of prices.

inferior good Any good that is consumed less as average incomes in an economy rise.

inflation A rise in the general level of prices. Galloping inflation (or hyperinflation) is an inflation which precedes at a high rate but perhaps for only a brief period. The rate of inflation generally increases during a galloping inflation. Creeping inflation is an inflation which lasts for a long time at a fairly steady pace.

insider dealing The illegal use of privileged information when trading on the stock market. For example, if someone knows that a takeover bid is about to be launched and starts buying shares because they think this will cause the value to increase.

insolvency The condition of being unable to pay debts or of having greater liabilities than assets.

intangible assets Assets that do not have an easily determined monetary value such as brand loyalty or intellectual property rights.

integration Firms within an industry are horizontally integrated if they all specialize in a single process, for example making tin cans. Firms within an industry are vertically integrated if each firm tends to carry through the production of a commodity from the raw material stage right up to the finished product. An industry in which the firms brewed beer, bottled it, and sold it in their own bars would be an example of vertical integration.

intellectual property A collective term for patents, copyrights, and trademarks.

interest rates The rates charged by a lender, such as a bank, to borrowers.

inverted yield curve An unusual market condition in which long-term US Treasury bonds yield less than short-term US Treasury bonds. It is often regarded as an indicator of imminent recession.

investment bank A bank that provides money for industry, generally by buying shares in companies.

invisible trade Service industries which earn foreign currency.

IPO An acronym for Initial Public Offer. The open sale of shares in a company prior to the company being listed on a stock exchange for the first time.

Islamic banking A form of ethical investments bound by the precepts of Islam, particularly the prohibition of interest payments.

junk bond A bond issued by a company or other entity with a low credit rating. Junk bonds are usually traded at a fraction of their face value.

laissez-faire The doctrine of leaving economic activity to market forces free of government interference.

leveraged buy out An acquisition largely funded by borrowed money.

liabilities Debts, including bank loans and money invested in the business by holders of bonds and shares.

limited liability If a company goes bankrupt and has limited liability, the owners of the company (the shareholders) are only obliged to pay back company debts with the money they have already invested in the firm. They will not be forced to sell their personal possessions to help pay debts.

liquidation The dissolution of a company such that its assets are made liquid (converted into cash) in order to pay any debts and the remainder is distributed among the companies shareholders.

liquidity The ease with which an asset can be converted into money. Cash is perfectly liquid but shares in a company are less liquid because they must be sold first before money is obtained. Assets such as property are even less liquid because they are harder to sell than shares.

long position Describes the trading position of an investor who owns a security. An investor in a long position hopes to make a profit because he is expecting the price of the security to rise. *See also* **short position**.

macroeconomics That branch of economics which studies the economy as a whole, e.g. the level of output, the level of employment, the level of inflation.

margin trading Investing in securities using borrowed money, often using the securities themselves as security against the debt.

market Any area of business where buyers and sellers are in contact with each other and where prices in one area affect prices in another area. A market need not be confined to a particular place, it could refer to an area of the economy, for example, the market for factory machinery or the market for foreign exchange.

market economy The economy of a country where prices are largely determined by supply and demand and whose government has little direct control over the means of production or trade.

market price The price, as determined by supply and demand, at which goods, service, etc., may be exchanged.

means of production Raw materials and means of labor used in the production process.

merger The joining together of two or more firms to form a single company.

microeconomics A branch of economics dealing with the study of units within the economy, e.g. firms, markets, and individual consumers.

mixed economy An economy where parts of the means of production or trade are both state and privately owned or controlled.

monetarism An economic policy based on controlling a country's money supply.

money market Financial institutions dealing with short-term loans and capital and with foreign exchange.

money supply The amount of money in an economy at a given moment. There are various ways in which the money supply can be defined. Narrowly defined, the money supply can mean the coins and bank notes in circulation and bank deposits where money can be withdrawn at short notice. A broader definition will also include savings accounts at banks and possibly bonds and shares.

monopoly Exclusive control of the market supply of a product or service.

monopsony A market in which there are multiple suppliers but only one buyer.

multiplier A ratio of changes of national income and employment to changes in expenditure.

national debt A country's outstanding debt, figured cumulatively over successive governments.

national income The total amount of income earned by all the people and institutions within a country from the production of goods and services (usually measured over a period of one year).

natural monopoly A monopoly that develops because of the unique nature of a business. For example, water supply is often regarded as a natural monopoly because it would be prohibitively expensive and wasteful to build competing distribution infrastructure.

oligopoly The control of a market by a small number of suppliers of goods or services.

open market operations The buying and selling of securities in order to control the money supply. This is normally done by the central bank. If the central bank wants to increase the money supply it will buy securities (in this case pieces of paper carrying the promise to repay the money) from the commercial banks giving the banks extra money. If the central bank wants to decrease the money supply it will sell securities to the commercial banks leaving them with less money.

opportunity cost The benefit that is sacrificed by choosing one course of action rather than the next best alternative, e.g. the opportunity cost sacrificed in building a road might be use of the land for farming.

option The right to buy or sell an asset at an agreed price.

planned economy *See* **command economy**.

pork-barrel politics Government spending intended to benefit a particular group in the expectation of political support.

preferred stock *See* **common stock**.

price fixing An illegal arrangement between competitors to set a common minimum price for their products. Price fixing is a conspiracy usually carried out by large corporations that dominate a particular market.

price mechanism The balancing of the forces of supply and demand in a market to produce a price.

prices policy Voluntary or statutory regulation of the level of increase in prices, usually with an aim of curbing inflation.

real wages Wages which are in terms of the goods and services money will buy as distinct from nominal wages which are simply wages in terms of money. If there is an inflation real wages may fall while nominal wages may rise.

red chip company A mainland Chinese company on the Hong Kong stock exchange.

rights issue When a company offers its existing shareholders the opportunity to buy newly issued shares at less than current market value.

scrip issue *See* **bonus issue**.

securities A general term covering both shares and bonds.

shares Pieces of paper which testify the ownership of part of a corporation. If 10,000 shares are issued and someone owns 1,000 shares, they own 1% of the company and they are entitled to 1% of company profits and 1% of the votes in the election of corporate officers or on corporate policy.

short position Describes the trading position of an investor who has sold a security that he does not yet own. An investor in a short position hopes to make a profit because he is expecting the price of the security to fall. *See also* **short selling**.

short selling The practice of selling shares that one does not own but that one has an agreement to purchase in the future. For example, if a hedge fund believes that the share price of a company is likely to fall it may agree with a broker to borrow 100 shares of that company today with the understanding that it will pay the market price for then in 30 days time. The hedge fund then sells these 100 borrowed shares at the current price with the expectation that when the 30-day period has expired it will pay less for them than it has received for selling them today.

smart money Funds managed by investors who tend to earn greater than average returns on their investments.

soft landing A period of economic slowdown that is successfully managed by a government so that it does not lead to a recession.

soft money Funds provided by a government or institution for a one-off project. Soft money is available only once and cannot be relied on as a source of future income.

spot price The price for a physical commodity to be delivered immediately as opposed to at some time in the future as is the case with futures trading.

stag An investor who buys shares in an IPO with the intention of selling them immediately dealing begins. *See also* **IPO**.

stagflation Rising prices combined with rising levels of unemployment.

stock exchange A market where shares in companies are bought and sold by brokers on behalf of investors.

stocks A synonym for shares.

subprime A term used to refer to any loan or credit product with terms and conditions that are less stringent than normal. For example, a mortgage product designed to be made available to customers with poor credit histories may be described as a "subprime mortgage."

subsidy Financial assistance given by a government to a business or individual enterprise.

supply-side economics Economic policies based on the idea that a national economy will benefit through a government making more money available for investment, especially through reducing tax levels.

takeover When one company takes control over another company by buying more than 50% of its shares. This gives it a majority of votes in the election of corporate officers or on corporate policy.

tariff A tax on imports.

taxation Compulsory payments by companies or individuals to the state. Direct taxes are on income and indirect taxes are taxes on commodities.

terms of trade The agreed conditions under which business is done.

Treasury A government department that is responsible for collecting, managing, and spending public revenue.

tunneling Illegally diverting company funds or lucrative contracts to a company insider or majority shareholder thereby lessening the value of the holdings of minor shareholders.

turnover Total money received in a given period. Turnover is usually the same as sales, or revenue, but it may be greater for some businesses.

value added tax A tax on the monetary value considered to be added to a product at each stage of its manufacture, added to the final price paid by consumers.

Wall Street The financial interests of the United States, considered as based in Wall Street, New York City, where the Stock Exchange and major banks are located.

World Bank An international cooperative financial organization that gives loans to developing countries.

yield The amount of profit made on an investment.

education

abecedarian A person who is learning the alphabet or the basic elements of a subject.

academe A place of learning, or the world of education in general.

academic A person who is a member of a college, university, or other institution of higher education.

academy A school, especially a private school, or a place where a particular subject is taught.

alma mater The school, university, or college where a person was educated.

alumna A woman who graduated from a particular school, university or college.

alumnus A man who graduated from a particular school, university or college.

autodidact A person who is self-taught rather than having received formal education.

baccalaureate A bachelor's degree.

bachelor A person who has been awarded a degree by a college or university after completing an undergraduate course of study.

bachelor's degree An academic degree awarded by a college or university to someone who has completed an undergraduate course of study.

bookish Fond of reading books or studying.

campus An area of ground or group of buildings belonging to a school, college, or university.

chair A post as a professor of a particular subject at a college or university.

chancellor A title given to the heads of some universities in the United States and the United Kingdom.

chapter house A building where a branch of a fraternity or sorority holds meetings.

coed A girl or woman student at a coeducational school, college, or university.

coeducational Teaching both male and female students at the same institution.

collegiate Belonging to or typical of a college or college students.

commencement A ceremony at which school diplomas or academic degrees are awarded to students.

computer-aided instruction Teaching in which extensive use is made of computers by teaching staff and students.

conservatory An institution that specializes in teaching one of the arts, especially music.

continuous assessment The assessment of a student's performance throughout the duration of a course rather than relying on an examination at the end of it.

correspondence course A course of instruction carried out by mail rather than attendance at an institution.

cram To study intensively for an examination or to prepare students intensively for an examination.

cum laude With honor, a Latin phrase meaning that a student has graduated with distinction.

curricular Included in a particular curriculum.

curriculum The complete range of courses of study available at a particular institution.

dean A person in charge of the administration in a college, university, or faculty.

detention Time spent by a student in school after classes, imposed as a punishment.

didactic Intended or inclining to teach or instruct people.

discipline Any particular field of knowledge or learning.

distance learning A form of studying a subject from home rather than by attending an institution, such as by correspondence or via computer links.

docent A lecturer in some colleges or universities, especially one who is not a regular member of a faculty.

doctor A person who has been awarded the highest academic degree in a particular subject by a college or university.

doctorate The academic degree of doctor, as awarded by a college or university.

don A lecturer at a British university or college, especially at Oxford or Cambridge.

donnish Characteristic of a university lecturer, especially in devotion to learning.

dropout A person who leaves a school or college without having completed the course of study.

elementary school A school for the first six or eight grades in a child's education.

emeritus Having retired from full-time work but retaining the title of the post held before retiring as an honorary title.

erudite Having or involving great scholarship or learning.

extracurricular Not included in the regular curriculum of a school, college, or university.

extramural Located or taking place outside the boundaries of a college or university.

faculty Any of the distinct branches of teaching at a college or university, or the body of teachers in a particular subject.

fellow A graduate student who is carrying out research in a particular subject and is paid to do some teaching.

fellowship The position of fellow at a college or university, or the money granted to one.

field trip An excursion by staff and students to study at first hand something of interest or relevance to a course.

finishing school A private school for girls at which students are taught social and cultural skills to equip them for life in society.

flunk To be unsuccessful in an examination or course of study, or to assess a student as being unsuccessful.

fraternity An organization of male students at a college or university, primarily for social activities.

freshman A student in the first year at a school, college, or university.

grade school An elementary school.

graduate To be awarded an academic degree or diploma by a school, college, or university. A graduate is a person who has been awarded such a degree or diploma.

graduation The awarding of an academic degree or diploma, or the ceremony at which this is carried out.

grammar school In the United States this means an elementary school; in the United Kingdom it means a secondary school with a particularly academic curriculum.

higher education Education beyond the level of secondary school, especially at a college or university.

high school A secondary school that includes grades from 9 to 12 or 10 to 12.

homiletic Intended to teach or instruct, especially in a moral and practical way.

interdisciplinary Involving two or more separate branches of learning.

intern A student who is studying a subject at an advanced level or a graduate who is being given practical training in a particular field.

intramural Located or taking place within the boundaries of a college or university.

Ivy League A group of long-established, academically respected colleges and universities in the northeast United States. These are: Brown, Columbia, Cornell, Dartmouth, Harvard, Princeton, the University of Pennsylvania, and Yale.

junior college A college that provides a two-year course equivalent to the first two years of a four-year undergraduate course.

junior high school A school that includes grades 7 and 8 and sometimes 9.

kindergarten A school or class for children from the ages of four through six, intended to prepare them for primary school.

kindergartner A child who attends a kindergarten, or a teacher at a kindergarten.

learning difficulties An impaired ability to learn, sometimes congenital and sometimes resulting from damage to the brain caused by injury or disease.

lexicon A dictionary or a list of vocabulary used in a particular field.

lowerclassman an underclassman

lycée A secondary school in France.

magna cum laude With high honors, a Latin phrase meaning that a student has graduated with high distinction.

major A field of study that a student specializes in, or a student that is specializing in a particular field. To major in something is to study it as a specialty.

master's degree An academic degree awarded by a college or university to someone who has studied a subject for at least one year beyond the bachelor's degree.

matriculate To enroll as a student at a college or university.

minor A field of study that a student is not specializing in and which requires fewer credits, or a student studying such a field. To minor in something is to study it as as a secondary field.

module A short course of study in a particular subject or in a particular area of a subject.

Montessori method An approach to teaching young children that stresses allowing them to develop at their own pace and cultivate their natural abilities through practical play.

multiversity A university that has many affiliated colleges or research institutions at separate campuses.

Oxbridge The British universities of Oxford and Cambridge considered as together forming an institution in British society, representing both academic excellence and social privilege.

Oxonian A student or former student of Oxford University.

parent-teacher association An organization that brings together the parents of children at a particular school and the teaching staff, intended to maintain good relations and communication between them and often to raise funds for the school.

parietal Living within or being in authority in a particular college.

pedagogue A teacher, often one who is considered dogmatic or pedantic.

pedagogy The profession or art of teaching.

playschool A nursery for preschool children.

postgraduate Involved in or undertaking study at an advanced level after having graduated from a college or university.

preparatory school In the United States, a private secondary school that prepares students for college; in the United Kingdom, a private school that prepares students for public school.

primary school In the United States, an elementary school for the first three or four grades; in the United Kingdom, a school for children under the age of eleven.

primer A book used to teach children to read, or one that covers the basics of a subject.

principal A person who is in charge of a school or other educational institution.

proctor A person who supervises at examinations and enforces discipline in a school.

professor A teacher at a college or university, especially the most senior in a particular field.

public school In the United States, any local primary or secondary school that is open to all; in the United Kingdom, a private, fee-paying, secondary school.

reader A member of the teaching staff at a British university who is senior to a lecturer but junior to a professor.

recess A period during the school day when there are no classes.

rector A title for the head of some schools, colleges, or universities.

reformatory A place where young people who have broken the law are confined to be disciplined and trained.

reform school a reformatory

Regius professor A professor at some British universities who has been appointed by the Crown to a chair established by royal patronage.

sabbath school A school held on the Sabbath for religious instruction.

scholar A learned person or a student, especially one who specializes in a particular field or who has received a scholarship.

scholarship Knowledge and learning, or a financial award made to a student to help fund attendance at a school, college, or university.

scholastic Involving or typical of schools, education, or scholarship.

secondary school In the United States, a school that students attend after elementary school and before going on to college; in the United Kingdom, a school for students between the ages of 11 and 18.

semester Either of two divisions of the academic year, each lasting from 15 to 18 weeks.

seminar A group of college or university students who are involved in advanced study or research under the guidance of a professor or tutor and who meet regularly for discussions or exchange of findings.

seminary A religious school where priests, ministers, or rabbis are trained.

senior high school A school that includes grades 10, 11, and 12.

sophomore A student in the second year of a college course, or a high-school student in the tenth grade.

sorority An organization of female students at a college or university, primarily for social activities.

special education Teaching for children whose needs cannot be met by the standard curriculum, for example children with learning difficulties.

substitute teacher A teacher who takes the place of another teacher who is absent from school for some reason, such as illness.

summa cum laude With the highest honors, a Latin phrase meaning that a student has graduated with the highest possible distinction.

Sunday school A school for religious instruction, usually held on church premises.

supply teacher The term used in the United Kingdom for a substitute teacher.

syllabus A summary of the important elements of a course of study or text. In the United Kingdom this also means the subjects studied in a particular course or at a particular institution.

tertiary education Education at a level above that of secondary or high school.

thesaurus A book that lists synonyms and related words but does not give definitions.

three R's Reading, writing, and arithmetic, considered as the basic elements of education.

trimester Any of three parts that the academic year is divided into in some colleges and universities.

underclassman A student in the first or second year of a secondary or college course.

undergraduate A student at a college or university who has not yet been awarded a degree.

law

acquittal The decision by a judge or jury that an accused person is not guilty of a crime.

actionable Able or likely to give rise to a legal action.

affidavit A declaration made in writing and under oath in the presence of an authorized person such as a notary public.

alternative dispute resolution An attempt to resolve a dispute without a court proceeding, for example, arbitration or mediation.

appellate court A court that is authorized to hear appeals and review decisions made by other courts.

arraignment The bringing of an accused person to a court to answer a charge that has been made.

attorney a lawyer

attorney general The chief law officer and legal advisor of a state or nation.

autopsy A scientific examination of a dead body carried out in order to determine the cause of death.

bailiff An official of a court, especially one who maintains order or is in charge of prisoners.

bar The railing that encloses the part of a courtroom where legal business is conducted, or a term for the legal profession and lawyers in general.

barrister A British lawyer who has been called to the bar and can plead in higher courts.

bench A judge or magistrate presiding in a court, or judges in general.

bylaws Rules of corporate governance.

canon law The body of laws governing the affairs of a Christian church.

case law Law based on previous judicial decisions and precedent rather than statutes.

certiorari An order sent from a superior court to an inferior one requesting a transcript of the proceedings of one of its cases for review.

circuit judge A judge of the Court of Appeal of one of the district judicial circuits

citation A summons ordering someone to appear in court.

codification The collection of a number of laws or legal principles into one organized body.

committal The act of entrusting something to someone, or of ordering someone to be confined.

common law The body of law based on court decisions, customs and practices rather than on statutes.

coram populo A Latin phrase meaning in the presence of the people.

coroner A public official who holds an inquest to investigate any sudden or suspicious death.

corpus delicti The body of a crime, or the essential facts that show that a crime has been committed.

corpus juris A collection of laws, especially laws of a country.

counsel A lawyer or team of lawyers conducting a case in court or giving legal advice.

counselor An attorney, especially one who is conducting a case in court.

court martial A military court appointed to try a person accused of an offense against military law, or a trial conducted by such a court.

court order An order from a court requiring someone to do or not do something.

cross-examination The questioning by a lawyer of a witness who has already been questioned by the opposing side, especially with a view to discrediting the witness's testimony.

decriminalize To declare that something that has been against the law is no longer considered a crime.

defendant A person against whom an action has been brought in court.

deposition An examination of a witness before a trial.

district attorney The state prosecuting officer in a particular judicial district.

exculpate To clear someone of any guilt or blame.

exhibit An object that is formally produced in court as a piece of evidence.

exonerate To free a person of any blame.

false arrest An arrest of a person that is unjustified or against the law.

false imprisonment The illegal or unjustified detention of a person.

felon A person who has committed a felony.

felony A serious crime, such as murder or rape. *Compare* misdemeanor.

Fifth Amendment An amendment to the United States Constitution establishing that, among other things, no person can be compelled to testify against himself or herself.

foreman A member of a jury who is appointed to preside over and speak for it.

forensic Belonging to or used in a court of law.

forensic medicine The use of medicine in legal proceedings, such as to establish a cause of death.

grand jury A special jury typically of between 12 and 23 people convened to decide whether or not there is enough evidence against an accused person to warrant a criminal indictment.

habeas corpus A writ requiring a person to be brought before a court so that it can be decided whether or not the person's detention is lawful.

highway patrol A division of the state police whose officers patrol public highways.

hung jury A jury that has been unable to come to an agreed verdict.

illicit Not allowed by law.

impanel To enroll people as members of a jury.

impeachment The charging of a public official before a quasi-political body with having committed an offense while in office.

indictment A written charge accusing someone of having committed a crime, presented by a grand jury.

injunction A court order that prohibits someone from doing something.

inquest A judicial inquiry, especially one into the cause of a sudden or suspicious death.

judge advocate general The senior legal officer in a branch of the United States armed forces.

judgment The official determination by a court of the rights and claims of the parties to a lawsuit litigated before it.

judicature The authority, jurisdiction, or function of a judge or a court.

judicial Belonging to, appropriate to, or characteristic of a court or the administration of justice.

judiciary A system of courts, or the judicial branch of a government.

juridical Belonging to the law, a judge, or the administration of justice.

jurisdiction The right to apply the law, or the area in which someone has this right.

jurisprudence The science or philosophy of law.

jurist A person with extensive knowledge or experience of law, such as a judge, a distinguished law professor, or lawyer.

juror A person who serves on a jury.

jury A group of citizens summoned to a court to hear a case and give a verdict.

justice of the peace A magistrate empowered to try some minor cases and administer oaths.

kangaroo court An illegal or dishonest court.

lawsuit An action brought in a court of law by one party against another.

legal aid Money or legal services granted to people who otherwise cannot afford to employ an attorney.

legislation A law, body of laws, or the process of making laws.

litigant A person who is taking part in a lawsuit.

litigation The process of initiating or contesting a lawsuit.

litigious Tending to initiate lawsuits frequently or too readily.

loophole A way of evading a penalty or obligation made possible by a legal ambiguity or omission.

magistrate A public officer who has the power to administer the law.

malfeasance Wrongdoing or misconduct.

malpractice Conduct by a professional or official person that is immoral or improper.

mandamus An order issued by a superior court requiring a lower court or public official to do something.

Miranda rights The rights that a person who is being arrested must be informed of, such as the right to remain silent or the right to have legal counsel.

miscarriage of justice A situation in which the administration of justice has failed or been mismanaged.

misdemeanor An offense that is less serious than a felony.

mistrial A trial that is invalid because an error has been made or because the jury is unable to agree on a verdict.

mitigating circumstances Factors that may be considered as lessening the extent to which an accused person is culpable.

natural law The body of law that is believed to be inherent in human nature.

nolo contendere A plea made by a defendant that is effectively equivalent to a plea of guilty but which does not prevent the defendant from denying the charge in subsequent proceedings.

notary public A person who is legally authorized to administer oaths, take affidavits, and witness documents.

offense An action that breaks a law, especially a crime.

ordinance An authoritative regulation or statute, especially one passed by a local authority.

peace officer A person whose job is to enforce the law and keep the peace, such as a sheriff.

perjury The deliberate telling of lies or failure to tell the complete truth while under oath in a court of law.

plaintiff A person who initiates a court action.

plea The answer given by a defendant in a court case to the charge that has been brought.

plea bargaining The practice of negotiating an agreement between the prosecution and defense in a criminal court case, by which a defendant pleads guilty to a lesser charge in return for the dropping of a more serious charge.

police commissioner A government offical in charge of a police department.

posse A group of citizens summoned by a sheriff to help in maintaining law and order.

postmortem examination an autopsy

power of attorney A legal instrument authorizing a person to act as agent for another, especially in financial or legal matters.

precedent A decision made by a court that is taken as authorization or a standard in a subsequent case.

prima facie Evident, or sufficient at first sight.

probate The process of legally establishing the validity of a person's will.

probate court A court whose authority is restricted to establishing the validity of wills or administering estates.

public defender An attorney who is appointed by the government to defend clients who cannot afford to pay for legal representation.

public prosecutor An official appointed by the government to act for the community or state in prosecuting criminal actions.

Queen's evidence In British courts, evidence given by a criminal against his associates in favor of the Crown.

recidivist A person who has committed crimes in the past and shows a tendency to relapse into crime at a later date.

recognizance A legal obligation to do something, such as appear in court at a later date, that someone enters into before a court or magistrate.

retrial A second trial of a case that has already been the subject of a trial.

solicitor In the United States, a lawyer; in the United Kingdom, a lawyer who is able to plead only in lower courts and is not a member of the bar.

Solicitor General A lawyer who handles all appeals to the Supreme Court for the Department of Justice.

state's evidence Evidence given for the prosecution in a state or federal trial, or a person who gives evidence for the state.

statute A law that is passed by a legislature.

statute book A list of all the laws passed by a legislature.

statute of limitations A statute that sets a time period during which legal proceedings must be begun.

statutory According to, authorized by, regulated by, or enacted by a statute.

statutory rape The crime of having sexual relations with a person who is below the statutory age of consent.

sub judice Currently being considered by a judge or a court of law.

subpoena A writ issued by a court ordering a person to appear before it. To subpoena someone is to make the person the subject of such a writ.

sui juris Considered in law to be fully competent to handle your own affairs.

suit a lawsuit

summons A written notice ordering a person to appear in court to answer a charge, give evidence, or serve on a jury. To summons someone is to issue the person with such a notice.

Supreme Court The highest federal court in the United States, with authority over all other courts, and to which appeals may be made against the judgments of lower courts.

surety A person who agrees to take legal responsibility for someone else's debts or obligations if that person defaults.

testimony Evidence given under oath by a person, especially statements made by a witness in court.

tort A wrongful act, done deliberately or through negligence, especially one that causes injury or damage and for which the injured party may bring a civil suit.

tortious Wrongful, especially in constituting or involving a tort.

tribunal A court of justice, often one set up to look into a specific matter.

vigilante A person who unlawfully takes the enforcement of law into his or her own hands.

violation The process or an act of breaking or disregarding a law.

warrant An authorization issued by a judge or magistrate allowing an officer to do something, such as search a premises or arrest a person.

witness stand A place, often raised or enclosed, in a court from which a witness gives testimony. In the United Kingdom this is called a witness box.

writ A written order issued by a court requiring a person to do or not do something.

politics

absolutism A political theory that all power should be in the hands of a single ruler.

activist A person who takes an active and often militant part in politics.

anarchism The political theory that all governments oppress the people and should be abolished.

autarchy A form of government in which one person has absolute and unlimited power.

autocrat A ruler who possesses absolute and unlimited authority.

Balkanization The division of a part of the world into smaller parts that are usually hostile to each other.

ballot A piece of paper or card used to make a vote, the right to vote, a total number of votes, or an act of voting.

banana republic A small country with an economy that is highly dependent on a single crop or resource, and is often ruled by a dictator or miltary junta.

bloc A group of countries or people that share the same interest or aims and usually act together.

bossism The domination of a political organization by powerful professional politicians.

brinkmanship The practice of holding out to the last minute for what you want in political negotiations, especially in international affairs, in the face of threats from a powerful opponent.

bureaucracy A system of government administration in which a hierarchy of nonelected professional officials is in control and often insists on strict adherence to standard procedures.

canvassing The process of trying to find out how people intend to vote or of trying to obtain their votes.

capitalism An economic system in which the means of production are privately owned and producers compete to maximize their profits.

card-carrying Being a member of a particular political party or organization.

caucus A meeting of members of a political party to choose candidates or delegates or decide on matters of policy.

centrist A person who holds moderate rather than left- or right-wing political views.

civics The study of the political rights and responsibilities of citizens and of the operation of government.

coalition An alliance between political parties, factions, or groups, especially a temporary one.

collectivism The belief that the means of production in a state should be controlled by the people.

communism A political belief that there should be no classes in society, that there should be no private ownership, and that the people should collectively control the means of production.

constituency The group of voters that an elected legislator represents, or the district where they live.

constituent Any of the residents represented by a particular elected legislator.

convention A meeting of members of a political party, especially of delegates to choose candidates for an election.

coup (d'état) The sudden overthrow of a government, often with violence.

cronyism The practice of appointing friends or supporters to political office irrespective of their abilities.

demagogue A person who gains the support of the public by making impassioned speeches that appeal to their emotions and prejudices.

democracy A form of government in which power is held by the people or exercised on their behalf by elected representatives.

despotism A form of government in which power is held by a single ruler and is often used tyrannically.

détente A policy or situation in which tension between rival nations is relaxed.

devolution The transfer of power from a central government to smaller units such as regional authorities.

dictator A ruler whose power is unlimited and is not challenged by a recognized opposition.

egalitarian Believing in or promoting equal political, social, and economic rights for all people.

electioneering The practice of working actively to secure votes for a candidate in an election.

Electoral College A group of electors who are chosen to elect the President and Vice President of the United States.

electorate All of the people who are entitled to vote in a particular election.

executive The branch of a government that puts into effect the laws and decisions made by that government.

executive session A session, usually closed to the public, of a legislative body during which it carries out executive business, such as the ratification of a treaty by the Senate.

Fabianism The political belief that socialism can be introduced by gradual reform rather than by revolution.

fascism A form of government in which a dictator rules,

opposition is suppressed, the economy is centrally controlled, and extreme nationalistic policies are pursued.

federalism A form of government in which power is held partly by a central authority and partly by a number of regional or state governments.

filibuster The practice of trying to delay the passage of legislation by making long speeches or using other obstructive tactics.

floating voter A person who does not always vote for the same political party.

franchise The right to vote in elections to form a government.

fringe group A group of people within a political party who hold extreme or minority views.

geopolitics The study of the ways in which geography and politics interact, especially in international affairs.

gerrymandering The practice of fixing the boundaries of electoral districts in a way that gives unfair advantage to a particular party.

Grand Old Party A nickname for the Republican Party.

grassroots People at a local or ordinary level, such as the ordinary members of a political party or the members of an electorate.

gunboat diplomacy The use of threats of military force, especially by a strong country to a weaker one, in diplomatic relations.

hardliner A person who pursues an uncompromising policy.

hustings Political campaigning, or a place where political speeches are made during an election.

imperialism A policy of gaining power over other nations by seizing their territory or dominating their economies.

junta A group of military officers who govern a country, often after having seized power in a coup d'état.

keynote address A speech made to a political gathering that focuses on points that are considered to be currently most important.

lame duck An elected representative or administration that has failed to win re-election but continues in power until the inauguration of the winner of the last election.

left The people or parties who support social and political reform with a view to improving the condition or increasing the power of the common people.

left-wing Supporting or belonging to the most liberal and egalitarian element of a political party or other group.

legislature The branch of a government that decides on the laws for a state.

Leninism The political theory of Vladimir Ilyich Lenin, especially his interpretation and modification of Marxism.

lobby A group of people who try to influence the decisions of a legislature in favor of a particular interest.

logrolling The practice of trading favors between politicians in order to ensure the passage of legislation or adoption of policy that favors a particular interest.

lumpenproletariat The lowest level of the proletariat, made up of criminals, vagrants, and the permanently unemployed.

majority leader The person who leads the majority party in the Senate or House of Representatives.

marginal A constituency in which elections tend to be won by a small margin and may therefore be likely to change hands.

Marxism The political theory of Karl Marx, including its analysis of society in terms of the class struggle and its belief in the replacement of capitalism by communism.

militant A person who plays an active and aggressive part in supporting a political party or cause.

minister A government officer who heads a department.

minority leader The person who leads the minority party in the Senate or House of Representatives.

monarchy A form of government headed by a hereditary ruler, such as a king or queen, or a country with this form of government.

mugwump A person who remains independent or neutral in politics.

oligarchy A form of government in which power is held by a small group of people.

partisan An enthusiastic, committed member of a political party, faction, or cause.

party hack A member of a political party who is not particularly brilliant but who can be relied upon for loyalty.

party line The policies of a political party, or a particular policy, which loyal members are expected to support.

plebiscite A vote in which the whole electorate is asked to decide on a particular issue.

plutocracy A form of government in which power is held by the rich.

political action committee A committee of special-interest groups, such as business or labor, formed to raise funds for the campaign of a political candidate.

politicize To make something become political in character.

politicking The practice of discussing or taking part in politics.

politico A person who is actively involved in politics or who seeks political office.

polity Any form of government or organized society.

poll The casting of a vote, the number of votes cast, or a place where voting takes place.

polling station A place where people go to vote during an election.

popular front A coalition of leftist political groups, especially any of those formed in Europe in the 1930s to oppose Fascism.

pork barrel A government project that brings investment and employment to a place represented by a particular member of a legislature.

power broker A person who controls a number of politicians or a large number of votes and uses this to influence political affairs.

precinct Any of the election districts into which a town or city is divided.

primary A meeting of the voters in a political party to choose delegates for a convention or nominees for office, or a preliminary election to nominate candidates for office.

proletariat The class in society who make a living by selling their labor and possess no capital.

proportional representation A system of assigning the number of seats in a legislature according to the proportion of the total votes that each party wins.

public servant A person who holds office in a government.

quango Quasi-autonomous non-governmental organization, an organization or agency that receives funding from a government but is able to act independently.

rabble-rouser A person who makes speeches that stir up the emotions of the public.

realpolitik An approach to politics that is not idealistic but ruthlessly opportunistic, especially in advancing the interests of a country.

Red a communist

referendum An instance of submitting an important public issue, such as a proposed piece of legislation, directly to the electorate in a vote.

republic A democratic state or form of government in which the head of state is elected rather than holding hereditary office.

returning officer An official in some countries, such as the United Kingdom and Canada, who is in charge of an election in a particular constituency, supervising the counting of the votes and announcing the result.

right The people or parties who support conservative or reactionary policies.

right-wing Supporting or belonging to the most conservative and reactionary element of a political party or other group.

runoff A second election held after a first election has failed to produce a clear result.

seat Membership of a legislative body, or, in Britain, a Parliamentary constituency.

secretary of state The head of a government department, for example foreign affairs or defense.

slate A list of the candidates belonging to a particular party who are standing in an election.

socialism A political theory advocating public ownership of the means of production and the sharing of political power by the whole community.

spin doctor A person whose job is to promote the best possible interpretation of a politician's acts or statements.

splinter group A faction that has broken away from a larger political group.

spoiled ballot A ballot paper that is invalid because the person voting has not marked it properly, whether inadvertently or deliberately.

spoils system The practice engaged in by a newly-elected government of rewarding its supporters with appointments to government office.

Stalinism The form of communist theory or practice associated with Joseph Stalin, typified by totalitarianism.

superpower A very powerful country, especially one with nuclear weapons.

swing A fluctuation in a pattern of voting.

syndicalism A political movement advocating the seizure of government by syndicates of labor unions united in a general strike.

technocracy A form of government in which power is in the hands of scientists and other technicians.

Third World All of the underdeveloped countries in the world considered as a whole.

ticket A list of election candidates belonging to a party.

totalitarianism A form of government in which the state controls every aspect of the individual's life and all opposition is suppressed.

Trotskyism The form of communist theory associated with Leon Trotsky, particularly his call for worldwide revolution.

tyranny A form of government in which a single ruler holds absolute power.

ward An electoral district of a town or city.

ward heeler A person who works for a political party within a particular ward.

philosophy

absolute Existing without depending in any way on other things; the opposite of relative.

atomism In Greek philosophy, the notion that matter is made up particles of solid matter moving in empty space.

cartesianism The philosophy of Descartes and his supporters which emphasized a radical division between matter and mind.

cynics A Greek school of thought which held that nothing can be known; it became associated with the disregard of material things.

determinism The theory that all events are caused, and that there is no free will.

dialectic In Greek philosophy, the art of testing whether assertions hold true. In Hegel, a system of logic proceeding from thesis to antithesis to synthesis.

dualism Any theory which distinguishes between two fundamentally different things, such as good and evil, mind and matter, etc.

empiricism The view that knowledge proceeds from experience.

epistemology The critical investigation of knowledge and its validity.

ethics The philosophical study of morality in human conduct, and of the rules which ought to govern it.

existentialism A practical philosophical tendency centered on the concrete realities of human life, rather than generalized abstractions.

free will Opposed to determinism, the belief that physical causes do not entirely shape the world, and that mental processes can act to influence things.

hedonism The belief that pleasure and the avoidance of pain constitute the highest good.

humanism A view originating in the Renaissance that reason must be autonomous from authorities such as the Church.

hypothesis A suggested explanation for events and phenomena.

idea An object in the mind. For Plato, the metaphysical pattern of which real objects are pale reflections.

idealism The notion that the objects of reality do not have independent existence but are constructs of the mind, or made up of ideas.

innate ideas Ideas which exist, pre-formed, in the mind at birth.

materialism The doctrine that all phenomena are explained by physical laws alone.

metaphysics A branch of philosophy dealing with questions of being.

mind-body problem The philosophical question of how mind and body are related, and whether mind is a non-physical substance.

monism The belief that all things are unified, or that they are all explained ultimately on one single principle or law.

neoplatonism Various schools of philosophy which took the philosophy of Plato as their starting-point.

nominalism The view that universals such as "the true" exist in name only and do not actually exist.

paradox A statement which seems to contradict itself or lead to absurdity.

phenomenology A philosophical doctrine established by Husserl; the science of appearances.

pluralism The belief that there are more than one or two substances in the world, such as mind and matter.

positivism A philosophical doctrine that we can only have knowledge of things we experience through the senses.

pragmatism An American philosophical school; the view that the meaning of things is in their practical relation to people.

realism A medieval doctrine that universals such as "the good" have real existence.

reality Whatever is accepted as having objective existence, independent of thought or language.

reductionism The attempt to explain complex phenomena in terms of simple laws or principles.

relativism The view that there are no absolute truths or values.

scepticism The view that there is no certain knowledge without justification.

scholasticism A term for the medieval philosophy taught in schools, and exemplified by Thomas Aquinas.

sensationalism The theory that all our knowledge derives ultimately from the senses

socratic Pertaining to the philosopical method and teachings of Socrates.

utilitarianism A philosophical school of thought arguing that ethics must be based on whatever brings the greatest amount of good to the greatest number of people.

psychology

amnesia Memory loss, sometimes due to a blow on the head or some other damage to brain function, or to neurotic disorder as a result of inner conflict.

analytical psychology The process of attempting to explain or relieve disturbance by looking into the unconscious forces governing behavior. The term is also used more specifically to refer to the school of Carl Jung.

archetype Jung used this term to refer to such universal concepts as the "here," which he saw as part of the collective unconscious—that part of the mind inherited from the experience of previous generations and common to us all.

association The technique of association involves reading out a list of words and encouraging subjects to respond with the first word coming to mind.

autism Children suffering from this condition appear withdrawn, as if lost in fantasy. No cause or cure has yet been found; but specialized teaching has enabled many to lead relatively normal lives.

autosuggestion The theory that if individuals can suggest a belief to themselves, they will come to believe it.

behaviorism A school of psychology that places great importance on learned behavior and conditioned reflexes.

castration complex A child's fear that he will lose his genitals as a punishment for fantasizing about them is often the basis of a castration complex, and the root of neurosis in some cases.

catalepsy A state of muscular rigidity maintained for long periods.

catatonia An extreme form of schizophrenia characterized by muscular rigidity or catalepsy, stereotyped mannerisms, refusal to communicate, and stupor.

catharsis The release of pent-up feelings and repressed emotions after a subject has begun to talk about problems during analysis.

complex An idea which is partly or wholly repressed, but which determines your opinion of yourself, may produce a complex. A woman may not consciously recall being teased as a child for being fat, for instance, but the idea may remain in her unconscious and as a result she may develop a complex about her appearance, whatever her adult build.

compulsion An irresistible urge, often a neurotic reaction, taking such forms as having to wash one's hands every few minutes or touching certain objects before leaving a room.

conversion reaction A form of hysteria in which repressed conflict is converted into symptoms such as deafness, blindness, or paralysis, without actual physical cause.

death wish According to Freud, in addition to a "drive to survive," we also have certain impulses known collectively as the death wish.

depersonalization Pathological loss of contact with reality.

deviation Conduct departing from the norm. Specifically, it is used to describe sexual perversions, such as a fetish or sadism.

displacement The man who gets angry at the office but is afraid to lose his temper there, may arrive home and let out all that pent-up aggression on the family. In a process known as displacement, he has directed his anger to a handy substitute.

double-bind Two contradictory responses from a person. Some schools hold that this is sometimes a root cause of schizophrenia.

ego That aspect of the mind most in touch with reality.

Electra complex A daughter's fixation on her father.

extroversion Concern with things outside rather than with your own thoughts and feelings. Jung first devised the term "extroversion—introversion" as a dimension along which people can be divided into psychological types.

folie à deux This mental disorder, present in two closely associated individuals at once, most commonly occurs in a husband and wife.

free association In this method, sometimes used in psychoanalysis, subjects are encouraged to let their thoughts wander, the final chain of associations often providing clues to the underlying disturbance.

id The part of the mind or personality that is governed by the pleasure principle, and which demands gratification.

individual psychology This school, founded by Alfred Adler, aims to reach an understanding of mental disturbance through the examination of early feelings of inferiority and subsequent compensatory activity, and to improve patterns of reaction.

industrial psychology The study of the effects of such things as working conditions, stress, morale, and rewards on the efficiency of workers.

inferiority complex Unconscious feelings of insignificance and insecurity hidden by excessively aggressive or other compensatory behavior.

inhibition Mental blockage occurring when the superego or voice of conscience prevents the individual from behaving in a particular way.

introversion A tendency to turn inward, first examined by Jung, which often results in avoidance of social contact, isolation and loneliness.

kleptomania Compulsive stealing, symbolic of an unconscious need, often sexual in origin.

libido The sex instinct or erotic desire.

masochism A disorder in which pleasure is derived from having pain, whether mental or physical, inflicted on oneself; it is sometimes associated with sexual activity.

megalomania Arising from exaggerated valuation of oneself, this state is characterized by delusions of grandeur.

nervous breakdown Any mental condition prohibiting normal functioning.

obsession A dominating idea or thought which takes over an individual.

Oedipus complex The repressed desire of a boy or man for a sexual relationship with his mother.

paranoia A psychotic disorder marked by imaginary persecution.

penis envy Repressed female desire to possess a penis as part of their own anatomy.

phantom limb Imagined sensations in a limb that has been amputated. These result from nerve ends in the stump which continue to convey misleading messages to the brain.

phrenology This pseudo-science developed in the 19th century and holds that certain characteristics—such as wit, normality, aggression or benevolence—are related to particular parts of the brain and can be recognized by bumps on the contour of the head.

pleasure principle The immediate satisfaction of urges and desires is, according to psychoanalytical theory, an overriding principle which remains with us even in adulthood to a marked degree.

psychiatrist A practitioner specializing in the diagnosis and treatment of mental and nervous disorders.

psychoanalysis A system of psychology aiming to discover and address the unconscious motivation for certain types of behavior.

psychodrama The acting out of relationships or feelings in an attempt to release and identify repressed emotions.

psychologist A practitioner who studies behavior and the way in which the mind actually works.

psychopath An unstable individual who is unable to adjust to society.

psychosomatic Describes physical disorders resulting at least partly from psychological factors.

psychotherapy Treatment that sets out to help a subject adjust to daily life.

reflexes Acts that occur involuntarily—such as blinking—are the result of a reflex response.

regression This term implies a return to an earlier stage of psychological development. In the course of therapy, regression hypnosis is sometimes used in order to uncover the possible root of some current problem.

repression Involuntary ejection of shameful emotions and memories from consciousness because they are too painful to bear; it may sometimes result in neurotic symptoms.

sadism A form of perversion, often sexual, involving pleasure through inflicting pain on another. Sado-masochism implies a tendency toward both sadism and masochism.

subconscious This term describes any mental process of which we are only dimly aware.

sublimation Freud first described this unconscious process whereby an instinctive urge is transformed so that it is more socially acceptable.

superego That part of the personality that exercises a prohibitive role, acting as the voice of conscience.

transference Psychoanalytical theory holds that through the process of transference, healing may take place. So it is that the psychoanalyst becomes the object of a patient's suppressed emotions—either love or hatred—while the transference is resolved.

unconscious This part of the mind is cut off from consciousness and is believed to be the seat of repressed emotions.

religions

Buddhism and Jainism

agama The canon of holy work.

ahisma The Jaina doctrine of non-violence and non-injury to any form of life.

ajiva A non-soul, or non-living substance.

bodhi tree also called a bo tree. The Buddha sat under the shade of this tree to meditate until he gained enlightenment.

bodhisattva A person who vows to become a Buddha by leading a virtuous and wise life. At the highest level, this is a person who postpones entering nirvana by doing charitable work.

bonze A Buddhist monk, especially in Japan or China.

buddha A word meaning awakened or enlightened one. It is a title and not a proper name. Buddhists believe that there have been many buddhas and that there will be many buddhas in the future.

dharma Saving truth. The Buddha's message of how to overcome suffering.

Digambara A Jaina sect who go naked on the final stages of their spiritual journey.

gompa A Tibetan word for a meditation room which contains a shrine, meditation cushions, and desks for sacred books.

jatakas Stories of the Buddha's past lives before he was born as Gautama.

jina A victor or conqueror; also a Tirthankara, a title given to the great Jaina teachers such as Mahavira.

jiva A living soul, or living substance.

karman A tenet of Jaina doctrine that all phenomena are linked together in a universal chain of cause and effect.

nirjana A process consisting of fasting, not eating certain kinds of food, control over taste, modesty, study, and meditation, and renunciation of the ego.

nirvana A state of ultimate wisdom and blessedness.

prayer wheel Especially in Tibet, a wheel with Buddhist prayers written on it. Each time someone makes it turn a complete revolution is equivalent to saying a prayer.

ratnatraya Jaina ethics of right knowledge, faith, and conduct. A Jaina follower must try to achieve and follow all three together.

relic A part of the body or something used or associated with a saint or other very important religious figure such as the Buddha.

shrine A cabinet or table which contains representations of the

Three Jewels. These are a statue, the holy books wrapped in cloth, and a stupa. The shrine also contains offering bowls, pictures of gurus, flowers, lights, statues of other buddhas. In Tibetan Buddhism the shrines are very ornate.

stupa A three-dimensional mandala used on a shrine. It represents the Buddha's mind.

sutra The Buddha's words or a guru's commentary on the Buddha's words.

Svetambaras One of the two Jaina sects. Their name means "white robed."

Tirthankaras Revealers of the Jaina religious path.

Christianity

Advent A period of time before Christmas, marking preparation for the coming of Christ.

Ascension Celebration of Jesus' ascension into heaven, forty days after Easter.

Christmas This celebrates the birth of Christ. The festival is held on the 25 December. The Nativity (depicting the birth of Christ) is a common theme for Christmas theater plays and celebrations.

clergy Religious leaders; a member of the Church.

College of Cardinals A body of the highest authority next to the pope in the Roman Catholic Church. The pope is elected from one of the cardinals, and is elected by them. They assist the pope in religious and non-religious affairs.

creeds Statements of Christian belief.

cross The main Christian symbol, reminding Christians of Jesus' sacrificial death and his resurrection. It is a symbol of good over evil.

crucifix A cross with the figure of the crucified Jesus, especially important to Roman Catholics.

crusades During the Middle Ages, Christian armies tried to recapture Jerusalem which had been conquered by Muslim Turks. These military expeditions were called crusades. They began before 1100 and ended in the late 1200s

doctors (of the Roman Catholic Church) These are saints whose doctrinal writings have special authority either by papal decree or by the Church's universal agreement. These include Gregory the Great, Augustine, Basil, John Chrysostom, and Gregory of Nazianus.

Easter A feast commemorating the death and resurrection of Jesus.

eucharist Also called communion, Mass, or Lord's Supper. A church service which remembers the Last Supper. The wine and the bread or wafer taken by the participants are symbols of Jesus' body and blood which he commanded that his followers eat and drink

evangelist A person who brings or announces good news; author of one of the gospels.

gentile A non-Jewish person.

glossolalia Speaking in tongues, taken as a sign in some Christian churches of inspiration by the Holy Spirit. Also called the gift of tongues.

gospel Good news, specifically the good news of the coming of the Kingdom of God. There are four gospels included in the New Testament.

Last Supper The traditional Passover meal which Jesus shared with his Apostles the night before his death. Jesus is said to have blessed bread and told the Apostles to "Take eat, this is my body." and passed wine saying, "This is my blood." These elements are part of the communion service.

Lent A period of spiritual discipline, fasting, and penance leading up to Easter.

monasticism Withdrawing from everyday life to concentrate on prayer and meditation.

parable A story told by Jesus to convey his religious message.

Pentecost Marks the coming of the Holy Spirit.

resurrection Rising from the dead. Reports of Jesus' resurrection convinced many people that Jesus was the Son of God.

sacraments Outward and visible signs of an inward faith, or ceremonies in which a spiritual benefit is given to an individual.

saints People who have died for the faith or who have been thought worthy of special honor and remembrance by the Church as examples to Christians, and in the Roman Catholic Church as mediators with God.

stations of the cross Plaques or pictures (about 14) placed around the walls of a Catholic church marking the stages of Jesus' journey to his crucifixion and burial. The stations are: Pilate's condemnation, Christ receives his cross, Christ falls to the ground, Christ meets his mother, Symon of Cyrene takes the cross, Veronica wipes Christ's face, Christ falls a second time, Christ tells the women of Jerusalem not to weep for him, Christ falls a third time, Christ is stripped, Christ is nailed to the cross, Christ dies on the cross, Christ's body is placed in arms of his mother, and Christ's body is entombed.

Trinity Three persons in one God. The belief that God is three persons—the father, the son who is Jesus, and the Holy Spirit which is the spirit of God's grace.

Hinduism and Sikhism

Adi Granth Sikh sacred book.

atman The essence or principle of life; reality in individual forms.

Bhagavad-Gita A philosophical work on ethics and the nature of God, forming part of Mahabharata.

Brahma The all-pervading power.

brahman A priest or teacher.

caste A system of class differentiation based on Hindu scriptures.

dharma Moral and religious duty, or the right way of living.

Diwali A four-day New Year festival.

five Ks The five items that Sikh males are supposed to wear or carry as symbols of their faith. These are: the kangha, a comb, the kara, a steel bangle, the kesh, beard and uncut hair (covered by a turban), the kirpan, a short sword, and the kuccha, short trousers.

gurdwara A Sikh temple.

guru A spiritual leader who embodies the teachings of his order and the founder-deity and receives pupils in his ashram.

Hare Krishna Movement This is another name for the International Society for Krishna Consciousness which was founded by Swami Prabhupada in 1965 following the teachings of a 16th-century holy man, Chaitanya.

karma Literally "action," this means the moral law of cause and effect governing the future. Bad actions lead to rebirth in the lower orders of being. Good behavior leads to rebirth in the higher orders.

khalsa A collective term for all baptized Sikhs. The word means "pure ones."

Mahabharata An ancient Sanskrit epic story of battle between Pandavas and the Kauravas.

moksha Release, or liberation from continuous rebirth.

monotheistic Believing in one god only.

nirvana A state of release from the cycle of reincarnation and absorption into the universal reality.

Om or **aum** The symbol of Hinduism and of Hindu dharma. It represents the divine reality of the universe and is the first sound which began creation. By chanting "om," Hindus identify themselves as part of the whole of creation.

puja A performed ceremony and prayer.

samsara The endless cycle of life, death, and rebirth governed by law and karma.

Sanskrit An ancient language of India, considered to be sacred.

untouchables Members of no caste. They are considered impure and treated as outcasts.

Vedas Four books forming the Hindu sacred texts.

Islam

ayatollah This is a title held by the highest religious leaders of the Shiite sect. Ayatollahs guide Shiites in spiritual and worldly matters. An ayatollah can become the leader of the nation.

hajj The pilgrimage to Mecca which all Muslims must achieve at least once during their life.

hejira Muhammad's escape from Mecca to Medina in AD 622.

Islamic decoration Calligraphy or geometric patterns. Islamic art never has pictorial representations. Verses from the Koran and the Shahada or the Bisamillah are often used for decoration.

Ka'aba The most sacred shrine of Islam. It stands in a corner of the Grand Mosque in Mecca. It is the point to which all Muslims turn when they pray. The Ka'aba has a black stone in one corner which is thought to be especially sacred. The Ka'aba is empty. A black cloth usually covers the outside.

muezzin A crier or caller to prayer who announces prayer times from the minaret of a mosque.

Muslim A follower of the religion of Islam. In Arabic, Muslim means one who submits (to God).

Shiites Muslims who believe that the legitimate line of succession from Muhammad is through his cousin, the caliph Ali, and his descendants. Most Shiites live in Iran.

Sunnites Muslims who believe that the first four caliphs who came after Muhammad were the legitimate successors.

Judaism

bar mitzvah A ceremony undergone by a Jewish boy when he is 13 showing that he is now a full member of the Jewish community. The event is celebrated in the synagogue.

cantor The person who chants prayers during worship in the synagogue.

chosen people The Jews or ancient Hebrews or Israelites believe themselves to be the nation chosen by God. They have made a convenant with God.

covenant An agreement made between God and the Israelites in which God promises to love and protect them, but requiring certain duties in return.

Creation God's Creation of the world as described in Genesis. The Creation took six days and on the seventh day God rested.

Day of Atonement The holiest day of the year, also called Yom Kippur, a day of fasting and prayer.

diaspora The dispersion and exile of Jews, first by the destruction of the kingdom of Israel and of the kingdom of Judah and later by improved communications, commercial opportunities and especially the spread of the Roman Empire. Jews were scattered throughout Europe, Asia, and later North America. This dispersion was sometimes forced, such as in the exile to Babylon in 586 BC and at the destruction of the Temple by the Romans in AD 70.

Exodus The flight of the Children of Israel from Egypt into the wilderness and eventually to Canaan.

huppa A canopy under which a bride and bridegroom stand during a traditional Jewish wedding ceremony.

Israelites The descendants of Jacob who made up the Twelve Tribes.

Jerusalem A holy city for Jews and the capital city of the ancient kingdom of Judah. The Western Wall is venerated as the only remaining part of the Temple.

kosher This means ritually correct or proper and applies to food which has been prepared following Jewish dietary laws.

manna Food that God gave the Israelites during their time in the wilderness after the food they had brought with them ran out. Manna appeared in the morning on the ground. It was small like hoar frost.

matzah Unleavened bread eaten at Passover.

menorah A candle holder with seven branches.

messiah The "promised" or "anointed one," a saviour who will deliver mankind from its sins. Jews believe that the messiah is yet to come.

Passover The deliverance of the Israelites from Egypt, and the annual festival kept in memory of the event.

patriarchs The forefathers of the Israelites and founders of the Jewish religion: Abraham, Isaac, Jacob, and Jacob's sons.

Pentateuch The first five books of the Hebrew Bible, called the Five Books of Moses.

Philistine A people who were the enemies of the Israelites in their settlement of the Promised Land in the Old Testament.

Promised Land The land that God promised to give to the descendants of Abraham, Isaac, and Jacob which was known as

Canaan or Palestine.

prophet Someone who brings a message from God to the people. They most frequently spoke of true worship of God, upright living, and the coming of the messiah.

rabbi A spiritual leader, teacher, and interpreter of Jewish law. Rabbis deliver sermons in the synagogue, give advice, and perform many other functions.

Sabbath The seventh day of the week in the Jewish religion, Saturday. It is a holy day and a day of rest.

shiva A seven-day period of mourning which the family enter into after a funeral.

siddur A prayer book used in the synagogue and for the chanting of prayers.

Star of David A symbol of Judaism and of Israel. It consists of two triangles which interlace to form a six-pointed star. In Hebrew it is called the shield of David.

Tabernacle The dwelling place of the tent of the Lord was the portable sanctuary made by the Children of Israel during years of wandering in the wilderness.

tallith A shawl worn by men for prayer.

Talmud With the Tenakh, Judaism's two most sacred collections of writings. This is a collection of legal and ethical writings, history, and folkore.

tefillin Small black boxes containing scriptures and worn on the forehead and left arm.

Tenakh The Hebrew Bible which is also Christianity's Old Testament.

Shinto

Amaterasu Omikami The most important divinity in Shinto mythology, the Sun goddess and ancestress of the imperial household. Her descendants unified the Japanese people.

kami This means mystical, superior or divine. It is a sacred and divine power assigned to various gods and dieties, but kami can be found in many things.

kojiki Means "records of ancient matters." It is one of the sacred Shinto scriptures.

makoto The truthful way or will of kami. Something which is only revealed to people through kami.

musubi The mysterious creating and harmonizing power of Kami.

nihon skoki "Chronicles of Japan" important, in some sense sacred, Shinto scripture.

shinto Literally means the "way of kami," the "way of the gods,"

or "way of higher forces." The word was used in the 6th
century to distinguish traditional religions from Buddhism.
torii A gateway at the entrance of a Shinto temple.

Modern religions and cults

charismatic With divinely given power or talent. The word is
often used to describe sect leaders capable of inspiring or
influencing people.
evangelical A word used to describe Christian Protestant groups
who place an emphasis on the infallibility of the Bible,
importance of conversion, and faith in reconciliation with God
because of the death of Christ for man's salvation.
millenarianism A belief in a period in the future of 1,000 years
when Jesus will come and rule the Earth. Millenarianism has
produced sects which date the "end" and others which want to
prepare people for Jesus' coming by spreading religion.
New Age An interrelated set of philosophical and spiritual beliefs
becoming more widespread since the 1980s. Important elements
are spiritualism, belief in reincarnation, alternative healing, and
astrology.
occult Magical or hidden. Supernatural or mystical happenings
or acts which do not form part of a recognized religion.
Witchcraft, divination, magic, Satanism are all considered to be
part of the occult.

sociology

alienation
Karl Marx

alienation A concept first introduced by Marx and since used in a variety of contexts. Loosely defined, it means the separation of the individual from important aspects of the external world accompanied by a feeling of powerlessness or lack of control. A person may feel alienated from themselves or from society.

animism A belief in the existence of spirits dwelling in natural phenomena such as animals, tree, mountains, or storms.

anomie A term introduced by Durkheim to refer to a situation where the conditions for happiness are absent. Durkheim argued that one of the conditions for happiness was that there should be clear norms governing social behavior. The absence of these norms resulted in anomie and unhappiness.

anthropology The study of the human race. Known in Britain as social anthropology. Anthropology differs from sociology largely because it developed from a different intellectual tradition. Early anthropologists were motivated by a desire to study primitive societies. On the other hand, the founding fathers of sociology (such as Durkheim, Weber, and Marx) were more concerned with an analysis of industrial societies.

aristocracy A ruling class which inherits wealth, special privileges, and titles; typically accompanied by a monarchy.

behavioral science Any of various scientific disciplines, including sociology and anthropology, that involve observing the actions of human beings.

bourgeoisie People who, in the capitalist system, own the means of production, i.e. those things which are used to produce commodities, such as factories, machinery, and finance. According to Marx, as society moved from feudalism to capitalism, the bourgeoisie replaced the aristocracy as the real power holders. A distinction is sometimes made between the petite bourgeoisie (small property owners such as tradesmen, shopkeepers, and craftsmen) and the haute bourgeoisie (large scale property owners such as company owners.)

caste A rigid class system based on common acceptance of a religious principle. For example, the ancient Indian caste system. Castes were defined in the Hindu religion. Membership of caste depends on birth, and movement between castes is only possible in some instances through marriage.

charisma A term introduced by Max Weber to describe an ability to lead and inspire through force of personality and without the aid of material incentives, coercion, or the authority of office.

charisma
Max Weber

clan A group of people who claim to be descended from the same ancestor through either male or female links or both. It may be impossible to trace these links.

class Karl Marx defined two classes: the bourgeoisie and the proletariat. Sociologists have since defined class to include such factors as power and education.

critical theory/critical sociology *See* **Frankfurt School.**

cult A religious organization or movement which deviates from the established religious tradition in the community.

deviance Divergence from the accepted social norms of behavior. Deviance can be beneficial to society if unorthodox behavior leads to creativity or innovation. Alternatively deviance may be harmful as in the case of crime.

endomy The practice of marrying within a particular group such as a tribe or social class.

estate A form of social stratification which is recognized by the legal system. Commonly, estates were formed around the following groups: the nobility, the clergy, the peasants.

ethnocentrism Invented by W.G. Summer to mean a "view of things in which one's own group is the center of everything and all others are scaled and rated with reference to it."

ethnography A branch of anthropology which gives a descriptive account of the way of life in a particular society usually as the result of an in-depth study through personal contact.

ethnology A branch of anthropology which focuses on classifying people and cultures and explaining how these groups became distributed.

ethnomethodology Associated with the sociologist Harold Garfinkel, ethnomethodology studies the ways in which people use everyday knowledge to interpret and understand the world and communicate with other people.

exomany The practice of marrying outside the social group such as the tribe or village.

extended family A family group which consists of parents and children and other relatives living together or in close contact. The extended family is larger than the nuclear family.

feudalism A term used to describe the social order in Europe from medieval times. Essentially the system consisted of an unarmed peasant population who were subservient to noblemen and warriors. Some sociologists have used the term to describe historical periods in other cultures, such as Japan.

Frankfurt school A term referring to members of the Frankfurt Institute of Social research founded in 1923. The institute draws on the work of early Marx, Freud, and Hegel to produce an approach to the social sciences and philosophy which is known as critical theory.

functionalism A school of sociological and anthropological thought which considers social institutions such as religion within the context of the social system as a whole.

haute bourgeoisie *See* **bourgeoisie**.

hermeneutics The study of the way in which we interpret and attempt to understand phenomena such as texts, works of art, actions, and gestures. Although originally part of philosophy, hermeneutics has had an important influence on sociology.

hunter-gatherer A human being depending on the hunting of animals, fishing, and gathering of wild fruits and seeds for survival. Hunter-gatherer societies represent at least 90% of human history.

ideology Any system of ideas and beliefs. Many writers, such as Marx, use the term to refer to a distorted system of beliefs and ideas.

institutions Patterns of behavior which become established over the course of time. Sometimes used to refer to large organizations that have established codes of behavior. It can also refer to important social entities such as the state, the church, the family, and the law, which operate along set patterns of behavior.

kinship The way in which people are related by birth or through marriage in different societies.

matriarchal Describes a society in which the positions of power or dominance are held mainly by women. No historical proof of a truly matriarchal society has been found.

matrilineal Used to describe a society in which descent is traced through women.

monogamy A rule which permits men and women to have only one marriage partner at a time.

norms Social norms are standards of behavior or ideas which are common to a group. Conforming to social norms increases a group's identity.

nuclear family A family group of just parents and children living together or in close contact without other relatives.

patrilineal Used to describe a society in which descent is traced through men.

petite bourgeoisie *See* **bourgeoisie**.

physical anthropology A branch of anthropology which studies the biological characteristics of man, such as genetic makeup, blood types and bone structure.

polygamy Marriage to more than one person at the same time. The most common form of polygamy is polygyny, where a man has several wives. A less common form is polyandry, where a woman has several husbands.

proleteriat A class of people who sell their labor and who do not own the means of production in a capitalist society.

rites of passage Rituals which accompany the passage of an individual from one social status to another, e.g. the transition from adolescence to full adulthood.

shamanism A shaman is a religious specialist but, unlike a priest, a shaman does not belong to a Church. Personal mystical experience forms the basis of the shaman's spiritual knowledge such as healing, protecting through magic, and offering spiritual guidance. The term originally comes from Siberia but anthropologists have used it to describe certain individuals in cultures all round the world.

social anthropology A branch of anthropology concerned with the study of linguistics, archaeology, ethnography, and ethnology.

social darwinism A term associated with Herbert Spencer (1820–1903) who applied Darwin's theory of evolution to the social sphere. This postulated that natural selection allows those members of society who are well adapted to their social environment to flourish while the others fall by the wayside.

socialization The shaping of human behavior through experience in social institutions.

social stratification The ranking of social groups in a hierarchy. Castes, classes, and estates are different forms of social stratification.

society A group of people who form a system of relationships and have their own culture.

sociobiology The study of the biological basis for human behavior.

structuralism Structural anthropologists see cultural forms (e.g. customs, language, and tools used by man) as projections into this world of the inner workings of the human mind. The task of anthropology is to decode these cultural forms to reveal the principles through which the human mind operates.

taboo A word of Polynesian/Melanesian origin which is used in anthropology to refer to an action, object, or space which society regards as forbidden. For example, in many societies, incest is taboo.

totemism Originally a North American term, totemism is used to refer to a mystical or ritual relationship between a social group and a class of objects such as a species of plant or animal.

voodoo A religious cult practiced in Haiti and in parts of the Caribbean, Brazil, and the southern states of America. Voodoo mixes beliefs and rites of Africa with elements from the Catholic religion.

social sciences

A A member of the highest grouping into which society is divided by occupation, typically a senior manager, administrator, or professional.

affluent society A society in which resources are not scarce and most people live in comparative prosperity.

agrarian Being or belonging to a society based on cultivating crops.

alienation A state in which a person feels detached from the outside world and sometimes from his or her own feelings.

alternative society A section of a society in which people adopt a lifestyle different from the mainstream, perceived as being unconventional, less materialistic, and often more natural.

angst A feeling of anxiety or apprehension, often without a specific or identifiable cause.

anomie A feeling of anxiety, hopelessness, and lack of purpose caused by the absence or breakdown of standards and values in society.

anthropology The scientific study of humankind, including origins, behavior, religion, institutions, and social and cultural development.

B A member of the second highest grouping into which society is divided by occupation, typically a person in middle management, or in the intermediate ranks of an administrative or professional occupation.

behavioral science Any scientific discipline in which the behavior of people or animals is studied, such as sociology or psychology.

benefit The term used in the United Kingdom for welfare payments.

benefit fraud In the United Kingdom, the deliberate claiming of welfare payments to which you are not entitled.

blue-collar Belonging to or typical of people who work for wages rather than salary, often in manual jobs for which work clothes are worn.

bourgeoisie The class in society who control the means of production, such as capitalists and large employers, and, according to Marxist theory, oppress the working class.

Brahmin A member of a class with high social and cultural standing, especially a member of one of the older New England families.

C1 A member of the occupation grouping typically consisting of junior managers, supervisors, and clerical workers.

C2 A member of the occupation grouping typically consisting of skilled manual workers or manual workers who are in charge of others.

caste Any of several social classes into which a society may be divided, usually according to wealth, profession, or hereditary rank.

class Any of several strata in a society, usually based on relative wealth, profession, or hereditary rank.

class conflict The idea, found in communist theory, that the classes in society are engaged in a struggle, especially of the bourgeoisie against the suppressed working class.

class warrior A person who is actively involved in the struggle between classes, such as a working-class political agitator.

classless society A society without divisions according to economic and social status, one of the goals of communism.

collective unconscious In the psychology of Carl Jung, an area of the unconscious mind that all members of a society share, including instincts and religious feelings.

consanguinity The state of being related to another person by blood or through a shared ancestor.

corporate sector The area of a state's economy that is dominated by large corporations.

counterculture A culture within a society, consisting of people, especially the young, who reject the values of the mainstream.

D A member of the occupation grouping typically consisting of semiskilled or unskilled workers.

demographics The characteristics of a human population, especially with regard to such factors as numbers, growth, and distribution, often used in defining consumer markets.

dink Either partner in a young professional couple who have not had children (double income, no kids).

disadvantaged Lacking in some or many of the basic necessities of life, such as a decent standard of living, good housing, and medical care.

downwardly mobile Tending to drop in social or economic status.

E A member of the lowest occupation grouping, typically consisting of the long-term unemployed, the old, or the chronically ill.

ecofreak A militant environmentalist, especially one considered as excessive.

economic determinism The belief that all activities, such as cultural and political ones, arise from the economic organization of society.

ecowarrior A militant environmentalist.

ennui A feeling of general dissatisfaction and listlessness caused by boredom or lack of activity.

environmentalist A person who is concerned about the destruction or degradation of the earth's environment through pollution and overuse of finite resources.

ethnic cleansing The deliberate removal or killing of a minority ethnic group within a country by a dominant ethnic group.

ethnic group A group of people who share a common race, religion, language, or other characteristic.

ethnic minority An ethnic group that is not the dominant one in a particular society, such as an immigrant population.

ethnicity A person's ethnic background.

ethnicize To make something, for example a police force, more representative of the diverse ethnic groups that make up a society.

ethnology The scientific study of human cultures or peoples, especially with regard to their origins, distribution, or characteristics.

extrovert A person whose interests are directed outwardly rather than inwardly.

feminist A person who believes that women should have the same rights as men.

focus group A group of people who are taken as representative of the larger population and whose opinions on various matters are studied by market researchers or political analysts.

folklore The traditional beliefs, legends, or stories passed by word of mouth within a society.

folk memory Past events remembered in common amongst the members of a society.

Freudian Typical of the psychology of Sigmund Freud, especially in stressing the importance of the influence of infantile sexuality on the later adult.

gemeinschaft A society with many common personal ties, such as family or religious beliefs.

gesellschaft A society whose ties are formal or practical rather than personal .

health insurance Insurance that a person takes out to pay for medical treatment.

income support In the United Kingdom, welfare payments made to the unemployed or people on low incomes.

industrial action A British term for job action.

industrialized Possessing large-scale industries as an important part of the economy.

introvert A person whose interests are directed inwardly rather than outwardly.

job action A strike or slowdown carried out by a workforce as a protest or attempt to secure concessions from an employer.

Jungian Typical of the psychological theories of Carl Jung, especially his belief in the important effect of race and culture on an individual's psychology.

Keynesian Typical of the economic theories of John Maynard Keynes, particularly of his belief that governments must use monetary and fiscal regulation to keep unemployment down.

matrilineal Tracing descent through the mother's line.

Medicare A health insurance program for people over 65 years old, under which the government pays the medical expenses of qualifying people.

meritocracy A society in which people acquire status through their achievements or abilities.

middle class The class of people in a society who are above the working class but below the upper class, typically composed of professionals and managers.

mores The common ideas, conventions, or customs of a particular society or social group.

National Health Service The British system of free or low-cost medical and dental treatment for qualifying people, paid for by taxation.

nationalism Devotion to your country and its interests, often involving striving for independence from a larger political unit.

nationality The country or nation to which a person belongs through birth or naturalization.

nationalization The conversion of something, especially an industry, from private ownership to government ownership.

nimby A person who objects to something considered undesirable, such as a halfway house or industrial plant, being established in his or her neighborhood while being happy for it to be set up elsewhere (not in my back yard).

occupation grouping Any of the groups based on what people do for a living into which a society can be divided, often used by market researchers or advertizers.

opinion poll A poll that asks a sample of people for their feelings on a particular issue, such as what they think of a political party or a commercial product.

paleoanthropology The scientific study of primitive human beings.

pariah A person regarded as being an outcast from society.

patrilineal Tracing descent through the father's line.

peer group A group of people who are approximately equal in age or social status.

pink-collar Being or typical of jobs that were traditionally held by women, such as secretarial posts.

pluralism A situation in which several different ethnic or cultural groups coexist within a society.

plutocracy A society in which power is in the hands of wealthy people.

political economy The social science that studies both politics and economics, and in particular the interrelationship between them.

post-feminist Arising out of feminism and developing feminist ideas further.

postindustrial Describing a country or economy in which traditional heavy industries have declined in importance and have been largely replaced by service industries.

private enterprise The area of business that is privately owned and not regulated by state control.

privatization The conversion of something, especially an industry, from state ownership to private ownership.

psychiatry The branch of medicine that deals with mental disorders .

psychoanalysis A form of psychiatric therapy in which the therapist attempts to explore the unconscious mind of the subject, and uses the findings to help resolve mental or emotional problems.

psychology The scientific study of human and animal behavior and mental processes.

psychosocial Involving both psychological and social elements.

public assistance Aid given in the form of money or food by a government to the needy or homeless.

public housing Housing owned by a government that is rented at minimum rates to the needy.

recession A temporary decline in economic activity.

relief Public assistance.

sectarian Belonging to or involving a particular sect, denomination, or faction, especially when seen as narrow-minded or dogmatic.

social anthropology The branch of anthropology that studies the cultural and social aspects of human communities.

social climber A person who tries to gain acceptance to a social stratum above the one he or she currently occupies.

social engineering The process of applying sociological principles to problems in society.

socialization The process by which an individual, especially a child, becomes adapted to the norms of society.

social psychiatry The branch of psychiatry that deals with the effect of society on mental disorders.

social psychology The branch of psychology that deals with the effect of society on human behavior.

social sciences A group of disciplines that study human society and the relationships between it and its members, including anthropology, economics, history, political science, psychology, and sociology.

social security A government program that provides money to the needy, such as the unemployed; the money that is provided.

social work Work intended to improve the conditions of the disadvantaged in society, including counseling.

societal Belonging to or typical of society, especially in its organization.

sociobiology The scientific study of the effects of biological factors on human behavior and the evolution of societies.

sociolinguistics The study of the relationship between language and society.

sociology The scientific study of human societies, including their functioning, origins, and development.

sociopath A person suffering from a personality disorder that involves extreme antisocial behavior.

status symbol Something that is considered to give someone prestige in society, especially a possession.

taboo A prohibition that a society places on a particular form of behavior.

underclass The lowest level in a society, consisting largely of the disadvantaged or permanently unemployed.

upper class The highest class in society, usually made up of the wealthy and those holding hereditary rank.

upwardly mobile Tending to rise in wealth or social status.

urbanization The process of changing a rural area into an urban one.

welfare Money or other forms of aid provided to the needy by government.

welfare state A social system in which the state takes responsibility for the social and economic wellbeing of its citizens, especially in matters of health and social security.

white-collar Belonging to or typical of workers who do not carry out manual labor and who are usually expected to dress formally.

working class The class in society that works for wages.

archaeology

Abbevillian Belonging to an early period of the Paleolithic Age, characterized by primitive stone axes.

Acheulian Belonging to a period of the Paleolithic Age during which symmetrical stone axes were made.

acropolis The citadel or fortified high point in an ancient Greek city.

Anasazi A member of a people who lived in what is now the southwestern United States until around AD 100 . The Anasazi were weavers and potters, and built cliff dwellings in canyons.

antediluvian Belonging to a time before the flood described in the Bible.

antiquarian A person who collects or studies antiquities.

antiquity A thing, such as a ruin or an object, that dates from ancient times.

archaeology The study of the history of humankind, based on material evidence from the past, especially ruins of buildings and artifacts.

archaeomagnetism A technique used to date ancient clay objects by measuring how much they have been magnetized by the earth's magnetic field.

Assyriology The study of the civilization and archaeological remains of ancient Assyria.

Aurignacian Belonging to a period of the Paleolithic Age during which primitive humans used bone and antler tools and made cave paintings.

Azilian Belonging to a Paleolithic culture in southern France and Spain.

Aztec A member of a people who ruled an empire in central Mexico and were overthrown by Spanish conquistadors under Cortès in the 16th century.

balk A strip of ground left unexcavated between two trenches dug at an archaelogical site.

barrow A large mound of earth heaped up over a prehistoric tomb.

bogman Any human body found preserved in a peat bog, such as in Ireland.

bracteate A thinly beaten gold or silver plate or dish.

broch A circular, drystone Iron Age tower containing living quarters, common in the north of Scotland and thought to have been used as a fortified home.

Bronze Age The period between the Stone Age and the Iron Age during which people discovered how to make tools and weapons from bronze.

burin A prehistoric flint tool like a chisel.

cairn A mound of stones built as a memorial or marker, often above a grave.

callais A type of green stone used in Neolithic and early Bronze Age times to make ornaments and beads.

carbon dating A technique used in determining the age of an archaeological find based on establishing how much it contains of carbon-14, which decays at a known rate.

cartouche An oval or oblong figure containing a royal or divine name in ancient Egyptian hieroglyphics.

caveman A prehistoric human being who lived in a cave, especially in the Paleolithic Age.

cave painting A painting or drawing made on the wall of a cave dwelling by primitive human beings. Often showing hunting scenes, particularly fine examples of these were discovered in caves near Lascaux in southern France.

celt A prehistoric stone or metal implement shaped like an ax head.

chalcolithic Belonging to a prehistoric period during which both stone and bronze tools were used.

cist A Neolithic tomb made of stone slabs.

clovis point A leaf-shaped flint projectile point with fluted sides belonging to a prehistoric culture of North and Central America.

crannog A dwelling built on a natural or artificial island in a lake or bog by ancient Celtic peoples in Ireland and Scotland. Such sites, often fortified, were chosen because they were easily defended.

Cro-Magnon man An early form of human being who lived in Europe in Paleolithic times.

cromlech A prehistoric circle of standing stones, sometimes encircling a mound.

cross-dating A method of establishing the age of archaeological finds or remains by comparing them with other finds or remains which sometimes have known dates.

cyclopean Built using massive, irregularly-shaped, uncemented blocks of stone, as was common in pre-classical ancient Greek architecture.

dig An archaeological excavation, or a site where one is being carried out.

dolmen A Neolithic structure consisting of a large flat stone supported horizontally on two or more upright stones, thought to have been used as a tomb.

earthwork An embankment of earth constructed as a fortification.

Egyptology The study of the civilization and archaeological remains of ancient Egypt.

eolith A primitive tool made of a roughly broken stone, especially flint.

Eolithic Belonging to the earliest period of the Stone Age, during which primitive human beings began to use stone tools and weapons.

fosse A ditch or moat dug as a fortification.

fossil The remains of a prehistoric plant or animal found preserved in a solid, mineralized form in rocks or, sometimes, frozen in ice.

fossilize To turn something into a fossil.

graffito A drawing or inscription carved or scratched onto a surface such as a rock or piece of pottery, or on the wall of an ancient building.

grave goods Tools, weapons, clothing, or other objects found in ancient tombs, presumably placed there for the deceased to use in the afterlife.

Gravettian Belonging to a Paleolithic culture in southwestern France in which people made small, pointed stone blades with blunt backs.

Helladic Belonging to a Bronze Age culture in Greece and the Greek Islands.

henge A circle of standing stones or wooden posts, often surrounding a burial chamber, dating from the Paleolithic Age or the Bronze Age.

Heroic Age A period in an ancient culture, such as in that of ancient Greece, during which the heros and demigods recorded in legend were believed to have lived.

hieroglyphics An ancient Egyptian form of writing using pictures and symbols to represent objects, names, or sounds, often found carved on monuments.

hillfort A prehistoric stronghold with ditches and ramparts, constructed on top of a hill.

hogback A Saxon or Viking tomb that curves down toward the ends and has sloping sides.

hut circle A circle of earth or stones that marks where a prehistoric hut once stood.

hypocaust A space beneath the floor in an ancient Roman villa in which hot air from a fire or furnace was circulated to heat the house.

Ice Age A period during which glaciers advanced to cover large parts of the earth's surface, the most recent occurring over 11,000 years ago.

Inca A member of a people who ruled a South American empire

centered on Peru and were overthrown by Spanish
conquistadors in the 16th century.

Iron Age The period in human history following the Bronze Age,
during which people discovered how to make iron tools and
weapons.

Java man A type of primitive human being that lived in the
Stone Age in Java.

kist *See* cist.

La Tène Belonging to an Iron Age Celtic culture in Europe dating
from the 5th to the 1st century BC, known for a characterictic
curvilinear style of decoration used in artifacts.

larnax An ancient Greek coffin made of terracotta and often
ornamented.

Levalloisian Belonging to a Stone Age culture in western Europe,
in which people made tools from flint by striking off flakes to
give one flat side and one domed side.

ley line A line, usually straight, joining two features in a
landscape, thought to have been a prehistoric pathway or to
have some kind of magical significance.

long barrow A mound of earth constructed over a Neolithic stone
tomb.

Magdelenian Belonging to the latest Paleolithic culture in
Europe.

Maya A member of a people who ruled an empire in what is now
southeast Mexico, Guatemala, and Belize. The Maya built
complex cities and great temples and developed mathematics,
hieroglyphic writing, and the use of a calendar.

megalith Any very large stone used in prehistoric buildings or
monuments, especially in western Europe.

megaron The large, rectangular, main room in a Bronze Age
Greek house.

menhir A prehistoric monument consisting of a single large
standing stone, found especially in the British Isles and
northern France.

Mesolithic Belonging to the middle period of the Stone Age,
during which people made small flint tools.

microlith A small prehistoric flint tool.

Minoan Belonging to a Bronze Age culture in Crete from around
3000 BC to 1100 BC.

monolith A single large block of stone as used in a prehistoric
monument.

Mousterian Belonging to a Paleolithic culture associated with
Neanderthal man, during which tools made from flaked flint
were used.

Mycenaean Belonging to a Bronze Age culture in mainland

Greece, the Greek islands, and Asia Minor, centered on the city of Mycenae.

Neanderthal man A type of primitive human being that lived in Europe in the Paleolithic Age.

neolith A stone tool belonging to Neolithic times.

Neolithic Belonging to the latest period of the Stone Age, during which polished stone tools were made and people began to grow crops and keep animals.

New Stone Age The Neolithic period.

obelisk A tall, four-sided, stone pillar, especially one erected as a monument in ancient Egypt.

Old Stone Age The Paleolithic period.

Olmec A member of a people of southern Mexico and the surrounding regions whose civilization predates the Maya.

paleolith A stone tool belonging to Paleolithic times.

Paleolithic Belonging to the earliest period of the Stone Age, during which primitive human beings emerged and the first stone tools were made.

paleontology The study of plants and animals that existed in prehistoric times, based on fossil remains.

palmette A design or ornament in the form of a stylized palm leaf, often used in ancient architecture.

palstave An ancient bronze implement like an ax head, made to fit into a split wooden handle.

Peking man A type of primitive human being, remains of which were found in China.

Piltdown man A supposed type of primitive human being based on remains found in England in 1912, later discovered to have been a hoax.

pithecanthropus A type of primitive human being.

pre-Columbian Belonging to the Americas in the period before the arrival of Christopher Columbus.

prehistoric Belonging to the period before writing or recorded history.

protohistory The study of a particular human culture in the period immediately before it developed writing or recorded history.

pylon A gateway to an ancient Egyptian temple.

pyramid A massive ancient Egyptian building erected over or containing a tomb, with four triangular sides tapering to a point at the top.

radiocarbon dating carbon dating

robber trench A trench at an archaeological site that originally contained stones that made up the foundation of a wall but which were taken away for some later use.

Rosetta Stone An inscribed basalt slab dating from around 196 BC, found near Rosetta, a town in northern Egypt, in 1799. Because it carried the same text in hieroglyphics, demotic Egyptian, and Greek, it was of vital use in deciphering hieroglyphics.

round barrow A mound of earth constructed over a Bronze Age tomb or site of a cremation.

Solutrean Belonging to a Paleolithic culture in Europe, coming between the Aurignacian and the Magdelenian, in which people made flint blades.

sondage A deep trench excavated at an archaeological site in order to make an initial examination of the different layers of earth.

souterrain Any underground passage or chamber.

standing stone Any large stone erected to stand upright, either alone or as part of a group, in prehistoric times.

stele An upright stone slab or tablet, often decorated or carved with inscriptions, common in prehistoric times.

step pyramid A type of pyramid with distinctly terraced rather than smoothly ascending sides.

stone circle A Neolithic or Bronze Age circular formation of standing stones, such as at Stonehenge, England, thought to have a connection with astronomical observation.

stratigraphy A section cut vertically in the ground and used, by examining the different layers, to determine the chronology of human artifacts or settlement remains that are found buried.

tholos A type of tomb, shaped like a beehive and built of unmortared stones, associated with the Mycenaean culture in ancient Greece.

Toltec A member of a people who ruled an empire in central and southern Mexico before being conquered by the Aztecs.

tribrach A prehistoric flint tool with three projections.

trilithon A prehistoric structure consisting of two large upright stones supporting a third horizontal stone.

tumulus An ancient grave mound or barrow.

vallum An ancient Roman rampart or wall made of earth or piled sods.

villa An ancient Roman country house with both residential and farm buildings arranged around a courtyard.

ziggurat An ancient Assyrian or Babylonian temple in the form of a pyramid with terraced sides tapering toward the top.

the zodiac

air One of the four elements; associated with the intellect and thought.

astrology The study of the coincidences between planetary positions and events. While it is said that planets "influence" events, the modern view is that coincidence is a more valid term. This view stems from the work of psychologist Carl Jung on synchronicity.

astrology

birthchart A chart showing the positions of the Sun, Moon and planets at the time of a person's birth, relative to the place of birth.

cardinal One of the three qualities; associated with receptivity, initiative and executive action.

earth One of the four elements; associated with practical reality.

element The elements represent general characteristics that are linked with certain zodiac signs. There are four elements: fire, air, earth and water.

fire One of the four elements; associated with activity and enthusiasm.

fixed One of the three qualities; associated with stability, determination and consistency.

horoscope A birthchart calculated according to the exact time of birth.

mutable One of the three qualities; associated with adaptability, adjustment and harmonization.

opposite signs The zodiac signs opposite each other on the zodiac wheel, as follows (and vice versa):

Sign	Opposite sign
Aries	Libra
Taurus	Scorpio
Gemini	Sagittarius
Cancer	Capricorn
Leo	Aquarius
Virgo	Pisces

planets The eight major bodies, apart from Earth, which move around the Sun: Mercury, Venus, Mars, Jupiter, Saturn, Uranus, Neptune and Pluto. It is an astrological convention to also include the Sun and the Moon when speaking of the planets, making ten astrological planets in all.

quality The qualities describe behaviors associated with certain zodiac signs. There are three qualities: cardinal, fixed and mutable.

rising sign The sign of the zodiac which is on the eastern horizon at the time of a person's birth. Also known as the Ascendent. This sign is said to indicate the general outlook, appearance, survival strategy and outer personality of people born at that time.

ruling planet Each zodiac sign is said to be especially "influenced" by one or more of the planets, as follows:

Sign	Ruling planet
Aries	Mars
Taurus	Venus
Gemini	Mercury
Cancer	Moon
Leo	Sun
Virgo	Mercury
Libra	Venus
Scorpio	Mars and Pluto
Sagittarius	Jupiter
Capricorn	Saturn
Aquarius	Saturn and Uranus
Pisces	Jupiter and Neptune

ruling planet
Zodiac signs

Aries
Taurus
Gemini
Cancer
Leo
Virgo
Libra
Scorpio
Sagittarius
Capricorn
Aquarius
Pisces

star sign Common misnomer for sun sign.

sun sign The sign of the zodiac occupied by the sun on the date of birth.

water One of the four elements; associated with sensitivity and emotion.

zodiac An imaginary band, viewed as if from the centre of the solar system, and divided into twelve segments of 30 degrees. Each segment is named after a nearby constellation of stars.

zodiac characteristics A group of characteristics associated with a sign, which have been built up from observation of events that happened when the sun was in that sign. The characteristics of people born under each sign also form a part of the astrological body of knowledge.

zodiac position The exact position of the Sun is given as between 0 and 29 degrees 59 minutes of each sign. The positions of the planets are also given in the same way. The positions at any particular time can be calculated in advance from astronomical tables.

fortune telling

aeromancy Divination by atmospheric conditions. There are several different forms, including austromancy, ceraunoscopy, chaomancy, and meteormancy.

ailuromancy Divination from cats.

alectryomancy A form of augury, in this case divination from the eating patterns of sacred chickens.

aleuromancy Divination using slips of paper baked in doughballs. The modern equivalent are Chinese fortune cookies.

alphitomancy Divination using cakes made of wheat or barley flour.

arachnomancy A form of augury, in this case divination from the appearance and behavior of spiders.

arithomancy A form of divination in which numbers are believed to exert an influence on our lives and personality. This is also called numerology or numeromancy.

astragalomancy A form of sortilege which in this case is divination using the bones of sheep.

astrology A form of divination using the stars and planets and involving the signs of the zodiac.

augury Divination based mainly on the appearance and behavior of animals. Haruspicy is sometimes considered part of augury.

austromancy A form of aeromancy, in this case divination using the wind.

belomancy A form of sortilege which in this case is divination by arrows.

bibliomancy A form of sortilege which in this case is divination from books and which includes rhapsodomancy. It is also called stichomancy.

botanomancy A form of pyromancy which in this case is divination by burning leaves and branches.

capnomancy A form of pyromancy which in this case is divination by smoke.

cartomancy A form of divination using modern playing cards.

catoptromancy A form of scrying which in this case involves divination by gazing into a mirror.

causinomancy A form of pyromancy which in this case is divination by objects cast into the fire.

cephalomancy A form of augury, in this case divination from the skull or head of a donkey or goat.

ceraunoscopy A form of aeromancy, in this case divination using thunder and lightning.

ceromancy Divination from melted wax.

chaomancy A form of aeromancy, in this case divination using aerial visions.

chirognomy Divination using the palm of the hand but which also includes an analysis of hand shape, fingers and fingernails. It is also called chirology, chiromancy, and palmistry.

clairaudience A form of clairvoyance which in this case is hearing the future ahead of time.

clairvoyance A form of divination by seeing the future ahead of time. There are many different forms of clairvoyance, including clairaudience, metagnomy, precognition, and psychometry.

cleidomancy A form of radiesthesia, which in this case is divination using a suspended key. Used in dowsing.

cleromancy An alternative name for sortilege.

coscinomancy A form of radiesthesia which in this case is divination using a suspended sieve.

crithomancy Divination using the markings on freshly baked bread.

cromniomancy Divination using onions.

crystallomancy A form of scrying which in this case involves divination with a crystal ball.

dactylomancy A form of radiesthesia which in this case is divination using a suspended ring. May be used in dowsing.

daphnomancy A form of pyromancy which in this case is divination by the burning of laurel leaves.

dowsing A method of divination used to locate things, often using special rods, under the earth, including water, mineral deposits, bodies, archaeological sites, cables, pipes, tunnels, lost property or hidden treasure. Dowsing may involve radiesthesia.

entomomancy A form of augury which in this case is divination from the appearance and behavior of insects.

geomancy Divination by the earth. This can mean use of actual earth, or earth-like substances such as sand.

graphology A method of assessing a person's character from their handwriting.

halomancy A form of pyromancy which in this case is divination by casting salt into a fire.

haruspicy Divination from the entrails of animals, one form of which is hepatoscopy; sometimes considered part of augury.

hepatoscopy A form of haruspicy which in this case is divination using the liver.

hippomancy Divination from horses.

hydromancy A form of scrying which in this case is divination by water. Pegomancy is a form of hydromancy.

I Ching An ancient Chinese text (also known as the Book of Changes) from which one's fortune can be predicted.

ichthyomancy A form of augury which in this case is divination from the shape and entrails of fish.

lampadomancy Divination using a single oil lamp or a torch flame.

lithomancy Divination using precious stones.

lychnomancy Divination from the flames of three wax candles.

metagnomy A form of clairvoyance which in this case is seeing future events when in a hypnotic trance.

meteormancy A form of aeromancy, in this case divination using meteors and shooting stars.

metoposcopy A method of assessing character and fortune from lines on the forehead.

moleoscopy A method of assessing character from moles on the body.

molybdomancy Divination using molten tin or lead.

myomancy A form of augury which in this case is divination from the color and movement of mice.

necromancy Asking the dead to answer questions about the future using automatic writing, a ouija board, or through a medium.

numerology A form of divination in which numbers are believed to exert an influence on our lives and personality. This is also called numeromancy or arithomancy.

oenomancy A form of augury which in this case is divination from the patterns made by wine.

oneiromancy A form of divination based on dreams.

ophiomancy A form of augury which in this case is divination from the color and movement of snakes.

Oriental astrology A form of eastern divination based on a 12-year cycle and involving 12 animals which, unlike the zodiac signs of western astrology, are not based on the configuration or movement of planets or stars.

ornithomancy Divination using the sound, appearance, and flight of birds.

palmistry Divination using the palm of the hand but which also includes an analysis of hand shape, fingers and fingernails. It is also called chirognomy, chirology, or chiromancy.

pegomancy A form of hydromancy which in this case is divination using a sacred pool or spring.

pessomancy A form of sortilege which in this case is divination by drawing or casting of specially marked pebbles. This is also called psephomancy.

phrenology Assessing character from the presence of bumps on

palmistry

the head, developed by F. J. Gall in the nineteenth century.

phyllorhodomancy Divination using rose petals.

physiognomy Character analysis using facial features.

precognition A form of clairvoyance which in this case is an inner paranormal knowledge of the future.

psephomancy Another word for pessomancy.

psychometry A form of clairvoyance which in this case involves divination about a specific person, brought about by holding an object belonging to them.

pyromancy Divination by fire. There are many different forms, including, botanomancy, capnomancy, causinomancy, daphnomancy, halomancy, pyroscopy, and sideromancy.

pyroscopy A form of pyromancy, which in this case is divination by burning a sheet of paper on a white surface and examining the resulting stains.

radiesthesia The use of a pendulum for divination. There are different forms, including cleidomancy, coscinomancy, and dactylomancy. Radiesthesia is often used when dowsing.

rhapsodomancy A form of bibliomancy which in this case is divination from a book of poetry.

runes Symbols of an ancient alphabet, used for divination.

scapulomancy A form of augury which in this case is divination from the patterns or cracks and fissures on the burned shoulder blade of an animal.

scrying Divination by gazing into a reflective surface. There are many different forms, including crystallomancy, catoptromancy, and hydromancy.

runes

sideromancy A form of pyromancy which in this case is divination by casting an odd number of straws onto iron brought to red heat in a fire and reading the patterns formed by straws, their movements, and the nature or the flames and smoke.

sortilege A form of divination by the casting or drawing of lots. There are many different types including astragalomancy, belomancy, bibliomancy, pessomancy, rhapsodomancy and stichomancy. It is also called cleromancy.

stichomancy A form of sortilege which in this case is divination using books. This is also called bibliomancy. Rhapsodomancy is a form of stichomancy.

tasseography Divination using tea leaves.

tephromancy Divination using the patterns formed in the ashes of burnt offerings made to the gods.

tyromancy Divination from cheese.

zoomancy A form of augury which in this case is divination from the appearance and behavior of any animal.

paranormal

anima/animus The spirit of the opposite sex within the subject (female in men, male in women).

apparition A ghost, or something that appears to be present.

astral body The consciousness of the soul independent of the physical body in which it resides.

astral projection A breaking free by the astral body, believed to occur just before death or during some dreams; also known as out-of-body experience.

astral trip A self-induced out-of-body experience in which the astral body is projected.

atman The divine cosmic principle of the monad.

aura The pulsating field of energy which surrounds living things.

automatic writing The writing of words or symbols without conscious intention, sometimes through a medium.

birth The initial moment of independent, conscious life.

body The biological, physical self.

body-mind A term encompassing the whole person.

creative anxiety State immediately preceding expression of a insight or creative thought.

daat Ultimate knowledge.

deja vu The sensation of repeating a previous experience (French for "already seen").

doppelganger The wraith (e.g. id, astral body, or shadow) of a living being (German for "double-goer.")

dowsing A method of locating something that is hidden or buried using a stick or pendulum.

eidolon An imprint or image of the body left after death on the astral plane (from the Greek for "image").

elementals Disembodied etheric forces including gnomes, sylphs and undines.

entelechy The physical achievement or realization of a potential.

etheric body An image of the monad; the life force.

extrasensory perception (ESP) Ability to perceive beyond the normal range of the senses.

gnomes The earth elementals.

hallucination A perception or image of an external object that is not there in reality.

hypnogogic state A state between waking and sleeping or vice versa, often characterized by hallucinatory images.

incubation The inducement of dreams.

individuality The spirit; another term for the monad.

intelligences In Cabbalism, the seven spirits guiding the soul through the Tree of Life.

invocation The calling down of a spirit to be manifested in a physical form.

kirlian photography A method of making a photographic image of an aura.

lost souls Souls that are out of contact with their monads and are thus unable to evolve further.

lucid dream A dream that can be induced or controlled and is characterized by the dreamer being aware that he or she is dreaming.

manas The monad's cosmic intelligence, or ability to understand.

matter The physical being.

medium Someone who serves as an intermediary between the living and the dead.

mind The thinking part of the physical body.

monad Spritual individuality that is reincarnated.

near-death experience (NDE) An occasion when the mind or soul leaves the physical body temporarily. *Compare* **out-of-body experience**.

out-of-body experience (OBE) An occasion when an individual separates from and views from above his or her physical body. *Compare* **near-death experience**.

precognition The ability to predict the future using extrasensory perception.

serial dream A dream which continues a theme or story as one of a series of dreams.

sylphs Spirits of the air.

undines Female water spirits.

magic

abracadabra A magic word perhaps derived from the name of the demon Abraxas. In numerology, the letters in the name Abraxas add up to 365, the number of days of the year.

air signs The zodiac signs Gemini, Libra and Aquarius, all of which are associated with the element Air.

alchemy The practice of turning base metals into gold but also of attaining spiritual perfection.

amulet A charm with magic power, made from a substance that protects against evil, such as wood, stone or metal and inscribed with magical characters or figures. They may be used to invoke the help of spirits and divert evil from the wearer but do not necessarily attract luck to the wearer or endow them with magical qualities.

anagogue A mystical interpretation of a word or passage in a text.

angel A form of good spirit residing in heaven.

anima female spirituality

animus male spirituality

asson A rattle used by voodoo priests and priestesses to summon the "loa," one of many vodoun gods.

athame A black-handled knife used by witches in magic ceremonies.

babalawo A priest of the highest order belonging to the Santería religion, similar to vodoun, with magic powers, including the ability to heal the sick, divine the future and punish wrongdoers.

bakor Also known as a "boko," this is a "houngan" involved in black magic.

Beltane An ancient Celtic festival held on May 1 at which ritual bonfires were lit and purification rites were carried out.

besom Also called a broomstick, this is a tool used by witches to help them fly. Modern witches use a besom to carry out ritual cleaning.

birth number An unchangeable number which, according to numerologists, reveals the influence of numbers at the time of birth.

black art Another name for black magic or witchcraft.

Black Book A book kept by the master of a coven into which the names of newly-initiated witches were written during the medieval sabbat.

black books Also called grimoires, these are handbooks of magic in which the names of demons are often set out, with instructions for their invocation and exorcism.

black cakes Cakes made from black millet and the flesh of unbaptized infants, believed to be presented to the Devil by witches during a medieval sabbat.

black magic Magic used for evil purposes.

black magician A magician who practices magic for the purposes of evil. In medieval times such a person may have been called a sorcerer.

black mass A black magic ceremony in which a perversion of the Roman Catholic Mass is used.

black witch A witch who practices magic for the purposes of evil. In medieval times such a person may have been called a sorcerer. In the Santería religion a black witch (also known as a "mayombero") is a "santero" who specializes in necromancy, revenge and the destruction of human life.

blasting rod Also called a rod or wand, this is a tool used by witches and magicians for conjuring and directing energy.

boko Also known as a "bakor," this is a "houngan" involved in Black Magic.

bokor A voodoo sorcerer.

Book of Shadows Also known as the Book of Spells, this is a book used by modern witches for recording spells and rituals, magic diagrams, recipes and anything associated with their art.

cabala Also known as the kabala, kabbalah and qabalah, this is an ancient Hebrew mystical doctrine, elements of which are sometimes used in witchcraft.

cantrip A Scottish word for a magic spell.

cauldron Associated with medieval witches, this is a large iron pot in which poisons, ointments and philtres were brewed.

cauldron

Celtic Tree Alphabet Also known as Ogham staves or Ogam staves, this is an ancient alphabet consisting of 25 symbols, described by Robert Graves in The White Goddess and used by modern druids for divination.

censer Used by witches and magicians, this is a small container used to burn incense, herbs, chemicals, wood, etc.

chalice Used in modern witchcraft, this is a cup or goblet often associated with the element Water.

charm Anything that protects against evil.

charm wand A glass rod resembling a walking stick, filled with seeds, used to protect a house from evil spirits.

circle of being The name used by some modern witches to describe a magic circle.

chalice

cone of power Also known as "raising the power," this is a heightening of awareness brought about in modern witch ceremonies by chanting and dancing.

conjuration A magic spell, or the practice of casting magic spells.

conjure To summon a devil or spirit using magic.

conjure man Also called a witch doctor, "jujuman," root doctor, "obeahaman" and leaf doctor, this is a priest and physician called upon by African tribal members and followers of religions such as vodoun, Santería and macumba. Conjure men practitioners who use their powers only for good are known as "ngangas."

cord A ceremonial cord made from silk, other natural material or nylon, used by some modern witches.

correspondences A system used by magicians for relating things—especially, planets, elements, signs of the zodiac and numbers—to each other.

coven A group of witches.

cunning folk Also known as white witches, these were medieval witches believed to practice magic for the purposes of good rather than evil.

dedication A term used by some witches for initiation.

demon An evil spirit that may take many different forms. In Western tradition they are sometimes referred to as infernal spirits and have been said to exist in hundreds of thousands. In other traditions they are thought to exist in billions.

demonic possession Possession by a demon, sometimes resulting in strange behavior such as the vomiting of strange objects.

deosil clockwise

devas Water elementals who live in streams, rivers, clouds and mists.

devils grease

devil's grease Also known as "unguentum sabbati" or witches' salve, this is a lotion believed to have been used by medieval witches to enable them to fly. The principal ingredient was thought to be infant flesh.

devil's mark A mark given to witches by the Devil during their initiation. (Note, this is different from a witch's mark).

Devil, the God's adversary, also called Satan Lucifer (the name he was given before he was thrown out of heaven for opposing God), Satan or Lucifer. The worst of all demons, he is portrayed in many different forms, often as a black goat, or with three horns, the taloned feet of a bird of prey, the claws of an alligator and a second face where his genitals would be.

Dianus Also known as the Horned God or "Janu," this is a fertility god worshiped by some modern witches who claim there is no relationship between this deity and the Devil.

doppelganger A ghostly double of a person who is still alive.

drawing down the moon A term used by some modern witches for the casting of a magic circle.

Druids Celtic people who, in Europe in ancient times, acted as judges, lawmakers and priests and practiced divination. Druids today use the Ogham staves as a means of divination.

Earth Mother Also known as the Great Mother, this is a deity worshiped by some modern witches.

ebbos In the Santería religion this is a counter spell cast by a "santero."

effigy Also called a "fith-fath," this is a doll-like image of a person made using material such as wax, clay or straw and used by witches and magicians for inflicting injury or death or for healing purposes. They are particularly important in love and death spells.

Druid

element One of four elements, Earth, Air, Fire or Water, believed to be particularly significant to magic ritual, for hundreds of years linked to other things (such as the planets and the signs of the zodiac), using a system of correspondences.

elementals These are disembodied beings that have no spirit and consist mainly of etheric forces. They are also sometimes called sprites.

elixir of life Also known as the Philosopher's Stone, this was a substance alchemists attempted to make in order to restore youth, prolong life and turn metals into gold.

enchanter A male sorcerer or magician.

enchantment A magic spell or the practice of casting magic spells.

enchantress A female magician or sorceress.

esbat One of thirteen modern witch rituals carried out during a full-moon.

evil eye Also known as overlooking or fascinating this is a worldwide belief in the ability of some people (especially witches) and animals to bring about harm by looking at someone.

exorcism A ritual performed to expel an evil spirit.

fairies Air elementals who live in light and thought.

familiar A low-ranking demon given to a witch by the Devil for the purpose of strengthening the witch's power. In medieval times familiars were commonly thought to be animals such as cats, dogs, rabbits and toads. In shamanism, a familiar is a spirit who protects a shaman from illness and unfriendly forces and is also known as a totemic animal, guardian spirit, power animal, or tutelary spirit.

fascinating *See* evil eye.

fates Air elementals who live in light and thought.

fetch An apparition or doppelganger.

fetish An object believed to hold magical or spiritual power, especially one used by a shaman.

fith-fath *See* **effigy**.

flying ointment *See* **devil's grease**.

gematria A magico-philosophical science of numbers found in the cabala and based on the 22 letters of the Hebrew alphabet.

genie A spirit that does the bidding of the person who summons or releases it.

ghost dance A Native American ceremonial group dance carried out as part of the observation of a religion that foretold the resurrection of ancestors and the disappearance of the white people.

gibbous moon Also called a humped Moon this is when the Moon appears between half and full.

gnomes Earth elementals who live in stones and trees.

gramarye An old word for magic or the occult.

Great Mother *See* **Earth Mother**.

gremlin A mythical creature believed to tamper with all kinds of machinery.

grimoires *See* **black books**.

guardian spirit *See* **familiar**.

Gypsy wise women Gypsy women with the power of divination.

hagridden Used to describe a person who is being harassed by a witch.

hakata Bones, dice, seeds or shells which, in religions such as vodoun, are used by a witch doctor for divination.

hand of glory The hand of a hanged man which, when dried according to specific ritual, can be used to cast a spell on others in which they fall into a death-like trance.

hexagram

hedgewitch A witch who practices alone rather than in a coven.

hex Another word for witchcraft, sometimes used to mean a spell or the sign of a star within a circle often painted on barn doors, perhaps as a means of warding off the evil eye.

hexagram A six-pointed star, also known as the Star of David, used in magic (especially black magic), representing the balance between masculine and feminine.

Horned God *See* **Dianus**.

houngan Also known as a voodoo priest, papa or papa-loa, in the vodoun religion this is a man who summons vodoun gods in order to divine the future or heal. A houngan involved in black magic is known as a "bakor" or "boko."

incubus

incubus A demon sent by the Devil to have sexual intercourse with sleeping women. Incubi are sex elementals and may be half human, half animal.

infernal hierarchy A proposed hierarchy for the demons in Hell.

infernal spirit Another name for a demon, an evil spirit residing in Hell and which may take many different forms.

instruments of the art Tools used by witches and magicians.

italeros A "babalawo" who practices divination using seashells.

Janu *See* **Dianus.**

jinn An Arab name for a spirit.

juju An object used in Africa as a charm, fetish, or amulet.

jujuman Also called a witch doctor, "obeahman," root doctor, conjure man and leaf doctor, this is a priest and physician called upon by African tribal members and followers of religions such as vodoun, Santería and macumba. Jujumen practitioners who use their powers only for good are known as "ngangas."

kabbala *See* **cabala.**

King's evil Another name for scrofula, a disease of the glands of the neck, which, during the Middle Ages was believed to be cured by the touch of a monarch.

kisengue A scepter (a human tibia bone wrapped in black cloth) given to a "mayombero" during his initiation ceremony.

kiss of shame Also known as osculum infame, the "obscene kiss," the practice of kissing the Devil's buttocks during a medieval sabbat.

lamia A mythological monster, half woman and half serpent, preying on human beings.

leaf doctor Also called a witch doctor, jujuman, root doctor, conjure man and "obeahaman," this is a priest and physician called upon by African tribal members and followers of religions such as vodoun, Santería and macumba.

loa The voodoo name for a god.

Lucifer Another name for the Devil.

lycanthrope Creatures that are half human, half animal, the most well-known of which is the werewolf.

mage An old word for a magician.

magic circle A circle used by witches and magicians to concentrate their powers and protect against psychic entities. Witches may call the circle the circle of being.

magic circle

magician A man who practices magic, perhaps using the cabala.

magic square A square made up of smaller squares each containing a number, popular with magicians for making talismans.

magus Originally meaning a priest of the Zoroastrian religion, this came to refer to a magician or sorcerer.

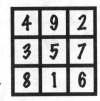

magic square

mam Also known as a "manman," "mambo" or voodoo priestess, in the vodoun religion this is a woman who summons vodoun gods in order to divine the future or heal.

mandrake A plant with a human-shaped root believed to have particularly magical qualities.

mayombero Also known as a black witch, this is a "santero" who specializes in necromancy, revenge and the destruction of human life.

medicine man Also called a shaman, this is someone with magic powers resulting from contact with the supernatural. Common in the religion of the Inuits, Maoris, Mongolians, Polynesians and Native Americans.

mojo A charm or amulet that is worn to protect the wearer against evil.

name number A changeable number which, according to numerologists, shows someone's acquired or developed personality traits.

necromancy The summoning of the dead for the purposes of divination.

nganga A special cauldron which holds the magical powers and potions of a mayombero.

ngangas Witch doctors who use their powers only for good.

ngozi A grudge-bearing spirit in vodoun religion.

numerology A form of divination in which numbers are believed to exert an influence on every facet of our lives and personalities.

nymphs Water elementals who live in streams, rivers, clouds and mists.

obeahman Also called a witch doctor, jujuman, root doctor, conjure man and leaf doctor, this is a priest and physician called upon by African tribal members and followers of religions such as vodoun, Santería and macumba. Obeahman practitioners who use their powers only for good are known as "ngangas."

occult The occult is the realm of magic and the supernatural, or any knowledge or practices involved in this.

ogham staves *See* **Celtic Tree Alphabet**.

olympic spirit One of seven spirits (Aratron, Bethor, Hagith, Och, Ophiel, Phalec, and Phul) closely related to the seven planets.

overlooking *See* **evil eye**.

pact with the Devil An agreement made by an individual with the Devil in which a person agrees to carry out evil deeds in return for wealth or power.

palindromes These are words or phrases that read the same backward or forward. They were often made into magic squares and were believed to have powerful magic properties.

papa Also known as a voodoo priest, "houngan" or papa-loa, in the vodoun religion this is a man who summons vodoun gods in order to divine the future or heal.

pact with the Devil

pentacle A five-pointed star within a circle, used as a means of protection by witches and magicians.

pentagram A five-pointed star used in many magic rituals including the invoking or banishing of spirits. In some positions it represents the Devil.

pentacle

periapt A charm or amulet worn to protect the wearer against evil.

philosopher's mercury According to alchemists this is mercury from which earth, air, fire and water have been removed. It is associated with prima materia, the substance from which all other matter is composed.

Philosopher's Stone Also known as the elixir of life this was a substance that alchemists attempted to discover or make in order to restore youth, prolong life and turn base metals into gold.

philtre A love potion originally made by combining wine, herbs and drugs.

possession The condition of being dominated by an evil spirit.

power animal Also known as a guardian spirit, tutelary spirit, totemic animal or familiar, this is a spirit who protects a shaman from illness and unfriendly forces.

prima materia According to alchemists this is the substance from which all other matter is composed. It was associated with philosopher's mercury, mercury from which Earth, Air, Fire and Water have been removed.

puffer An alchemist who concentrated solely on turning base metals into gold. The term later came to be used to describe any kind of alchemist.

qabalah *See* cabala.

raising the power Also known as the cone of power this is a heightening of awareness brought about in modern witch ceremonies by chanting and dancing.

resguardo In the Santería religion this is a protective talisman made by a "santero."

ring of gyges A magic ring believed to make the wearer invisible.

rod Also called a wand or blasting rod, this is a tool used by witches and magicians for conjuring and directing energy.

root doctor Also called a witch doctor, jujuman, conjure man, "obeahaman" or leaf doctor, this is a priest and physician called upon by African tribal members and followers of religions such as vodoun, Santería and macumba. Root doctor practitioners who use their powers only for good are known as "ngangas."

runes Ancient symbols of Nordic and Germanic origin, used for divination.

sabbat A seasonal festival celebrated by witches.

salamanders Fire elementals who live in flames.

santero A priest or priestess belonging to the Santería religion, similar to vodoun, with magic powers, including the ability to heal the sick, divine the future and punish wrongdoers. The highest order of priest is the "babalawo."

Satan Another name for the Devil.

Satan Lucifer Name of the Devil before he was thrown out of Heaven for opposing God.

Seal of Solomon Also known as the Star of Solomon, this is a hexagram within a circle, used by witches and magicians to help protect against demons.

Satan

shaman Sometimes called a medicine man, these are people who have magic powers resulting from contact with the supernatural. Common in the religion of the Inuits, Maoris, Mongolians, Polynesians and Native Americans. In some cases, they may be female.

sigil A symbol representing a spirit.

sky clad A term used by modern witches to describe being naked.

sigils

snakestone A naturally-occurring stone with glass-like qualities believed by some to be the hardened saliva of adders and used to protect against evil.

sorcerer In medieval times this term was used to describe almost anyone who practiced science or set up a laboratory. Some use the term to describe a black witch or black magician. A sorceress is the female equivalent.

spell Words which when written or spoken have magic power. Some spells are cast without the use of words, but usually rely on the use of special signs and rituals.

spirit A term used to mean different things in different cultures. It may mean the independent part of a person that survives after death; in magic it tends to refer to a supernatural being without a body.

Spirits of Solomon Seventy-two spirits which, according to legend, were shut up in a brass vessel by King Solomon of Israel and later released by the Babylonians.

sprite A name sometimes used for an elemental.

Square of Jupiter A magic square consisting of 16 smaller squares, which when added up horizontally, vertically or diagonally total 34. It is often used as a talisman where the qualities of the planet Jupiter are required.

Square of Mars A magic square consisting of 25 smaller squares, which when added up horizontally, vertically or diagonally total 65. It is often used as a talisman where the qualities of the planet Mars are required.

Square of Mercury A magic square consisting of 64 smaller squares, which when added up horizontally, vertically or diagonally total 260. It is often used as a talisman where the qualities of the planet Mercury are required.

Square of Saturn A magic square consisting of 9 smaller squares, which when added up horizontally, vertically or diagonally total 15. It is often used as a talisman where the qualities of the planet Saturn are required.

4	9	2
3	5	7
8	1	6

Square of Saturn

Square of the Moon A magic square consisting of 81 smaller squares, which when added up horizontally, vertically or diagonally total 369. It is often used as a talisman where the qualities of the Moon are required.

Square of the Sun A magic square consisting of 36 smaller squares, which when added up horizontally, vertically or diagonally total 111. It is often used as a talisman where the qualities of the sun are required.

Square of Venus A magic square consisting of 49 smaller squares, which when added up horizontally, vertically or diagonally total 175. It is often used as a talisman where the qualities of the planet Venus are required.

Star of David A six-pointed star (hexagram) used in magic (especially black magic) and representing the balance between masculine and feminine.

Star of Solomon Also known as the Seal of Solomon, this is a hexagram within a circle, used by witches and magicians to help protect against demons.

Succubus A demon sent by the Devil to have sexual intercourse with sleeping men, Succubi are sex elementals and may be half human, half animal.

Superior spirits of Hell Six of the most important demons of Hell (Lucifuge, Satanachia, Fleuretty, Sargatanas, Nebiros and Agaliarept) who between them are thought to command many thousands of lesser demons.

sylphs Air elementals who live in light and thought.

talisman An amulet engraved with characters that attract occult influences, often used to perform a specific act, such as healing. They bring good luck and avert danger. Unlike an amulet (which is passive) a talisman must be waved, kissed, touched or used in some similar way.

totemic animal Also known as a guardian spirit, power animal, tutelary spirit, or familiar, this is a spirit who protects a shaman from illness and unfriendly forces.

tutelary spirit *See* **totemic animal**.

undines Water elementals who live in streams, rivers, clouds and mists.

unguentum sabbati *See* **devil's grease**.

vampire A corpse that returns to life at night to suck people's blood.

vévé In voodoo this is a symbol representing a god (loa).

vodoun Another name for voodoo.

voodoo priest Also known as a "houngan," "papa" or "papa-loa," in the vodoun religion, this is a man who summons vodoun gods in order to divine the future or heal.

voodoo priestess Also known as a "mambo," "manman" or "mam" in the vodoun religion, this is a woman who summons vodoun gods in order to divine the future or heal.

wand Also called a rod or blasting rod, this is a tool used by witches and magicians for conjuring and directing energy.

warlock A Scottish term meaning demon, wizard or magician and used in medieval times to describe male *witches* but rarely used by male witches themselves today.

white magic Magic that is performed for the purposes of good rather than evil.

white magician A magician who practices magic for the purposes of good.

warlock

white witch Also known as "cunning folk," these were medieval witches believed to practice magic for the purposes of good rather than evil. The term is also used by some to describe a modern witch.

wicca A name used by some modern witches for their cult.

wiccecraft An Anglo-Saxon term meaning "craft of the wise."

widdershins counter-clockwise

witch From the Anglo-Saxon wicca, meaning "the wise one;" a person who practices witchcraft.

witchcraft From the Anglo-Saxon wiccecraft meaning "craft of the wise."

witch doctor Also called an "obeahman," "jujuman," root doctor, conjure man and leaf doctor, this is a priest and physician called upon by African tribal members and followers of religions such as vodoun, Santería and macumba. Witch doctors who use their powers only for good are known as "ngangas."

witches' salve *See* **devil's grease**.

witches' tools Items used by witches, including the athame, censer, chalice, cord, pentacle and wand.

witch

witch's mark A place on a witch's body from where his or her familiar feeds.

wizard A man who practices magic.

zombie Corpse brought back to life by a voodoo sorcerer (bokor).

Physical world

5

geography

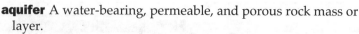

abyssal plain A level tract of the deep ocean floor.

air mass A fairly uniform mass of air covering a large area and containing air of, for example, polar or tropical origin.

Antarctic Circle A line of latitude approximately 66.5° south of the equator; the southern hemisphere's equivalent of the Arctic Circle.

aquifer

aquifer A water-bearing, permeable, and porous rock mass or layer.

archipelago A large group of islands, or a sea that contains one, for example the Aegean.

Arctic Circle A line of latitude, approximately 66° north of the equator, north of which the Sun does not rise at least one day in winter or set at least one day in summer; the northern hemisphere's equivalent of the Antarctic Circle.

atoll A ring-shaped coral reef enclosing a lagoon.

aurora An electrical discharge producing curtains of light seen at high latitudes in the night sky.

avalanche A great mass of snow that suddenly slides down a slope.

badlands Arid, barren, hilly land that is deeply eroded by gullies.

bar A sandy or shingly ridge that lies across a river mouth or a bay.

barrier island A long, low, narrow, sandy island separated from the mainland by a lagoon.

bay A wide inlet in a sea or lake, but smaller than a gulf.

beach The sloping strip of land between high and low water marks.

butte A flat-topped, steep-sided mountain or hill smaller than a mesa.

cape A pointed mass of land jutting into the sea.

cartography The making of maps.

cave A hole in the Earth's crust, produced by water erosion or lava.

cirque A mountain hollow eroded by snow and ice. It may contain snow or a lake.

cliff A steep, erosion-resistant rock face, as in gorges and on some coasts.

col A natural pass in a mountain range.

continent One of the world's great unbroken land masses.

continental shelf A shallow sea bed; the submerged edge of a continent.

contour line A line on a map that connects points of equal height.

Coriolis force The tendency of the Earth's rotation to turn winds and currents to the right in the northern hemisphere and to the left in the southern hemisphere.

creep The gradual downslope movement of soil or rock fragments, due to gravity.

cuesta A ridge with a steep slope on one side, and a gentle dip slope on the other.

delta Flat, alluvial land at a river mouth where it splits into many streams called distributaries.

denudation The wearing away of the land surface by the sum of such processes as weathering and erosion.

desertification The process by which land that has been farmed or inhabited becomes changed into desert, usually through climatic change or overfarming.

drumlin A half-egg-shaped hill of glacial deposits, formed under moving glacial ice.

dune A sand ridge or mound formed where wind heaps up the sand in a desert or on a low sandy coast.

equator An imaginary line around the Earth midway between the poles.

dune

equatorial zone The belt between latitudes 10°N and 10°S of the equator.

erg An area in a desert where there are shifting sand dunes, for example in the Sahara.

erosion The removal of loose mineral particles by wind, water, and moving ice.

estuary A broad, low, river mouth, usually where the coast has sunk or sea level has risen.

fjord A long, narrow, steep-sided sea inlet invading a glaciated valley.

geyser A periodic fountain forced up by the pressure of steam produced by hot rocks heating underground water.

glaciation (1) The effects on land of ice sheets or glaciers that erode rocks and deposit the rock debris. (2) A time when ice sheets develop and spread.

glacier A mass of ice that creeps down a valley, scouring its floor and sides.

gorge A deep, narrow, steep-sided valley, formed where a river erodes the floor far faster than the sides.

graben *See* **rift valley.**

ground water Subsurface water filling pores in rock. It flows under gravity.

gulf A very big and deep coastal inlet, larger than a bay.

gorge

gully A narrow channel worn in a hillside by running water. Gullies abound in land prone to soil erosion.

guyot A flat-topped submarine mountain formed by a subsiding volcanic island.

headwall A steep slope at the head of a cirque or valley.

hogback A long, narrow ridge that is steep on both sides.

horn A steep-sided, pyramidal mountain peak formed by the backward erosion of the headwalls of several cirques.

horse latitudes Subtropical belts of atmospheric high pressure; calm regions in both hemispheres between the westerlies and the trade winds.

horst A high block of land between parallel faults, caused by the block having risen or the land on either side having sunk.

iceberg A floating mass of ice that has broken off the end of a glacier and fallen into the sea.

ice sheet An immense mass of ice covering a large land area.

International Date Line The line of longitude (with local deviations) 180° E or W, where the date changes by a day. East of the line it is one day earlier than west of the line.

island A piece of land completely surrounded by a river, lake, sea, or ocean.

isthmus A narrow neck of land that joins two larger areas of land.

karst Limestone landscape with a largely bare, rocky surface and rivers that flow through underground caves.

lagoon A shallow area of water partly or wholly cut off from the sea by a strip or strips of land.

lake A large sheet of water surrounded by land or, more rarely, ice.

landform A distinctive natural configuration of the land surface.

landlocked Entirely surrounded by land, such as an inland sea or a country.

landslide The sudden slide down a slope or cliff of a mass of rocks or soil.

latitude Location north or south of the equator.

llano A large area of usually treeless, grassy plain in South America.

longitude Location east or west of the prime meridian.

magnetic poles Points on the Earth's surface sought by a magnetic compass needle. Their positions vary.

map projection A device for showing the Earth's curved surface on a flat sheet.

massif A mountain mass of ancient rocks partly dissected into separate peaks.

meander A curve in a river that swings in wide loops from side to side.

Mercator projection A type of cylindrical map projection in which the lines of latitude and longitude intersect at right angles.

meridian A line of longitude passing between the poles at right angles to the equator.

mesa A relatively small plateau capped by resistant horizontal rocks.

meteorology The study of the atmosphere and its behavior, especially with reference to weather.

midoceanic ridge A submarine mountain chain formed of upwelling molten rock.

mirage An optical illusion caused by the bending of light passing between air layers of differing density.

moraine Rock debris moved or dumped by a melting glacier or ice sheet.

mountain A mass of land higher than a hill and standing significantly above its surroundings. A mountain summit is small compared to its base.

ocean The great sheet of salt water surrounding the Earth's landmasses; also its subdivision into the Pacific, Atlantic, Indian, and Arctic oceans.

ocean current A horizontal flow of water through the ocean. Warm and cold surface currents redistribute the Sun's heat more evenly around the Earth.

oceanic trench A deep, narrow trough in an ocean floor.

oceanography The study of oceans, including seawater, the ocean floor, and marine plants and animals.

parallel Any of the imaginary lines of latitude that circle the Earth parallel to the equator.

peneplain A nearly flat land surface almost worn down to sea level.

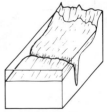

oceanic trench

peninsula A narrow strip of land that is almost surrounded by water.

permafrost Permanently frozen ground found in polar and subpolar zones.

pingo A hillock produced in polar regions by an underground ice "blister" pushing up the surface above.

plain A large tract of almost level land.

plateau A large area of high land with a fairly flat top and steep sides.

polar zones The regions that lie 75–90° north and south of the equator.

poles The ends of the Earth's axis, forming its northernmost and

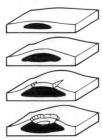

pingo

southernmost points: the North Pole and South Pole. Their locations do not correspond exactly with the North and South magnetic poles that are produced by the Earth's magnetic properties.

prairie An extensive open area of flat grassland, especially in the central plains of North America.

prime meridian An imaginary north-south line of longitude that passes through Greenwich, England, and is used as the basis for longitudinal measurements on the globe.

rainforest An area of dense tropical evergreen forest with a very heavy annual rainfall.

rapids A steep section of river where water flows faster than elsewhere.

ravine A long, narrow, steep-sided depression in the Earth's surface, between a gully and valley in size.

reef A ridge of rocks or coral that is usually submerged in the sea.

relief

relief Differences in height for any area of the Earth's surface.

ria A drowned river valley, forming a long, narrow, funnel-shaped inlet at right angles to the sea.

rift valley A long narrow trough where land has sunk between two in-facing parallel faults; also called a graben.

savannah An area of flat grassland in a tropical or subtropical region.

sea A subdivision of an ocean, or a large landlocked expanse of salt water.

ria

selva *See* **rainforest**.

spit A low strip of sand or shingle, one end joined to land, the other poking into the sea or across a bay.

stalactite A "stone icicle" formed on a cave ceiling from dissolved calcium carbonate deposited as dripping water evaporates.

stalagmite A calcium carbonate column on a cave floor formed in the same way as a stalactite.

steppe An extenive flat area of grassland, especially the semiarid plains of eastern Europe.

strait A narrow strip of sea that links two larger areas of sea.

subcontinent A large area of land that is part of a larger continent but is considered to form a distinct entity, especially India.

subtropical zones Latitudes between the tropics and temperate zones. They lie about 25–35° North and 25–35° South.

swell A long, symmetrical undulation of the surface of the sea.

taiga An area of coniferous evergreen forest lying south of the tundra in Europe and Asia.

talus (scree) Loose rock fragments fallen from a cliff.

temperate zones Latitudes broadly between subtropical and polar zones.

tides The regular rise and fall of sea level mainly due to the Moon's gravitational pull on the Earth.

topography The surface features of a particular place, or a description of these.

toponymy The place names used in a particualr region or language.

tropical zones Latitudes lying roughly 10–25° N and 10–25° S.

tsunami A high-speed wave set off by an earthquake, landslide, or volcanic eruption and towering on reaching some coasts; also called seismic sea wave.

tundra An area between the tree line in Arctic regions and the polar ice, with low-growing vegetation and permanently frozen subsoil.

valley A long depression worn in the land by a river or ice, or sunk between faults.

veldt Any extensive open area of grassland in southern Africa.

wadi A normally dry desert watercourse.

water cycle The circulation of water from sea to air and back again. This involves evaporation, condensation, and precipitation, and may include surface runoff, rivers, and glaciers.

waterfall A stream falling over a cliff-like step in the bedrock.

watershed Land drained by a river and its tributaries.

water table The upper surface of rock saturated by ground water. Wet and dry weather make the table rise and fall.

wave A disturbance moving through the surface of land or water.

weathering The decay and break up of rocks on the Earth's surface by natural chemical and mechanical processes.

geology

abyssal rock *See* **plutonic rock**.

age A subdivision of geological time.

amphibole Any of a group of rock-forming ferromagnesian silicates.

andesite A dark, fine-grained rock, taking its name from the Andes Mountains.

anticline An upfold in the rocks.

Archean eon The first eon in Earth's history (4.6–2.5 billion years ago).

arenit A sandstone with sedimentary particles of between 0.06 mm and 2 mm across.

asthenosphere A dense, plastic layer of mantle below the lithosphere.

basalt A fine-grained extrusive rock. Oceanic crust is largely basalt.

batholith An immense, dome-shaped, deep-seated mass of intrusive igneous rock.

bauxite The main ore from which aluminum is extracted.

bed A sedimentary layer of rock that is more than ½ in (1 cm) thick.

bedding plane/surface The surface between two beds of sedimentary rock.

bedrock The mass of solid rock that lies beneath the regolith.

boss A small mass of intrusive igneous rock with a circular surface.

brash A mass of rubble or stone fragments.

breccia A sedimentary rock made of sharp-edged fragments naturally cemented together.

Cambrian period The first part of the Paleozoic era: 590 to 505 million years ago.

carbonates Plentiful minerals that contain metal combined with oxygen and carbon. They include calcite, aragonite, and dolomite.

bedrock

Carboniferous period The penultimate period of the Paleozoic era: 360 to 249 million years ago.

Cenozoic era The geological era after the Mesozoic era. It is sometimes known as the age of mammals and began 65 million years ago.

chalk A white, soft form of limestone.

chert A type of sedimentary rock made up of of tiny quartz crystals.

clasts Rock fragments, such as those that form mud, sand, and gravel.

clay Sheet-like silicates held together by water. Clays tend to be plastic when wet and hard or powdery when dry.

coal A rock that is mostly carbon and readily burns. It consists of layered plant remains compacted by pressure over millions of years.

conglomerate A type of sedimentary rock made up of pebbles and larger rounded stones, cemented together by sandy material.

continental drift The theory that continents have drifted around the face of the Earth.

core The dense, intensely hot ball of rock below the Earth's mantle. The outer core, 1400 mi (2240 km) thick, is probably molten iron and nickel with some silicon. The inner core, 1540 mi (2440 km) across, may be iron and nickel at 3700 °C. Extreme pressure prevents it from becoming liquid.

craton An ancient part of a continent that has remained undeformed by mountain-building activity.

Cretaceous period The third and last period of the Mesozoic era: 144 to 65 million years ago.

crust The hard outer skin of rock forming the ocean floor and the continents. Continental crust averages 20 mi (33 km) thick. Oceanic crust is less than 6.2 mi (10 km) thick.

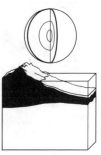

crust

crystal A mineral that has solidified with geometrically arranged atoms and external symmetry.

Devonian period The fourth period of the Paleozoic era: 408 to 360 million years ago.

diagenesis The chemical and physical process by which sediment is turned into rock.

dike A vertical sheet of igneous rock that has intruded across older rocks.

diorite A coarse-textured igneous rock, mainly comprising feldspar and pyroxene.

discontinuity A zone that marks a boundary between different layers of the Earth, such as between the mantle and the core, and where the velocity of seismic waves changes.

dike

dolomite A mineral or sedimentary rock made of calcium magnesium carbonate.

earthquake A sudden shaking of the ground when stressed rocks move along a fault. Volcanic eruptions trigger some earthquakes.

earth science Geology, or any of the other sciences that study the physical phenomena of the Earth.

Eocene epoch The second part of the Tertiary period: 55 to 38 million years ago.

epoch A time unit within a geological period.

era A time unit within an eon. An era contains at least two periods.

erathem The rocks formed during a geological era.

evaporite Rock formed of crystals precipitated by the evaporation of salt-saturated water.

facies Features of the appearance or composition of a rock representing a local environment.

fault A fracture zone where one rock mass has moved against another.

feldspar Any of a group of minerals comprising aluminum silicates and a metal (calcium, potassium, or sodium).

flint Dark, smooth, shiny chert.

fold A bend in rock layers, formed when pressure has made them plastic.

foliated Formed of leaves of flaky, layered minerals aligned during metamorphism.

foredeep A long basin filling with sediment eroded from an active mountain system nearby.

fossil The remains or trace of an organism preserved in sedimentary rocks.

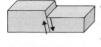

gabbro A dense, dark, coarse-grained, intrusive igneous rock that largely consists of feldspar and pyroxene.

fault

gangue Valueless minerals in ore.

gemstone A mineral valued for its beauty, durability, scarcity, and suitability for cutting into a gem.

geochemistry The study of substances in the Earth and their chemical changes.

geochronology earth's history

geode A hollow nodule of rock lined inside with crystals.

geodesy The scientific study of the size and shape of the Earth.

geology The scientific study of the Earth, especially its rocks and minerals and their development.

fold

geophysics The study of the structure and development of the Earth.

gneiss A coarse-grained metamorphic rock with minerals in wavy layers.

granite An intrusive igneous rock rich in quartz and feldspar, often with mica.

gypsum A mineral or rock composed of calcium sulfate and water.

halite Rock salt: sodium chloride.

hematite iron oxide

Holocene epoch The second (present) part of the Quaternary period: 10,000 to the present.

hornblende A variety of amphibole.

hornfels A type of granular, fine-grained metamorphic rock.

hypabyssal Describes rock that has solidified as an intrusion before reaching the Earth's surface.

ice age A time when ice sheets covered much of the Earth. The present Ice Age is only one of several ice ages.

igneous rock The term for a rock formed when molten rock cools and hardens. Extrusive, or volcanic, igneous rock cools on the surface as lava. Intrusive igneous rock forms when molten rock cools underground.

isostasy The state of balance of the Earth's crust as it floats on the denser mantle. Mountains are balanced by deep roots of crustal rock.

joint A crack in rock, formed along a line of weakness.

Jurassic period The second (middle) period of the Mesozoic era: 213 to 144 million years ago.

laccolith A lens-shaped mass of intrusive igneous rock that pushes overlying rocks into a dome.

laterite A type of reddish soil, found in tropical or subtropical regions that has been leached of its soluble minerals.

lava Molten rock when it appears at the Earth's surface.

leaching A process by which soluble constituents of soil are removed by liquid passing through it.

limestone Sedimentary rock composed mainly of calcium carbonate.

limnology The study of bodies of water that are inland, such as lakes.

lithification A process that changes sediments into solid rocks, essentially compaction and the precipitation of a mineral cement.

lithosphere The term used to describe the Earth's crust coupled with the rigid upper mantle.

lithospheric plate An independently moving slab of the lithosphere.

lopolith A saucer-shaped intrusion (some are huge) between rock strata.

magma Molten rock that is formed below the surface of the Earth's.

mantle The dense, hot rock layer, 1800 mi (2900 km) thick, below the crust. Some parts of it are semi-molten and able to flow.

marble A metamorphic rock formed from recrystallized limestone or dolomite.

Mesozoic era The geological era between the Paleozoic and Cenozoic eras: 248 to 65 million years ago. It is sometimes called the "Age of Dinosaurs."

metamorphic rock Sedimentary or igneous rock altered by great

mantle

heat or pressure, e.g. limestone changed to marble.

mica A rock-forming silicate.

mineral A natural inorganic substance with distinct chemical composition and internal structure.

mineralogy The study of minerals.

Miocene epoch The fourth part of the Tertiary period.

Mississippian period In North America, the first part of what is generally called the Carboniferous period: 360 to 321 million years ago.

nappe A recumbent (flopped over) fold that has sheared through, with its upper limb forced far forward.

Neogene period The second part of a revised two-part division of the Cenozoic era. It runs from the Miocene epoch to the Holocene: 24.6 million to 2 million years ago.

obsidian A glassy volcanic rock.

nappe

oceanography The study of oceans and their life.

Oligocene epoch The third part of the Tertiary period: 38 to 24.6 million years ago.

olivine A dark green silicate.

oolite Sand consisting of rounded grains of carbonate known as ooids.

Ordovician period The second period in the Paleozoic era: 505 to 438 million years ago.

ore A metal-rich mineral deposit.

orogeny A phase of mountain building.

Paleocene epoch The first part of the Tertiary period: 65 to 55 million years ago

paleoecology The study of the relationship between prehistoric plants, animals, and their surroundings.

Paleogene period The first part of a revised two-part division of the Cenozoic era: 65 to 24 million years ago.

paleogeography The study of the Earth's past geography.

paleomagnetism The magnetic alignment of particles in rock that occurred when the rock formed. It reflects the Earth's magnetic field at the time.

paleontology The study of fossilized prehistoric plants and animals.

Paleozoic era The first part of the Phanerozoic eon, 509 to 248 million years ago.

pangaea The prehistoric supercontinent that formed late in the Paleozoic era and broke up in the Cenozoic era.

Pennsylvanian period In North America, the second part of what is generally called the Carboniferous period: 320 to 286 million years ago.

peridotite A coarse-grained igneous rock, mainly of olivine and pyroxene, such as dunite.

period A geological time unit within an era.

Permian period The last period of the Paleozoic era: 286 to 248 million years ago.

petrifaction The process by which organic materials become fossilized.

petrography The description and classification of rocks.

petroleum Mineral oil composed of hydrocarbons formed in the Earth's crust.

petrology The study of rocks.

Phanerozoic eon The "age of visible life"—the fossil-rich past 590 million years of Earth's history.

plate tectonics The study of how lithospheric plates move around.

Pleistocene epoch The first (ice age) part of the Quaternary period: 2 to 0.1 million years ago.

Pliocene epoch The last part of the Tertiary period: 5 to 2 million years ago.

plutonic rock Igneous rock from deep below the Earth's surface.

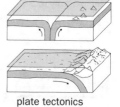

plate tectonics

Precambrian The period containing all of Earth's history before the Cambrian period.

Proterozoic eon The second eon in Earth's history: 2.5 billion to 590 million years ago.

puddingstone A type of conglomerate rock.

pyroxene Any of a group of rock-forming silicate minerals.

quartz A hard silicate mineral.

quartzite Sandstone that has been changed over time to solid quartz rock.

Quaternary period The second (present) period of the Cenozoic era: 2 million to the present.

radiocarbon dating Radiometric dating based on the decay of the isotope carbon-14. It is used to date organic materials less than 70,000 years old.

radiometric dating Dating rocks by the known rate of decay of radioactive elements that they contain.

regolith The layer of soil and broken rock that covers the bedrock.

rock Any solid mass that is composed of minerals, forming a part of the Earth's crust.

rock units Rocks grouped by their characteristics, not by time. The units include (from major to minor) groups, formations, and members.

sandstone A sedimentary rock formed of naturally cemented sand grains.

saprolite A deposit of decomposed rock, clay, or silt that has remained in its original place.

schist A metamorphic rock rich in flattened, aligned minerals. It comes from slate and basalt.

scoria Fragments of dark lava that resemble cinders.

sedimentary rock Rock formed from accumulated sediments. Examples are clay, sandstone, and limestone.

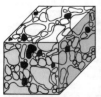

seismograph An instrument used to detect and record movements of the ground, especially during Earth tremors.

seismology The study of Earth tremors.

series The rocks formed during a geological epoch.

shale A type of layered sedimentary rock formed chiefly from

sedimentary rocks

clay.

silicates The most plentiful group of rock-forming minerals, usually consisting of silicon and oxygen combined with a metal. They include feldspar, mica, and quartz.

sill A horizontal sheet of igneous rock intruded between sedimentary rock layers.

Silurian period The third period of the Paleozoic era: 438 to 408 million years ago.

sill

slate A fine-grained metamorphic rock formed from shale. It splits along lines of weakness produced by deformational pressure.

soil Broken rock fragments, often mixed with decayed organic matter.

spreading ridge A submarine mountain chain built by magma that rises to plug a widening gap between two diverging lithospheric plates.

stage The rocks formed during a geological age.

stock Like a batholith but smaller.

stratigraphy The study of stratified (layered) rocks.

stratum A single sedimentary layer.

subduction The sinking of one lithospheric plate's leading edge below another lithospheric plate. This occurs below deep ocean trenches.

superposition The principle that, in undisturbed layered rocks, the higher a stratum, the younger it is.

syncline A downfold in the rocks, creating a trough.

system The rocks formed during a geological period.

talus A mass of rock debris forming a slope at the bottom of a cliff.

tectonics The geological study of large structures such as mountains.

tektites Small, black, glassy pieces of sedimentary rock, melted

tektites

by the impact of an ancient meteorite.

Tertiary period The first period of the Cenozoic era, comprising the epochs from the Paleocene to the Pliocene: 65 to 2 million years ago.

till Sediment dumped by a glacier.

tillite Rock formed from till.

travertine Calcium carbonate deposited by water, as in stalactites.

Triassic period The first period of the Mesozoic era: 248 to 213 million years ago.

tuff A rock made up of compacted volcanic ash; also known as tufa.

unconformity A level where sedimentary rocks cover an older rock surface partly removed by erosion. The level marks a time gap.

uniformitarianism The principle that present geological processes are the key to past events in Earth's history.

varves Paired (fine and coarse) layers annually deposited in a glacial lake.

vein A crack in rock containing a mineral deposit.

volcano A hole or fissure in the ground from which lava and other volcanic products emerge.

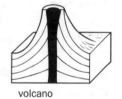

volcano

meteorology

American Hurricane Center An organization in Miami, Florida which sends out specially equipped aircraft to measure conditions.

anemometer An instrument which is used to measure wind speed.

anti-cyclone An area of high pressure where the winds are spiraling outward. The pressure is highest in the center, and the weather produced is often bright and clear.

atmosphere The name given to the layer of gases around the Earth and other heavenly bodies.

backing A term referring to when wind changes direction anticlockwise, such as backing from south to south-east.

Beaufort scale (wind scale) A scale that rates the force of wind from 0 to 12, a rating of 0 being absolute calm and one of 12 being hurricane force.

cirrus Light, feather-shaped white clouds that usually form at 4–6 mi (7.6–10km).

climate The average weather of a region or place measured for all seasons over a number of years. There are three important areas: tropical, temperate and polar.

cloud A mass of tiny droplets formed when water vapor condenses as warm, moist air moves upwards where the temperature is lower. The bottom of the cloud is the dew point.

col The area of intermediate pressure that separates cyclones or depressions.

cold front The boundary between a mass of cold air moving into an area of warm air. The warm air is forced to rise and cumulus clouds are formed.

convection The upward motion of a body of air which transfers heat from ground level to the upper part of the atmosphere.

cumulus White clouds that have a cotton wool-like appearance, usually formed at 2–3 mi (3–5km) as warm air rises.

cyclone A low-pressure tropical storm with high speed rotating winds.

depression An area of low pressure where the winds are spiraling inward. Also known as a low.

dew Water droplets formed from the condensation of water vapor in the atmosphere.

dew point The point at which air saturated with water vapor produces condensation which forms dew.

dust devil An intense low-pressure system which creates a column of fast-moving wind laden with dust.

anemometer

climate

☐ Polar
■ Temperate
☐ Tropical

fog A phenomenon that occurs at ground level when very small droplets of water are formed, by condensation, on dust in the air as a result of air cooling rapidly.

forecast Prediction of the weather conditions in the near future based on data collected in the past and computer modeling techniques.

front The boundary between air masses that have contrasting temperature and humidity.

glazed frost A layer of transparent—or "black"—ice.

greenhouse effect The term given to the heating of the Earth's surface caused by infrared radiation trapped in the atmosphere.

haar Sea mist or fog that occurs over cold bodies of water.

hoar frost Term given to the white dusting caused by ice crystals.

humidity A measure of the amount of water vapor in the atmosphere.

hurricane A severe tropical storm rated 12 on the Beaufort scale.

hygrometer A piece of equipment for measuring the percentage humidity of the air.

ice The solid form of water as it freezes when the temperature is below 32°F (0°C).

inversion layer A layer of warm air overlying an area of cold, so that temperature increases with height.

ionosphere The upper layer of the atmosphere that lies above the stratosphere and is about 217 mi (350km) thick.

isobar A line drawn on a map linking places with the same atmospheric pressure.

isohyet A line drawn on a map linking places that have the same rainfall.

isotherm A line drawn on a map linking places that have the same temperature.

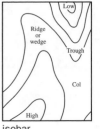

isobar

jet stream A narrow corridor of fast-moving air at high altitude.

land breeze A wind caused by a convection current during the evening. The air mass over the sea cools down more slowly than that over adjacent land causing the denser cool air to push out over the sea and creating a breeze.

mist A phenomenon that occurs at ground level when very small droplets of water are formed by condensation as a result of air cooling rapidly.

monsoon A regular wind that reverses direction with the changing of the seasons.

nimbus Thick grey generally shapeless clouds that form at about 1.3 mi (2km).

occluded front The term for when a cold front overtakes the warm front in a depression.

precipitation A term for the formation of water droplets, as water vapor in the air condenses, that are large enough to start to fall. If the temperature is above 32°F (0°C) it will fall as rain, below this temperature it will fall as snow, sleet, or hail.

rain Precipitation falling from clouds in the form of water drops.

relative humidity A percentage scale to measure the level of humidity in the atmosphere: from 0% which indicates the air is absolutely dry to 100% which indicates the air is saturated.

ridge An area of high pressure between two depressions.

sea breeze A wind caused by a convection current during the day. When the air mass over land heats up it rises drawing in the cooler air overlying the sea, creating a breeze.

snow Precipitation falling from clouds where the temperature is below 32°F (0°C).

space The zone beyond the outer layer of the atmosphere.

stratosphere The layer of atmosphere that lies above the tropopause and is about 15.5 mi (25km) thick.

stratus Layers of low clouds often covering a large area, usually formed in calm weather.

thermal A rising column of warm air.

tornado An intense cyclone where the spiraling wind-speed reaches over 200 miles (320km) per hour.

trade wind A wind that blows in the same direction during a particular season or seasons.

tropopause The thin layer of the atmosphere, about 3 mi (5km) thick, that lies between the troposphere and the stratosphere.

troposphere The layer of the atmosphere lying nearest the Earth which varies in thickness from 11 mi (18km) at the equator to 6.2 mi (10km) at the poles.

trough An elongated area of low pressure between two areas of high pressure.

typhoon An intense cyclone in the China Sea where the spiraling wind-speed reaches over 100 miles (160km) per hour.

veering A term given to when wind changes direction clockwise, for example south-west to west.

warm front The term used to describe the boundary between a mass of warm air moving into an area of cold air over which it rises.

waterspout An intense low-pressure system which creates a column of fast-moving wind laden with water.

wedge A narrow area of high pressure between two depressions.

whirlwind An intense area of low pressure moving in a circular motion caused by a convection current that occurs over hot land such as in deserts.

Wind scale *See* **Beaufort scale.**

The Sciences

astronomy

asteroids

astronomical unit

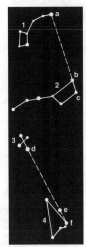

celestial poles

aberration Apparent changes in the position of a celestial body, brought about by the movement of the earth in relation to it.

absolute magnitude A star's size when seen from a distance of 10 parsecs.

achondrite A type of stony meteorite.

aerolite A meteorite composed mainly of silica.

albedo The proportion of incoming light that is reflected by a celestial body, e.g. the Moon reflects 7% of the sunlight that it receives.

almucantar A circle on the celestial sphere that is parallel to the horizontal plane.

anthelion A luminous area like a halo sometimes seen in the sky opposite the sun.

aphelion The point in a planet's orbit at which it is farthest from the Sun.

apolune The point in an orbit of the Moon at which the orbiting object is farthest from the Moon.

asteroids Lumps of metal or rock in many sizes concentrated in parts of the solar system.

astrobleme A mark left on the surface of the Earth by the impact of a meteorite.

astronomical unit (au) The mean Sun to Earth distance, equal to 92,955,807 mi (149,597,870 km). Agreed internationally in 1964, but its value has altered.

aurora The orthern and southern "polar lights" sometimes seen in Earth's upper atmosphere and created by solar particles striking atoms.

big bang theory The idea that the universe began with an explosion 13–20 billion years ago. According to the theory, formulated in 1927, the universe is still expanding. It is now obsolete to some extent. *Compare* **steady state theory**.

black hole An object with large mass but small size, from which no light can escape; formed in the first moments in the life of the universe. Also called a collapsar.

bolide A large and extremely bright meteor.

celestial poles The North and South Celestial Poles are the equivalents in the sky of the North and South Poles on Earth. Earth's axis joins the North and South Poles; extended northward it points to the North Celestial Pole, and extended southward it points to the South Celestial Pole.

The North Celestial Pole is roughly marked by the star Polaris in the constellation Ursa Minor (the Little Dipper).

Polaris is only three-quarters of one degree away from the true pole. To find Polaris, find Ursa Major (the Big Dipper) and extend the imaginary line joining the two stars known as the Pointers.

There is no star marking the South Celestial Pole; the nearest star visible to the naked eye is Sigma Octantis. To find the South Celestial Pole, find the constellation of the Southern Cross and extend the imaginary line joining the two stars that form its longer arm.

chromosphere A layer of gas that lies above the photosphere of a star, such as the Sun.

collapsar *See* **black hole.**

comet A dust, gas, and ice body that orbits the Sun and develops a long, bright tail on nearing the Sun.

constellation An apparent grouping of prominent stars. Stars have been divided into the artificial groups called constellations for over 2000 years.

corona The Sun's gaseous outer layer that emits solar wind and is visible as a halo during a total solar eclipse.

cosmogony The study of the origin and development of the universe.

cosmology The study of the universe.

critical density The amount of matter and energy in the universe which if exceeded will delay and even reverse the universe's expansion.

curved space The concept that light takes a curved path through space near massive objects

cusp Either of the two points of a crescent moon.

declination A star's angular distance in degrees N or S of the celestial equator. Equivalent to the Earth's latitude.

eccentric Describes an orbit that deviates from a circular path, such as an elliptical orbit.

eclipse of the Moon This occurs when the Earth is in a direct line between the Sun and Moon. The Moon is then in the Earth's shadow and cannot receive any direct sunlight. It becomes dim and appears coppery-red in color. There are never more than three eclipses of the Moon in a year.

eclipse of the Sun From the Earth, the Sun and Moon appear to

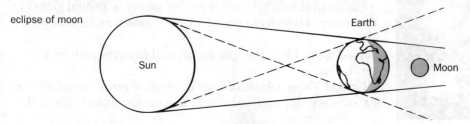

eclipse of moon

Sun

Earth

Moon

be about the same size: the Sun is about 400 times as big as the Moon but is also 400 times farther away from the Earth. When the Moon is in a direct line between the Sun and the Earth, the Moon's disk-shaped outline appears to cover the Sun's bright surface, or photosphere. The part of the Earth directly in the Moon's shadow sees a total eclipse of the Sun; areas around it see a partial eclipse. There are different types of exclipse: total, partial and annular.

ecliptic The Sun's apparent path across the sky.

elongation angle As seen from the Earth, the angle between the Sun and a planet or the latter and a satellite.

ephemeris A table that shows the coordinates of a celestial body at various specific times.

equinox "Equal night," the two points at which the ecliptic intersects the celestial equator to produce the seasonal spring (vernal) equinox and autumnal (fall) equinox.

evection Irregularity in the movement of the Moon caused by variations in the orbit of the Sun.

exosphere The outermost layer of the atmosphere of a planet.

extraterrestrials Living creatures from other worlds. Some scientists calculate that our civilization stands alone in the universe. Others contend that there could be many thousands of worlds inhabited by intelligent beings. Even so, all of them would be too distant to reach by astronaut-controlled space exploration.

facula A large bright spot that appears on the photosphere of the Sun.

galactic shapes

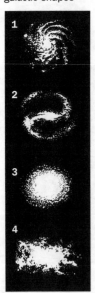

flocculus A cloudlike mass of gases appearing on the surface of the Sun.

Fraunhofer lines Dark lines seen on the Sun and other stars, named after their 1814 Bavarian discoverer.

galactic coordinates The relative location of our galaxy's components in latitude and longitude (degrees and min) measured in relation to the celestial equator which is itself a projection of the Earth's equator.

galactic shapes Galaxies are classified by their shape. The four main classes are:

1 **Spiral** These galaxies resemble pinwheels, with spiral arms trailing out from a bright center. Our galaxy is a spiral galaxy at the center of which is a cluster of stars known as the Milky Way.

2 **Barred spiral** Here, the spiral arms trail from the ends of a central bar.

3 **Elliptical** These galaxies do not have spiral arms. About 60% of galaxies are elliptical, varying in shape from almost spherical

(like a soccer ball) to very flattened (like a football).

4 Irregular About 10% of galaxies are irregular with no definite shape.

galaxy Galaxies are collections of stars and planets and clouds of gas or dust that form "islands" in the emptiness of space. A recent theory claims much of this is occupied by invisible dark matter. Most galaxies are found in groups; very few are found on their own.

gravitational collapse What happens to a star when its hydrogen and other energy supplies are unable to maintain gravitation. The collapse's result can be a black hole, white dwarf, neutron star, or supernova.

Halley's comet A comet that orbits the Sun about every 76 years. It was first recorded in 240 BC, was last seen in 1986, and is next due in 2061.

heliosphere The area of space occupied by the Sun's magnetic field and gases.

HR (Hertzsprung–Russell) diagram A graph (devised 1911–13) plotting stars' colors against their brightness in descending order, with the Sun midway in the sequence.

Hubble's Constant/Law, Hubble flow In 1924, Edwin P. Hubble discovered that the farther away a galaxy is, the faster its apparent speed. The speed-to-distance ratio is the constant, now measured at 30–60 mi/sec (50–100 km/sec) per million parsecs.

insolation The solar radiation that strikes the Earth or another planet.

International Astronomical Union (IAU) A world body founded in 1919.

ionosphere The area of the Earth's atmosphere in which ionization caused by solar radiation affects the transmission of radio waves.

Kepler's laws Three laws (1609–19) formulated by German astronomer Johann Kepler. (1) The planetary orbits are elliptical. (2) A planet's velocity is greater the nearer it is to the Sun. (3) The square of a planet's orbital period is proportional to the cube of its distance from the Sun.

light year (ly) The distance traveled by light in a year, equal to 5.878 trillion mi (9.4605 trillion km) or 63,290 au. Defined in 1888.

local group of galaxies A cluster of more than 24 galaxies, including our Milky Way. Andromeda is the largest galaxy.

luminosity A star's essential brightness.

Magellanic Clouds Two Milky Way satellite galaxies visible to the human eye in the southern hemisphere and found by

Europeans during the first circumnavigation of the world (1519–22).

magnetosphere The region near the planet possessing a magnetic field, which determines the motion of the charged particles in this region. Earth, Saturn, Jupiter, Uranus, and Mercury are the solar system planets known to have magnetospheres.

magnitude A star's brightness measured as either absolute magnitude or apparent magnitude. The latter states brightness in the sky on a scale from -26.8 (the Sun, brightest) to +25 (the faintest).

mare (pl. maria) A large dark area observed on the surface of the Moon or a planet.

meteorite A rock or metal lump that has fallen to Earth; thought to be asteroid debris.

meteoroid A solid body moving through space that is smaller than an asteroid.

meteors Tiny cometary fragments observable as "shooting stars" when burning up in the Earth's atmosphere. About 100 million meteors a day enter the Earth's atmosphere.

Milky Way The spiral galaxy home of our solar system. Its 150 billion stars extend for 500,000 light years and have existed for about 12 billion years.

nebula A dust and gas cloud formed in space that is a source of stars. Sometimes used to refer to other galaxies, when their stars appear indistinct.

nebula

neutron star The smallest but densest kind of star, apparently resulting from a supernova explosion that compressed the star's particles into subatomic neutrons. A neutron star 15 mi (25 km) across can equal the Sun's mass.

nova A star that briefly grows intensely bright.

nucleosynthesis The synthesis of heavier chemical elements from hydrogen nuclei in the interior of a star.

oblate Describes a planetary shape in which the equatorial distance is greater than the distance between the poles. The Earth is an oblate planet.

orbit The curving path that one space object takes around another.

parsec (pc) The distance at which 1 au would measure 1 sec of arc, equal to 19.16 trillion mi (30.857 trillion km) or 206,265 au or 3.26 ly (1).

periastron The point in the orbit of an object around a star at which the object is at its closest to the star.

perihelion The point in a planet's orbit at which it is closest to the Sun.

perturbation One space body's gravitational effect on another's orbit.

phases of the Moon The Moon produces no light of its own: it shines because it reflects sunlight. The amount of the lit half that can be seen from the Earth changes from day to day. These regular changes are known as phases of the Moon. The interval between one new Moon and the next is 29 days, 12 hr, 44 min, 3 sec.

photosphere The visible outer layer of a star, especially of the Sun.

plage An intensely hot and bright area in the chromosphere of the Sun.

planetary path The paths taken by the nine planets in our solar system.

planetary ring Planetary rings, made up of millions of particles, are known to orbit the planets Jupiter, Saturn, Uranus, and Neptune. They are rarely more than a few hundred yards in thickness but may be many thousands of yards wide. Saturn is thought to have more than 1000 separate rings.

planetary ring

planetary rotations Planets rotate in different ways.

1 The Earth The Earth's mean distance from the Sun is 93 million mi (150 million km). The Earth orbits the Sun in 365.25 days. Meanwhile, the Earth rotates every 23 hr 56 min.

2 The Moon It takes 27.3 days for the Moon to complete one orbit of the Earth. Because it takes exactly the same time for the Moon to turn once on its own axis, the same side of the Moon always faces the Earth. The far side of the Moon can be seen only from space.

planetary rotations

3 The Sun The Sun, like the Earth, rotates on its axis. Because the Sun is made of gas it can rotate at different speeds at different latitudes: it rotates more slowly at its poles than at its equator. Rotation periods are approximately 34–7 days at its poles and 24–6 days at its equator.

planetary satellites A satellite is a companion body that orbits a planet. Earth's satellite is the Moon. Planetary satellites are the known satellites orbiting each planet. Venus and Mercury do not have satellites.

pulsar A rapidly rotating neutron star that gives off regular bursts of radio waves.

quasars Short for "quasi-stellar radio sources," these are very remote but extremely bright objects, thought to be at the hearts of galaxies existing on the fringes of the universe. The first of more than 600 was discovered in 1963.

radar astronomy The use of radar to track objects in the solar system. Beyond Saturn, the signal is too weak.

radio astronomy The collection and analysis of radio waves from space, a technique that began in 1937.

red giant A star 10–100 times the Sun's size.

red shift An effect by which the faster an object moves away from Earth the redder its light spectrum becomes.

reflector A telescope that has a concave mirror to focus light back to an eyepiece. Isaac Newton built the first one in about 1668.

refractor A telescope with a lens that refracts light onto a particular point that is magnified for the eye.

right ascension (ra) A space object's angular distance to the east of the vernal equinox.

sidereal period The time taken for a planet to complete one orbit of the Sun.

sidereal time Time measured by Earth's rotation against the stars.

sky map A map of the constellations seen from the northern or southern hemisphere.

solar system Our solar system consists of nine planets. The diameter of each planet, at its equator, is given here.

a Mercury 3,031 mi (4,878 km)
b Venus 7,521 mi (12,104 km)
c Earth 7,926 mi (12,756 km)
d Mars 4,222 mi (6,795 km)
e Jupiter 88,732 mi (142,800 km)
f Saturn 74,565 mi (120,000 km)
g Uranus 31,566 mi (50,800 km)
h Neptune 30,137 mi (48,500 km)
i Pluto 3,725 mi (5,995 km)

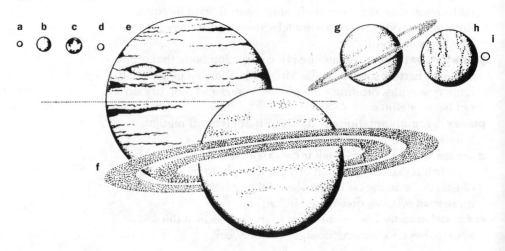

star An object that is maintained by its own gravity and shines due to the radiant energy produced by the nuclear fusion at its core.

star type Stars are often referred to in terms of their color (red, orange, yellow, blue, white), comparative size (dwarf, giant, supergiant), and brightness. Blue and white stars are hotter than the yellow Sun; orange and red stars are cooler. Here are some examples of star types:

1 Sirius B A white dwarf: diameter 100 times smaller than the Sun's.

2 Barnard's Star A red dwarf: diameter 10 times smaller than the Sun's.

3 Sun A yellow dwarf.

4 Capella A yellow giant: diameter 16 times larger and brightness 150 times greater than the Sun's.

5 Rigel A blue-white giant: diameter 80 times larger and brightness 60,000 times greater than the Sun's.

6 Betelgeuse A red supergiant: diameter 300—400 times larger and brightness 15,000 times greater than the Sun's.

steady state theory The theory that the universe has always existed and been expanding. This theory, which was formulated in 1954, has been largely rejected in favor of the big bang theory.

stellar aberration A star's apparent elliptical course around its true position as Earth orbits the Sun.

stellar wind The flow of plasma into space from the surface of a star.

sunspot One of many relatively cool dark spots that appear periodically on the surface of the Sun.

supercluster A group of neighboring clusters of galaxies.

supernova A star that explodes and leaves a neutron star remnant.

variable star A star that varies in brightness because of internal changes or because it is periodically eclipsed by other bodies.

white dwarf (star) A roughly Earth-sized and compacted remnant of a star that has collapsed but is not yet a neutron star.

white hole A hypothetical reverse of a black hole, from which matter emerges.

zodiac A zone divided into 12 constellations along the ecliptic.

sunspot

biology

absorption Uptake of substances, such as digested food and oxygen, into cells.

active transport An energy-requiring process which carries substances across cell membrane against a concentration gradient.

adaptation An inherited feature that increases an organism's chances of survival.

adenosine triphosphate (ATP) A substance that supplies the immediate energy needs of cell.

aerobic respiration Respiration using oxygen.

algae Plantlike organisms, mainly microscopic but also including seaweeds.

alleles Two or more genes which control the same characteristic.

alternation of generations A life cycle (e.g. mosses, ferns) in which a haploid generation alternates with a diploid generation.

amino acids Molecular building blocks of proteins.

anaerobic respiration Respiration without oxygen.

anatomy Study of the structure of organisms.

angiosperms Flowering plants.

annual A plant with a one-year life cycle.

anther A pollen-producing part of flower, found at the tip of the stamen.

antibody A protein released by blood cells to destroy invading foreign organisms or substances.

antigen A molecule recognized as foreign by the body's immune system, causing the release of antibodies.

artery

artery A blood vessel that carries blood away from the heart.

arthropods A very large phylum of animals that have exoskeletons and jointed limbs, including insects and crustaceans.

asexual reproduction Reproduction requiring one parent. Offspring are identical to the parent.

autotroph Organism (e.g. plant) that can make its own food from simple inorganic molecules.

bacteriophage A virus that infects and destroys the cells of bacteria. Also called phage.

arthropods

bacterium (pl. bacteria) A very small, single-celled, prokaryotic organism.

biennial A plant with a two-year life cycle.

biochemistry Study of the chemistry of life processes.

biology Study of living things.

botany Study of plants.

bryophytes A group of plants that includes mosses and liverworts.

capillaries Microscopic blood vessels that link the arteries to the veins.

carbohydrates Compounds composed of carbon, hydrogen, and oxygen. Some are energy-rich (e.g. glucose, starch); others are structural (e.g. cellulose).

carnivore A meat-eating organism.

carpel A female sex organ of flowering plants, which consists of stigma, style, and ovary.

cell The basic unit of all living things.

cell membrane The outer boundary of a cell.

cell wall The nonliving covering around cells of plants and some bacteria.

cellulose A carbohydrate of which plant cell walls are made.

central nervous system The brain and spinal cord of vertebrates.

centriole Either of two organelles near the nucleus involved in cell division.

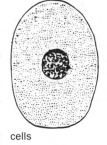

cells

chlorophyll A green pigment that "traps" sunlight for photosynthesis; found in plants and some protists.

chloroplast A structure inside a cell that contains chlorophyll.

chromosome A coiled thread of DNA found in the nucleus of a cell.

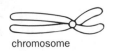

chromosome

cilium (pl. cilia) A microscopic, hairlike projection from some cells.

circadian rhythm The regular recurrence of life activities in 24-hour cycles.

class A group of organisms that is a subdivision of a phylum, e.g. mammals.

conifers Cone-bearing trees and shrubs.

connective tissue Tissue that connects parts of the body, e.g. adipose tissue.

continuous variations Variations within a species that do not fall into distinct categories, e.g. height in humans.

convergent evolution Evolution of similar features in unrelated organisms as adaptations to similar lifestyles, e.g. wings in birds and bats.

cotyledon A seed leaf that provides food for an embryo plant.

cuticle A waterproof, waxy outer covering found, for example, on leaves and insects.

cytology Study of cells.

cytoplasm The region of a cell between the nucleus and membrane, containing the organelles.

deciduous tree A tree that loses its leaves each year in the autumn.

deoxyribonucleic acid (DNA) A molecule found in a cell nucleus that carries genetic information.

dicotyledon A flowering plant that has two cotyledons in its seed.

digestion The breakdown of large food molecules into smaller ones prior to absorption.

diploid Having two sets of chromosomes in the nucleus.

discontinuous variations Variations within a species that fall into distinct categories, e.g. eye colors.

divergent evolution Evolution of dissimilar features in closely related organisms as adaptations to dissimilar lifestyles, e.g. insect mouth parts.

dominant In genetics, used to describe a trait or gene that suppresses expression of its paired trait or gene.

ecdysis The molting of the exoskeleton of arthropods.

ecology Study of the relationships between living things and their enviroment.

egestion The removal of indigestible food from the body.

embryo A plant or animal that is at an early stage of its development.

embryology Study of development of embryos.

endocrine gland A ductless gland that secretes hormones.

endoplasmic reticulum A system of internal membranes in a cell.

endoskeleton An internal skeleton, usually made of bone and cartilage.

entomology Study of insects.

enzyme A biological catalyst.

epidermis The protective outer layer of plants and animals.

epiphytes Plants that grow on other plants without being parasites.

epithelium A type of animal tissue that covers inner and outer surfaces.

ethology Study of animal behavior.

eukaryote An organism whose cells have a nucleus and membrane-bound organelles.

evolution Change in the characteristics of a population of organisms over time.

excretion The removal of the waste products of cell metabolism.

exoskeleton The hard outer covering of some animals, e.g. insects, crustaceans.

fats Energy-rich compounds made from one glycerol and three fatty acid molecules.

fauna All animals occupying a major geographical region.

fermentation The breakdown of carbohydrates by anaerobic respiration.

fertilization The union of male and female gametes to form a zygote.

flagellum A whiplike organelle of locomotion in sperm cells and some unicellular organisms.

flora All plants occupying a major geographical region.

flower The specialized reproductive shoot of a flowering plant.

fruit A ripened ovary of a flowering plant, containing seeds.

fungus (pl. fungi) A member of the kingdom Fungi, a group of nonmotile saprophytes and parasites.

gamete A sex cell, e.g. sperm, ovum.

gene A piece of DNA molecule that determines a hereditary characteristic.

genetics Study of heredity.

genotype The genetic makeup of an organism.

genus A group of closely related species.

germination The start of the development of a plant from seed or spore.

gestation period The time between fertilization and birth.

gland An organ that secretes one or more substances along ducts (exocrine) or into the bloodstream (endocrine).

haploid Having one set of chromosomes in the nucleus.

hemoglobin An oxygen-carrying pigment found in the red blood cells of vertebrate animals.

herbaceous Describes a plant with little or no wood.

herbivore A plant-eating animal.

hermaphrodite An animal that produces male and female gametes.

heterotroph An organism that obtains food by feeding on other organisms, e.g. animals, fungi.

heterozygous Possessing two different alleles of a particular gene.

fungi

hibernation A dormant state, with a reduced metabolic rate, adopted by certain mammals and reptiles to survive winter.

histology Study of tissues.

homeostasis Maintenance of a stable internal environment inside an organism.

homozygous Possessing identical alleles of a particular gene.

hormone A chemical messenger that is produced in one part of an organism and acts in another part.

hybrid The offspring of two parents differing in one or more inherited characteristics.

immunity Resistance to disease.

immunology Study of immune systems.

incubation Keeping eggs or embryos warm (e.g. by sitting on them) in preparation for hatching.

inflorescence A flowering shoot.

instinct Inherited behavior that is not dependent on experience.

invertebrate An animal without a backbone, e.g. an earthworm, or locust.

kingdom In biological taxonomy, the highest level in the hierarchy, e.g. plants, animals.

life cycle The sequence of events between the start of one generation and the start of the next.

lysis The destruction of cells, for example those of bacteria by a bacteriophage.

invertabrate

meiosis A type of cell division that halves the number of chromosomes in a cell, e.g. in the production of sex cells.

meristem Plant tissue consisting of rapidly dividing cells.

metabolism All of the chemical reactions taking place inside an organism.

metamorphosis Change in the form of certain organisms between the juvenile and adult stages, e.g. tadpole and frog.

micro-organism A very small organism, e.g. a protist or bacterium.

mimicry The adoption by one species of the structure or behavior of another to gain protection.

mitochondrion (pl. mitochondria) A rod-shaped organelle inside a cell that is a site of energy release.

mitosis A type of cell division that produces two cells identical to the parent cell.

monocotyledon A flowering plant with one cotyledon in its seed, e.g. grasses.

multicellular Composed of many cells.

mutation Inheritable change in a gene's DNA.

mycelium A mass of "threads" (hyphae) that form a fungus.

natural selection The process that favors the survival and reproduction of organisms that are best adapted to their environment.

nitrogen fixation The conversion of nitrogen gas to nitrates by some bacteria.

nucleus A cell organelle that contains the chromosomes and directs cell activities.

omnivore An animal that eats both plants and animals.

organ A structure composed of several tissues that performs a specific function, e.g. stomach, leaf.

organelle A specialized structure inside a cell, e.g. a chloroplast.

organism An individual living thing.

osmosis Movement of water through a selectively permeable membrane, e.g. a cell membrane.

ovule A structure inside a plant ovary containing female gamete. It develops into seed after fertilization.

ovum (pl. ova) A female gamete or egg.

parasite An organism living on or in, and feeding on, another organism.

parthenogenesis The production of young from unfertilized eggs.

parasite

pathogen A disease-causing organism.

perennial A plant that lives for several years, e.g. oak.

peristalsis Rhythmic contractions in the walls of tubular organs that push the contents onward, e.g. food in the intestine.

phage *See* **bacteriophage**.

phagocytosis A process of a cell actively engulfing other cells or food particles.

phenotype The physical appearance of organism that results from the interaction between a genotype and the environment.

phloem Tissue that carries food in plants.

photoperiodism The response of plants to changes in day length, e.g. flowering.

photosynthesis Food production by plants and algae using sunlight, carbon dioxide, and water.

phylum A major group of organisms that is a subdivision of a kingdom, e.g. mollusks.

physiology Study of how organisms work.

phytoplankton A type of plankton that consists of floating aquatic plants.

plankton Microscopic aquatic organisms that float near the surface of water.

plasmolysis Shrinkage of a plant cell caused by water loss.

pollen Spores produced by plants, containing male gametes.

pollination In flowering plants, the transfer of pollen from anther to stigma.

prokaryotes Organisms whose cells have no nucleus or membrane-bound organelle, e.g. bacteria.

proteins Molecules made up of long chains of amino acids. They are important as enzymes and in cell structure.

protists A group of mostly unicellular plantlike and animal-like organisms that belong to the kingdom Protista.

protozoan A unicellular organism such as an amoeba, belonging to the Protist kingdom.

pupa A stage in metamorphosis that follows the larval stage.

recessive In genetics, used to describe a trait or gene that is expressed only when its paired trait or gene is identical.

reflex action Simple behavior in which a stimulus evokes a response without involving the brain, e.g. a knee jerk.

respiration Chemical reactions inside a cell that break down food molecules to release energy.

ribonucleic acid (RNA) A molecule that transfers information essential for protein synthesis from DNA.

ribosomes Small particles inside cells that are sites of protein synthesis.

saprophyte An organism that feeds on dead organic material, e.g. a mushroom.

saprozoic Feeding by absorbing dissolved nutrients, as do protozoans.

secretion The natural production and release of a useful substance.

seed An embryonic plant and its food supply.

selectively permeable membrane A membrane that allows some molecules to pass through it but not others

sexual reproduction Reproduction involving the fusion of two gametes.

spawn To lay many small eggs, as do fish, for example.

species A group of similar organisms that can interbreed and produce fertile offspring.

spermatozoon (pl. spermatozoa) The male gamete of animals.

spiracle A hole through which a creature breathes, such as in the abdomen of an insect.

sporangium A structure in which spores are produced and stored.

spore A small reproductive body from which a new organism can grow, such as in nonflowering plants, certain bacteria, algae, and fungi.

stamen The male reproductive organ of a flower.

stigma The pollen-receptive tip of the female reproductive organ of a flower.

stimulus Any change that evokes a response from an organism.

sugars Soluble, sweet-tasting carbohydrates, e.g. sucrose, glucose.

symbiosis The living together of two organisms from different species for mutual benefit.

system A group of organs that function together to perform specific functions, e.g. the digestive system.

taxis The response of a protist or lower animal to directional stimulus, usually involving movement, either towards the stimulus or away from it.

taxonomy Classification of organisms.

thallophyte A plantlike organism that resembles a thallus, such as a fungus.

thallus A type of plant that is not separated into stem, leaves, and roots.

tissue A group of similar cells that performs a particular function, e.g. muscle.

translocation The movement of food through the phloem of a plant.

transpiration Evaporation of water from leaves.

tropism Directional growth movement of a plant in response to a stimulus.

turgor The internal tension that keeps a non-woody plant upright, created by the pressure of water in its tissues.

unicellular Consisting of one cell.

vacuole A saclike, fluid-filled cell organelle used for storage.

vein A blood vessel that carries blood toward the heart.

vertebrate An animal with a backbone, e.g. fish, reptile, mammal.

vestigial organ An organ retained during evolution but no longer useful, e.g. the human appendix.

virus An almost lifelike, extremely small particle made of protein and nucleic acid. It needs to parasitize a living cell in order to reproduce.

vitamins A group of substances that are essential in small amounts in the diet.

viviparous Giving birth to live young.

warning coloration Bright pattern of markings indicating that an animal is unpleasant to eat.

xylem Tissue in plants that carries water and mineral salts from the roots to the rest of the plant.

vertebrate

yolk The part of animal egg cell that serves as a food source for the embryo.

zoology Study of animals.

zooplankton A type of plankton consisting of small animals, such as corals.

zygote A fertilized egg cell produced during sexual reproduction.

environmental issues

acceptable daily intake (ADI) A human's safe daily intake of any chemical, in milligrams per kilogram of body weight.

acid rain Rain acidified by sulfuric, nitric, and other acids that form when water and sunlight react with sulfur dioxide, nitrogen oxides and other pollutants released by burning fossil fuels. Acid rain can poison lakes, kill forests, and corrode buildings.

acid rain

additive A chemical added to a food undergoing an industrial process.

agrochemicals The chemical fertilizers and pesticides underpinning modern agriculture.

air pollution Contamination of the air, especially by smoke or gases from vehicles, factories, and power stations. It can cause disease, kill plants, and damage structures.

algal bloom Explosive growth of algae in water over-enriched by nutrients from sewage, artificial fertilizers, etc. Effects can include the mass death of fish.

alternative technology Methods of using resources more efficiently and with less damage to the environment than orthodox technology.

Antarctic Treaty An international agreement (1959) to ensure the peaceful use of Antarctica and ban waste dumping and nuclear testing.

artificial fertilizer Mineral fertilizer usually containing nitrogen, phosphorus and potassium compounds. Overuse can harm soil structure and pollute water supplies.

bioconcentration The concentration of pollutants, especially pesticides, in the living tissue of organisms at the top end of a food chain.

biodegradable Capable of being broken down by such living agents as bacteria. Some plastics are biodegradable.

biodiversity Variety of life forms.

biogas Gas fuel that is obtained from living matter, such as ethanol from sugarcane or methane from decaying organic substances.

biological control Controlling pests by biological not chemical means, as by introducing predators or, as with flies, sterilizing males.

biomass The chemical energy in growing plants, hence biomass fuels (firewood, dried dung, and biogas).

biosphere Earth's living things and their environment.

biosphere reserve A conservation area of two (or more) zones with limited human activity (research, tourism, etc).

captive breeding The breeding of rare animals in zoos or parks, especially to help preserve species that are threatened by extinction in the wild.

carbon dioxide A gas in air. In the carbon cycle, plants make food with carbon dioxide, and breathing, burning, and decay return it to the air. *See* **greenhouse gases**.

carcinogen Any cancer-causing agent.

carrying capacity The population of living things that an ecosystem can support without impairing its stability.

catalytic converter A device removing certain pollutants from exhaust gases of vehicles running on unleaded gasoline.

CFCs *See* chlorofluorocarbons.

Chernobyl Site of the worst nuclear reactor accident, in 1986 in the Ukraine (part of the then USSR).

chlorinated hydrocarbons Highly toxic pesticides including Aldrin, DDT and dieldrin, now largely banned in the West.

chlorofluorocarbons (CFCs) Compounds of chlorine and fluorine once much used as aerosol propellants and refrigerants, and in foam packaging; now known to deplete the ozone layer and act as greenhouse gases.

conservation Protecting the environment.

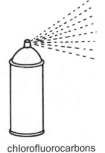

chlorofluorocarbons

contamination Spoiling by contact.

croplands Arable farmlands.

DDT Dichloro-diphenol-trichloroethane. A pesticide with dangerous bioconcentration effects that is banned in much of the West, but still used in developing countries.

debt-for-nature swap Cancellation of the debts of developing nations in return for their commitment to environmental conservation.

desertification Fertile land becoming unproductive desert, often due to overcropping and overgrazing.

dioxin Any of dozens of highly toxic contaminants of products including or involving chlorinated phenols.

ecosystem A community of living things and their environment (pond, tree, forest, etc).

endangered species Any species of plants and animals in danger of extinction.

eutrophication The over-enrichment of water by nutrients (e.g. from chemical fertilizer or sewage), causing overgrowth and decay of plants, deoxygenation of water, and the death of its organisms.

food chain A series of different life forms linked by what they eat and what eats them.

food web A mesh of interlinked food chains.

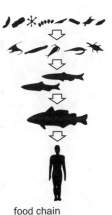

food chain

Gaia hypothesis A theory that the biosphere acts as a self-sustaining, self-regulating organism. British scientist James Lovelock named it after a Greek Earth goddess.

genetic diversity The diversity of living species, also of genetic variations within one species. It helps life forms to persist in face of epidemic diseases or harsh climatic change.

geothermal energy Useful heat obtained by pumping water past hot underground rocks.

GNP Gross national product: a measure of national wealth including overseas income.

greenhouse effect Alleged human-made atmospheric warming by accumulating gases trapping solar heat below them rather like a greenhouse roof. *See* **greenhouse gases**.

greenhouse gases Carbon dioxide, methane, chlorofluorocarbons, nitrous oxide and low-level ozone. *See* **greenhouse effect**.

green movement A popular movement urging production and use of environmentally harmless consumer goods. Green politicians would curb economic and population growth and protect the natural environment.

green revolution A program launched in the 1960s to boost world food supplies with new, high-yielding hybrid cereals.

habitat The type of place where an animal or plant normally lives.

hazardous waste Toxic industrial and other wastes, posing major disposal problems.

heavy metals Elements including cadmium, lead and mercury, all poisonous. Careless dumping can create local health hazards.

herbicides Weed-killing chemicals such as paraquat, a highly toxic contact poison.

irradiated food Food preserved by exposure to ionizing radiation. Critics say partly-rotted food would still contain toxins.

landfill Disposal of hazardous or other waste by tipping it in a hole in the ground. Consequences can be an explosive methane build-up and contaminated water supplies.

lean-burn engine An automobile engine that curbs nitrogen oxide exhaust emissions.

London Dumping Convention Agreement (1975) controlling the dumping of waste from ships and aircraft. (Also called the Convention on the Prevention of Marine Pollution by Dumping of Waste and Other Matter.)

low-impact technology Technology with minimal effect on the environment.

migration corridor A protected strip of natural habitat through which wild animals are able to migrate.

monoculture Extensive cultivation of one crop. It maximizes use of farm machinery, but increases risks of crop disease, pest infestation, and impaired soil structure.

mutagens Chemicals causing mutations, i.e. genetic changes (often harmful) in a living organism's offspring.

national park An area that is preserved chiefly for its outstanding natural beauty or scientific importance.

nature reserve An area set aside chiefly to protect its wild plants and animals.

nitrate A nitrogen compound essential for plant growth, but liable to contaminate water supplies where nitrate fertilizer is washed into rivers or seeps underground.

nitrogen cycle The natural circulation of nitrogen (including nitrogen compounds) from air to consuming organisms (plants, animals and bacteria) and back to air.

noise pollution Persistent loud noise (as from traffic, machinery, audio equipment) causing discomfort and perhaps even deafness.

nuclear accident An accident involving a nuclear power plant, perhaps with an escape of harmful radioactivity.

nuclear waste Radioactive waste produced by the nuclear industry. Safe long-term disposal of this waste presents major problems.

nuclear winter The prolonged period of cold, dark weather likely on a global scale if a large-scale nuclear war produced immense dust clouds shutting out light from the Sun.

organic farming Farming without artificial fertilizers or pesticides. Organic farming involves manuring with plant or animal wastes and the biological control of pests and weeds. *See* **biological control**.

organophosphates Organophosphorus compounds, used as pesticides, which act as nerve poisons and can severely affect wildlife.

overfishing Harvesting fish stocks faster than breeding can make good the deficit.

overgrazing Letting livestock graze land so heavily that the soil loses fertility, grass grows sparsely and soil erosion may take place.

ozone layer A belt of ozone gas in the upper atmosphere. This ozone filters out incoming ultraviolet radiation liable to damage the chemicals all living things are made of. Holes appearing in the ozone layer above polar regions have been blamed on chlorofluorocarbons (CFCs).

PCBs Polychlorinated biphenyls. Compounds once much used in electrical products, but highly toxic and now difficult to dispose of because extremely stable.

pesticides Chemicals that kill plant, animal and other pests, and may also pollute food and water supplies. Well-known toxic pesticides include Aldrin, Chlordane and DDT. *See* **chlorinated hydrocarbons, organophosphates**.

plutonium Element produced in large quantities by nuclear reactors; also used in nuclear weapons.

pollution Introducing harmful substances or other agents into the environment.

population explosion The explosive worldwide growth of human population since the industrial revolution.

population pyramid A diagram showing successive age groups as a pyramid of horizontal bars. Each bar's length shows the relative size of one age group.

radioactivity The emission of rays and subatomic particles from the nuclei of certain elements decaying into others, notably uranium and its decay products, down to, but excluding, lead. Radioactivity from nuclear bombs and installations, and even certain rocks, can injure living tissues.

Ramsar Convention An international agreement (1971) to protect wetlands. (Also known as the Convention on Wetlands of International Importance especially as Waterfowl Habitat.)

recycling Conserving by reusing (directly or after reprocessing) such used materials as aluminum, glass and paper.

renewable resources Crops, fish, timber, solar, and wind energy and other resources that can be used without exhausting them.

reprocessing The extraction of plutonium (for military use) and unused uranium from the nuclear fuel of a reactor.

salinization Making soil too salty for growing land plants. Salinization is a problem in some irrigated soils of hot dry climates. Evaporation concentrates sucked-up salts in the soil's upper levels.

scrubber Equipment curbing air pollution by removing toxic gases from chimneys; used in power stations burning fossil fuels.

smog Air pollution caused by combined smoke and fog or (photochemical smog) by sunlight acting on vehicles' exhaust gases.

solar power The Sun's energy exploited by solar panels, collectors or cells to heat water or air or to generate electricity.

sustainable development Economic progress without damage to ecosystems.

Tropical Forest Action Plan A scheme to conserve tropical forests, devised in 1987 by UN agencies, the World Bank and the World Resources Institute. Critics claim it favors industrial forestry.

unleaded gasoline Lead-free gasoline, promoted to reduce a damaging accumulation of lead in the environment.

uranium A highly radioactive element used in thermonuclear reactors.

urbanization Growth of towns and cities: a global trend. Huge unsanitary slums are a feature of fast-growing cities in the developing world.

waldsterben (forest death) Damage to trees caused by air pollution and secondary infection.

tropical forest

waste disposal Removing and destroying or storing damaged, used or other unwanted domestic, agricultural or industrial products and substances. Disposal includes burning, burial at landfill sites or at sea, and recycling.

water pollution Contamination of rivers, lakes and seas by fertilizers, pesticides, sewage, and oil or toxic waste from ships and factories.

wave power The energy in sea waves exploited to generate electricity.

urbanization

wetlands Bogs, marshes, swamps, flood plains, and estuaries. Many have high and varied populations of plants and animals.

wind power The energy in wind exploited by aerogenerators to generate electricity.

World Conservation Strategy A strategy launched (1980) by the IUCN and WWF to help nations protect ecosystems.

World Heritage sites Designated natural and cultural sites internationally recognized as of outstanding importance.

chemistry

acid A solution of a substance in water which has a pH of less than 7.

actinides (actinoids) The name of the group of elements with atomic numbers from 89 (Actinium) to 103 (Lawrencium).

adsorption The process by which molecules of gases or liquids become attached to the surface of another substance. Desorption is the opposite process.

aerosol Extremely small liquid or solid particles suspended in air or another gas.

aliphatic Describes organic compounds composed of carbon atoms in straight or branched chains.

alkali A solution of a substance in water which has a pH of more than 7 and has an excess of hydroxyl ions in the solution.

allotrope An elements (such as oxygen, which can exist in its normal form and as ozone) which can exist with different physical properties while in the same physical state.

amine Any of a series of organic compounds of nitrogen, such as ethylamine.

amphoteric Describes a substance which exhibits properties of both an acid and a base.

anhydrous Containing no water; applied to salts without water of crystallization.

anion An ion that carries a negative charge, especially one migrating to an anode during electrolysis.

anode Electrode carrying the positive charge in a solution undergoing electrolysis.

aqueous Containing water

aromatic compound **aromatic compounds** The group of hydrocarbons derived from benzene (C_6H_6) which have a ring structure.

atomic number Or proton number (Z) The number of protons in the nucleus of an atom. If not electrically charged, this is equal to the number of electrons in its shells.

atomicity The atomicity of an element is the number of atoms in one molecule of the element

autocatalysis The action as a catalyst by one of the products of a chemical reaction.

azeotrope (azeotropic mixtures) A mixture of liquids which boils without a change in composition. When it boils it gives off a vapor whose composition is the same as the liquid.

base (Usually a metal oxide or hydroxide) A substance existing as molecules or ions which can take up hydrogen ions. When a base reacts with an acid it forms a salt and water only.

Brownian movement The random motion of microscopic particles suspended in a gas or liquid.

buckyball molecule An allotropic form of carbon (also known as a buckminsterfullerene). It has a cage structure and has the formula C50, C60, and C70.

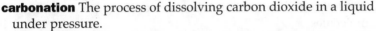

buckyball molecule

buffer solution A solution which can maintain an almost constant pH value when dilute acids or alkalis are added to it.

calorific value The energy value of a food or fuel, given by the heat evolved when a unit amount (1 gram or 1 kg) is completely burnt in oxygen.

carbonation The process of dissolving carbon dioxide in a liquid under pressure.

carbonization Anaerobic destructive distillation. Coal forms coke in this process; wood forms charcoal.

catalyst A substance which alters the rate of a chemical reaction. It takes part in the reaction but remains chemically unchanged by it.

cathode The electrode carrying the negative charge in a solution undergoing electrolysis.

cation An ion that carries a positive charge, which is attracted by the negatively charged electrode, the cathode, during electrolysis.

caustic Describes an alkaline substance which burns or corrodes organic material

change of state The physical process where matter moves from one state to another. Examples of such changes are melting, evaporation, boiling, condensation, freezing, crystallization, and sublimation.

chemiluminescence Light that is radiated during a chemical reaction

chemurgy The branch of chemistry that deals with the development of new chemical products from organic raw materials.

chlorofluorocarbons Compounds formed when some or all of the hydrogen atoms in a hydrocarbon have been replaced with chlorine and fluorine.

chromatography A way of separating and identifying mixtures of solutes in a solution.

coagulation The grouping together of small particles in a solution into larger particles. Such a solution eventually coagulates with the particles forming either a precipitate or a gel.

colloid A substance made of very small particles whose size (1-100 nm) is between those of a suspension and those in solution.

combustion The chemical term for burning, usually in oxygen.

concentration A measure of the quantity of solute dissolved in a solution at a given temperature.

condensation The process by which a liquid forms from its vapor.

conjugate solutions Solutions of two substances which are partially miscible will form two conjugate solutions in equilibrium at a certain temperature.

cracking The process used in the petroleum industry to convert large-chain hydrocarbon molecules to smaller ones. The process uses heat and catalysts.

cross-linking Chemical bonds between adjacent polymer molecules.

crystal A substance with an orderly arrangement of atoms, ions or molecules in a regular geometrical shape.

cytochemistry The branch of chemistry that deals with the study of cells.

decomposition The process of breakdown of a chemical compound into less complex substances.

dehydration A chemical reaction to remove a water molecule from a compound.

crystal

deliquescence The way in which a solid substance absorbs water from the atmosphere. The process can continue until the substance passes into solution.

deuterium An isotope of hydrogen. Its nucleus contains one proton and one neutron and has a relative atomic mass of two.

diffusion The process of rapid random movement of the particles of a liquid or gas which eventually form a uniform mixture.

dispersion Small particles distributed in a fluid.

dissociation The breaking down of a molecule into smaller molecules, atoms or ions.

dissolving The adding of a solute to a solvent to form a uniform solution.

distillation A process in which a solution (or a mixture of liquids whose boiling points are widely differing) is heated to a particular temperature to produce a vapor. This vapor is condensed, forming a pure liquid (the distillate) which has a single boiling point.

effervescence The production of bubbles which rise to the surface in a liquid.

efflorescence The way in which a hydrated crystal loses water of crystallization to the atmosphere, making its surface become powdery.

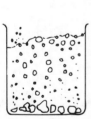
effervescence

effusion The process by which a gas under pressure moves through a small aperture into an region of lower pressure.

electrode A conductor which allows current to flow through an electrolyte, gas, vacuum, dielectric, or semiconductor.

electrolysis The process by which an electrolyte is decomposed when a direct electric current is passed through it between electrodes.

electrolysis

electrolyte A substance which forms ions when molten or dissolved in a solvent and which carries an electric current during electrolysis.

electron One of the three basic subatomic particles. It is very light and orbits round the nucleus of an atom. It has a negative charge.

electrophoresis The movement of charged particles, colloidal particles or ions through a fluid under the influence of an electric field.

element A substance which cannot be split into simpler substances using chemical methods

elementary particles The particles from which atoms are made. Neutrons and protons are found in the nucleus of the atom. Electrons form a cloud around the nucleus.

emulsifier A substance which both assists the formation of an emulsion and stabilizes it when formed.

emulsion A colloidal dispersion in which small droplets of one liquid are dispersed within another, such as oil in water or water in oil.

enantiotropy The transformation of one allotrope, or form, of a substance into another by a change in temperature. Such a change is reversible.

endothermic change A chemical reaction which absorbs heat from the surroundings.

enthalpy A measure of the stored heat energy contained in a substance.

equilibrium The state of a reversible chemical reaction at which the forward and backward reactions take place at the same rate

ester An organic compound formed from an alcohol and an organic acid.

eutectic mixture A mixture of two or more substances which melts at the lowest freezing point of any mixture of the components. This temperature is the eutectic point. The liquid melt has the same composition as the solid.

evaporation The process in which a liquid changes state to vapor. It can occur at any temperature up to the boiling point of the liquid.

exothermic change A chemical reaction which releases heat to the surroundings.

fatty acid A monobasic acid, especially one found in animal fats or vegetable oils.

filter A device containing a porous material, for example, paper or sand, which can remove suspended solid particles from a fluid.

filtrate Clear liquid which has passed through a filter.

fission A process (spontaneous or induced) during which a heavy atomic nucleus disintegrates into two lighter atoms which together have less mass than the total initial material. This lost mass is converted to energy, the amount is given by Einstein's equation $E=mc_2$.

flocculation The grouping together of colloidal particles to form a precipitate which may float in the liquid.

fluid A substance which can flow because its particles are not fixed in position. Liquids and gases are fluids.

fluorescence The emission of light from an object which has been irradiated by light or other radiations. Energy is absorbed by the object and then re-radiated at a longer wavelength than the incident light.

foam A dispersion of gas in a liquid or solid.

functional group The atom (or group of atoms) present in a molecule which determines the characteristic properties of that molecule.

fusion (melting) The process by which a change of state from solid to liquid occurs.

gel A colloidal solution which has formed a jelly. The solid particles are arranged as a fine network in the liquid phase.

half-life A substance which undergoes exponential decay decays by the same ratio in equal intervals of time. The constant ratio is the half-life. The rate of radioactive decay of a substance is defined by its half-life.

halide A compound which a halogen makes with another element. Metal halides are ionic; nonmetal halides are formed by covalent bonding.

halogenation The introduction of one or more halogen atoms into the structure of an organic molecule.

halogens The elements fluorine, chlorine, bromine, iodine, astatine.

heterogeneous reaction A chemical reaction taking place between substances in different physical states, e.g. solids, liquids and/or gases.

homogeneous reaction A chemical reaction taking place between substances which are in the same physical state, e.g. solid, liquid or gas.

homologous series A series of related organic compounds.

humidity The measure of the amount of water vapor in air, given as either the absolute or relative humidity.

hydrate A salt containing water of crystallization, e.g. $CuSO_4.5H_2O$.

hydride A compound formed between hydrogen and one other element.

hydrocarbons Organic compounds which contain carbon and hydrogen only.

hydrogenation The addition of hydrogen to another compound, usually an unsaturated organic compound. Unsaturated oils are hydrogenated to form margarine.

hydrolysis The process by which a chemical compound decomposes through reaction with water.

hydrophilic Water-loving. In solution, refers to a chemical or part of a chemical that is highly attracted to water.

hydrophobic Water-hating. Refers to a chemical or part of a chemical that repels water.

hygroscopic Describes a substance which absorbs moisture from the air without becoming liquid.

immiscible Describes substances which do not mix and form more than one phase when brought together.

incandescence The emission of light by a body which is strongly heated.

inert A substance which is either very or completely unreactive. Nitrogen and the noble gases are inert.

inorganic Not relating to living organisms, or not containing hydrocarbon groups.

immiscible

insoluble Describes a substance which does not dissolve in a particular solvent under certain conditions of temperature and pressure.

ion An electrically charged atom or group of atoms.

ionization The process by which an atom becomes an ion by either losing or gaining one or more electrons.

isomers Different (usually organic) compounds having the same molecular formula and relative molecular mass but some different properties, as they have different three-dimensional structures.

isomorphism The existence of two or more different substances which have the same crystal structure.

isotonic Describes solutions which have the same osmotic pressure.

isotopes Atoms of the same element (all chemically identical) having the same atomic number but containing different numbers of neutrons, giving a different mass number.

lanthanides Elements with an atomic number of 57 through 71. Also called rare-earth elements.

latent heat The quantity of heat which is absorbed or released by a substance during a change of state (fusion or vaporization) at constant temperature.

law A rule describing certain natural observable phenomena or the relationship between effects of variable quantities.

litmus paper Paper impregnated with litmus, a lichen-derived powder that changes color according to the acidity or basicity of a substance it comes into contact with. Litmus paper is thus used to test for acidity or basicity.

luminescence Light emission from a substance caused by an effect other than heat. Fluorescence and phosphorescence are forms of luminescence.

mass number The total number of protons and neutrons (nucleons) in the nucleus of an atom.

melting

melting The change of state from solid to liquid. It occurs when the particles in the solid lattice have gained sufficient energy to break the bonds which hold them in the lattice.

metalloid An element which has both metallic and nonmetallic properties.

metastable Describes a system which appears to be stable, but which can undergo a rapid change if disturbed.

miscible Describes liquids which mix together completely.

mixture A system which consists of two or more substances (solid, liquid, or gas) present in any proportions in a container. There is no chemical bonding between substances. A mixture can be separated using physical methods. The formation of a mixture does not involve a change in temperature.

molality The concentration of a solute giving the number of moles of solute dissolved in 1 kg of solvent.

molarity The concentration of a solution giving the number of moles of solute dissolved in 1 dm^3 of solution.

mole The amount of a substance which contains the same number of entities (atoms, molecules, ions, any group of particles, but the type must be specified) as there are atoms in 0.012 kg of the carbon-12 isotope. The actual number is known as the Avogadro number, which has a value of 6.023×10^{23}.

molecule The smallest part of an element or chemical compound which can exist independently with all the properties of the element or compound. It is made up of one or more atoms bonded together in a fixed whole number ratio.

monoacid An acid that has one replaceable hydrogen atom.

monobasic Describes an acid, for example hydrogen chloride, that has only one replaceable hydrogen ion in a molecule.

monomer A basic unit from which a polymer is made.

monotropy The condition in which an element can exist in more than allotrope but one is always more stable under all conditions. The other forms are metastable.

neutral Describes a solution whose pH is 7. It is neither acidic nor alkaline.

neutralization The reaction of an acid and a base forming a salt and water.

neutron One of the three basic particles in an atoms. It is found in the nucleus and has zero charge.

noble gas Any of a series of elements that are mostly inert and monatomic, for example argon and helium.

nucleon A proton or neutron.

nucleus The small (about 10^{-14} m diameter) core of an atom. All nuclei contain positively charged protons, and all but hydrogen contain neutrons which have zero charge.

nuclide A particular isotope of an element, identified by the number of protons and neutrons in the nucleus.

organic Relates to either living organisms, or compounds containing carbon (except carbonates, hydrogen carbonates and carbon dioxide).

osmosis The movement of solvent molecules through a semipermeable membrane from a dilute solution to a more concentrated solution.

osmotic pressure The pressure that must be applied to a solution, when separated from a more dilute solution by a semipermeable membrane, to prevent the inflow of solvent molecules.

oxidation A substance is oxidized if it gains oxygen, loses hydrogen, or loses electrons.

oxide A compound consisting of oxygen and another element only. They can be either ionic or covalent and there are four types of oxide—acidic, basic, neutral and amphoteric.

ozone One of the two allotropes of oxygen, existing as O_3. It is a bluish gas with a penetrating smell.

petrochemical A chemical that is derived from petroleum or natural gas.

petrochemistry The branch of chemistry that studies petroleum and petroleum derivatives.

pH A scale which gives a measure of the acidity of an aqueous solution. A neutral solution has a pH of 7; an acidic solution has a lower value, and an alkaline solution a higher value.

phase Part of a system whose physical properties and chemical composition are consistent and are separated from other parts of the system by a boundary surface.

phosphorescence The emission of light by an object, and the persistence of this emission over long periods, following irradiation by light or other forms of radiation.

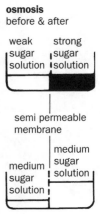

osmosis
before & after

weak sugar solution | strong sugar solution

semi permeable membrane

medium sugar solution | medium sugar solution

photocatalysis The speeding up or slowing of a chemical reaction by light.

photochemical reactions Chemical reactions which are initiated by a particular wavelength of light.

photolysis The decomposition or disassociation of a compound when exposed to light of a certain wavelength.

phototropy The ability of certain substances to change color reversibly on exposure to light of a certain wavelength.

plasticizer A substance added to polymers and other materials to increase their flexibility.

polar molecule A molecule which has a positive charge at one end and a negative charge at the other.

poly- prefix meaning many. Used in the naming of chemical compounds.

polymer A material containing very large molecules which are built up from a series of small basic units (monomers). There can be between hundreds and hundreds of thousands of basic units in a polymer.

polyunsaturated Describes fats or other carbon compounds that contain many unsaturated bonds.

porous Able to allow the passage of water, air, or other fluids.

precipitate An insoluble substance formed by a chemical reaction.

proton One of the three basic particles in the atom, found in the nucleus with the neutron. It has positive charge.

pyrolysis The decomposition of a substance by heat.

qualitative Describes a statement, or analysis, which gives the composition of an item, not the amounts present.

quantitative Describes a statement, or analysis, which gives the amounts of an item present.

radical A group of atoms forming part of many molecules. They are very reactive as they have an incomplete electron structure.

radioactivity The spontaneous disintegration of certain isotopes accompanied by the emission of radiation (a-rays, b-rays, c-rays).

rare-earth elements *See* **lanthanides.**

reactant A substance present at the start of chemical reaction which takes part in the reaction.

reaction A process in which substances react to form new substances. Bonds are broken and re-formed in chemical reactions.

redox chemistry A process in which one substance is reduced and another is oxidized at the same time.

reduction The reverse of oxidation.

reforming The catalytic conversion of hydrocarbon molecules into other products

regelation The melting of ice when subjected to pressure and

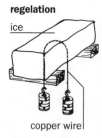
regelation
ice
copper wire

refreezing on removal of that pressure.

residue The solid remaining after the completion of a chemical process.

reversible reaction A chemical reaction which can proceed in either direction. It does not reach completion but achieves dynamic equilibrium.

saturated compounds Chemical compounds which contain no double or triple bonds in their structure.

saturated solution A solution where there is an equilibrium between the solution and its solute.

semipermeable membrane A substance which allows solvent molecules to pass through but not solute molecules.

sol A liquid solution or suspension of a colloid.

soluble A relative term which describes a substance which can dissolve in a particular solvent.

solute A substance which dissolves in a solvent to form a solution.

solution A uniform mixture of one or more solutes in a solvent. It usually refers to solids dissolved in liquids but can also refer to gases in liquids, gases in solids, etc.

solvation The process of interaction between ions of a solute and the molecules of the solvent. This process is known as hydration when the solvent is water.

solvent A substance, usually a liquid, in which a solute dissolves to form a solution.

states of matter

states of matter The three states are solid, liquid, and gas.

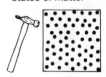

stereoisomerism Isomers of a compound which have the same formula and functional groups and differ only in the arrangements of groups in space are stereoisomers.

stoichiometry The calculation of the proportions in which elements or compounds (molecules) react with each other.

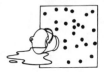

structural isomer Molecules which are structural isomers have the same molecular formula but have different molecular structures. They may contain different functional groups.

sublimation The reversible process by which a substance in a solid state changes directly to a gas.

supersaturated solution A solution which contains a higher concentration of solute than does a saturated solution at that temperature. A supersaturated solution is metastable.

surface tension Within a liquid, molecules attract each other equally in all directions. At the surface, however, there is no force attracting them outwards, so the molecules are pulled towards the interior of the liquid.

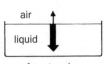

air

liquid

surface tension

surfactant (surface active agent) A substance (for example a detergent) added to a liquid which can alter its spreading or wetting characteristics by lowering its surface tension.

suspension A type of dispersion in which small solid particles are dispersed in a liquid or gas.

synthesis The formation of chemical compounds by constructing them directly from their elements or from other simple compounds.

tautomerism Tautomerism occurs when a compound exists as two different structural isomers that are in dynamic equilibrium with each other.

thermal decomposition The breaking down of a chemical compound by heat into smaller components which do not recombine on cooling.

thermal dissociation The breaking down of a chemical compound by heat into smaller components which recombine to form the original compound on cooling.

thermoplastic Describes a substance which becomes flexible when heated and hardens on cooling with no change in its properties.

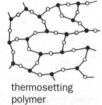

thermosetting
polymer

thermosetting polymer A polymer which has a structure of interlinked chains. They cannot be softened by heat but are decomposed by it.

titration A method of quantitative analysis.

triple point The conditions of temperature and pressure at which the three phases of a substance (solid, liquid, and gas) are in equilibrium.

tritium An isotope of hydrogen. Its nucleus contains one proton and two neutrons and thus has a relative atomic mass of three.

unsaturated compounds Chemical compounds which contain one or more double or triple bonds in their structure.

unsaturated solution A solution in which the solvent is able to absorb more solute at a particular temperature.

valency The number of electrons required by an atom to form a stable molecule or radical.

vapor Gas which is below the temperature at which it can be liquefied by pressure (the critical temperature).

vaporization The process of change of state of a solid or liquid to a vapor.

variable A condition, such as temperature, concentration and pressure, which can be changed in a chemical reaction.

volatile Describes a substance which readily turns into a vapor.

water of crystallization The exact number of water molecules which are chemically bonded to a molecule of a salt within a hydrated crystalline compound.

zymurgy The branch of chemistry that deals with fermentation processes, for example in brewing.

physics

acceleration Rate of change in velocity, measured in feet (meters) per second per second $(ft(m)/sec^2)$.

acoustics The study of sound waves.

adhesion A force of attraction between molecules.

aerodynamics The study of the flow of gases, especially air.

alpha particle A helium nucleus that has a positive electric charge.

alternating current A rapidly reversing electric current.

ampere/amp The unit of electric current in the international system.

amplifier An electronic device that increases the strength of a signal.

amplitude A wave's greatest displacement from equilibrium.

anode A positive electrode.

Archimedes' principle The principle that a body submersed in a liquid loses weight equal to that of the volume of liquid that it displaces.

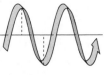

amplitude

atom The smallest part of an element capable of taking part in a chemical change.

atomic number The number of protons in the nucleus of an atom.

atomic weight *See* **relative atomic mass**.

barometer An instrument for measuring atmospheric pressure.

beta particle An electron emitted by an isotope undergoing radioactive decay.

boiling point The temperature at which a liquid's vapor pressure equals external pressure.

Boyle's law The principle that at a constant temperature the volume of a given mass of gas is inversely proportional to its pressure.

buoyancy The upthrust (upward force) on a body placed in a fluid.

Calorie/calorie A calorie is the amount of heat needed to raise the temperature of a gram of water by 1°C. A Calorie (kilocalorie) is 1000 calories.

capacitance A system's electrical capacity for storing an electric charge.

capillarity The rise or fall of a liquid in a narrow tube, caused by the relative attraction of its molecules for each other and the tube wall.

cathode A negative electrode.

cathode-ray tube A vacuum tube and cathode forming the

picture tube in television receivers.

Celsius The centigrade temperature scale in which water freezes at 0°C and boils at 100°C.

centripetal force A force that acts radially inward on an object moving in a circular path.

concave curving inward

condensation The change from vapor into liquid.

conduction (1) The transfer of heat from molecule to molecule. (2) The flow of electrons from atom to atom through a conductor.

conductor (1) An object conducting heat. (2) A substance conducting an electric current.

concave

conservation of mass and energy The principle that, in any system, the sum of mass plus energy is constant.

conservation of momentum The principle that, in any system, linear or angular momentum is constant unless an external force acts on the system.

convection Heat transfer by means of currents circulating through fluids.

convex curving outward

coulomb The unit of electric charge, defined as the quantity of electricity conveyed by one ampere in one second.

curie A unit used to measure the activity of a radioactive substance.

current The flow of electricity through a conductor.

convex

decay The breakdown of a radioactive substance, producing daughter (decay) products.

decibel A logarithmic unit of sound intensity.

density Mass per unit volume.

diffraction An effect caused when, after passing an obstacle or through a narrow slit, waves (e.g. of light) interfere with each other and may bend or spread.

diffusion The mixing of substances due to the motion of their particles.

diode An electronic device with two electrodes; often used as a rectifier.

direct current An electric current that always flows in the same direction.

döppler effect Apparent change in the frequency of light waves or sound waves due to the relative motion of the observer and the source of the waves.

efficiency The ratio of a machine's energy output to energy input.

Einstein's law The law of the equivalence of mass and energy, expressed as $E = mc^2$ or energy equals mass times the velocity of light squared.

elasticity The ability of a substance that has been deformed to regain its original size and shape when the deforming stress is removed.

electricity Phenomena related to static electric charges and electric currents.

electrode A terminal that conducts electricity toward or away from a conductor in a circuit.

electrolyte A dissolved substance conducting, and decomposed by, an electric current.

electromagnet A temporary magnet produced when electric current flows through wire that has been coiled around soft iron.

electromagnetic radiation Waves of energy associated with electric and magnetic fields.

electromagnetism The study of electric and magnetic fields and their interaction.

electron A subatomic particle carrying a negative charge.

electronics The use and study of electricity in semiconductors.

energy The capacity for doing work.

engine A device converting one form of energy into another, especially mechanical energy.

evaporation Conversion of a liquid to a vapor, below its boiling point.

Fahrenheit scale The temperature scale which measures the melting point of ice at 32° and the boiling point of water at 212°.

fallout Radioactive matter which has fallen to Earth after a nuclear explosion.

farad A unit of capacitance. A conductor has a capacitance of one farad if a charge of one coulomb changes its potential by one volt.

ferromagnetism The magnetic property of cobalt, iron, nickel, and some alloys.

fiber optics The use and study of light transmission through fine, flexible glass and plastic tubes.

fission The splitting of an atom's nucleus to release subatomic particles and energy.

fluid A (gas or liquid) substance which takes the shape of its container.

flux A flow of particles, a fluid, or an electric or magnetic field.

force Something applied which alters a body's state of rest or motion.

freezing Change of state from liquid to solid.

frequency Number of cycles or waves per second.

fundamental particles Theoretically indivisible subatomic particles grouped as matter particles (electrons, muons, taus, neutrinos, and quarks) and force particles (W and Z bosons, gluons, gravitons, and photons).

fusion 1) Melting. 2) A nuclear reaction forming a heavier nucleus from light atomic nuclei and in the process releasing nuclear energy.

g A unit of acceleration in free fall due to gravity. On Earth this is about 32 feet per second per second (9.81 m/sec²).

gamma rays Penetrating extreme shortwave radiation emitted in decay of some radioactive substances.

geiger counter A device for measuring radioactivity.

gravitation The mutual attraction between bodies, due to their masses.

gravity Intensity of gravitation measured at the surface of a star, planet or other heavenly body.

half-life The time in which half the atoms in a radioactive isotope decay.

heat A form of energy passed between bodies of differing temperature.

hertz A unit of frequency with a value of one cycle per second.

hydrodynamics The study of moving liquids and fluids.

hydrostatics The study of the forces in stationary liquids and fluids.

gravity

induction (electromagnetic) The process of inducing a voltage in an electrical conductor by changing the magnetic field around it.

inertia A body's tendency to maintain a state of rest or of uniform motion.

infrared radiation Invisible heat radiation emitted from hot bodies.

integrated circuit A tiny electrical circuit that is made up of a semiconductor chip with several electronic components.

interference The effects of imposing one set of waves on another.

ion An electrically charged atom or group of atoms.

isotopes Atoms of an element with an identical number of protons but differing numbers of neutrons.

joule A unit of work or energy transfer. One joule is equal to work done by a force of one newton moved about 1 m in the direction of the force.

kelvin scale An absolute temperature scale in which 0 K (zero kelvin) equals -459.67°F (-273.15°C), absolute zero, and 273.15 K corresponds to 32°F (0°C).

kinetic energy The energy possessed by moving bodies.

latent heat Heat released or absorbed when a substance changes state without a change in temperature.

lens A device causing light rays or subatomic particles to converge or diverge as they pass through it.

lever A rigid bar turned about a fixed point (fulcrum) to support or move a load; a simple form of machine.

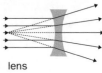

lens

light Electromagnetic radiation with wavelengths visible to the eye.

lux A unit of illumination equal to a luminous flux of one lumen spread over 1 sq m.

machine A device performing work, especially where a smaller force or effort moves a greater load.

lever
a fulcrum
b load
c effort

mach number A unit of velocity. Mach 1 is the speed of sound; Mach 5 is described as hypersonic.

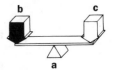

magnet A substance able to attract iron and which produces a magnetic field.

magnetic field An area of magnetic influence.

magnetism Forces of attraction and repulsion associated with magnets.

mass The amount of matter in a body.

mass-energy equation *See* **Einstein's law**.

mass number The number of nucleons (protons and neutrons) in the nucleus of an atom.

mechanical advantage The ratio of load to effort produced by a machine.

mechanics The study of how objects move under the influence of forces.

microwaves Electromagnetic radiation between radio and infrared wavelengths.

moment The turning effect produced by a force acting around a point.

momentum Mass multiplied by velocity.

motor A machine that converts electrical energy into mechanical energy.

neutron A subatomic particle with roughly the mass of a proton and no electric charge.

newton The unit of force giving a mass of 1 kg an acceleration of about 1 m per second per second.

nuclear energy Energy released by the conversion of matter to energy during a chain reaction caused by nuclear fission or fusion in a bomb or reactor.

nucleus An atom's positively charged core containing one or more protons and (except in hydrogen) one or more neutrons.

ohm The unit of electrical resistance.

optics The study of light and its uses.

oscillation A repetitive vibration with a regular frequency.

Pascal The unit of pressure produced when one newton acts on about 1 sq m.

Pascal's principle The principle that pressure applied to any part of an enclosed fluid acts without loss on all other parts of the fluid.

pendulum A suspended weight swinging regularly under gravity's influence.

permeability The ability of a substance to let another substance pass through it.

photon A unit or quantum of electromagnetic radiation.

physics The study of matter and energy.

pitch Sound frequency.

Planck's law The principle that lectromagnetic radiation consists of units (quanta or photons).

plasma A gas with roughly equal numbers of negative and positive ions.

pneumatics The study of the mechanical properties of gases.

polarization In transverse waves, vibrations confined to one plane.

poles Two points of a magnet where magnetism seems concentrated.

potential difference The energy difference that tends to make an electric charge or current move. It is measured in volts.

power The rate of energy transfer.

pressure Force per unit area.

prism A transparent, solid object, with at least two plane faces, that bends a light beam and splits it into its component colors.

proton A positively charged subatomic particle.

quantum mechanics A system of mechanics that supplanted Newtonian mechanics in the study of subatomic particles.

quantum theory The theory that electromagnetic radiation consists of units called quanta or photons.

rad A unit of radiation absorbed from a radioactive source.

radiation Electromagnetic and radioactive energy emitted as rays, waves, or particles.

radioactivity The emission of subatomic particles and rays due to the disintegration of the atomic nuclei of certain isotopes of some elements.

radioisotope An isotope that is radioactive.

rectifier An electrical device that converts alternating current into direct current.

refraction The bending of a sound wave or ray of light as it passes from one medium to another.

relative atomic mass (atomic weight) The mass (quantity of matter) of atoms.

relativity, theory of Einstein's two-part theory involving the idea of a four-dimensional space–time continuum.

resistance The ratio between the potential difference across a conductor and the current that is carried. It is measured in ohms.

semiconductor A substance with properties between those of an electrical insulator and a conductor at room temperature, but with conductivity modified by temperature and impurities; crucial in modern electronic devices.

SI units An international system of scientific units (Système International d'Unités) based on the kilogram, meter, and second.

solenoid A wire coil partly surrounding an iron core. When current flows through the wire it produces an electromagnetic effect.

sound The phenomenon produced by certain pressure waves reaching the ear.

spectrum A band of electromagnetic radiation with components separated into their relative wavelengths.

strain Deformation due to stress.

superconductivity The increase in electrical conductivity and decrease in resistance, in certain substances, at very low temperatures.

surface tension The cohesion of a liquid's surface caused by the inward attraction of its molecules.

temperature Degree of "hotness" measured in Celsius, Fahrenheit, etc.

thermodynamics The study of heat and heat-related energy.

transducer A device that converts one kind of wave signal into another.

transformer A device transferring an alternating current from one circuit to another.

transistor A semiconductor device used, as a rectifier, amplifier or switch.

ultrasonics The study of frequencies higher than those we can hear.

ultraviolet radiation Electromagnetic radiation that has a wavelength between that of visible light and that of X-rays.

unified field theory A proposed theory, still being sought after, that will relate electromagnetic, gravitational, and nuclear fields.

vacuum A space without matter.

vapor A gas that becomes a liquid under increased pressure.

vector A quantity that is direction as well as magnitude.

velocity Rate of motion in a particular direction.

viscosity In fluids, the resistance to flow.

volt The unit of potential difference.

watt The unit of power: one watt equals one joule per second.

wave A disturbance or pulse moving through space or a medium.

wavelength

wavelength The crest-to-crest (or some comparable) distance between two waves.

weight The pull of gravity on an object. Weight is measured in newtons.

work Force multiplied by distance; work is measured in joules.

X-rays Electromagnetic radiation with a wavelength between those of ultraviolet light and gamma rays.

mathematics

acre A measure of land: originally the amount of land that a yoke of oxen could plough in a day. Equal to 4840 yd^2.

ampere (A) The unit for measuring electric current.

amu *See* **atomic mass unit**.

ångström (Å) A unit of length, used mainly to measure the wavelength of light. Named after the Swedish physicist A.J. Ångström (1814–74). Equal to 10^{-10} m (10^{-8} cm).

apothecaries' system A system of weights used especially by pharmacists.

are (a) A unit of measure equal to an area of 100 m^2 (1 are = 100 m^2). *See* **hectare** (ha): 100 are = 1 ha.

astronomical unit (au) A unit of measure based on the distance between the Earth and the Sun. Approximately equal to 1.5 x 10^8 km.

atomic mass unit (amu)
   chemical A unit of mass equal to $\frac{1}{16}$ of the weighted mass of the three naturally occurring neutral oxygen isotopes. 1 amu chemical = $(1.660 \pm 0.000\ 05)$ x 10^{-27} kg. Formerly called the atomic weight unit.
   international A unit of mass equal to half of the mass of a neutral carbon-12 atom. 1 amu international = $(1.660\ 33 \pm 0.000\ 05)$ x 10^{-27} kg.
   physical A unit of mass equal to $\frac{1}{16}$ of the mass of an oxygen atom. 1 amu physical = 1.660 x 10^{-27} kg.

atto- A prefix meaning a quintillionth (10^{-18}). For example, 1 attometer = 1 quintillionth of a meter.

avoirdupois system A system of weights based on the 16-ounce pound and the 16-dram ounce.

baker's dozen An amount of 13.

billion (bil) A number equal to 10^9.

bolt A measure of length, usually for fabric. A bolt of wallpaper equals 16 yd and a bolt of cloth equals 40 yd.

British thermal unit (BTU) The measure of heat needed to raise the temperature of one pound of water by 1° F. Equal to 252 calories.

bushel (bu) A measure of dry volume. In the US, 1 bu = 8 gal (64 US pt); in the UK, 1 bu = 8 gal (64 UK pt). The measures are not to be confused: 1.03 US bu = 1 UK bu.

caliber A unit of length used to measure the diameter of a tube or the bore of a firearm, in increments of $\frac{1}{100}$ in or $\frac{1}{1000}$.

calorie (cal) A measure of heat energy representing the amount of heat needed to raise the temperature 1 g of water by 1°C.

Also called "small calorie": 1000 cal = 1 kcal or Cal. *See* **joule, kilocalorie**.

centi- Prefix meaning a 100th or $\frac{1}{100}$ in the metric system; e.g., a centiliter (cl) is a unit of volume equal to $\frac{1}{100}$ (0.01) liter.

centrad A measure of a plane angle, especially used to measure the angular deviation of light through a prism. 1 centrad = $\frac{1}{100}$ (0.01) radian.

century A measure of time equal to 100 years.

chain A measure of length equal to 22 yd. Also known as Gunter's chain.

engineer's chain A measure of length equal to 100 ft.

nautical chain A measure of length equal to 15 ft.

square chain A measure of area equal to 484 yd^2.

chaldron A measure of volume. 1 chaldron = 36 bu.

cord A unit of dry volume, especially used for timber. Equal to 128 ft^3.

cubic units (cu or 3) These signify that three quantities measured in the same units have been multiplied together. For example, with a three-dimensional rectangular object, the height, breadth, and length may be multiplied togther to give its volume, which is then measured in cubic units.

cubit A unit of length approximately equal to 18 in. Originally based on the distance from the tip of the middle finger to the elbow.

cup A measure of volume (either liquid or solid) used especially in cooking. 1 cup = $\frac{1}{2}$ pt, 8 fluid ounces (16 tbsp).

day

mean solar day A measure of time representing the interval between consecutive passages of the Sun across the meridian, averaged over one year. 1 day = 24 hr (86,400 sec).

sidereal day A measure of time approximately equal to 23 hr, 56 min, 4.09 sec. A sidereal day represents the time needed for one complete rotation of the Earth on its axis.

deca- Prefix meaning ten in the metric system; e.g., a decameter is a measure of length equal to 10 m.

decade A measure of time equal to 10 years.

deci- Prefix meaning $\frac{1}{10}$ in the metric system; e.g., a deciliter (dl) is a measure of liquid volume equal to $\frac{1}{10}$ (0.01) litre.

decibel (dB) A measure of relative sound intensity.

degree (°)

geometrical A unit of measure of plane angle equal to $\frac{1}{360}$ of the circumference of a circle (1 circle = 360°).

temperature A measure of temperature difference representing a single division on a temperature scale.

digit One of ten Arabic symbols representing the numbers 0 to 9.

Also used in astronomy as a unit of measure equal to half the diameter of the Sun or Moon. Used in ancient Egypt as a measure of length: 1 digit = 1 finger width.

dozen A counting unit equal to 12.

drachm A unit of weight in the apothecaries' system. 1 drachm = ⅛ apothecaries' ounce (60 grains).

dram (dr) A unit of mass equal to 1/16 oz.

  fluid dram A unit of liquid volume. 1 dr = ⅛ fl oz.

dry Used to distinguish measures of dry (solid) volume as opposed to liquid (fluid) volume.

dyne A unit of force equal to that needed to produce an acceleration of 1 centimeter per second in a mass of one gram. Replaced in the international system by the newton (N): 1 dyne = 10^{-5} N.

electronvolt (eV) A unit of energy representing the energy acquired by an electron in passing through a potential difference of 1 volt. 1 eV = $(1.6 \pm 0.000\ 07) \times 10^{-19}$ J.

erg A unit of energy equal to the energy produced by a force of 1 dyne acting through a distance of 1 cm. Replaced in the inernational system by the joule (J): 1 erg = 10^{-7} J.

fathom (fm) Unit of length, especially used to measure marine depth. 1 fm = 6 ft. Originally based on the span of two outstretched arms.

feet per minute A unit of speed representing the number of feet traveled in 1 min.

femto- A prefix meaning 1 quadrillionth (10^{-15}).

firkin A unit of volume, used especially to measure beer or ale. 1 firkin = 9.8 US gal.

fluid Used to distinguish units of liquid (fluid) volume as opposed to dry (solid) volume.

fluid dram *See* **dram**.

fluid ounce *See* **ounce**.

foot (ft) A unit of length equal to 12 inches.

furlong (fur) A unit of length equal to ⅛ mile (660 ft).

gallon (gal) A unit of liquid volume equal to eight pints. The US and UK gallons should not be confused: 1UK gal = 1.2 US gal.

gauge A unit of length used to measure the diameter of a shotgun bore; e.g., six-gauge equals 23.34 mm. Originally based on the number of balls of certain size in a pound of shot.

giga- A prefix meaning one billion (10^9). For example, 1 gigameter = 1 billion meters.

gill A unit of liquid volume. In the UK, 1 gill = ¼ UK pt; in US (gi), 1 gi = ¼ US fl pt. The two should not be confused: 1 UK gill = ½ US gi.

grade (g) A measure of plane angle in geometry. $1^g = 0.9°$.

grain (gr) A unit of mass measurement, used especially in the apothecaries' system. 1 grain = $\frac{1}{7000}$ lb (avoirdupois); 480 grains = 1 ounce troy; 24 grains = 1 pennyweight.

gram (g) A unit of mass or volume measurement. 1 g = 0.001 kg.

gross A counting measure equal to 144 (or 12 dozen).

hand A unit of length, used especially to measure horses' height. 1 hand = 4 in.

hectare (ha) A measure of area, usually of land, equal to 10,000 m².

hecto- Prefix meaning 100; e.g., a hectometer (hm) is a unit of length equal to 100 m.

hertz (Hz) A unit of frequency measurement equal to one cycle per second.

horsepower (hp) A unit of work representing the power needed to raise 550 lb by 1 ft in 1 s.

   metric horsepower A unit of power representing that needed to raise a 75-kg mass1 meter in one second.

hour (hr) A unit of time measurement equal to 60 min (3600 s).

hundredweight (cwt) A unit of mass equal to 112 lb; 1 hundredweight troy = 100 pounds troy; 1 hundredweight = 4 quarters.

   short hundredweight (sh cwt) Equal to 100 pounds.

inch (in) A unit of length equal to $\frac{1}{12}$ ft.

inches per second A unit of speed representing the number of inches traveled in one second.

joule (J) A unit of energy equal to the work done when a force of one newton is applied through a distance of one meter. Used instead of calorie: 1 J = 0.239 cal. Named after the British physicist J.P. Joule (1818–89).

karat A unit of weight equal to 200 mg (3.1 grains). Also used as a measure of gold purity (per 24 parts gold alloy).

keg A unit of volume, used especially for beer, equal to approximately 30 gal. Also used as a measure of weight for nails, equal to 100 lb.

kelvin (K) A scale of temperature measurement in which each degree is equal to $\frac{1}{273.16}$ of the interval between 0 K (absolute zero) and the triple point of water. K = °C + 273.16. Named after William Thomson, Lord Kelvin (1824–1907).

kilo- A prefix meaning 1000; e.g., a kilogram (kg) is a unit of mass equal to 1000 grams.

kilocalorie (kcal or Cal) A unit of energy measurement representing the amount of heat required to raise the temperature of one kilogram of water by 1°C. Also called the "international calorie." 1 kcal = 1000 cal.

See **calorie.**

kilometer (km) A unit of length equal to 1000 m.

kiloparsec A unit of distance used to measure the distance between galactic bodies. 1 kiloparsec = 3260 light years.

kilowatt (kW) A unit of power equal to 1000 watts (W).

kilowatt-hour (kWh) A unit of energy equal to the energy expended when a power of 1 kW is used for one hour.

knot (kn) A nautical unit of speed equal to the velocity at which one nautical mile is traveled in one hour. 1 kn = 6076 ft per hour.

lakh An Indian counting unit equal to 100,000.

lambda (λ) A unit of volume measurement. 1 λ = 1 microliter (10^{-6} litre).

league A unit of length equal to 3 miles.

light year A unit of length (distance) representing the distance traveled by electromagnetic waves (light) through space in one year. 1 light year = 9 trillion miles.

liter (l) A unit of volume measurement equal to the volume of one kilogram of water at its maximum density. 1 l = 1000 cm^3.

magnum A measure of volume, used especially for wine or champagne. 1 magnum = $\frac{2}{5}$ US gal.

mega- A prefix meaning one million; e.g., a megaton is a unit of weight equal to one million tons.

megahertz (MHz) A unit of frequency equal to one million cycles per second.

meter (m) A unit of length equal to 100 cm.

meters per minute (m/min) A unit of speed measurement representing the number of meters traveled in one minute.

metric system A system of measurement based on the meter.

metric ton *See* **tonne**.

micro- A prefix meaning one millionth; e.g., a microliter is a unit of volume equal to one millionth of a liter.

micron (μm) A unit of length equal to $\frac{1}{1000}$ (0.001) mm. Also called the micrometer.

mile (mi) A unit of length equal to 1760 yd.

   nautical mile (n mi) A unit of length used in navigation. In the metric system, one nautical mile (international) = 1852 m.

   sea mile A unit of length distinguished from the nautical mile. 1 sea mile = 1000 fathoms (6000 ft).

miles per hour (mph) A unit of speed representing the number of miles traveled in one hour.

millennium A period of time equal to 1000 years.

milli- Prefix meaning one thousandth or $\frac{1}{1000}$; e.g., one millimeter (mm) is a unit of length equal to $\frac{1}{1000}$ (0.001) of a meter.

minim A unit of volume, applied to liquids. 1 minim = $\frac{1}{480}$ fl oz.

minute
    geometric (') A unit of measure for plane angles. $1' = \frac{1}{60}°$.
    time (min) A unit of time measurement equal to 60 seconds.
    60 min = 1 hr.
month
    lunar A unit of time equal to four weeks (2,419,200 sec).
    sidereal *See* **year, sidereal.**
    tropical *See* **year, tropical.**
nano- A prefix meaning one billionth (10^{-9}). 1 nanometer = 1
    billionth of a meter.
nautical mile *See* **mile.**
newton (N) A unit of force which, when applied, accelerates a
    mass of one kilogram by one meter per second per second. This
    unit has replaced the dyne: $1 N = 10^5$ dynes. Named after Isaac
    Newton (1642–1727).
ohm (|) A unit of electrical resistance. One ohm equals the
    resistance across which a potential difference of one volt
    produces a current flow of one ampere. Named after the
    German physicist G.S. Ohm (1787–1854).
ounce (oz) A unit of mass equal to $\frac{1}{16}$ lb.
    fluid ounce A unit of liquid volume measurement. In the US,
    1 fl oz = $\frac{1}{16}$ US pt; in the UK, 1 fl oz = $\frac{1}{20}$ UK pt.
    metric ounce A unit of mass equal to 25 grams. Also called a
    mounce.
    ounce troy A unit of mass in the troy system. Equal to $\frac{1}{12}$
    pound troy.
pace A unit of length/distance equal to about three feet, used in
    ancient Rome.
palm A unit of length used in ancient Egypt, equal to the width of
    an average palm of the hand (4 digits).
parsec (pc) A unit of length used for measuring astronomical
    distances.
    1 parsec = 3.26 light years.
pascal (Pa) A unit of pressure equal to the force of one newton
    acting over an area of one square meter.
peck (pk) A unit of dry volume. 1 peck = 2 gal.
pennyweight (dwt) A unit of weight in the troy system equal to
    $\frac{1}{20}$ ounce troy (24 grains).
perch *See* **rod.**
pi (π) Symbol and name representing the ratio of a circle's
    circumference to its diameter. Its value is approximately 3.14.
pica A unit of length, used by printers, approximately equal to
    $\frac{1}{6}$ in.
pico- A prefix meaning one trillionth (10^{-12}). For example, 1
    picometer = 1 trillionth of a meter.

pint (pt) A unit of volume. Two kinds of pint are used: 1 fl pt = ⅛ gal; 1 dry pt = ¹⁄₆₄ gal.

point A unit of length, used especially by printers, approximately equal to ¹⁄₇₂ in.

pole *See* **rod**.

pound (lb) A unit of mass equal to 453.59 g.
pound force A unit of force equal to 32.174 poundals.
pound troy (lb tr) A unit of mass in the troy system. 1 pound troy = 12 ounces troy.

poundal A unit of force equal to that needed to give an acceleration of one foot per second to a mass of one pound.

PSI Pounds per square inch: a unit for measuring pressure. One PSI equals the pressure resulting from a force of one pound force acting over an area of one square inch. *See* **pound**.

quart (qt) A unit of volume, usually for liquids. 1 qt = 2 fl pt.
dry quart (dry qt) A unit of measure for dry (solid) volume .

quarter (qr)
mass quarter A unit of mass. 1 quarter = ¼ US ton (500 lb).
quarter troy (qr tr) A unit of weight equal to 25 troy pounds.

rad A short form of radian, a unit of measure for plane angles. *See* **centrad**.

ream A unit of volume, used to measure paper in bulk. One ream equals about 500 sheets.

rod
area rod A unit of area equal to 30 ¼ yd². Also called a square perch or a square pole.
length rod A unit of length equal to 5½ yd. Also called a perch or a pole.

rood A unit of area equal to ¼ acre (1210 yd²).

score A counting unit equal to 20.

scruple A unit of mass in the apothecaries' system equal to 20 grains.

second A unit of time equal to ¹⁄₆₀ minute.
geometric (") A measure of plane angle equal to ¹⁄₃₆₀°.
sidereal A unit of time equal to ¹⁄₈₆ 400 of the interval needed for one complete rotation of the Earth on its axis.

square units (sq or ²) These signify that two quantities measured in the same units have been multiplied together. For example, to find the area of a square or rectangle, length and breadth are multiplied together to give the area, which is measured in square units.

stere A unit of volume, especially used for measuring timber. 1 stere = 1 m³.

tablespoon (tbsp) A unit of volume used in cooking and equal to

1.5 centiliters (3 tsp). 16 tbsp = 1 cup.

teaspoon (tsp) A unit of volume used in cooking and equal to 0.5 centiliter. 3 tsp = 1 tbsp.

tera- A prefix meaning one trillion (10^{12}). For example, 1 terameter = 1 trillion meters.

ton A unit of mass. In the US, 1 ton = 2000 lb. In the UK, 1 ton = 2240 lb. Called a long ton in the US.

ton troy (ton tr) A unit of mass equal to 2000 pounds troy.

tonne (t) A unit of mass equal to 1000 kg. Also called a metric ton.

tonne of coal equivalent A measure of energy production/consumption based on the premise that one tonne of coal provides 8000 kilowatt-hours (kWh) of energy.

trillion A number equal to 10^{12}.

troy system A system of mass measurement based on the 20-ounce pound and the 20-pennyweight ounce.

volt (V) A unit of electromotive force and potential difference, equal to the difference in potential between two points of a conducting wire carrying a constant current of one ampere (A), when the power released between the points is one watt (W). Named after the Italian physicist Alessandro Volta (1745–1827).

watt (W) A unit of power equal to that available when one joule of energy is expended in one second. 1 W = 1 volt-ampere; 746 W = 1 horsepower (hp). Named after the Scottish engineer James Watt (1736–1819).

X-unit (x or XU) A unit of length used especially for measuring wavelength. 1 x-unit ≈ 10^{-3} ångström (10^{-13} m).

yard (yd) A unit of length equal to three feet. 1 yard = 3 ft (36 in).

yards per minute (ypm) A unit of speed representing the number of yards traveled in one minute.

year A unit of time measurement determined by the revolution of the Earth around the Sun.

> **anomalistic year** Equals the time interval between two consecutive passages of the Earth through its perihelion (365 days, 6 hr, 13 min, 53 s).

> **sidereal year** Equals the time that it takes the Earth to revolve around the Sun from one fixed point (usually a star) back to the same point (365 days, 6 hr, 9 min, 9 sec).

> **tropical year** Equals the time interval between two consecutive passages of the Sun, in one direction, through the Earth's equatorial plane (or from vernal equinox to vernal equinox; 365 days, 5 hr, 48 min, 46 sec).

physiology: the human body

abdomen The large body cavity below the thorax, lined by the peritoneum. It contains the stomach, intestines, liver, gallbladder, pancreas, spleen, kidneys, and adrenal glands.

abduction Movement of a limb away from the body's midline, or of a digit away from a limb's axis. Abductor muscles are muscles that contract to move part of the body outward.

absorption The transfer of digested nutrients from the alimentary canal into blood or lymph.

accommodation The eye's ability to change the convexity of its lens in order to focus on objects at different distances.

acetabulum A socket in the hip bone to take the rounded head of the femur.

acetylcholine A neurotransmitter that triggers activity by muscles or secretory glands.

acoustic Relating to sound or hearing.

adduction Movement of a limb toward the body's midline, or of a digit toward a limb's axis. Adductor muscles are muscles that contract to move part of the body inward.

abdomen

adenoids Masses of lymphoid tissue in the upper throat that form part of the body's defense against infection.

adenosine triphosphate (ATP) A compound that stores chemical energy in cells.

adipose fat tissue

adrenal glands (or suprarenal glands) Two endocrine glands, one on each kidney. The medulla and cortex of the adrenal glands secrete different hormones.

adrenaline *See* **epinephrine**.

aerobic respiration In living cells, a process that uses oxygen to break down complex molecules into simpler ones, releasing energy.

afferent Directing to a part of the body. The afferent nerves of the peripheral nervous system send impulses to the central nervous system.

agglutination Clumping of red blood cells or antigens, caused by the action of antibodies.

agranulocytes *See* **leukocytes**.

aldosterone An adrenal gland hormone that acts on the kidneys to help maintain the balance of salt in the body.

alimentary canal (or gastrointestinal tract) The digestive tract: a tube with its ends at the mouth and the anus.

alveolus One of the lungs' tiny air sacs at the outer ends of the terminal bronchioles; also the bony socket supporting a tooth.

alveolus

amino acids Organic compounds that form the ingredients of proteins.

anabolism Chemical reactions in the body that use energy to build complex molecules from simpler substances.

anaerobic respiration In living cells, a process that without using oxygen breaks down complex molecules into simpler substances, releasing energy.

androgens Male sex hormones produced by the testes and adrenal glands.

anterior In front of; ventral.

antibodies Substances produced by the body and giving immunity against specific antigens.

antidiuretic hormone (ADH) A hormone made by the hypothalamus and released from the pituitary gland. By making the kidneys reabsorb water, it limits urine output and helps control the body's water balance.

antigens Substances that on entering the body trigger the production of antibodies.

anus The lower end of the rectum, forming the outlet of the alimentary canal. It is normally closed by a sphincter.

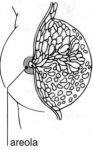
areola

aorta The largest artery, arising from the left ventricle of the heart.

apocrine glands Sweat glands that produce body odor. They occur in the armpits and genital area and become active at puberty.

appendix (or vermiform appendix) A short, slim, wormlike tube opening into the cecum but closed at the other end. It contains lymphoid tissue, which is involved in immunity.

aqueous humor Watery fluid filling the chamber of the eye in front of the lens.

arachnoid A web-like membrane: the middle of the three meninges covering the brain and spinal cord.

areola The pigmented ring around a nipple.

arteriole A small artery supplying blood from a main artery to a capillary.

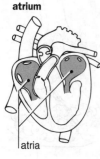
atrium

artery A blood vessel transporting blood from the heart to elsewhere in the body.

astrocyte A star-shaped type of cell that supports neurons in the brain and spinal cord. *See* **neuroglia**.

atrium (pl. atria) Either of the two upper chambers of the heart, which receive blood from the veins.

atria

auditory tube *See* **eustachian tube**.

auricle The external ear flap or pinna; also an appendage to an atrium of the heart.

autonomic nervous system Part of the peripheral nervous

system not under conscious control. It operates smooth muscle, cardiac muscle, and glands. *See* **parasympathetic nervous system; sympathetic nervous system**.

axilla the armpit

axon The extension of a neuron, taking impulses away from the cell body.

backbone *See* **vertebral column**.

Bartholin's glands A pair of glands flanking the outlet of the vagina. They produce a lubricating fluid.

basal ganglia Paired structures deep in the forebrain. They help to coordinate and control willed muscle movements.

basal metabolic rate The minimum rate at which a body needs to produce heat energy to stay alive when at rest.

basilar membrane A structure of the inner ear.

basophil A type of white blood cell readily stained by basic dyes.

bile A greenish-yellow fluid that emulsifies fats. It is produced by the liver and stored in the gallbladder.

bladder A sac, especially the muscular bag inside the pelvis where urine collects before being expelled from the body.

blastocyst (or blastula) A hollow ball of cells formed from a morula about five days after fertilization.

blastula *See* **blastocyst**.

blood A sticky red fluid made up of colorless plasma, red blood cells (erythrocytes), white blood cells (leukocytes), and platelets (thrombocytes).

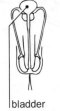

bladder

blood pressure The pressure of blood against blood-vessel walls, especially the walls of arteries.

blood type Any of various types of blood (notably A, B, AB, O, Rh-positive, Rh-negative) named for the antigen(s) they do or do not contain. Mismatched blood transfusions cause adverse reactions in recipients.

bone Dense connective tissue hardened by deposits of calcium carbonate and calcium phosphate.

bone marrow Soft red and yellow substances that fill cavities in bone. Red bone marrow forms blood. Yellow bone marrow contains fat.

bowel *See* **large intestine**.

Bowman's capsule (or glomerular capsule) Part of a nephron in a kidney: a little cup surrounding a glomerulus. *See* **glomerulus, kidney, nephron**.

brain The body's chief control center, containing billions of interconnected nerve cells.

brain stem A stalklike part of the brain, between the cerebrum and spinal cord. It contains the midbrain, pons, and medulla oblongata.

brain waves Patterns of electrical activity within the brain.

breast *See* **mammary gland**.

breastbone *See* **sternum**.

bronchiole A tiny subdivision of a bronchus, ending in the little air sacs called alveoli.

bronchus (pl. bronchi) Either of the two tubes branching from the lower end of the trachea and forming the main airways to and from the lungs.

bursa A fluid-filled sac that reduces friction when one body part moves against another, as at a knee joint.

calcaneus The tarsal bone that comprises the heel bone. *See* **tarsus**.

calcitonin A hormone produced by the thyroid gland. It lowers the calcium level in blood.

calorie A calorie (c) is the amount of heat needed to raise the temperature of 1 gram of water by 1°C. A Calorie (C) is a kilocalorie, or 1000 calories (c). The energy content of foods is usually given in Calories (kilocalories).

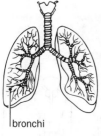
bronchi

capillary The tiniest type of blood vessel, connecting an arteriole and a venule.

carbohydrates Organic compounds containing carbon, hydrogen, and oxygen. They include starches, sugars, and cellulose. Carbohydrate foods provide energy. *See* **disaccharides, monosaccharides, polysaccharides**.

cardiac Relating to the heart.

cardiac muscle Involuntary striated muscle, found only in the heart. *See* **muscle**.

carotid artery Either of the two main arteries in the neck, one on each side.

carpus The wrist's framework comprising eight small bones called carpal bones.

cartilage Gristle; dense, white connective tissue cushioning bones and supporting parts of the ear and respiratory system.

catabolism Chemical reactions in the body that break down complex food substances into simpler substances, releasing energy.

cecum A blind pouch in the colon where the colon starts from the lower end of the ileum.

cell The basic unit of the body. Most cells comprise a nucleus surrounded by cytoplasm within a membrane.

cellulose A fibrous carbohydrate forming the cell walls of plants. It is indigestible to humans, but stimulates peristalsis.

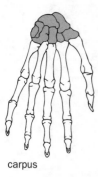
carpus

central nervous system The brain and spinal cord.

centriole One of a group of tiny tubules near the nucleus of a cell. Centrioles play a part in cell division. *See* **mitosis**.

cerebellum The largest part of the hindbrain, sprouting below the back of the cerebrum. It helps produce smoothly controlled and coordinated muscular movements.

cerebral cortex The cerebrum's thin outer layer of gray matter. It consists of neurons' cell bodies and dendrites.

cerebral hemisphere Either of both halves of the cerebrum.

cerebrospinal fluid A clear fluid filling the brain's ventricles and surrounding the brain and spinal cord to protect them from injury.

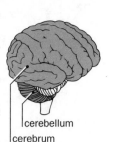
cerebellum
cerebrum

cerebrum The upper, major part of the brain, with two hemispheres, and including the diencephalon. It handles consciousness, learning, memory, emotions, sensations, and voluntary movements.

cervical Relating to a neck or cervix.

cervix A neck, especially the neck of the uterus where it opens into the vagina.

chemoreceptor A sensory organ that responds to a chemical stimulus. Chemoreceptors give us our senses of taste and smell.

cholecystokinin A hormone that causes the gallbladder to contract and so release bile into the duodenum.

cholesterol A fatty substance produced and used by the body and ingested in food. High levels of certain types of cholesterol can narrow blood vessels, impairing circulation.

chorion The embryo's outer membrane, which helps to form the placenta.

choroid The eyeball's dark middle layer.

chromosome A rodlike body containing genes, and appearing in a cell nucleus as the cell divides.

chyme The creamy mass of partly digested food and gastric juice found in the stomach and small intestine during digestion.

cilia Tiny hairlike projections from cells, which make lashing movements and help to propel a cell through its medium.

citric acid cycle *See* **Krebs cycle**.

clavicle Either of the two collarbones, linking the scapulae to the sternum.

clitoris An erectile, pea-sized organ above the opening of the vagina. It is highly sensitive and is involved in female sexual response.

coagulation blood clotting

coccyx Four fused vertebrae forming the "tail" of the backbone.

cochlea Part of the inner ear concerned with hearing: a canal coiled like a snail's shell and linked to the acoustic nerve.

coenzyme A nonprotein compound that activates an enzyme to speed up a biochemical reaction.

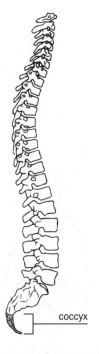
coccyx

collagen A fibrous protein, the chief protein constituent of connective tissue.

colon The part of the large intestine between the cecum and rectum.

complement Proteins in blood plasma activated by and helping to dissolve foreign cells such as bacteria.

cones Receptor cells in the retina. They sense bright light and function in daylight. *See* **retina**.

connective tissue The body's most widespread type of tissue: supporting, linking, storing, and holding organs in place. It includes blood, bone, and cartilage.

corium *See* **dermis**.

cornea A transparent convex membrane forming part of the eye's outer coat in front of the iris and pupil.

corpus A distinctive mass of tissue; the major part of an organ.

corpus callosum The band of nerve fibers joining both hemispheres of the cerebrum.

corpuscles A term often used for the red and white blood cells.

corpus luteum Yellow endocrine tissue formed in the ovary from a ruptured Graafian follicle. *See* **Graafian follicle**.

cortex The outer layer of an internal organ, notably of the brain and each kidney.

corticosteroids Cortisone and other hormones produced in the cortex of each adrenal gland. Corticosteroids help to control the balance of salts and sugars in the body.

cranial nerves Twelve pairs of nerves linking the underside of the brain with parts of the head, neck, and thorax. Some feed sensations from the eyes, nose, and ears to the brain.

cranium The part of the skull that contains the brain.

creatinine A nitrogenous waste product excreted in urine.

cutaneous Relating to the skin.

cuticle Epidermis; dead skin at a nail root.

cytoplasm A cell's jellylike contents except for the nucleus.

cytotoxic Any substance that is toxic to cells.

dendrites Treelike processes of neurons, which receive impulses from other neurons and send them to the neuron's cell body.

dentine Bony tooth tissue that encloses the pulp chamber and root canals.

deoxyribonucleic acid (DNA) A nucleic acid in the cell's chromosomes, which contains the cell's coded genetic instructions. *See* **gene**.

dermis (or corium) The layer of skin below the epidermis, containing nerves, blood vessels, glands, and hair follicles.

diaphragm A muscular sheet used in breathing. It separates the thorax and abdomen.

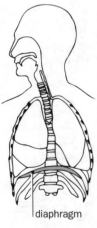

diaphragm

diastole The interval between two of the heart's contractions as it supplies blood to the body. *Compare* **systole**.

diencephalon The "between brain" area of the forebrain between the midbrain and cerebral hemispheres. It includes the thalamus and the hypothalamus.

digestion The chemical and mechanical breakdown of foods into simple substances that can be absorbed by the body.

disaccharides Sugars formed from two monosaccharide molecules, such as lactose, maltose, and sucrose.

distal Away from the point of origin of a limb or other structure. *See* **proximal**.

DNA *See* **deoxyribonucleic acid**.

dopamine a neurotransmitter

dorsal Relating to the back. *Compare* **ventral.**

duodenum The upper part of the small intestine, where most chemical digestion takes place.

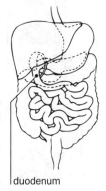
duodenum

dura mater *See* **meninges**.

ear The organ of hearing and balance. *See* **external ear, inner ear, middle ear**.

eardrum *See* **tympanic membrane**.

ectoderm An embryo's outer germ layer, which develops into structures including the brain and skin. *See* **endoderm, mesoderm.**

efferent Directing away from a part of the body. Efferent nerve fibers carry signals away from the central nervous system.

electrolytes Chemicals (e.g., salts, acids, and bases) that conduct electric current when they are dissolved in water.

embryo A young animal in an early phase of development. In humans the phase lasts from the third through the eighth week after fertilization.

embryo

enamel A tooth crown's hard outer layer.

endocrine glands Ductless glands, producing hormones that travel through the bloodstream to target cells where they affect metabolism. *See* **exocrine glands**.

endoderm An embryo's inner germ layer, producing some internal organs and the linings of the digestive and respiratory systems. *See* **ectoderm, mesoderm.**

endometrium The mucous membrane that lines the uterus and is shed during menstruation.

endorphins Peptides in the brain that act as natural painkillers. *See* **enkephalins**.

endothelium The cell layer lining the inside of the circulatory and lymphatic systems.

enamel

enkephalins Peptides in the brain that act as natural painkillers. *See* **endorphins**.

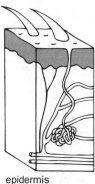

epidermis

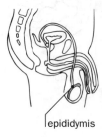

epididymis

enzymes Biological catalysts: proteins that speed up chemical reactions in the body without themselves undergoing change.

eosinophil A type of white blood cell that takes up the red dye eosin.

epidermis The skin's outer layer.

epididymis (pl. epididymides) A coiled tubule on each testis where sperm are stored and mature.

epiglottis A cartilage flap behind the tongue that is closed during swallowing to stop food entering the larynx.

epinephrine (or adrenaline) A hormone produced by the adrenal glands to prepare the body for "fight or flight" in conditions of stress.

epiphyses The ends of a long bone.

epithelium The layer of cells covering the body's surface and lining the alimentary canal and respiratory and urinary tracts.

erythrocytes Red blood cells, which transport oxygen and carbon dioxide in hemoglobin.

esophagus The muscular tube through which food travels between the pharynx and stomach.

estrogen A collective name for female sex hormones made in the ovaries, which produce female secondary sexual characteristics and stimulate growth of the lining of the uterus.

ethmoid bone A bone forming the side walls of the nose.

eustachian tube (or auditory tube) A tube between the middle ear and the throat. It helps to equalize air pressure.

excretion The removal of feces, urine, and other wastes from the body via the colon, kidneys, lungs, or skin.

exocrine glands Sweat glands and other glands that release their products through ducts to a surface or cavity. *See* **endocrine glands**.

external ear The ear's auricle (pinna) and external auditory canal between the auricle and the tympanic membrane (eardrum).

exteroceptor A sense organ responding to stimuli from outside the body.

eye The sense organ that converts light into electrical signals, which pass to the brain to be interpreted as visual images.

fallopian tubes (or uterine tubes or oviducts) The tubes through which ova (eggs) travel from the ovaries to the uterus.

fascia A fibrous layer of connective tissue. Such layers join skin to the tissues beneath and form sheaths around individual muscles.

fascicle (or fasciculus) A bundle of muscle or nerve fibers.

fats One of the three main types of food, rich in stored energy.

fatty acids Chains of carbon and hydrogen atoms forming

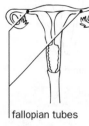

fallopian tubes

molecules that are the basic building blocks of fats.

feces The body wastes discharged from the rectum. They are made up of indigestible food, bacteria, and secretions.

femur The thigh bone.

fertilization (or conception) The joining of a sperm with an ovum.

fetus An unborn mammal from when its adult features become recognizable. In humans, this is in the ninth week of development.

fibrin A fibrous protein providing the framework on which blood clots form.

fibrinogen A soluble protein in blood, converted to insoluble fibrin by the enzyme thrombin which thus triggers clotting.

fibula The long, slim bone at the outer side of the leg. *See* **tibia**.

fissure A split or groove.

follicle A small secreting cavity or sac. Ova (egg cells) develop in follicles in the female ovaries. *See* **hair follicle**.

follicle-stimulating hormone (FSH) A hormone that stimulates the maturation of ovarian follicles in females and sperm production in males. FSH is produced by the pituitary gland.

fontanel A soft spot in an infant's head where skull bones have not yet fused together.

foramen A hole in a bone or between two body cavities.

forebrain The front part of the brain comprising the diencephalon and telencephalon.

foreskin (or prepuce) Loose skin covering the glans (bulbous end of the shaft of the penis).

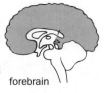
forebrain

fossa A shallow depression.

fovea A small pit, especially that in the retina where vision is clearest.

frontal bone The forehead bone.

fructose (or levulose) A source of energy found in sweet fruits. *See* **monosaccharides**.

gallbladder A pear-shaped bag where bile is stored, under the liver.

gametes Sex cells: ova and sperm.

ganglion A mass of nerve cell bodies outside the central nervous system.

gastric Relating to the stomach.

gastrointestinal tract *See* **alimentary canal**.

gastrulation The formation of a tube-shaped embryo with three germ layers. *See* **ectoderm, endoderm, mesoderm**.

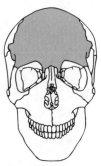
frontal bone

genes Basic biological hereditary units, consisting of DNA and located on chromosomes. Genes contain coded instructions that control how organisms and their descendants develop.

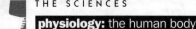
genitalia sex organs

germ layers An early embryo's three cellular layers, giving rise to all body tissues. *See* **ectoderm, endoderm, mesoderm**.

gestation (or pregnancy) The period from conception to birth, which in humans lasts about 280 days.

gland A structure that produces a secretion. *See* **endocrine glands, exocrine glands**.

glomerular capsule *See* **Bowman's capsule**.

glomerulus A convoluted mass of blood-filtering capillaries in a nephron. *See* **kidney, nephron, tubule**.

glottis In the larynx, the gap between the vocal cords.

glucagon A hormone that breaks down glycogen to glucose. It is produced by the pancreatic islets.

glucocorticoids Hormones that control the metabolism of fats and carbohydrates. They are produced in the cortex of each adrenal gland.

glucose (or dextrose) A simple sugar: the form of carbohydrate absorbed from the alimentary canal, supplied by blood to the muscles and converted for storage to glycogen.

gluteal Relating to the buttocks.

glycogen A carbohydrate stored in the liver. It is produced from, but more complex than, glucose. *See* **monosaccharides, polysaccharides**.

goblet cells Goblet-shaped cells producing mucus and found in mucous membranes.

gonadotrophins Gonad-stimulating hormones made by the pituitary gland.

gonads Primary reproductive organs: the ovaries and testes.

Graafian follicle (or vesicular follicle) A type of tiny vesicle in the ovary which encloses a developing egg. *See* **corpus luteum**.

granulocytes White blood cells with cytoplasm that contains granules. *See* **leukocytes**.

gray matter Parts of the central nervous system comprising cell bodies with axons and dendrites lacking a myelin sheath.

growth hormone (or somatotrophin) Growth-stimulating hormone produced by the anterior (front) pituitary gland.

hair follicle The tiny sheath in which a hair grows up through the skin.

Haversian canals (or osteonic canals) Tiny canals in bone, containing nerves and blood vessels and surrounded by concentric rings of cells.

heart The hollow, muscular, fist-sized organ that pumps blood around the body. It lies between the lungs, behind the sternum.

hematopoiesis (or hemopoiesis) The production of blood cells in red bone marrow.

hemoglobin The iron-rich, oxygen-transporting pigment in red blood cells which gives them their color.

hepatic Relating to the liver.

hindbrain Brain structures below the midbrain. The hindbrain comprises the pons, medulla oblongata, and cerebellum.

hip bones (or Innominates) Flared bones forming the pelvis. Each hip bone comprises three fused bones: the ilium, ischium, and pubis. *See* **pelvis**.

hindbrain

histamine A hormone in almost all body tissues, released by antigen—antibody reactions. Its effects include making blood vessels expand and leak.

homeostasis The body's internal balance, produced by a regulatory system that maintains more or less stable temperature, blood pressure, electrolyte levels, etc.

hormones Chemical substances released into the blood by endocrine glands to influence tissues in other parts of the body.

humerus The upper arm bone.

hymen A perforated membrane that may cover or partly cover the entrance to the vagina.

hypophysis *See* **pituitary gland**.

hypothalamus A structure in the diencephalon, above the midbrain. Its centers control emotion, hunger, and thirst, and it releases hormones that trigger the production of other hormones by the pituitary gland.

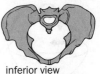

hip bones (female)

inferior view

anterior view

ileum The last part of the small intestine, after the jejunum and before the cecum.

ilium The uppermost of the three fused bones that form the hip bone.

immune system The body's system of defenses against infective organisms or other foreign bodies invading the body.

immunity The body's effective resistance against a disease-causing organism. Immunity can be innate or acquired by producing antibodies. *See* **antibodies, antigens**.

immunoglobins Proteins that are produced by lymphocytes and act as antibodies.

implantation The process by which a blastocyst attaches itself to the lining of the uterus.

inflammation Heat, pain, redness, and swelling in infected or injured tissue. It occurs as blood vessels dilate in response to damage and as white blood cells engulf microorganisms and dead tissue.

inguinal Relating to the groin.

inner ear The cochlea and vestibular system, respectively dealing with hearing and balance. *See* **cochlea, vestibular system, vestibule**.

innominate bone *See* **hip bone**.

inorganic substances Chemical substances (e.g., salts, water) not containing carbon.

insulin A hormone that lowers the level of glucose in blood. Insulin is produced in the pancreas. *See* **pancreatic islets**.

integument skin

interferon Immune system proteins that help to protect cells against attack by some kinds of viruses.

interneurons Nerve cells that carry impulses beween sensory and motor neurons. They occur only in the central nervous system.

interoceptor A type of sensory nerve ending found in internal organs and responding to changes inside the body.

interstitial cells Cells in the testes that produce the male sex hormone testosterone.

intervertebral disk The fibrocartilaginous disk between two vertebrae.

intestine *See* **large intestine, small intestine**.

involuntary muscle *See* **smooth muscle**.

iris The circular colored part of the eye surrounding the pupil. Muscle fibers that make the iris contract alter pupil size, and so the amount of light entering the eye.

ischium The bone forming the lower, rear part of a hip bone: the part that you sit on.

islets of Langerhans *See* **pancreatic islets**.

isometric Describes contraction that increases the internal tension in a muscle without shortening it.

isotonic Describes contraction that maintains the same tension in a muscle and shortens it.

jejunum The middle part of the small intestine, between the duodenum and ileum.

joint A place where two or more bones meet. Bones at a joint may be fixed or they may move against one another.

keratin A hard, waterproof protein found in the epidermis, hair, and nails.

kidney A bean-shaped organ that filters wastes from blood to form urine. The two kidneys lie in the upper rear of the abdomen, one on each side of the vertebral column.

kilocalorie *See* **calorie**.

Krebs cycle (or citric acid cycle) A series of biochemical reactions in living cells that break down carbohydrates, releasing energy. *See* **catabolism, metabolism**.

labia "Lips": the labia majora and labia minora are respectively the outer and inner lip-like skin folds outside the vagina.

lacrimal Relating to tears; also the name of a small bone in each

types of joint

ball-and-socket

hinge

saddle

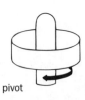

ellipsoidal

pivot

eye socket.

lactation Milk production by the mammary glands.

lactic acid A waste product of anaerobic respiration that accumulates in muscles during exercise.

large intestine (or bowel) The lower part of the alimentary canal, comprising the cecum, colon, and rectum. The large intestine absorbs water and eliminates wastes as feces.

larynx The cartilaginous voice box containing the vocal cords. It lies in the middle of the front of the neck, at the top of the trachea and below the pharynx.

lateral Toward the side.

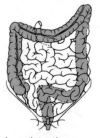

large intestine

lens A biconvex transparent structure behind the iris. It bends light rays entering the eye and so helps to focus them on the retina.

leukocytes White blood cells. They help to combat injuries and attack microorganisms invading the body. Types include granulocytes (eosinophils, neutrophils, and basophils) and agranulocytes (lymphocytes and monocytes).

ligament Fibrous tissue that connects bones.

limbic system Part of the forebrain encircling the brain stem and largely involved in emotional responses.

lipase An enzyme that digests fat.

lipids Organic compounds including fats, oils, and cholesterol.

liver The largest organ inside the body, in the right upper part of the abdominal cavity. Its many functions include manufacturing bile and glycogen, and so helping to digest and store food. *See* **bile, glycogen**.

lumbar region the lower back

lungs The two organs of respiration, filling most of the chest cavity inside the rib cage and above the diaphragm. Each lung resembles a "tree" with hollow bronchi, bronchioles, and alveoli as "branches," "twigs," and "leaves."

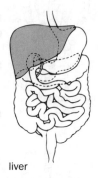

liver

luteinizing hormone (LH) A hormone that in females helps to make ova mature and triggers ovulation, and in males makes testes produce testosterone. LH comes from the pituitary gland and acts with FSH. *See* **follicle-stimulating hormone**.

lymph A transparent fluid much like blood plasma. It leaks from blood vessels into tissue spaces and is collected by the lymphatic system.

lymph nodes "Knots" in the lymphatic system, which contain lymphocytes and macrophages that filter the lymph passing through the nodes.

lymphatic system A network of vessels that return lymph from body tissues to blood and filter out harmful particles on the way.

lymphocytes White blood cells produced in the lymph nodes. They produce antibodies.

macrophages Large cells that scavenge cell debris and foreign bodies. They occur largely in connective and lymphatic tissue.

mammary glands Milk-secreting glands in female breasts. Each gland comprises many lobules linked by ducts leading to a nipple.

mandible The lower jawbone.

maxillae Two bones forming the upper jaw.

mechanoreceptors Pressure-sensitive sensory receptors, responding to touch or sound or shifts in the body's balance.

medial Toward the middle.

medulla The inner part of some organs, including the kidneys; a name for bone marrow.

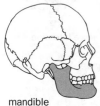

mandible

medulla oblongata The lowest part of the brain stem, which contains the vital centers controlling heartbeat and respiration.

meiosis Two successive cell divisions that halve the number of chromosomes in the resulting cells, which are sex cells (ova or sperm). *See* **mitosis**.

melanin A dark pigment occurring in skin and hair.

melatonin A hormone influencing the onset of puberty, the menstrual cycle, and the body's daily activity cycle. *See also* **pineal gland**.

membrane A thin lining or layer.

menarche When a girl starts menstruating, usually at about 13 years of age.

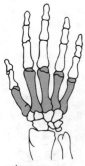

metacarpus

meninges Three protective membranes surrounding the brain and spinal cord. From the inner to the outer membrane they are: the pia mater, arachnoid, and dura mater.

menopause When a woman stops menstruating because she has passed childbearing age. This is usually between the ages of 45 and 50.

menstruation The monthly flow of blood and uterine lining from the vagina of nonpregnant females between menarche and menopause.

mesoderm An embryo's middle germ layer, which develops into the bones and muscles. *See* **ectoderm, endoderm**.

metabolic rate The body's energy expenditure per unit of time.

metabolism The array of continuous chemical changes that maintain life in the body. *See* **anabolism, catabolism**.

metacarpus The five metacarpal bones located between the wrist and the fingers.

metatarsus The five metatarsal bones located between the ankle and the toes. *See* **metacarpus**.

micturition urination

metatarsus

midbrain The top of the brain stem, between the diencephalon and the pons. It is largely a relay station for sensory impulses.

middle ear An air-filled chamber between the outer ear and inner ear. It amplifies sound waves and transmits them to the inner ear. *See* **ossicles, tympanic membrane**.

mineralocorticoids Hormones (e.g., aldosterone) produced by the adrenal cortex. They help to regulate mineral metabolism and the level of fluid in the body.

minerals Inorganic substances present in many foods. Very small quantities of minerals are needed to help maintain growth and health.

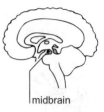

midbrain

mitochondria Structures in a cell's cytoplasm that play a major role in the breakdown of food molecules to release energy.

mitosis Ordinary cell division in which both daughter cells have as many chromosomes as there were in the parent cell. *See* **meiosis**.

monocytes A type of large white blood cell. *See* **leukocytes**.

monosaccharides Simple sugars, such as fructose and glucose. They are the building blocks of carbohydrates.

mons pubis In females, a fatty pad over the point where both pubic bones meet.

morula The ball of cells produced from a fertilized cell after three days. *See* **zygote**.

motor neuron (or motoneuron) A nerve cell that carries messages from the central nervous system to a muscle or gland. *See* **efferent**.

mucous membranes The mucus-secreting linings of the digestive, respiratory, reproductive, and urinary tracts.

muscle Tissue that shortens to make part of the body move. Most striated muscle is voluntary (under conscious control). Smooth muscle is involuntary (under automatic control). *See* **cardiac muscle, skeletal muscle, smooth muscle, striated muscle**.

mutation Change in a gene or genes of a living cell. A mutation in some way changes the cell's characteristics and will be inherited. *See* **chromosome, genes**.

muscle (smooth)

myelin The fatty white substance forming an insulating sheath around many nerve fibers.

myocardium Cardiac muscle forming the middle layer of the heart wall.

myosin A contractile protein occurring in muscle.

nares The nasal openings: nostrils.

nasals The pair of bones forming the upper end of the bridge of the nose.

navel *See* **umbilicus**.

nephron The basic filtration unit in a kidney. *See* **glomerulus, tubule**.

nerve A group of nerve fibers.

nerve fiber a neuron's axon

nervous system The coordinated networks of neurons that control the body. *See* **autonomic nervous system, central nervous system, peripheral nervous system**.

neural tube Embryonic tissue that gives rise to the brain and spinal cord.

neuroglia Cells in nerve tissue that support the cells that convey nerve impulses.

neurohypophysis The posterior part of the pituitary gland.

neuron A cell that conveys electrochemical impulses. Neurons form the basic units of the nervous system. *See* **axon, dendrites**.

Neurotransmitters Chemicals released by neurons to stimulate or inhibit activity in other neurons or in glands or muscles.

neutrophil The most plentiful type of white blood cell. *See* **leukocytes**.

nipple The conical projection on a breast, which contains the outlets of the milk ducts.

noradrenaline *See* **norepinephrine**.

norepinephrine (or noradrenaline) A neurotransmitter affecting various kinds of activity in the body, including blood flow.

nucleic acids Molecules that store genetic information. They form the DNA and RNA in living cells. *See* **deoxyribonucleic acid, ribonucleic acid**.

nucleus The control center in most types of cell, which contains coded genetic instructions. *See* **chromosome, genes**.

occipital bone A bone at the back of the skull with a hole in it for the spinal cord.

olfactory Relating to smell.

oocyte An immature ovum (egg).

optic Relating to the eye.

organ Part of the body made of different tissues that performs a particular task.

organelles Tiny structures performing particular tasks in a cell's cytoplasm. *See* **mitochondria, ribosomes**.

organic substances Compounds that contain carbon. Common examples are carbohydrates, fats, and proteins.

osmosis Diffusion of a fluid (e.g., water) through a semipermeable membrane.

ossicles Tiny bones, especially the malleus, incus, and stapes in the middle ear.

osteocytes Mature bone cells.

neuron

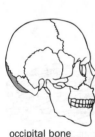

occipital bone

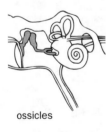

ossicles

osteonic canals *See* **Haversian canals**.

otoliths Tiny calcium carbonate crystals in the inner ear. *See* **vestibular system**.

outer ear The ear's auricle (pinna) and external auditory canal.

oval window A membrane-covered opening between the middle ear and inner ear.

ovarian cycle The monthly cycle by which eggs develop and are released from the ovary in females between puberty and the menopause.

ovary A walnut-sized sex organ which produces ova (eggs). Females have two ovaries, one on each side of the uterus.

oviduct *See* **fallopian tubes**.

ovulation The release of a ripe egg from a female's ovary. *See* **ovarian cycle**.

ovum (pl. ova) An egg; a female sex cell.

oxidation A chemical reaction involving loss of electrons. In the human body, oxidation occurs when breathed-in oxygen combines with molecules in food to produce energy, water, and carbon dioxide.

palate The roof of the mouth.

pancreas A tongue-shaped gland located in the abdomen that produces glucagon, insulin, and pancreatic juice. *See* **glucagon, insulin, pancreatic islets, pancreatic juice.**

pancreatic islets (or islets of Langerhans) Scattered endocrine regions in the pancreas that produce glucagon and insulin.

pancreatic juice Juice made in the pancreas that contains enzymes that help to digest all types of food.

papilla A tiny nipple-shaped projection.

parasympathetic nervous system The part of the autonomic nervous system that controls rest and digestion.

parathyroid gland Any of four pea-sized endocrine glands on the thyroid gland. They produce parathyroid hormone.

parathyroid hormone (or parathormone) A hormone that controls blood calcium level. It is produced by the parathyroid glands.

parietal bones Two fused bones forming the top of the skull.

patella The kneecap.

pathogen A microorganism that causes disease.

pectoral Relating to the chest.

pelvis A bony basin formed by the two hip bones, the sacrum, and the coccyx; also the core of a kidney, containing the broad upper end of a ureter.

penis The male organ of urination and copulation.

pepsin A protein-digesting enzyme in the stomach.

pericardium The two-layered membrane enclosing the heart.

pelvis (male)

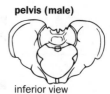

inferior view

perineum The part of the body between the anus and the genitals.

peripheral nervous system A network of nerves linking the brain and spinal cord to other parts of the body. Some control voluntary acts, others automatic responses. *See* **autonomic nervous system, somatic nervous system**.

peristalsis Waves of muscular contraction that force substances through passageways, such as the alimentary canal.

peritoneum The slippery membrane lining the abdomen and its organs.

phagocytes Those white blood cells and other cells that perform phagocytosis.

phagocytosis A process by which certain cells engulf and destroy foreign particles or microorganisms such as bacteria.

phalanges Finger and toe bones.

pharynx The throat.

photoreceptors Light-sensitive cells in the retina. *See* **cones, rods**.

pia mater *See* **meninges**.

pineal gland An endocrine gland in the diencephalon. It produces melatonin.

pituitary gland (or hypophysis) A two-part endocrine gland on the sphenoid bone in the skull. It controls other endocrine glands.

placenta An organ formed in the uterus during pregnancy to nourish the fetus and remove its waste products.

plasma The fluid part of blood.

platelets (or thrombocytes) Disk-shaped structures in blood that promote clotting.

pleura The double membrane that covers the lungs and lines the chest wall.

polysaccharides Linked monosaccharides, as in starch, glycogen, and cellulose.

pons A bridgelike structure, especially the brain stem between the midbrain and medulla.

posterior Behind; to the rear.

prepuce *See* **foreskin**.

progesterone A hormone that helps prepare the uterus to receive a fertilized egg.

pronation Turning the palm downward.

proprioceptors Mechanoreceptors in joints, muscles, and tendons. They help in the sensation of body position and body movements.

prostaglandins Fatty acids with local hormone-like and other effects. They occur in most tissues.

prostate gland A gland below the bladder in males. It produces a sperm-activating fluid that forms nearly a third of the semen's volume.

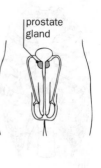
prostate gland

proteins Complex nitrogenous compounds built from amino acids; essential constituents of living cells. Protein foods are vital for the growth and repair of the body.

protoplasm Cytoplasm plus nucleoplasm (the substance that forms the cell nucleus).

proximal Near the point of origin.

puberty The time in life when someone is becoming sexually mature.

pubes The hairy area covering the pubis.

pubis Part of a hip bone: one of a pair that meet at the front of the pelvis.

pudendum *See* **vulva**.

pulmonary Relating to the lungs.

pulse The regular throbbing of an artery, which can be felt as it expands each time the heart pumps blood through it.

pupil The hole in the middle of the iris, through which light enters the eye.

pylorus The narrow exit from the stomach into the duodenum, closed by a ring of muscle until food in the stomach is liquidized.

radius One of the two bones of the forearm.

receptors Sensory nerve endings that receive and transmit stimuli.

rectum The last part of the colon, where feces collect before leaving the body.

reflex action The body's automatic, involuntary response to a stimulus.

renal Relating to the kidney.

respiration A term with several different meanings: (**1**) breathing; (**2**) taking up oxygen and giving out carbon dioxide; (**3**) deriving energy from food with or without oxygen. *See* **aerobic respiration, anaerobic respiration**.

respiratory system In humans, the mouth, nose, pharynx, larynx, trachea, bronchi, bronchioles, alveoli, and lungs.

reticular formation A system of nerve cells in the brain stem, controlling consciousness.

retina The back of the eyeball where neurons convert light into electrical impulses that pass through the brain. *See* **cones, rods**.

ribonucleic acid (RNA) Nucleic acids that help to produce proteins in living cells.

ribosomes Tiny structures that synthesize proteins in cell cytoplasm. *See* **organelles**.

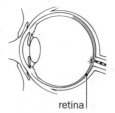
retina

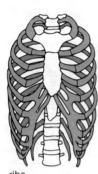
ribs

ribs Twelve pairs of curved bones that protect the chest cavity and that rise to enlarge it, helping to draw air into the lungs.

RNA *See* **ribonucleic acid**.

rods Receptor cells in the retina that sense dim light. *See* **retina**.

round window A membrane-covered opening between the middle ear and inner ear.

saccule *See* **vestibular system**.

sacrum Five fused vertebrae joined to the two hip bones.

sagittal Relating to a length wise division of the body or of a body part.

salivary glands Paired glands in the mouth and cheeks. They produce saliva, which moistens food and starts the process of digestion.

scapula (pl. scapulae) Either of the two shoulder blades.

sclera The white outer coat of the eyeball.

scrotum The sac that contains the two testes.

sebaceous gland An exocrine gland in the skin that produces sebum (an oily secretion).

secretions Fluids or solids produced or concentrated in glands.

semen Fluid containing sperm and secretions from accessory male sex glands.

semicircular ducts *See* **vestibular system**.

seminal vesicles Paired accessory male glands providing sperm with energy-rich fluid that forms the largest component of semen.

seminiferous tubules Coiled tubes producing sperm in the testes.

sensory neurons Neurons that send signals to the central nervous system.

septum A wall between body cavities.

serotonin A neurotransmitter in the brain, involved in sleep, mood, etc.

serum Blood plasma that does not contain clotting factors but does contain antibodies.

sex chromosomes The X and Y chromosomes, genetically determining gender: normally XX produces females and XY produces males.

sex chromosomes

sigmoid S-shaped, as in part of the colon.

sinoatrial node (or SA node) Special cells in the heart wall, forming its natural pacemaker.

sinus A cavity or hollow, as in the skull's air-filled nasal sinuses and in the channels draining venous blood from the brain.

skeletal muscle Muscle attached to bones and under voluntary control. *See* **striated muscle**.

skeleton The bony framework that protects and supports the body's soft tissues.

skin The body's waterproof covering; its largest organ, with two main layers: the epidermis and dermis. *See* **dermis, epidermis, subcutaneous tissue**.

skull Twenty-two bones forming the frame of the head. All interlock rigidly except the hinged lower jawbone (mandible).

small intestine Part of the alimentary canal between the stomach and the large intestine. It includes the duodenum, jejunum, and ileum. Most digestion occurs in the small intestine.

smooth muscle Involuntary muscle without the striated fibers of skeletal muscle. It automatically operates internal organs such as the stomach, bladder, and blood vessels.

somatic nervous system The part of the peripheral nervous system that sends motor impulses to skeletal muscles.

somatotrophin *See* **growth hormone**.

sperm Male sex cells.

sphenoid A bone in the skull base.

sphincter A ring-shaped muscle that contracts to close an orifice.

spinal cord The cable of nerve tissue running down inside the vertebral column and linking the brain with most of the body.

spinal nerves Thirty pairs of nerves and one single nerve springing from the spinal cord.

spine *See* **vertebral column**.

spleen A large organ behind the stomach. It filters and stores blood.

striated muscle Muscle consisting of striped fibers. *See also* **cardiac muscle, skeletal muscle**.

sternum the breastbone

steroids Chemically related substances with various metabolic effects. They include adrenal hormones, sex hormones, and cholesterol.

stomach A muscular bag-like part of the alimentary canal between the esophagus and small intestine. It stores and churns food and produces gastric juice, which partly digests food and kills germs.

striated muscle Muscle made of striped fibers. *See* **cardiac muscle, skeletal muscle**.

subcutaneous tissue The sheet of connective tissue below the dermis.

supination Turning the body to lie on the back, or turning the palm upward.

suprarenal glands *See* **adrenal glands**.

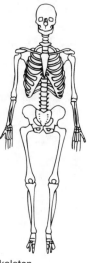

skeleton

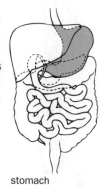

stomach

suture An immovable fibrous joint between bones of the skull.

sweat glands Glands located in the epidermis, which produce perspiration.

sympathetic nervous system The part of the autonomic nervous system that prepares the body to cope with stress.

symphysis A cartilaginous joint.

synapse The junction between two neurons.

synovial joint A freely movable joint with a cavity lined by synovial membrane and lubricated by synovial fluid.

systole A contraction of the heart. *Compare* **diastole**.

talus An ankle bone: part of the tarsus.

tarsus The seven small tarsal bones which help to form and support the ankle, heel, and instep. *See* **calcaneus, talus**.

taste buds Tiny sensory organs of the tongue and palate.

teeth Up to 32 bone-like structures in the jaws. Different types (incisors, canines, premolars, molars) are specialized to pierce, tear, crush, and/or grind food.

telencephalon The "end brain" front subdivision of the forebrain, which contains the cerebral hemispheres.

temporal bone One of a pair of bones forming the skull's lower side walls.

tendons Bands of fibrous connective tissue joining muscles to bones.

testicle *See* **testis**.

testis (or testicle; pl. testes) One of a pair of primary male sex organs that manufacture male sex cells (sperm).

testosterone A sex hormone mainly made in the testes. It stimulates the development of male sexual characteristics and other features.

thalamus A brain structure above the hypothalamus. It sends sensory impulses to the cerebral cortex, links sensations with emotions, and affects consciousness.

thermoreceptors Receptors that sense changes in temperature.

thigh bone *See* **femur**.

thoracic Relating to the chest.

thorax The chest: the body between the neck and the abdomen.

thrombocytes *See* **platelets**.

thymus A lymphoid endocrine gland in the chest involved in immunity.

thyroid An endocrine gland in the neck. *See* **calcitonin, thyroxine**.

thyroxine A hormone made in the thyroid that is important for growth and mental development.

tibia The shinbone.

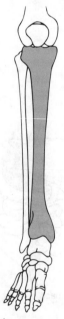

tibia

tissue Part of the body made of similar cells that perform a particular task.

tongue A mobile, muscular organ in the mouth, involved in tasting, chewing, swallowing, and speech.

tonsils Areas of lymphoid tissue around the entrance to the throat.

tooth *See* **teeth**.

trachea (or windpipe) The tube between the larynx and the bronchi.

tubule A tiny tube, as in the collecting tubules and convoluted tubules of the kidney.

tympanic membrane (or eardrum) A membrane between the external and middle ear.

ulna One of the two bones of the forearm.

umbilical cord The cord that joins a fetus to a placenta.

umbilicus (or navel) An abdominal scar left by removal of the umbilical cord after birth.

urea The chief nitrogenous waste product excreted in urine.

ureters The tubes conveying urine from the kidney to the bladder.

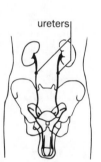

ureters

urethra The passage taking urine from the bladder to outside the body.

urinary system The kidneys, ureters, bladder, and urethra.

urine Liquid waste excreted by the kidneys.

uterine tubes *See* **fallopian tubes**.

uterus (or womb) A hollow muscular organ in females, above the bladder. Inside it, a fertilized ovum develops into a baby.

utricle *See* **vestibular system**.

uvula A conical tag hanging from the back of the palate. It helps to keep food out of the nasal cavities.

vagina The muscular passage between the vulva and cervix (neck of the uterus).

vascular Relating to or richly supplied with vessels, especially blood vessels.

vas deferens (or ductus deferens; pl. vasa deferentia) One of a pair of muscular tubes that are the sperm's outlet from the epididymis.

vein A blood vessel that transports blood from capillaries back to the heart.

venous Relating to veins.

ventral Relating to the abdomen or front of the human body. *Compare* **dorsal**.

ventricle A cavity, especially either of the two lower chambers of the heart, or one of the four cavities in the brain.

venule A small vein.

vermiform appendix *See* **appendix**.

vertebra A bone of the vertebral column.

vertebral column (or backbone or spine) The column of vertebrae between the skull and the hip bones, supporting the body and shielding the spinal cord. It has five sections: cervical, thoracic, lumbar, sacral, and coccygeal. *See also* **coccyx, sacrum.**

vesicle A small sac or bladder that contains liquid.

vesicular follicle *See* **Graafian follicle.**

vestibular system The part of the inner ear dealing with balance. It includes two sacs (saccule and utricle) containing gravity-sensitive otoliths, and three fluid-filled semicircular ducts which register movement.

vestibule A space before a passage begins, as in the inner ear beyond the oval window, between the semicircular ducts and cochlea.

villus (pl. villi) A minute fingerlike projection. Huge numbers line the small intestine, vastly increasing its surface area.

visceral Relating to internal organs.

vital capacity The amount of air expelled from the lungs after taking a deep breath.

vitamins Essential nutrients needed in tiny amounts to prevent deficiency diseases.

vitreous humor A jellylike substance in the eyeball, between the lens and the retina.

vocal cords Two belts of elastic tissue stretched across the larynx which produce sounds when air rushes past them.

voluntary muscle *See* **skeletal muscle.**

vulva (or pudendum) The external female genitals.

white matter Myelin-sheathed nerve fibers.

windpipe *See* **trachea.**

womb *See* **uterus.**

zygomatic bone The cheekbone.

zygote A fertilized egg, formed by the union of a sperm with an ovum.

physiology: disorders of the body

achondroplasia An inherited condition resulting in short stature. There is defective cartilage growth and defective ability to form bones.

ankylosing spondylitis A disease in which joints become inflamed and later fuse.

arthritis The term used to refer to a variety of inflammatory or degenerative diseases that damage joints. Acute forms are commonly caused by bacterial invasion. Examples of arthritis (not of acute forms) include osteoarthritis, rheumatoid arthritis, and gouty arthritis.

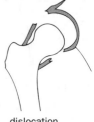

dislocation

bone cyst A cavity in bone, usually filled with fluid.

bunion The swelling of the joint between the big toe and first metatarsal bone, caused by wearing ill-fitting shoes.

fracture
a closed
b open
c complicated

bursitis The inflammation of a bursa (lubricating sac between bones, tendons, and muscles), usually caused by excessive stress or friction.

disk prolapse *See* **slipped disk.**

dislocation An injury in which bones are forced out of their normal positions, at a joint. Dislocations can occur when an injury tears ligaments that keep two bone surfaces in place.

displacement Another word for dislocation.

fracture A break in a bone. There are three types: closed, open, and complicated (closed or open).

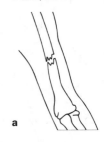

a

gouty arthritis A form of arthritis caused by urate crystals (formed from uric acid) deposited in the soft tissues of joints. Uric acid is a waste product, normally eliminated without any problems.

kyphosis Abnormal outward curvature of the upper spine.

lordosis Abnormal inward curvature of the lower spine.

Lyme disease A disease caused by bacteria transmitted by bites from ticks. It results in arthritis, especially in the knee joint.

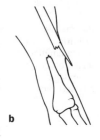

b

osteoarthritis Often referred to as degenerative joint disease, its specific cause is unknown. A current theory is that enzymes are released that break down cartilage in the joint. Cartilage repair is an ongoing process, but in those with osteoarthritis, more cartilage is broken down than is repaired.

osteomalacia A group of disorders caused by lack of vitamin D. With insufficient minerals, bones soften and weaken. Weight-bearing bones may bend or fracture.

osteomyelitis Infection of bone marrow and of the bone, usually

c

caused by bacteria, resulting in inflammation.

osteoporosis A group of diseases in which the resorption of bone outpaces the deposit of bone. Bones become lighter and more porous, making them susceptible to fracture.

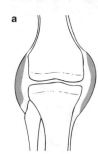

osteosarcoma Also called osteogenic sarcoma. A form of bone cancer arising in the long bone of a limb. Osteoblasts (bone cells) multiply and form tumors.

Paget's disease A disease that involves the abnormal formation and resorption of bone. Bones become soft, weak, thickened, and deformed.

rheumatism Any painful state in bones, ligaments, joints, tendons, or muscles.

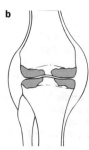

rheumatoid arthritis A chronic inflammatory disorder affecting joints, especially those of the fingers and toes, and causing severe swelling. Marked by exacerbations (flare-ups) and remissions (decrease in severity of symptoms). It is an autoimmune disease (the body's immune system attacks its own tissues).

rickets The disease of osteomalacia in children. Growing bones cannot calcify due to lack of nutrients, so their ends become visibly enlarged.

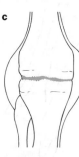

scoliosis Abnormal curvature of the spine to the side.

slipped disk Also called disk prolapse. The pulpy center of one of the disks that sits between the vertebrae oozes out and may press on an adjacent nerve, causing pain.

Muscular

rheumatoid
arthritis
a Inflammation
b Erosion of
   cartilage
c Fused joint

ataxia Lack of coordination of the muscles.

atrophy The wasting or withering of muscle.

Bell's palsy *See* **facial palsy**.

Bornholm disease (or pleurodynia) A viral infection that causes pain and overall swelling. It requires a long convalescence.

bursitis Inflammation of the sac (bursa) lubricating a joint. It can be caused by calcium deposits on a tendon, but is generally a result of continuous friction, pressure, or other injury.

cardiomyopathy Disease of the heart muscle.

convulsions Involuntary contractions of a group of muscles caused by an imbalance in the neurological system.

cramp A painful involuntary muscle spasm, which may result from loss of salt owing to excessive sweating or from deficient blood supply to the affected area.

crossed eyes A condition, also known as strabismus, that can be caused by a muscular imbalance in the muscles controlling eye movement.

facial palsy Also known as Bell's palsy. Often temporary paralysis of the facial muscles affecting one eyelid and one side of the forehead and mouth. The paralysis can be caused by injury to, or infection of, the nerve.

fibrositis Pain in muscles around joints. When this occurs in the lower back it is sometimes called lumbago. The cause is not known, but tension and bad posture may be to blame.

gangrene (gas) A type of gangrene involving bacterial infection, usually of a wound, leading to muscle death.

leiomyoma A noncancerous tumor of smooth muscle. Fibroids are common leiomyomas that occur in the uterus.

muscular dystrophy An inherited disorder in which there is a progressive wasting of muscle.

myasthenia gravis Weakness in skeletal muscles caused by an abnormality that prevents muscles from contracting.

myoclonus Rapid, involuntary spasm or jerks of a muscle or muscles, occurring during movement or rest. It can occur as a result of a brain disorder or epileptic fit, and may be linked with diseases of the nerves and muscles.

myoma A benign tumor of muscle.

myopathy A muscle disease, usually degenerative, but sometimes caused by drug side-effects, chemical poisoning, or by chronic disorder of the immune system. The muscles generally fail to function fully.

myositis Inflammation of muscle tissue, causing weakness, tenderness, and pain.

myotonia The inability of a muscle to relax after the need for contraction has passed.

pleurodynia *See* **Bornholm disease**.

poliomyelitis (also known as polio) A virus infection of groups of muscles, with severe symptoms. Vaccine is available against this.

rhabdomyolysis Destruction of muscle tissue, accompanied by the release into the blood of myoglobin (oxygen-carrying red muscle pigment). A common cause is a crushing muscle injury.

rhabdomyosarcoma A rare cancer of the skeletal muscle.

spasm A sudden, involuntary contraction of the muscle lasting a short time.

sprain An injury in which the ligaments reinforcing a joint are stretched or torn.

stitch A sharp pain in the side that can occur during strenuous exercise.

tendinitis The inflammation of tendons. It can be caused by overuse of a muscle or group of muscles.

tenosynovitis Inflammation of the sheath around a tendon caused by rheumatism or bacterial infection.

tetanus A disease caused by bacterial infection in which muscles are severely affected. Causes stiffness, contractions, and spasms.

tic The involuntary twitching of a muscle normally under voluntary control. Generally a sign of anxiety or insecurity, a tic begins as a deliberate movement that gradually becomes unconscious.

whiplash injury Tearing of the muscles and ligaments around the cervical (neck) vertebrae by sudden head movement, often resulting from automobile accidents.

wrist ganglion A lump in the wrist produced by a cyst affecting a tendon.

Circulatory: heart and blood disorders

angina pectoris A condition characterized by pain in the chest and sometimes the left arm, especially during times of stress or exertion. The cause is inadequate oxygen to the heart, sometimes a result of narrowed coronary arteries.

arrhythmia Abnormal heart rate or rhythm: tachycardia (faster than normal heart rate) and bradycardia (slower than normal heart rate). It is caused by a disruption of the heart's conduction system, which generates and transmits electrical impulses in the heart. It can be caused by coronary artery disease, stress, exertion, or some drugs.

cardiac arrest A point at which the heart ceases to beat effectively.

cardiac arrhythmia A disturbance in the electrical impulses to the heart which results in an irregular rhythm or rate of heartbeat.

cardiomegaly Enlargement of the heart. There are a number of causes.

cardiomyopathy A term used for a disease of the heart's muscle, resulting in a decrease in the heart's efficiency to contract and circulate blood.

carditis Inflammation of the heart.

congenital heart defects Heart defects in newborn babies including ventricular septal defect (the wall between two ventricles does not form properly), coarctation of the aorta (the aorta is narrowed), pulmonary stenosis (the pulmonary semilunar valve is narrowed), and tetralogy of Fallot (multiple defects).

constrictive pericarditis A condition in which the pericardium (lining) of the heart is scarred or otherwise diseased, preventing the heart from expanding properly.

cor pulmonale Disease of the heart caused by disease of the blood vessels to the lungs or disease of the lungs themselves.

endocarditis Inflammation of the endocardium (inner heart lining) often resulting from infection by bacteria.

epicarditis Inflammation of the epicardium (outer lining of the heart).

fibrillation Rapid, irregular contractions of the heart.

fibrosis of cardiac muscle Scarring of heart muscle.

heart attack *See* myocardial infarction.

heart block A condition in which the electrical impulses in the heart are blocked at points in the conduction system.

heart failure Pumping by the heart of less blood than the body needs causing inability to supply the oxygen demands of the tissues. It results in congestion of blood and lack of nutrition to tissues.

hypertension High blood pressure, often caused by stress, arteriosclerosis, or heart disease.

hypotension Low blood pressure, often causing faintness when someone stands suddenly.

ischemia Reduced blood supply to a part of the body or to an organ, especially the brain.

leukemia Cancer of the white blood cells. It affects the tissues involved in the production of blood, such as the bone marrow and lymph nodes.

mitral valve prolapse Improper closure of the mitral valve (the valve between the left atrium and ventricle). Also called floppy valve syndrome.

myocardial infarction Commonly called heart attack, a condition in which obstruction of blood flowing to the heart muscle results in tissue death. It is most often caused by atherosclerosis of the coronary arteries.

myocarditis Inflammation of the myocardium (main heart muscle) that can weaken the heart, impairing its function.

palpitations A sensation of a heartbeat that is rapid or irregular in some way. Can be caused by drugs, emotions, or heart disorders.

porphyria A group of disorders that all cause excess of the nitrogenous factors in hemoglobin (which transports oxygen) in the blood. The symptoms are severe.

shock The effect of lack of blood following an injury, including sudden lowering of blood pressure.

Stokes-Adams syndrome A sudden attack of unconsciousness accompanying heart block.

stroke The effect of a fault in the blood flow through the brain, caused either by a burst blood vessel or by an obstruction to the blood supply. Recovery of a victim's faculties may be protracted.

valvular stenosis Narrowing of a heart valve, which causes the heart to work harder to push blood around the body.

varicose vein A vein, usually on the leg, that has become swollen and twisted by internal pressure.

Defense systems

AIDS (Acquired Immune Deficiency Syndrome) An immunological disorder in which the body's immune response system becomes defective, leaving the sufferer open to opportunistic infections and some forms of cancer, such as Kaposi's sarcoma. It is caused by infection with the HIV virus, transmitted mainly through sexual intercourse or infected blood products.

allergies or hypersensitivities A hypersensitive reaction occurs when the body's immune system causes damage to tissue cells by fighting off a "threat"—such as pollen—that may actually be quite harmless.

autoimmune disorder A condition in which a person's immune system begins to attack the healthy organs and cells of his or her own body. Autoimmune disorders can cause a variety of diseases.

elephantiasis Infestation of the lymph vessels by parasitic worms that are transmitted by mosquito bite. It can cause gross swelling.

Grave's disease An autoimmune disorder which leads to an overactive and enlarged thyroid gland.

Hashimoto's thyroiditis An autoimmune disorder in which the cells of the thyroid gland are attacked. This interferes with the production of hormones by the thyroid gland, causing fatigue and weight gain.

hay fever An allergic reaction to pollen and other forms of airborne dust, often seasonal.

Hodgkin's disease A disorder of the lymphatic system in which the lymphoid tissue multiplies rapidly. This can damage the immune system and can result in infections, which are normally considered minor, becoming fatal.

multiple sclerosis (MS) A disease that is thought to be caused by an autoimmune disorder. It attacks the protective coverings of nerve fibers in the brain and spinal cord. Symptoms vary in severity but can include paralysis.

pernicious anemia Anemia is the lack of hemoglobin (oxygen-carrying part of blood). Pernicious anemia is due to a lack of vitamin B_{12}, and is often caused by an autoimmune disorder.

rheumatic fever A serious allergic reaction to bacterial infection, usually tonsilitis, with severe symptoms.

rheumatoid arthritis An autoimmune disorder which attacks the joints and surrounding tissues, causing them to become painful, swollen, stiff, and even deformed.

severe combined immunodeficiency (SCID) A birth defect in which babies lack sufficient T-cells and B-cells (white blood cells). These cells are vital to the working of the immune system. Sufferers have little or no protection against disease.

systemic lupus erythematosus (SLE) A systemic (not localized) autoimmune disorder. It particularly affects the joints, skin, lungs, and kidneys.

Rheumatoid arthritis
The synovium (membrane lining the capsule of a joint) becomes inflamed. Inflammation may then spread to the bone and cartilage.

Key:
a capsule
b inflamed synovium
c bone
d cartilage

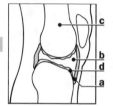

Respiratory

asbestosis A lung disease caused by the inhalation of fibers of the building material asbestos. They penetrate the lungs and eventually cause thickening of the lung tissue, which interferes with its functioning.

asthma A condition involving narrowing of the bronchioles (small airways in the lungs). This leads to recurrent attacks of breathlessness. Often these are triggered by an allergic reaction, but in some cases the cause is not known.

bronchitis Inflammation of the bronchi (tubes leading from the trachea into the lungs). It can be either acute (a short-lived, sudden attack) or chronic (a long-term condition). Acute bronchitis is normally caused by a viral infection. The main cause of chronic bronchitis is tobacco smoking.

asthma

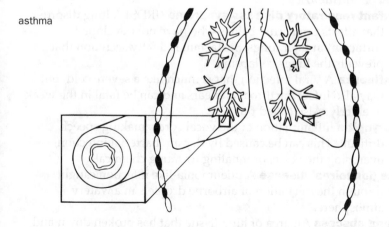

common cold A viral infection that causes inflammation of the respiratory tract lining. It is often accompanied by a runny nose, sore throat, sneezing, and headaches.

coryza A technical term for the common cold.

cystic fibrosis An inherited disease that involves oversecretion of a heavy mucus (thick, slimy fluid) that clogs the respiratory passages. Sufferers are more prone to catching fatal respiratory infections.

emphysema A disease in which the alveoli (tiny air sacs) of the lungs are damaged. Their separating walls are destroyed and the alveoli are enlarged. This leads to a decrease in the surface area available for gas exchange, and breathing becomes very difficult. The major cause of emphysema is tobacco smoking, but pollution and hereditary factors may also be involved.

enphysema

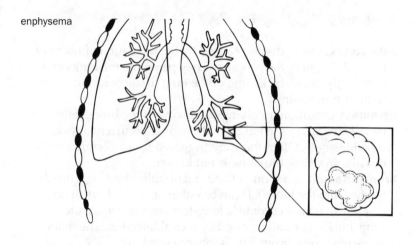

flu *See* **influenza.**

infant respiratory distress syndrome (IRDS) A lung disorder that affects premature babies who have not developed surfactant in their lungs. Surfactant is a fatty secretion that prevents the lungs collapsing.

influenza A viral infection that is much like a severe cold, but may also infect the throat and ears and can be fatal in the weak or elderly. Also called flu.

laryngitis Inflammation of the vocal cords, making speech difficult. This can be caused by dry air, bacterial infection, overusing the voice, or inhaling irritating chemicals.

Legionnaires' disease A pneumonia-like infection caught through the inhalation of airborne droplets in a watery atmosphere.

lung abscess An area of lung tissue that has broken down and become a pus-filled cavity. It is usually caused by inhalation of foreign material that gets trapped in the lung tissue, causing infection and inflammation. It causes coughing, fever, and chest pain, and can lead to blood poisoning. Treatment is usually with antibiotic drugs.

lung cancer Tobacco smoking is the main cause of lung cancer. Tiny, hairlike cilia line the respiratory tract and help protect the lungs from chemicals. Smoking eventually destroys their ability to do this. It is the chemicals present in the smoke, however, that cause cancer.

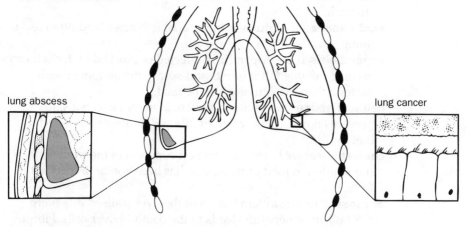

lung abscess

lung cancer

pertussis A disease, also known as whooping cough, mainly affecting babies and children. It is caused by a bacterium and is spread by airborne droplets produced by coughing. It causes persistent and often severe coughing spasms and leads to inflammation of the respiratory tract. Children are now vaccinated against pertussis as infants.

pleurisy Inflammation of the pleura (fluid-secreting coverings of the lungs). It may involve secretion of excess fluid (i.e. pleural effusion), which puts pressure on the lungs. Pleurisy is caused by infection or disease of the lungs.

pneumonia Inflammation of the lungs most often due to viral or bacterial infection. It may be accompanied by pleurisy.

pulmonary embolism A condition in which an embolus (blood clot, formed in a vein) breaks off and blocks a pulmonary artery which supplies blood to the lungs. It can result in pain, breathlessness, and sudden death.

rhinitis Inflammation of the nasal lining often accompanied by sneezing and runny nose. It can be caused by a viral infection (a cold, for example) or allergic reaction (for example, to pollen).

sinusitis Inflammation of the sinuses, usually caused by an infection.

tracheitis Inflammation of the trachea (the windpipe in the throat).

tuberculosis An infectious disease that mainly affects the lungs. It is caused by a bacteria that is often spread from person to person through sneezing and coughing.

whooping cough *See* **pertussis.**

Digestive

acid stomach The effect of a surplus of digestive juices in the stomach.

anal fissure A painful tear in the anal sphincter (and often rectal lining).

appendicitis If the appendix is infected or blocked by feces it can become inflamed. If it bursts and sprays the abdomen with bacteria then the situation can be fatal.

celiac disease Sensitivity to gluten, a protein in cereals. It prevents normal absorption of fats and necessitates a special diet for life.

cholera A severe bacterial infection common in the tropics, transmitted in food or drink that has been contaminated with feces.

cirrhosis Chronic inflammation of the liver (caused by severe alcoholism or hepatitis) leads to the death of liver cells. Fibrous scar tissue can build up and interfere with the liver's functioning.

colic Abdominal pain caused by temporary intestinal obstruction.

colitis Inflammation of the large intestine or colon. It may result from a viral or bacterial infection, causing pain and severe diarrhea.

constipation A condition in which food residue spends too long in the large intestine, too much water is absorbed and it becomes dry and difficult to pass. Lack of exercise or fiber, stress, or laxative abuse can lead to constipation.

diarrhea "Watery stools" can be caused by any condition that causes food residue to be rushed through the large intestine too quickly to allow water absorption. This may be due to bacterial irritation of the canal.

diverticulitis A lack of fiber in the diet can lead to the formation of diverticula (small projections of the large intestine lining through its wall). If these become inflamed then diverticulitis results.

dysentery A bacterial or amoebic infection causing bloody diarrhea, transmitted by infected food or water.

gallstones Formed when the cholesterol or pigment content of bile becomes crystallized. If the crystals obstruct any of the ducts, they can cause acute pain and jaundice.

gallstones
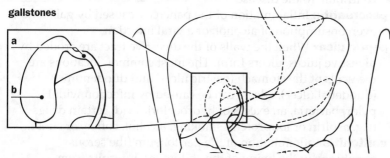

Gallstones can obstruct the cystic duct (**a**) leading from the gallbladder (**b**).

gastritis Inflammation of the stomach wall. It can be caused by an excess of hydrochloric acid and can lead to gastric ulcers.

gastroenteritis Inflammation of the stomach and intestines, commonly through virus infection.

halitosis "Bad breath" can be caused by tooth decay, any condition that inhibits saliva secretion, or poor dental hygiene.

heartburn Burning chest pain occurring when acidic gastric juices flow into the esophagus from the stomach. This can be caused by obesity, excessive consumption of food or alcohol, pregnancy, or hiatus hernia.

hemorrhoids Known as "piles," these are distended blood vessels of the anus. They are caused by conditions that put pressure on the veins such as lack of fiber in the diet or pregnancy.

hepatitis B Inflammation of the liver caused by infection with the hepatitis B virus carried by the blood.

hiatus hernia A condition in which the top of the stomach protrudes through the diaphragm. It causes heartburn as control is lost over the sphincter linking the esophagus to the stomach.

irritable bowel syndrome A condition in which the muscle movement in the large intestine is disturbed, resulting in pain and bowel irregularity. Its cause is unknown.

jaundice Accumulation of bile pigment in the blood leading to yellowing of body tissues, including the skin and the whites of the eyes. Jaundice is an indication of many liver and bile disorders, including blocked bile or hepatic ducts.

kwashiorkor Severe malnutrition in infants and young children caused by dietary deficiency, with such effects as emaciation, loss of skin color, and a bloated stomach.

mumps Inflammation of the parotid salivary glands, caused by a

hemorrhoids
a internal,
b external, and
c prolapsed.

a
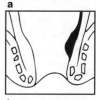

b
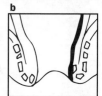

c

virus that is spread in saliva.

pancreatic cancer The presence of a malignant tumor in the pancreas. Smoking and a diet high in fats or alcohol may contribute to the disease.

pancreatitis Inflammation of the pancreas, caused by gallstones, overconsumption of alcohol, or a viral infection.

peptic ulcer When the walls of the digestive tract are eroded by digestive juices, ulcers form. The most common locations are the walls of the stomach (gastric ulcer) and duodenum (duodenal ulcer). Ulcers can be caused by infection with H. pylori bacteria, an excess of hydrochloric acid, certain drugs (e.g. aspirin or ibuprofen), smoking, alcohol, coffee, or stress.

peritonitis Inflammation of the peritoneum (the serous membrane in the lining of the abdomen). It results from bacterial infection within the abdomen, caused by perforation of the stomach or intestine. It causes severe pain, muscle spasms, fever, vomiting, and sometimes shock.

piles *See* **hemorrhoids.**

proctitis Inflammation of the anus and rectum, caused by, for example, intestinal infection, injury, and allergy.

pyloric stenosis A condition in which the pylorus (valve from stomach to small intestine) is narrowed, obstructing the passage of food. It can be caused by thickening of the muscle at the pylorus (in infants especially), or by scarring or the presence of a tumor.

strangury Obstruction of the flow through a vessel caused by outside pressure, especially through the intestine at the point of a hernia.

tooth decay Plaque (film of sugar and bacteria) weakens the protective enamel of teeth. Bacterial action then attacks the tooth structure, leading to cavities and even tooth loss.

typhoid fever A bacterial infection of the intestines, causing a rash, fever, and diarrhea, possibly leading to pneumonia. A vaccine is available against this.

Disorders of the brain and nerves

Alzheimer's disease The progressive degeneration of the brain resulting in dementia (mental deterioration).

amnesia The inability to memorize and/or to recall previously memorized information. This can be caused by damage to the brain resulting from physical injury or disease.

anencephaly A condition in which a child is born with an incomplete brain. There is no mental life as we know it. Usually, death occurs soon after birth or the child is stillborn.

carpal tunnel syndrome A condition characterized by pain and
tingling, or numbness, in the thumb and fingers. It can affect
either or both hands. The cause is unknown, although it is
known to result from pressure on the median nerve in the wrist.

cerebral edema Swelling of the brain often resulting from head
injury.

cerebral palsy The poor control over, or paralysis of, voluntary
(under conscious control) muscles resulting from damage to the
developing brain. Categories of disability caused by cerebral
palsy include: diplegia , in which all four limbs are affected but
the legs more severely than the arms; hemiplegia , in which the
limbs on only one side of the body are affected; and
quadriplegia, in which both arms and legs are severely affected.

concussion A slight injury to the brain that causes a temporary
loss of consciousness.

dyslexia A disorder in which the brain has difficulty with
reading, writing, and counting. Intelligence is not affected, but
letters in words may appear transposed or reversed, for
example.

encephalitis An infection of the brain with severe symptoms,
caused by a virus.

epilepsy Recurrent and abnormal seizures caused by abnormal
and irregular discharges of electricity from the millions of
neurons (nerve cells) in the brain.

headache Any pain in the head. Many factors that affect the
nervous system can produce a headache, including damage to
the brain and its blood vessels, infection of the ears, eyes, and
nose, and tension in muscles that results in a constriction of
their nerves.

insomnia Difficulty in falling or staying asleep. It can be caused
by stress, drinking too much coffee, or taking too little exercise,
or it may be a symptom of a physical or mental disorder.

Lou Gehrig's disease *See* **motor neuron disease**.

ME *See* **myalgic encephalomyelitis**.

meningitis Inflammation of the linings of the brain (meninges)
usually caused by a virus.

migraine A severe headache often accompanied by blurred
vision and nausea. It can be caused by stress or certain foods, or
the tendency may have been inherited.

motor neuron disease A condition in which the nerves in the
brain and spinal cord that control muscular activity degenerate.
Muscles become weak and may waste away. Also known as
Lou Gehrig's disease.

myalgic encephalomyelitis (ME) A condition of fatigue,
malaise, and stress. Its cause is unknown but it may be

associated with recent lung or stomach infection.

neuralgia Pain in a nerve, usually caused by injury or inflammation.

sciatica Pain from buttock to thigh caused by pressure on the sciatic nerve.

Disorders of the eye and ear

cataract An opaque area that forms within the lens of the eye.

conjunctivitis Inflammation of the transparent surface of the eye (conjunctiva).

deafness The total or partial inability to hear. It can be caused by a variety of factors including diseases such as otosclerosis, blockage of the ear canal by wax, damage to the eardrum, damage to the bones of the middle ear, and damage to nerves that take messages from the ear to the brain.

earache Any pain in the ear, most often caused by an infection of the middle ear.

glaucoma A condition in which pressure within the eye increases, compressing the retina and the optic nerve and causing pain and sometimes blindness.

hyperopia (farsightedness) Light rays focus behind, rather than on, the retina. The eye sees distant objects clearly, but nearby objects appear blurred. It can be corrected with a convex lens.

labyrinthitis Inflammation of the inner ear, usually caused by infection.

Menière's disease Fluid accumulates in the inner ear, causing deafness, vertigo, and tinnitus. The cause of the fluid increase is usually not known.

motion sickness Physical discomfort brought about by prolonged movements of the organs of balance within the ear. The symptoms may include headaches, nausea, and vomiting.

myopia (nearsightedness). Light rays from distant objects are focused in front of, rather than on, the retina and so appear blurred. It can be corrected with a concave lens.

Hyperopic eye
a light rays focusing behind the retina
b corrective convex lens

Myopic eye
a light rays focusing in front of the retina
b corrective concave lens

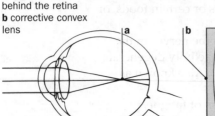
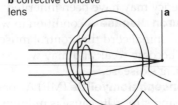

nyctalopia (night blindness) The inability to see well in dim light.

otalgia Any form of earache.

otitis media An infection of the middle ear that sometimes causes damage to the eardrum and loss of hearing. It is often caused by bacteria entering the middle ear via the eustachian tube (tube that connects the middle ear to the nasal cavity).

otosclerosis The immobilization of the tiny stapes bone in the middle ear caused by the formation of excess bone tissue around the oval window, resulting in progressive deafness.

perforated eardrum A tear or erosion of the eardrum, often resulting from middle ear infection.

presbycusis Deafness in elderly people caused by deterioration of tiny hair cells in the cochlea.

retinal detachment A condition in which the light-sensitive inner layers at the back of the eye become detached from the outer layers.

retinal hemorrhage Bleeding into the retina caused by diabetes mellitus, hypertension, or by blockage of the vein that drains blood from the retina.

retinal tear A tear in the retina caused by injury or general degeneration.

retinal vein (or artery) occlusion Blockage of the central vein or artery of the retina that sometimes results in blindness.

retinitis Inflammation of the retina.

retinitis pigmentosa Degeneration of the light-sensitive cells of the retina.

retinoblastoma Cancer of the retina.

strabismus (squint) Condition in which one eye does not look "straight," but turns in (convergent) or out (divergent). It is caused by a lack of balance between the muscles that control the eyes or a failure of the nervous system to cope with the effects of overfocusing the eyes.

strabismus

Convergent squint

Divergent squint

stye A painful, red, bacterial infection around the stem of an eyelash.

tinnitus A ringing or buzzing sound in the ears.

toxocariasis The infestation of humans by the worm toxocara canis, which lives in the intestines of dogs. It can infect and destroy the retina.

toxoplasmosis Infection by a parasite that can affect the retina.

trachoma Chronic and contagious conjunctivitis caused by an organism resembling both a virus and a bacterium.

vertigo Dizziness and lightheadedness, often caused by an infection of the inner ear that damages the organs of balance.

Urinary

anuria Condition in which no urine is produced.

calculi *See* **stones.**

cystitis Inflammation of the bladder, often due to bacterial infection, causing frequent and painful urination.

diuresis An increased or excessive flow of urine.

dysuria Painful or difficult urination.

ectopic kidney A kidney in an abnormal position (such as two kidneys on one side).

edema An abnormal increase in interstitial fluid, resulting in swollen tissues.

enlarged prostate The prostate gland in men can become enlarged due to cancer or infection or, commonly, because of fibrous glandular cells within the gland multiplying. It can lead to urine retention, which in turn can lead to infection.

enuresis The medical term for bed-wetting involving the involuntary emission of urine.

epispadias and hypospadias Conditions in which the male urethral opening is in the wrong place on the penis.

glomerulonephritis Inflammation of the glomeruli (part of the kidneys' filtering network).

gout A condition in which uric acid solidifies into crystals in the joints. Kidney tissue may also be affected.

hematuria The presence of blood in the urine.

hemophilia An inherited disorder of males passed on by females, in which the absence of a clotting factor in the blood means that bleeding becomes hard to stop.

incontinence Condition resulting from various causes, including injury or old age, in which urination cannot be voluntarily controlled. It may be temporary or permanent.

kidney failure Failure of a kidney to perform properly due to kidney disease, burns, injury, shock, heart attack, drugs, and other factors.

nephrotic syndrome A condition in which the glomerulus part of the nephron within kidneys does not work properly and protein escapes from the blood into urine, and fluid accumulates in body tissues.

nocturia Excessive urination during the night.

polycystic disease An inherited disease resulting in kidney cysts that prevent proper kidney function.

polyuria Excessive urination.

pyelonephritis Kidney infection caused by bacteria.

stones Stones, also called calculi, formed from substances that have precipitated out of urine. They can occur in the kidneys, ureters, or bladder and may require surgery.

uremia Poisoning by toxins accumulating in the body.

urethritis Inflammation of the urethra often resulting from bacterial infection.

urinary tract infection (UTI) Term for any infection in the urinary tract, including cystitis and pyelonephritis. It can be caused by an infection or by something obstructing the flow of urine, such as an enlarged prostate gland (in men), stones, or a tumor.

a 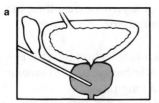 b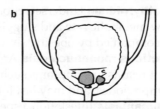

Urinary tract infection
a an enlarged prostate gland and
b bladder stones.

Endocrine

Addison's disease A condition caused by undersecretion of adrenal steroid hormones, resulting in weakness, nausea, low circulation, and bronzing of the skin.

adenoma A tumor of a gland.

adrenogenital syndrome Oversecretion of adrenal sex hormones, resulting in intense masculinizing of the body.

Aldosteronism Overproduction of the adrenal hormone aldosterone, resulting in a decrease in the body's potassium store.

cretinism Dwarfism and mental retardation caused by too little thyroxine in childhood.

Cushing's syndrome A condition caused by oversecretion of glucocorticoid hormones from the adrenals, resulting in a redistribution of body fat and other effects.

diabetes insipidus A condition in which, usually, the pituitary in the brain is faulty and the kidneys do not absorb enough water, resulting in a high urine output and intense thirst.

diabetes mellitus A condition characterized by frequent thirst and urination, caused by excess sugar in the blood. Results from a lack of insulin.

gigantism Oversecretion of growth hormone in childhood, resulting in taller-than-average stature. If the oversecretion occurs in adulthood, the condition is *acromegaly*, resulting in a thickening of facial bones and fingers.

glandular fever *See* **infectious mononucleosis**.

goiter An abnormal growth of thyroid tissue due to lack of iodine, causing a bulge in the neck.

gynecomastia Excessive growth of the male mammary gland caused by oversecretion of feminizing hormones.

hypersecretion Overproduction (of a hormone). Underproduction is called hyposecretion.

hyperthyroidism Oversecretion of thyroxine, resulting in increased metabolic and heart rates, circulation, and blood pressure.

hypoglycemia Low blood sugar, which can cause anxiety, tremors, weakness, and even unconsciousness and death.

hypothyroidism Undersecretion of thyroxine, resulting in a very low metabolic rate and sluggish activity, sometimes accompanied by obesity.

infectious mononucleosis An acute infection by a herpes virus that results in symptoms such as lethargy, painful swollen lymph nodes, and may last for a long time.

leishmaniasis Infestation, especially of the liver and spleen, by parasitic protozoa transmitted by sandfly bites.

myxedema Accumulation of water in skin resulting from thyroid hormone deficiency in adults.

nephritis Inflammation of a kidney.

pituitary dwarfism Undersecretion of growth hormone from the pituitary gland in childhood, resulting in smaller-than-average stature.

seasonal affective disorder (SAD) A condition resulting from changes in the body's level of the hormone melatonin. The level varies seasonally: it is higher in winter and lower in summer, when increased daylight inhibits its production. Symptoms include tiredness and depression.

Simmond's disease Undersecretion of pituitary hormones during adulthood, resulting in symptoms of deficiency of thyroid, adrenal, and sex hormones.

tetany Muscle twitches, spasms, and convulsions resulting from a lack of calcium in the blood. It may be caused by a dysfunction in the parathyroid glands (hypoparathyroidism).

Thyrotoxicosis Overactivity of the thyroid gland, often due to an autoimmune disease of the thyroid.

Reproductive

amenorrhea The abnormal absence of menstruation.

cervical cancer Cancer of the cervix (neck of the uterus).

cervical erosion A roughening of the cervical opening (os).

cervical polyps Benign tumors (usually harmless tissue growths) in the cervix.

cervicitis Inflammation of the cervix.

chlamydia A sexually transmitted disease caused by a bacterium.

displaced uterus A condition in which the uterus is not in the normal position. It might be tilted backward (retroverted) or dropped downward (prolapsed).

dysmenorrhea Painful menstruation usually caused by contraction of the uterus.

endometriosis The growth of endometrial (uterus-lining) cells outside the uterus.

fibroids Benign tumors of the uterus.

genital herpes A sexually transmitted disease caused by a virus.

genital warts Warts on the genital organs caused by a virus and spread through sexual contact.

gonorrhea A sexually transmitted disease caused by bacteria.

hydrocele An accumulation of fluid around the testes.

impotence Inability to maintain an erection and so have sexual intercourse.

infertility Inability to conceive a child; also called sterility.

inguinal hernia (indirect) Part of the intestine bulges into the inguinal canal—the channel through which testes drop into the scrotum before birth.

nonspecific urethritis *See* **urethritis.**

orchiditis Inflammation of a testis.

ovarian cysts Sacs of mucus (thick, slimy fluid) or fluid that grow within ovaries.

ovarian tumors Tumors of the ovaries, benign or malignant (harmful).

pelvic inflammatory disease (PID) Bacterial infection of the pelvic organs, especially the uterus, uterine tubes, or ovaries.

premenstrual syndrome (PMS) Physical and/or emotional discomforts experienced by some women before, during, and/or after menstruation.

prostatitis Inflammation of the prostate gland due to infection of the genitourinary tract.

salpingitis Inflammation of the Fallopian tubes caused by bacterial infection.

sexually transmitted disease (STD) Any disease (also called venereal disease) that is spread primarily through sexual intercourse. STDs include gonorrhea, syphilis, chlamydia, genital warts, and genital herpes.

syphilis A sexually transmitted disease caused by bacteria.

thrush A fungal infection that can affect the genital area.

undescended testes Condition in which the testes, which usually develop in the abdomen and descend into the scrotum about eight weeks before birth, fail to descend.

urethritis Inflammation of the urethra caused by gonorrhea or bacteria entering the urinary system. Nonspecific urethritis can be due to germs or a reaction to chemicals in the vagina of the sexual partner.

vaginitis Inflammation of the vagina sometimes caused by a sexually transmitted disease.

vulvitis Inflammation of the vulva.

Skin, hair and nails

abscess A pus-filled cavity; in the skin this is known as a pimple, pustule, or boil, depending on the size or the position.

acne This is often caused by the action of hormones on the oil glands. The glands become overactive and pimples develop, often accompanied by inflammation. If an oil gland is blocked by sebum (oily secretion), then it appears as a whitehead on the surface of the skin. If the external opening of the duct is evident, it will appear as a blackhead.

albinism An inherited condition in which people are born with defective melanocytes (pigment-producing cells). The skin, hair, and sometimes eyes lack color and the person is sensitive to sunlight.

alopecia Patchy loss of hair that can be hereditary or caused by disease or stress.

athlete's foot A fungal infection causing the skin between the toes to itch, crack, and peel.

birthmarks
a Mole
b Port-wine stain
c Spider nevi

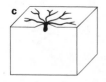
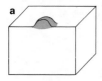

birthmarks Also called nevi, these are pigmented blemishes; they include moles , freckles, port-wine stains , spider nevi , and Mongolian spots.

blackhead *See* acne.

blister A blister is a fluid-filled pocket within the epidermis (upper layer of the skin) or between the epidermis and dermis (lower layer of the skin). It can be caused by friction, burns, or some skin diseases.

body odor If sweat is not washed off the skin, after a few hours bacterial activity will lead to unpleasant body odor.

boils Inflammation of hair follicles and oil glands that has spread to the dermis. They are often caused by bacterial infection.

burns A burn is tissue damage and cell death caused by exposure of the skin to high temperatures, electricity, excessive sunlight, and certain chemicals. A first-degree burn damages only the epidermis. Second-degree burns damage both the epidermis and the top of the dermis. This can cause blisters to appear. Third-degree burns damage all of the skin's layers and possibly underlying tissues as well. Severe burning can often be fatal as the body is made vulnerable to infection and fluid loss.

candidiasis *See* moniliasis.

chancre A painless ulcer which is often a symptom of syphilis.

chancroid A bacterially inflamed sore caused by a sexually-transmitted disease.

chicken pox A virus infection of the whole body. The rash starts on the back and chest. The disease may cause shingles in adults.

cold sore A recurring blister on the face, especially around the lips, caused bya virus.

contact dermatitis Inflammation of the skin due to irritants or allergic reaction. Irritants can be chemicals, metals, certain plants, or drugs. Symptoms can vary in severity from itching to cracks and bleeding.

cyst An abnormal fluid-filled sac in the skin or tissues, with many causes and types.

eczema Inflammation of the skin causing itching and scratching. It can be due to an allergic reaction, but sometimes there is no apparent cause.

epidermolysis bullosa (EB) An inherited disorder in which the skin is faulty or inadequate. The layers of the skin separate easily if damaged or touched, and then blister. Sufferers are prone to infection.

first-degree burns *See* burns.

herpes simplex The name of the virus that causes both cold sores and similar sores on the genitals that are sexually transmitted.

hives A skin condition, also known as urticaria, characterized by raised swellings that itch and burn. It is caused by allergies and sometimes injury or cold.

impetigo A skin infection characterized by raised, blister-like lesions, especially around the nose and mouth. These lesions rupture and form a yellowish crust.

keloid A protruding scar produced by the continuing production of scar tissue in the healing of a wound.

measles *See* rubella.

moniliasis A fungal infection that affects moist skin areas; also called candiasis.

onychogryphosis A condition, mostly afflicting elderly people, in which the nails become thick and disfigured.

plantar wart A wart that has been forced by pressure into the sole of the foot.

prickly heat A fine rash caused by dead skin cells blocking the pores of sweat glands.

psoriasis A condition in which areas of skin thicken, redden, and often develop a silvery, scaled top layer. This develops because new cells are being produced at a faster rate than normal. The cause is unknown, but an attack can be triggered by stress or infection.

ringworm A fungal infection characterized by patches of ring-shaped, reddened skin.

rubella A viral disease, also known as measles, that produces an irritant rash over the whole body, starting at the head. Vaccination is available against this.

scabies An infestation of mites that burrow into the skin of the hands, feet, or groin, causing an allergic reaction.

scarlet fever A severe bacterial infection giving rise to body rash and hair loss. Also called scarlatina.

seborrhea A condition involving excessive production of sebum by the oil glands. Combined with dermatitis (itchy, scaly rash), it is a common cause of dandruff (the shedding of dead skin from the scalp as white flakes). Cradle cap is a form of seborrhea common to babies.

second-degree burns *See* burns.

shingles A severe and painful form of chicken pox suffered mostly by adults aged over 50. It demands a lengthy convalescence.

skin cancers There are three common forms of skin cancer. Basal cell carcinoma is a proliferation of skin cells in the epidermal or dermal layer. It forms round, shiny lumps on the skin. Squamous cell carcinoma first affects the keratin-producing cells of the skin. It appears as small, scaly, red, raised patches. Malignant melanomas are raised or flat colored patches on the skin made of cancerous melanocytes (pigment-producing cells). The most common cause of skin cancers is ultraviolet radiation (from excessive exposure to sun, for example). Infection, frequent irritation, certain chemicals, and physical trauma, however, can also sometimes lead to skin cancer.

warts
a Filiform wart
b Plantar warts
c Venereal wart

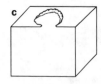

stretch marks If the skin is stretched too much (for example, during pregnancy or by rapid weight gain), then the dermis may be torn. This can be seen on the skin as lines called stretch marks, or striae – at first red, turning silvery white.

third-degree burns *See* burns.

urticaria *See* hives.

vitiligo Uneven coloring of the skin caused by loss of melanocytes and an uneven production of melanin (pigment). This results in lighter patches of skin surrounded by areas of the normal skin color. It is thought to be caused by a disorder of the immune system.

warts These are localized growths of the epidermis caused by a viral infection. They include filiform warts, plantar warts, and venereal warts.

whitehead *See* acne.

medicine

Types of drug

amebicidal drugs Used to prevent or treat amoebic infections.

amphetamines Drugs which stimulate the brain, and are used to treat drowsiness or hyperactive children; they are potentially addictive.

anabolic steroids Synthetic hormones that promote an increase in muscle size.

analgesics A class of drugs that relieve pain.

androgen A natural steroid hormone, such as testosterone, that controls male sex characteristics.

anesthetics Used to reduce or numb sensation, and promote painless sleep.

anorectics Used to reduce appetite. Most are potentially addictive and their use is now rare.

antacids Used to neutralize stomach acidity; prolonged use is inadvisable.

antiarrhythmic drugs Used to improve the regularity of the heartbeat.

antibacterial drugs Used to prevent or treat bacterial infections.

antibiotics Used to prevent or treat infection by various agents; most are ineffective against viral infections, however.

anticholinergic drugs These inhibit certain nerves from relaxing groups of muscles; some side effects.

anticoagulants Used to reduce or prevent blood clotting.

anticonvulsants Used to reduce or prevent convulsive seizures, such as those caused by epilepsy.

antidepressants Used to reduce or treat mental depression. The two main types are MAOI drugs and tricyclic antidepressants.

antidiuretics Used to reduce or prevent the formation or output of urine.

antiemetics (also called antinauseants) Used to prevent nausea and thus vomiting; mainly used by travelers to combat motion sickness.

antifungal drugs Used to prevent or treat fungal infections, locally (on the skin) or systemically.

antihelminthics Used to prevent or treat infestation by parasitic worms.

antihypertensive drugs Used to prevent or treat high blood pressure, and thus heart and circulatory disease.

antimalarial drugs Used to prevent or treat the various forms of malaria.

antinauseants Another name for antiemetics.

antipruritics Used to reduce or prevent itching of the skin or mucous membranes.

antipsychotic drugs Used to calm patients who are psychologically disturbed.

antipyretics Used to reduce high body temperature (fever).

antirheumatics Used to reduce or relieve the effects of rheumatism.

antiserums These are inoculations containing antibodies to a specific infection.

antispasmodics Used to prevent the contraction of smooth muscle, mainly in the treatment of bronchial and bladder disorders.

antitubercular drugs These are used in combination to treat tuberculosis.

antitussives Used to reduce or prevent coughing; some contain opiates.

antivenins Serums containing specific antibodies used to treat snakebite.

antiviral drugs These treat infections by individual groups of viruses.

anxiolytic drugs These relieve the anxiety states of medically diagnosed patients.

appetite suppressants These are occasionally used to treat obesity. Most are potentially addictive and are therefore rarely administered.

barbiturates A group of potentially addictive sedatives and anesthetics, with severe side effects. Many were formerly used as tranquilizers. The best known are pentobarbital, phenobarbital, and amobarbital (all subject to abuse).

benzodiazepines A large group of drugs that affect the brain. Some are used as sedatives or anxiolytics, others as muscle relaxants or anticonvulsants. The best known are diazepam, nitrazepam, and loprazolam.

beta blockers These drugs inhibit the body's normal reaction to stress, and are thus used mostly as antihypertensives.

beta receptor stimulants These drugs increase the body's normal reaction to stress, and are mostly used to strengthen the heartbeat or to widen respiratory passages.

bronchodilators These act to widen the bronchioles.

cephalosporins Antibiotics related to penicillin, used to treat bacterial infections.

chelating agents These are used to treat metal poisoning by absorbing metals in the bloodstream.

contraceptives Used to prevent conception. There are several types which may be taken orally.

corticosteroids Natural or synthetic hormones that assist metabolism, act in relation to stress, or maintain the salt-and-water balance in the body.

cytotoxic drugs Used to destroy cells, mainly in cancer chemotherapy.

decongestants Used to reduce mucus in the air passages of the nose.

depressants Used to reduce reactions in the body and relax muscles.

diuretics These increase the output of urine and so reduce body fluid levels.

emetic drugs These are used to promote vomiting.

estrogens The name for the female sex hormones produced by the ovaries.

hemostatic drugs Used to prevent or reduce bleeding; they are mostly injected or infused.

hormone supplements Prescribed to make up for a lack of natural hormones.

hypnotics These act on the brain to promote sleep.

imidazoles A group of antifungal drugs, used mainly to treat infections of the skin and mucous membranes.

keratolytic drugs used to treat scaly, horny areas of skin in conditions such as psoriasis and eczema.

laxatives Used to promote easy defecation.

MAOI drugs (monoamine oxidase inhibitors). a group of antidepressants. Highly effective, they require dietary precautions.

mucolytic drugs Used to promote the coughing up of sputum, so clearing air passages.

muscle relaxants Used to reduce or paralyze muscles; much used during surgery.

mydriatic drugs These drugs dilate the pupils of the eyes and are useful to oculists.

narcotics Technically, any drugs that cause stupor. The term is used also of sedatives and hypnotics, particularly the opiates. In law, however, the term describes illegal recreational drugs in general.

NSAIDs (nonsteroidal anti-inflammatory drugs). Used to treat or reduce inflammation. "Nonsteroidal" means they do not contain hormones, unlike some other types of anti-inflammatory drugs.

opiates Derivatives of opium, mainly used for sedative or narcotic effects.

parasympathomimetics Used to relieve the body's stress

reactions, such as in slowing the heart, widening the blood vessels, etc.

penicillins A group of antibiotics used to treat bacterial infections.

progestogens Synthetic female sex hormones.

Rauwolfia alkaloids Drugs used as antihypertensives. They were also once used as antipsychotic drugs.

respiratory stimulants Used to promote breathing in severely traumatized patients.

scabicides Used to treat infestations by itchmites.

sedatives These are used to calm patients and make them drowsy. Many are hypnotics used in smaller doses; some are potentially addictive.

sulfonamides Used to prevent the growth of bacteria, mainly in the treatment of urinary infections.

sulfonylureas These reduce the levels of glucose in the blood and are used to treat diabetes mellitus.

sympathomimetics Used to evoke the body's stress reactions, for example, speeding up the heart, or constricting the blood vessels.

tetracyclines A group of antibiotics that treat conditions caused by a range of infective organisms.

thiazides A group of diuretics.

tranquilizers A class of drugs ranging from sedatives to antipsychotic drugs.

uricosuric agents Used to reduce the uric acid in the body, and thus to treat gout.

vaccines These oblige the body to create its own antibodies to specific infections.

vasoconstrictors These narrow the blood vessels and so increase blood pressure.

vasodilators These widen the blood vessels and so reduce blood pressure.

Vinca alkaloids Cytotoxic drugs used to prevent the replication of cells.

Types of medical specialist

allergist Specialist in conditions resulting from extreme sensitivity to substances or environments.

anesthesiologist Specialist in the science and administration of anesthesia.

cardiologist Specialist in conditions and diseases related to the heart and circulation.

dentist Specialist in the care of the teeth and gums, and the treatment of oral disease and decay.

dermatologist Specialist in conditions and diseases affecting the skin.

endocrinologist Specialist in conditions and diseases of the hormonal glands, such as the pituitary, thyroid, pancreas, ovaries, or testicles.

gastroenterologist Specialist in diseases relating to the digestive system.

genetic counselor A specialist adviser on the chances of a child inheriting genetic malformation.

gerentologist Specialist in the effects and problems coming with old age.

gynecologist Specialist in conditions and diseases of the female body, particularly the reproductive system.

hematologist Specialist in the composition and analysis of blood.

histologist Specialist in the size, shape, and constitution of cells.

nephrologist Specialist in conditions related to the kidney.

neurologist Specialist in the treatment of conditions related to the nervous system.

obstetrician Specialist in pregnancy and related conditions (often also experienced in gynecology).

oncologist Specialist in the nature and treatment of cancer.

ophthalmologist Specialist in conditions and diseases related to the eyes.

optician Specialist in the fitting and adjusting of eye glasses and contact lenses.

optometrist Specialist in the testing eyes and prescribing of lenses to correct vision.

orthodontist Specialist in the branch of dentistry for treatment of crooked or misaligned teeth.

orthopedist Specialist in conditions and diseases of the bones, joints, and spine.

osteologist Specialist in the structure and diseases of the bones.

otorhinolarynologist Specialist in conditions of the ear, nose, and throat.

pathologist Specialist in the structural and functional changes caused by disease.

pediatrician Specialist in the diseases and disorders of babies and children.

peridontist Specialist in the branch of dentistry for treatment of conditions of the supporting structures of the teeth.

physiotherapist Specialist in the promotion of mobility in those handicapped by illness or accident, usually by external manipulation.

podiatrist Specialist in conditions and diseases related to the foot.

pulmonologist Specialist in conditions and diseases affecting the lungs.

radiologist Specialist in the use and interpretation of X-ray photography.

rheumatologist Specialist in conditions and diseases of the muscles and skeletal system, especially those affecting the joints.

urologist Specialist in conditions and diseases of the genito-urinary system.

medicine: surgical procedures

abduction A movement outward from the center of the body or of a limb.

abortion The termination of a pregnancy before the fetus is viable (able to survive outside the uterus).

abscess A pus-filled cavity in the body, usually caused by infection.

achillorrhaphy Suturing the Achilles tendon.

adduction A movement inward toward the center of the body or of a limb.

adenectomy Surgery to remove a gland.

adenoidectomy Surgery to remove the adenoids.

adhesion Abnormal joining of tissues caused by inflammation, resulting in scarring.

adipectomy Surgery to remove fatty tissue.

adrenalectomy Surgery to remove an adrenal gland.

amniocentesis Withdrawal of some of the amniotic fluid surrounding the fetus in order to diagnose congenital abnormalities.

amniotomy Rupturing the membrane surrounding the fetus, usually in order to induce labor.

amputation Surgery to remove a limb.

analgesics Painkilling drugs.

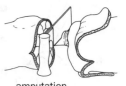

amputation

anastomosis Surgery to join two tube-like organs, such as pieces of intestine.

anesthesia Loss of sensation, including to pain, often induced before surgery. Includes general, local, spinal and epidural anesthaesia.

aneurysmectomy Surgery to remove an aneurysm.

angiectomy Surgery to remove part of a blood vessel.

angiography A diagnostic method of viewing the blood vessels after injecting a substance that is opaque to X-rays.

anoxia Lack of oxygen, often caused by an obstruction to the blood supply.

anterior Toward or at the front.

antibiotic A drug given to combat or prevent infection by destroying bacteria in the body.

anticoagulant A drug used to decrease the clotting ability of the blood, especially after heart surgery.

anti-inflammatory A drug used to combat inflammation and so decrease pain or discomfort.

antrectomy Surgery to remove a chamber or cavity, especially of bone.

bunionectomy
A Possible site of incision.
B The bony overgrowth (**a**) is trimmed, the bursa (**b**) is removed, and the phalanx (**c**) is cut away.
C The joint is then straightened and a new mobile joint forms in the gap (**d**).

A

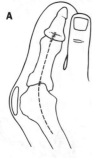

B

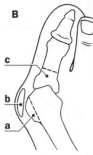

C

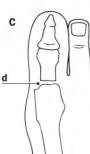

aortotomy Surgery to cut open the aorta.

appendectomy Surgery to remove the appendix.

apronectomy Surgery to remove excess abdominal fat.

arrythmia Irregularity in the heartbeat.

arterioplasty Surgery to repair an artery.

artery A vessel carrying blood from the heart to the rest of the body.

arthroscopy A diagnostic method of examining the inside of a joint using an illuminating instrument such as a fiberoptic endoscope.

aseptic Sterile; free of dangerous microorganisms, especially describing the conditions in which surgery is performed.

aspiration The use of suction to remove fluid from a body cavity, for example using a tube or syringe.

atherosclerosis A disease of the arteries caused by buildup of fatty deposits. It is sometimes treated with coronary bypass surgery.

atrophy A wasting away and/or emaciation, caused by aging, disease, infection, or injury.

augmentation Enlargement, as in cosmetic surgery to enlarge a woman's breasts.

autograft Skin graft using skin from patient receiving the graft. *Compare* **homograft**.

balloon angioplasty Surgery to expand narrowed arteries by inserting a catheter.

barium enema A diagnostic method of examining the rectum and colon using X-rays after inserting a contrast medium of barium sulfate liquid paste.

barium meal A diagnostic method of examining the internal organs of the digestive tract using X-rays and a contrast medium of liquid barium sulfate which is swallowed by the patient.

benign Used to describe an abnormal growth, such as a tumor, that will not spread to other tissues or organs and so is usually nonfatal. *Compare* **malignant**.

biopsy Surgery to remove a tissue sample for laboratory examination.

blepharectomy Surgery to remove an eyelid.

blepharoplasty Surgery to remove bags under the eyes, usually for cosmetic reasons.

bunionectomy Surgery to remove a bunion.

burrholes Holes made in the skull during a surgical opening of the skull.

carcinoma A malignant growth or tumor of cancerous surface tissues.

cardiac catheterization A method of examining or treating conditions of the heart and the arteries by the insertion of a catheter.

cardiomyotomy Surgery to open the heart muscle.

catheter A fine, plastic tube used in diagnostic procedures to examine internal organs and passages or as a drain to empty organs such as the bladder.

cauterization A method of destroying tissue by burning, used during surgery.

cephalotomy Another term for craniotomy.

cerebral angiography A diagnostic method of examining the blood vessels of the brain using X-rays and an opaque solution passed through a catheter.

cerebrospinal fluid A fluid that surrounds the spinal cord and brain.

Cesarean section Surgery to delivery a baby through an incision in the mother's abdomen.

chemosurgery Surgery using chemicals.

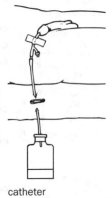

catheter

chemotherapy Treatment of disease, especially cancer, and infection using drugs or chemical agents.

cholangiostomy Surgery to open a bile duct.

cholecystectomy Surgery to remove the gallbladder.

chondrectomy Surgery to remove cartilage.

circumcision Surgery to remove the penis foreskin, often for religious reasons.

closure The closing of a surgical incision immediately after surgery.

colectomy Surgery to remove the colon.

colostomy Surgery to bring the colon to a specially created opening on the outside of the abdomen to allow it to act as an "artifical anus" in evacuating the contents of the bowel, often when the colon has had to be severed or removed.

Computerized Axial Tomography
a X-ray
b X-ray detectors

colpectomy Surgery to remove the vagina.

Computerized Axial Tomography (CT scan) A diagnostic method of examining the inside of the body (especially the brain) using hundreds of X-ray images that are combined by computer to build up a detailed picture.

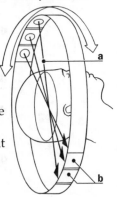

cone biopsy A surgical method of removing a cone-shaped piece of the cervix for analysis in a laboratory.

congenital Used to describe a condition or disease that is present at birth.

congestive heart failure Heart failure affecting either the right or left sides of the heart.

contracture Shortening of a muscle or tendon because of disease or injury and resulting in distortion and discomfort.

coronary artery bypass
a Deficient blood supply
b Bypass graft

coronal Relating to the crown of the head.

coronary Relating to a crown, as in the coronary arteries whose branches spread above the heart.

coronary artery bypass Surgery to create an alternative route of blood flow to the heart.

cosmetic surgery Any surgery carried out to enhance patient's appearance.

cranial Relating to the skull or head.

craniectomy Surgery to remove part of the skull.

craniotomy A surgical method of making an opening in the skull; sometimes performed on a fetus during a difficult birth; also called cephalotomy.

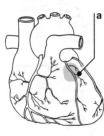

cryosurgery A method of destroying tissue by freezing, used during surgery.

cryptorchidopexy Surgery to treat a testicle that has failed to descend normally by bringing it down and securing it into the scrotum.

crystography A diagnostic method of examining the bladder using X-rays and an opaque solution that is injected into the bladder.

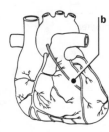

CT scan See **Computerized Axial Tomography.**

curettage A surgical method of scraping out a thin layer of tissue for analysis or disposal. See **D & C.**

cystectomy Surgery to remove the bladder; also used to refer to surgery to remove a cyst.

cystoscope A type of endoscope used to examine the inside of the bladder.

D & C Stands for dilatation and curettage, surgery to widen the cervix and scrape out tissue from inside uterus; used to treat abnormal bleeding.

debridement A surgical method of removing contaminated tissue.

decompression A method of removing or relieving pressure, such as by opening the skull to relieve pressure that has built up inside it.

denervation A surgical method of cutting or removing the nerve supply to an organ.

diagnostic Used to describe a procedure or method that is undertaken to identify a disease or some other cause of symptoms.

dialysis A method of compensating for poorly functioning kidneys by using a machine to artificially remove waste products from the blood.

diathermy A method used during surgery to allow cutting without excessive bleeding, using a high-frequency electric current.

dilatation The expanding or enlarging of a part of the body. *See* **D & C.**

dissection Surgical separation of tissues.

distal Toward the extremities of the body.

drainage A method of withdrawing excess fluid or pus from the body.

drip *See* **intravenous drip.**

duodenectomy Surgery to remove the duodenum, part of the intestine.

ECG *See* **electrocardiogram.**

echocardiography A diagnostic method of examining the heart's structure using ultrasound (high-frequency) waves.

echography A diagnostic method of examining the chest area using ultrasound (high-frequency) waves to produce a recording, called an echogram.

EEG *See* **electroencephalogram.**

electrocardiogram (ECG) A recording of the pattern of the electrical impulses of a patient's heart made using electrocardiography

electrocardiography A diagnostic method of examining the electrical impulses through the heart using electrodes attached to the chest and to a recording device to make an electrocardiogram.

electroencephalogram (EEG) A recording of the pattern of the electrical impulses of a patient's brain made using electroencephalography.

electroencephalography A diagnostic method of examining the electrical impulses of the brain using electrodes attached to the head and to a recording device to make an electroencephalogram.

electromyography A diagnostic method of examining the electrical activity of the muscles using metal probes that are inserted into the muscles.

embolectomy Surgery to remove a blockage in the bloodstream (embolus), often performed as emergency surgery.

endarterectomy Surgery to clear a blocked artery to restore proper blood flow.

endoscopy Examination of the internal organs (usually the esophagus and stomach) for diagnostic or surgical purposes using a thin illuminated instrument (endoscope). Endoscopy for other procedures uses specific names, e.g., laparoscopy, sigmoidoscopy.

endoscopy

enterocolostomy Surgical joining of the colon to the small intestine.

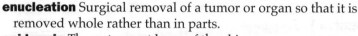
enucleation Surgical removal of a tumor or organ so that it is removed whole rather than in parts.

epidermis The outermost layer of the skin.

episiotomy A surgical cut made in the perineum to enlarge the vaginal opening during childbirth.

estrogen Any of several sex hormones responsible for female sex characteristics; produced in the ovaries and, to lesser degree, in the testicles.

eversion A turning outwards.

extension The straightening of a limb or other body part.

fenestration A surgical method of making a hole in or perforating something.

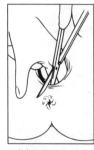
episiotomy

flexion A bending or being bent, as of a joint.

frontal Toward or of the front of the body or body part; relating to the forehead.

fusion A surgical method of joining.

gastrectomy Surgery to remove the stomach, either part or whole.

GI series *See* **upper gastrointestinal (GI) series.**

graft A surgical method of taking some material (such as skin or bone) from somewhere and adhering it somewhere else in order to repair or help regenerate damaged tissue. *See* **autograft, homograft.**

hematoma A blood-filled swelling.

hemorrhage Abnormal excessive bleeding, inside or outside the body.

hemorrhoidectomy Surgery to remove hemorrhoids.

hepatectomy Surgery to remove either the whole or a part of the liver.

herniorrhaphy Surgery to repair a hernia.

homograft A skin graft that uses skin from a person other than the patient receiving the graft. *See* **autograft.**

hysterectomy Surgery to remove the uterus.

ICU *See* **intensive care unit.**

ileostomy A method of creating an opening in the abdominal wall and attaching the ileum to this opening, through which intestine is emptied.

immobilization The fixing and holding in place (using traction or splints) of a fractured limb or damaged joint to allow healing to take place.

intensive care unit (ICU) An area of a hospital where seriously ill patients are kept under constant medical care and observation.

intravenous drip A device for supplying fluid directly into a patient's vein from a sterile container, usually on an upright stand, especially for medication or nourishment. The rate of flow can be controlled and adjusted.

intravenous pyelography (IVP) A diagnostic method of examining the urinary system using X-rays and an opaque solution injected into the veins to produce images called pyelograms.

intubation Inserting a tube in an organ or body passage, usually through the larynx in order to administer anesthaesia.

iridectomy Surgery to remove part of the iris of the eye.

irreducible Incapable of being restored to a former condition or position.

isotope scan A diagnostic method of examining the interior of the body using a scanner and radioactive material injected into the veins and organs.

IV *See* **intravenous drip**.

IVP *See* **intravenous pyelography**.

jejunectomy Surgery to remove the jejunum, part of the intestine.

laparoscopy A diagnostic method of examining a patient's abdomen (including the reproductive organs) using an endoscope

laparotomy Surgery to make an incision in the abdominal wall for surgery.

laryngectomy Surgery to remove the larynx.

lateral Toward or at the side.

lipectomy Surgical removal of fatty tissue.

liposuction Surgical removal of subcutaneous fat from a part of the body by suction, usually for cosmetic reasons.

lithonephrotomy Surgery to remove a kidney stone.

lobectomy Surgery to remove a lobe, such as a lobe of a lung.

lobotomy Surgery to remove part of the brain.

lumbar puncture A method of obtaining cerebrospinal fluid for diagnostic purposes by injecting a needle between two vertebrae at the base of the spine; also used for administering drugs for treatment or anesthesia.

lumpectomy Surgery to remove a tumor in the breast. *Compare* **mastectomy**.

lymphadenectomy Surgery to remove a lymph node.

lymph nodes Small oval-shaped bodies grouped in certain areas of the body, including the armpits, groin, neck, and abdomen, that produce antibodies to fight the spread of infection.

Magnetic Resonance Imaging (MRI) A diagnostic method of examining the inside of the body, tissues, or organs using radio waves to produce maps or images.

malignant Used to describe cancerous growth that will spread to

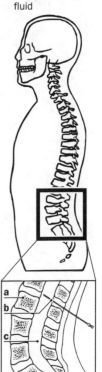

lumbar puncture
a Vertabrae of lower back
b Lumbar puncture needle
c Cerebral spinal fluid

surrounding tissues and, if not totally removed, may be fatal. *Compare* **benign.**

mammography A diagnostic method of determining the presence of breast cancer using X-rays.

mammoplasty Surgery to reduce, enlarge, or rebuild one of a woman's breasts.

mastectomy Surgery to remove a breast.

mastoidectomy Surgery to remove the mastoid bone.

medial Toward the midline of the body.

meninges Three layers of membrane—the pia mater, arachnoid mater, and dura mater—that surround the brain and spinal cord.

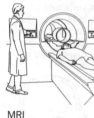

mastectomy

meniscectomy Surgery to remove cartilage from the knee (meniscus).

metastasis The spread of an abnormal growth, especially cancer, from one part of the body to another.

MRI *See* **Magnetic Resonance Imaging.**

myectomy Surgical removal of muscle.

myelography A diagnostic method of examining the space around the spinal cord (for example, to detect prolapsed disks) using X-rays and a contrast medium injected by lumbar puncture.

myringotomy Making an incision in eardrum to release fluid trapped inside.

MRI

narcotic Any of various drugs used to induce sleep and relieve pain.

nasogastric tube A thin, flexible, rubber or plastic tube passed through the nose and into the esophagus and stomach, used either to draw out digestive fluid or to provide nutrition in a liquid form.

necrotomy Surgery to remove dead bone.

nephrectomy Surgery to remove a kidney.

neurotomy Cutting a nerve to relieve pain.

obliteration A method of completely removing tissue, especially by surgery or radiation.

omentum A part of the peritoneum, consisting of membrane that suspends from the abdomen to cover the intestines.

oophorectomy Surgery to remove one or both ovaries.

ophthalmoscope An instrument used to examine the inside of the eye by means of a light shone through the iris.

orchiectomy Surgery to remove one or both testicles.

ostectomy Surgery to remove bone.

otoscope A tool for examining the inside of the outer ear canal and eardrum by the shining of a light.

palmar On the palm of the hand.

pancreatectomy Surgery to remove the pancreas gland.

paracentesis Removal of fluid from a body cavity for examination or treatment.

parathyroidectomy Surgery to remove the parathyroid.

perforation A hole formed by erosion in an organ or passageway of the body.

pericardectomy Surgery to remove the pericardium, the membranous sac around the heart.

pericardium A membranous sac surrounding the heart.

perineum The pelvic floor, especially referring to the area of muscle and tissue between the vaginal opening and the anus that is susceptible to tearing in childbirth.

peripheral Toward the surface.

peritoneum A membrane that lines the wall of the abdomen and covers the organs within the abdomen.

PET scan *See* **Positron Emission Tomography**.

phlebotomy The procedure of puncturing a vein, used to withdraw blood.

plantar On the sole of the foot.

pneumonectomy Surgery to remove a lung or some tissue from a lung.

polyp A tissue growth projecting from the skin or mucous membrane, such as inside the nose.

polypectomy Surgery to remove a polyp.

Positron Emission Tomography (PET scan) A diagnostic method of examining tissues within the brain using a radioactive isotope injected into the bloodstream

posterior Toward or at the back.

proctoscopy A method of examining the anus and rectum using an endoscope inserted through the anus.

prolapse The slipping of an organ or tissue into an abnormal position, as with a prolapsed uterus or prolapsed intervertebral disk.

pronation The turning to a face-down or palm-down position.

prostatectomy Surgery to remove the prostate.

prosthesis An artificial attachment to replace a body part, such as a limb or organ.

proximal Toward the point where a limb is attached to the body.

pulmonary Relating to the lungs.

radiation therapy (also called radiotherapy) A method of treating disease, especially cancer, using X-rays or radioactivity to destroy malignant growths.

radioisotope scan (also called radionuclide scan) A diagnostic method of examining an internal organ by injecting a radioactive isotope and following its progress within the patient's body.

reduction A surgical method of restoring an original relationship, for example by manipulating bones or hernias back into the original position.

respirator A machine that maintains regular breathing by pumping air in and out of the lungs.

revascularization Restoring the blood supply to a part of the body.

rhinoplasty Surgery to change the shape of the nose, usually for cosmetic reasons.

rhizotomy Cutting nerve roots from spinal cord, used to relieve pain.

rhytidectomy Cosmetic surgery to remove wrinkles from the face.

sagittal Relating to the median plane or a parallel plane of the body.

saline drip A saline isotonic solution supplied to a patient by intravenous drip.

salpingectomy Surgery to remove or sever one or both fallopian tubes.

shunt A bypass, often used by surgeons to divert blood supply around an obstacle or obstruction.

sigmoidoscopy A diagnostic method of examining the rectum and colon using a special type of endoscope called a sigmoidoscope.

splenectomy Surgery to remove the spleen.

stapedectomy Surgery to remove a diseased stapes (a small bone in the ear).

sterilization Surgery to prevent conception, often permanently, though some methods are reversible. *See* **hysterectomy, tubal ligation, vasectomy**.

stethoscope A tool used for listening to the sounds made by the internal organs, especially the heart and lungs, from outside the body.

stoma An artificial opening (as in an abdomen) made during surgery.

supination A turning to a face-up or palm-up position.

suppository A tablet inserted into the anus or vagina that dissolves to administer a drug treatment or anesthesia.

suture Thread (with needle attached) used to close incisions made during surgery.

synovium A membrane that lines a joint or surrounds a tendon and releases fluid allowing for joint movement.

tap A method of withdrawing fluid from the body, as in a spinal tap.

testosterone A sex hormone that is responsible for male sex characteristics. It is produced naturally in the testicles and is often synthesized for medical use.

thermography A diagnostic method of examining the inside of the body using a heat-sensitive camera

thoractomy Surgical opening of the chest wall, either between the ribs or by splitting the breastbone, to gain access to lungs and heart.

thorascope A special type of endoscope used to examine the lung cavity.

thrombectomy Surgery to remove a blood clot.

thrombosis A condition involving blood clotting within an artery or vein and possibly cutting off or obstructing the flow of blood.

thrombus A blood clot on the lining of a blood vessel, such as an artery or vein.

thyroidectomy Surgery to remove the thyroid gland, either part or whole.

tonsillectomy Surgery to remove the tonsils.

tracheostomy A method of making an artificial opening in the trachea (windpipe) to maintain a patient's breathing.

traction The treatment of broken bones by first pulling them apart and then restricting them in order to maintain proper alignment.

transfusion A method of introducing fluid, especially blood, into the body.

transplantation The surgical method of transfering or grafting tissues or organs from one part of a patient's body to another or to another patient.

tubal ligation Surgery to tie off the fallopian tubes in order to cause sterility.

tracheostomy

ultrasound scan A diagnostic method of examining internal organs using high-frequency sound waves, for example in monitoring the development of a fetus.

upper gastrointestinal (GI) series A diagnostic method of examining the esophagus, stomach, and intestines using X-rays and a barium meal

vagotomy Surgery to reduce the level of acid in a patient's stomach .

valvotomy A surgical procedure to separate heart valves that have become fused.

vasectomy Surgery to sever the vas deferens in order to cause sterility.

venipuncture The surgical opening of a vein using a small instrument.

venography A diagnostic method of examining the inside of veins using X-rays and an opaque solution injected into the veins.

X-rays Short-wavelength streams of photons used to penetrate a patients's body tissues for diagnostic purposes, such as to produce an X-ray image of the inside of the body, or as a form of therapy, such as to destroy diseased tissue.

medicine: alternative healing

absent healing Also known as distant healing, this is healing at a distance. Sometimes this forms part of faith healing (also called spiritual healing).

acupoint (also called acupuncture point, pressure point or tsubo). Any of the key points on the meridians where nerves feel uncomfortable when the flow of energy through the body is blocked.

acupressure (also known as shiatsu). A therapy in which pressure is applied to specific points on the body along acupuncture meridians, using techniques that include a gentle form of rolfing.

acupuncture A traditional Chinese method of healing which involves the insertion of fine needles to specific points in the skin.

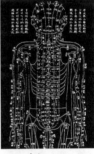

acupoint

acupuncture point *See* acupoint.

agni In Ayurvedic medicine this is the digestive fire which converts the five bhutas into doshas.

Alexander technique A method of retraining the body's movements in order to improve posture, and named after its originator, Frederick Matthias Alexander.

allopathic medicine Orthodox medicine.

amna An ancient Japanese system of massage that has existed for about 2000 years, in which the hands and feet are rubbed and manipulated.

anthroposophical medicine A holistic approach to health and illness based on the teachings of Rudolf Steiner who believed the word "anthroposophy" should be understood to mean awareness of one's humanity.

anthroposophy From the Greek "anthropos," meaning man, and "sophia," meaning wisdom. Rudolf Steiner said anthroposophy should mean awareness of one's humanity.

applied kinesiology A type of kinesiology which uses muscle testing in relation to all body functions.

aromatherapy Using essential plant oils to improve physical and mental well-being, often involving massage.

acupuncture

art therapies A group of therapies including art therapy, dance movement therapy, drama therapy, music therapy and sound therapy.

art therapy Using the spontaneous creation of art as a means of self-expression in order to improve emotional well-being. Individuals are encouraged by a therapist to express their feelings through collage-making, drawing, modeling, painting, or sculpting.

asanas Poses that form part of yoga.

astral body In anthroposophical medicine this is one of four aspects of man (the other three being physical, the etheric body, and the ego) and represents the emotions.

astrological diagnosis Also known as medical astrology, this is the use of astrology to aid the diagnosis and treatment of illness.

aura An energy field perceived as surrounding the human body which aura analysts describe as a cloud of light that radiates from a person, rather like the phosphorescence of some sea creatures.

aura analysis Analysis of a person's aura, by direct observation or using a Kilner screen or a Kirlian photograph.

auricular therapy Also known as auriculotherapy, this is treatment of the ear to bring about healing in other parts of the body.

autogenic From the Greek word meaning "coming from within," and relating to therapies such as autogenic training.

autogenic training Developed by a Berlin psychiatrist and neurologist, Dr Johannes H. Schultz, this is a method of profound relaxation training aimed at relieving stress, enabling the body to heal itself.

autosuggestion Also known as Couéism, this is a form of self-hypnosis developed by Emile Coué in 1885 which relys on the repetition of a positive mantra.

awareness through movement Part of the Feldenkrais Method these are a series of exercises taught to groups of pupils and involving slow, simple movements designed to make people aware of their habitual patterns of movement.

Ayurveda From the Sanskrit words "ayur," meaning life, and "veda," meaning knowledge, a traditional Indian text referring to ayurvedic medicine.

Ayurvedic medicine A holistic system of traditional Indian medicine from which most of western medicine has been derived.

Bach Flower Essences/Remedies Named after their originator, Englishman Dr Edward Bach, these are 38 preparations made from wild flowers and plants, used in a treatment based on homeopathic principles, designed for use at home to treat mental attitudes.

balneology A hydrotherapy treatment, this is the therapeutic use of natural spring waters or mineral waters.

Bates method A series of exercises designed to improve the eyesight and developed by William H. Bates between 1900 and 1931.

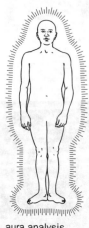

aura analysis

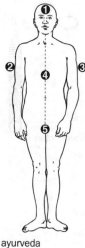

ayurveda

behavior therapy A variety of techniques, including aversion therapy, in which a patient is treated by conditioning to remove neuroptic symptoms.

Bhutas In Ayurvedic medicine these are the five elements from which all things are made—air, fire, earth, ether, and water—and which correspond to one of the senses (touch, sight, smell, sound, taste) and to a planet (Mercury, Mars, Jupiter, Saturn, Venus).

biochemics Developed in the 1870s by Dr Wilhelm Heinrich Schuessler, this is a system of therapy which aims to restore and maintain the body's natural mineral salts.

bioenergetic therapy Helping people to change habitual postures and body movements in order to unblock the body's energy (called bioenergy) and improve physical and emotional health.

bioenergy Term used to describe energy within the body as viewed by bioenergetic therapists.

biofeedback Also called neurological feedback, this is a therapy in which clients learn to control "involuntary" body fuctions (such as heart rate and blood pressure) using information made available through the use of special monitoring equipment.

biogenetics The use of exercises to relieve muscle tension and release emotions

biorhythm diagnosis The use of three human energy cycles—emotional, physical and mental, collectively known as biorhythms—to predict the times when someone will feel high and low energy.

breathing therapy A method used in relaxation therapy.

chakras Seven centers of intense energy located down the spine known as sahasrana, ajna, vishudda, anahata, manipuraka, swadhisthana, and muladhara. According to Hindu philosophy they are invigorated through yoga.

chakra therapy The use of gemstones to bring about positive changes in the energy flow within and between chakras; a form of color therapy in which colors are related to chakras on the spine.

chakras

Chi *See* Qi

chiropractic From the Greek "cheiro" and "praktikos," meaning "done by hand," this is a manipulative therapy based on the diagnosis and treatment of mechanical joint disorders and their effects on the nervous system.

clinical ecology The treatment of disorders believed to result from a person's reaction to their environment.

colonic irrigation Also called colonic hydrotherapy, this is a method of cleansing the intestines using warm water injected into the rectum.

color therapy Using color to bring about healing and sometimes involving chakra therapy.

combination remedies Used in biochemics, these are remedies which combine between three and five of the twelve different tissue salts identified by Dr Wilhelm Heinrich Schuessler in the 1870s.

conception vessel One of 14 meridians used in Chinese medicine.

Couéism Also known as autosuggestion, this is a form of self-hypnosis developed by Emile Coué in 1885 which relys on the repetition of a positive mantra.

cranial osteopathy A technique used by osteopaths to gently manipulate the eight bones of the skull.

cranio-sacral therapy Manipulation of body tissues in order to bring about a balance in the body's cerebrospinal fluid.

crystal therapy The use of naturally occuring crystals for healing purposes.

cupping A method of heat stimulation in which small, warm cups, bowls or drums are placed on the skin in order to increase local blood supply.

cymatics The use of sound waves to heal.

dance movement therapy The psychotherapeutic use of movement to bring about positive changes in a person's emotional, cognitive and social integration.

digestive/movement system In anthroposophical medicine this is one of three systems (the other two being the nerve/sense system and the rhythmic system) which together link the physical, etheric body, astral body and ego.

distant healing *See* absent healing.

do-in A form of Chinese self-massage.

dosha In Ayurvedic medicine the name given to one of three constitutional types (vata, pitta, and kapha), each converted from two Bhutas (elements) by agni and collectively known as tridoshas.

dream therapy Using dreams to help analyze and overcome emotional problems.

effleurage A gentle technique used in massage that involves stroking with the palms of the hands.

ego In anthroposophical medicine this is one of four aspects of man (the other three being the astral body, physical, and the etheric body) and represents an individual's spiritual core.

encircling The use of circles for healing purposes.

encounter therapy A form of group therapy, the intention of which is to help individuals improve their relationships with others.

energy lines (also called meridians). Fourteen channels through which the body's energy flows.

essential plant oils (also called essential oils) The oils that give plants their distinctive smell these are extracted and used in aromatherapy.

etheric body In anthroposophical medicine this is one of four aspects of man (the other three being the astral body, the ego, and the physical body) and represents that part of an individual that opposes the force of gravity, allowing growth upward, away from the earth.

eurythmy Developed by Rudolf Steiner, this is a system of promoting self-expression through music and may be used by practitioners of anthroposophical medicine.

faith healing (also called spiritual healing).When the power of a god or spirit serves as a healing force.

Feldenkrais method Developed by Moshe Feldenkrais, this is a series of exercises designed to realign the skeleton and make the body move with minimum effort and maximum efficiency, improving posture and general health.

feng shui The positioning of buildings, rooms and objects to achieve harmony with nature.

fertility amulet An object made of wood, stone, metal or other substance, and believed to improve fertility. Often amulets are inscribed with magical characters and figures and are expected to invoke the help of great spirits associated with a culture or religion.

faith healing

flotation therapy Floating in a tank of warm water in order to induce a state of deep relaxation.

flower essences Used in Bach Flower Remedies (also known as Bach Flower Essences) these are those parts of plants and flowers thought to contain healing properties.

frictions A technique used in massage in which pressure is applied to a small area, often using small circular movements.

gate control theory A theory which states that pain may be relieved by the application of pressure to certain parts of the body because the brain receives messages concerning pressure faster that it receives messages concerning pain. In other words, once a pressure message has reached the brain, the "gateway" for further (i.e. pain) messages is closed.

gem essence therapy The use of essences made by immersing gemstones in water and leaving them in the Californian sunshine so that their vibrational qualities percolate the water.

g-jo A form of acupressure practiced in the west.

governor vessel One of 14 meridians used in Chinese medicine.

hacking A stimulating technique used in massage in which the sides of the hands are used in a chopping motion to invigorate and increase blood flow to an area.

healing amulet An object made of wood, stone, metal or other substance and believed to protect the owner from illness or injury or to dispell illness.

healing shrine A place believed to have healing properties – such as Lourdes.

herbalism

herbalism The use of certain plants for medicinal purposes, now called phytotherapy. A herb is usually defined as a plant whose stem does not become woody and persistent, but dies down to ground level after flowering.

holistic In health care, a term used to describe treatments of the whole person: mind, body and spirit.

homeopathy A system based on the principle of "like curing like," which aims to treat the whole person and is the opposite of allopathic medicine in that it does not aim to suppress the symptoms of illness.

hydrotherapy The use of water to heal. A variety of techniques are used, including balneology, thalassotherapy and thermalism.

hypnosis Commonly used in hypnotherapy, this is an altered state of consciousness that can be induced by the self or by another person and during which conscious control is relaxed, making the contents of the unconscious more accessible. Hypnosis is from the Greek word "hypnos," meaning "sleep."

hypnotherapy Using hypnosis to improve health.

interdermal needles Very small, delicate acupuncture needles, used for insertion into points on the head and ears.

ion therapy Using ions (charged air particles) to prevent and cure illness and disease.

iridology Examining the eye's iris in order to diagnose conditions of the body.

jitsu Used in treatments such as shiatsu, this word describes an over-activity in the flow of life energy as identified at tsubos.

kappa In Ayurvedic medicine this is one of three doshas (the other two being pitta and vata) and resulting from the combination of the Bhutas earth and water by agni.

Ki *See* Qi

Kilner screen A special type of glass developed by the British scientist Walter J. Kilner in 1920 and used to observe the aura in aura analysis.

kinesiology From the Greek word "kinesis," meaning "movement," this was originally a method used by physiotherapists for testing a person's range of movement and the tone of their muscles but which is today referred to as applied kinesiology, which uses muscle testing in relation to all body functions.

Kirlian photography A method of recording the aura of people and plants onto photographic paper without the use of a camera and used for aura analysis. The technique was developed in the 1930s by Russian engineers Valentina and Semyon Kirlian.

kyo Used in treatments such as shiatsu, this word describes a depletion in the flow of life energy as identified at tsubos.

laying on of hands A technique used in spiritual healing in which the healing power of a god or spirit is channelled through the hands of the healer to the patient.

leeching The use of bloodsucking leeches for medical purposes, such as drawing off blood or preventing coagulation at a wound.

life force energy An alternative name for the etheric body.

macrobiotics A dietary system first devised by a Japanese doctor, Sagen Ishizuka, in which a diet of grains, brown rice, and vegetables is used for healing and illness prevention.

magnetic field therapy The modern use of magnets for healing purposes.

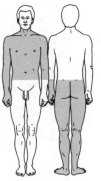

manipulative therapies A group of therapies in which practitioners use their hands to bring about positive changes in a person's physique and which include the Alexander Technique, bone setting, chiropractic, the Feldenkrais method, kinesiology, the laying on of hands, massage, osteopathy, polarity therapy, reflexology, rolfing, therapeutic touch and traction.

mantra A letter, word, sound, or phrase which may be used in meditation and repeated continually as you breath in or out. The best known mantra is "Om."

magnetic field therapy

marma massage A form of massage in which the therapist attempts to press marmas (107 points which in ayurevedic medicine correspond to organs in the body).

massage From the Greek word "massein," meaning "to knead," this is a manipulative therapy designed to relax, stimulate and invigorate the body by kneading, stroking, and pressing the soft tissues of the body.

mazdaznan A practice of healing based on the philosophy of two great prophets and of the Ahura Mazda, the creative intelligence of ancient Middle Eastern thought.

medical astrology Also known as astrological diagnosis, this is the use of astrology to aid the diagnosis and treatment of illness.

meditation Training one's attention or awareness to bring mental processes under voluntary control, of which there are various types including Transcendental Meditation.

megavitamin therapy Also once termed orthomolecular medicine, this is the use of large doses of vitamins to improve physical and mental health.

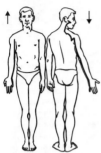

meridians

meridians (also called energy lines). Fourteen channels through which the body's energy flows.

mesmerism Name given to a type of therapy developed by Franz Mesmer who believed he had the ability to harness the magnetic forces of the planets and who some believe to be the originator of hypnotism.

metamorphic technique Also called prenatal therapy, this is the manipulation of the feet, hands, and head to help people come to terms with long-term problems, perhaps stemming from the nine months spent in the womb.

miasmas Emanations from leftover vestiges or previously acute conditions, such as childhood measles, or by toxins from current conditions, such as influenza or a period of worry or grief.

miraculous healing A type of faith healing in which cures appear to be miraculous. Examples of the healing power of Jesus are often described as miracles.

mother tincture Used in Bach Flower Remedies (also known as Bach flower essences) this is a preparation of spring water in which flower essences have been impregnated, together with a few drops of brandy.

moxa The dried leaves of Chinese wormwood used in moxibustion.

moxibustion A method of heat stimulation in which burning moxa is placed on or near the skin, or to the top of acupuncture needles.

music therapy A means of promoting self-expression through improvised music-making with the aim of facilitating positive changes in behavior and emotional well-being.

Native American healing

Native American healing The healing concepts and rituals of North American Indian tribes.

naturopathy A system which aims to treat the underlying cause of illness by encouraging the body to cure itself.

nerve/sense system In anthroposophical medicine this is one of three systems (the other two being the digestive/movement system and the rhythmic system) which together link the Physical, etheric body, astral body and ego.

Neurofeedback *See* **biofeedback**.

ojas In Ayurvedic medicine this is the life energy force which flows around the body and is the equivalent of the Chinese Qi and Japanese ki.

orgone therapy Part of Reichian Therapy designed to restore the body's energy.

orthomolecular medicine Now called megavitamin therapy, this is the use of large doses of vitamins to improve physical and mental health.

orthomolecular psychiatry The use of large doses of vitamins to improve mental health.

Oriental massage Non-western massage such as reiki, tuina and Thai massage.

osteopathy From the Greek words "osteo-" meaning bone, and "-pathy" meaning disease, this is a therapy that uses manipulation of the bones and muscles to alleviate pain, especially in the back.

orgone Therapy

panchakarma In Ayurevedic medicine this is a type of cleansing involving enemas, induced vomiting, nasal inhalation and purging.

past lives therapy A therapy based on the belief in reincarnation and that by addressing troublesome events in former lives clients may be helped to resolve their problems in the present.

pattern therapy The use of certain shapes, proportions and positions to positively influence well-being, as in pyramid healing.

pétrissage A technique used in massage in which fleshy areas of the body are kneaded in order to stretch and relax tight muscles.

phytotherapy From the Greek "phyton" meaning "plant" and "therapeuein" meaning "to take care of, to heal," this is the term used to describe medical herbalism.

pitta In Ayurvedic medicine this is one of three doshas (the other two being kapha and vata) and resulting from the combination of the Bhutas fire and water by agni.

polarity therapy The use of diet, self-help techniques and manipulation to re-balance the body's vital energy flow.

polarity therapy

pranayama Breathing exercises that form part of yoga.

prenatal therapy *See* **metamorphic technique**.

press needles Acupuncture needles designed to stay in the skin for several days and which can be pressed or manipulated by the patient as required.

pressure point *See* **acupoint**.

primal therapy A means of helping people to come to terms with negative experiences of childhood.

prismatic needles Acupuncture needles about $2^1/_2$ inches long, used in the treatment of acute diseases.

psionic medicine A system of medicine that combined orthodox medicine with radiesthesia in order to tackle the original causes

primal Therapy

of disease, avoiding the use of synthetic chemicals.

psychic healing The use of psychic powers for healing purposes such as in radiesthesia, radionics and psychic surgery.

psychic surgery A form of psychic healing particularly popular in Brazil and the Philipinnes in which healers claim to be able to perform surgical operations using no anesthetic or instruments and causing no pain.

psychodrama A therapy which aims to help individuals release their emotions by acting out real life situations.

psychosynthesis A form of self-development in which people are helped to discover the true aspects of their identities and to take control over all aspects of their personalities.

pyramid healing A type of pattern therapy in which pyramidal structures are used for healing purposes.

Qi (also known as Chi or Ki) In Chinese medicine this is the life energy force which flows around the body via meridians, or energy lines and is the equivalent of the Indian ojas.

radiesthesia From the French word meaning "dowsing," radiesthesia is the search for something using a divining rod or pendulum and is used as a diagnostic technique in psionic medicine and radionics.

radionics Treatment used to bring about positive changes in a person's energy field and often involving radiesthesia.

rebirthing A therapy in which clients are asked to reenact their own births.

reflexology Developed from zone therapy, this is a method of bringing about relaxation, balance and healing through the stimulation of specific points on the feet, or the hands.

reflex point Nerve endings commonly stimulated during reflexology treatments.

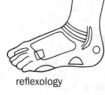
reflexology

Reichian therapy The use of movements designed to systematically release physical tension and repressed emotions, developed by psychiatrist Wilhelm Reich and incorporating orgone therapy.

reiki As a type of oriental massage this is a form of touch therapy in which the therapist senses which parts of a person's body are emitting weak energy by laying their hands close to or on the sites.

relaxation therapy Term used to describe a variety of techniques used to induce relaxation.

rhythmic system In anthroposophical medicine this is one of three systems (the other two being the digestive/movement system and the nerve/sense system) which together link the Physical, etheric body, astral body and ego.

rolfing Also called structural integration, this is a form of deep massage designed to correct posture, developed by Ida Rolf.

sclerology Analysis of the sclera (white of the eye) which is usually part of an iridology asessment.

seven-star needle A hammer 4-6 inches long, the head of which contains seven (or sometimes five) standard slim acupuncture needles. It is used in acupuncture for gently hammering over the skin surface.

shamanic healing Healing carried out by a primitive and tribal doctor known as a shaman, from the Tunguso-Manchurian word, "saman," meaning "he who knows."

shen tao A form of acupressure where a practitioner uses light finger pressure to tap subtle energy patterns.

shiatsu *See* acupressure.

spiritual healing *See* faith healing.

structural integration Also called rolfing, this is a form of deep massage designed to correct posture, developed by Ida Rolf.

shamanic Healing

Swedish massage A popular form of western massage originally called Swedish Movement Treatment and developed by Swedish gymnast Per Henrik Ling and combining therapeutic massage with exercises for muscles and joints.

T'ai-chi ch'uan A non-violent martial art in which exercises are used to stabilize the forces of yin and yang and improve overall well-being by easing the internal flow of life energy known as Chi.

thalassotherapy From the Greek word, "Thalassa," meaning "sea," this is the tonic effect of time spent in the sea or in sea water.

therapeutic touch A healer (rather than a therapist) uses their hands to bring about healing, by placing them directly on a patient's body or a small distance away from it. Contrary to the practices of faith healing and the laying on of hands, therapeutic touch healers do not necessarily believe they are channeling the power of a god or a spirit.

T'ai-chi ch'uan

thermalism In health care this is the use of the pressure of moving water of various temperatures to massage the muscles and stimulate the circulation.

tissue salts Salts which occur naturally in the body, twelve of which were identified by Dr Wilhelm Heinrich Schuessler in the 1870s and used as part of a therapy known as biochemics.

transactional analysis Concerned with the transactions between individuals, this form of therapy analyzes how we communicate, and aims to help people realize and express their needs more clearly.

transcendental meditation A form of meditation in which a mantra is used.

tridoshas In Ayurvedic medicine the collective name for the three constitutional types (vata, pitta, and kapha).

triple burner Also called the triple heater, this is one of 14 meridians used in Chinese medicine and controls the endocrine gland.

tsubo *See* **acupoint.**

tuina Used in China alongside acupuncture and herbal medicine, this is a form of intense, deep massage used to balance energy flow.

vata In Ayurvedic medicine this is one of three doshas (the other two being pitta and kapha) and resulting from the combination of the Bhutas air and ether by agni.

visualization therapy The use of mental images to improve overall health and well-being.

yang A word originating from the Old Chinese and meaning earth, the force of contraction. Yang is the opposite of yin.

yin A word originating from the Old Chinese and meaning heaven, the force of expansion. Yin is the opposite of yang.

yoga From the sanscrit word for "union," or "oneness," yoga is a system of spiritual, mental and physical well-being and of which there are many types, including bakti, hatha, jnana, karma and raja. Yoga involves asanas and pranayama.

zone therapy Developed by American surgeon Dr William Fitzgerald, this is an early western form of reflexology in which healing can be brought about by massaging certain zones in the foot.

yoga

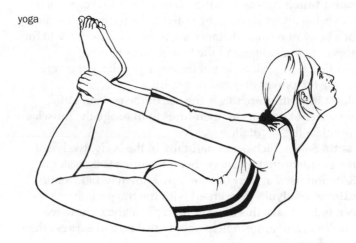

Technology

communications

alphabet Normally a set of graphic symbols which, either singly or in combinations, represents the sounds of a language. Alphabetic writing appears to have begun around 1700 BC. Its inventors are thought to have been the Egyptians, Phoenicians, or Hittites. The word comes from the first two letters of the Greek alphabet, alpha and beta.

attachment A computer file that is sent along with an e-mail message.

auto-responder A system used in handling e-mail that automatically replies to received messages.

ballpoint pen A fountain pen with a ball that rotates at the end of an ink reservoir, delivering the ink in a constant stream. Original invention attributed to John Loud in the US in 1888. The first practical ballpoint pen was invented by Georg Biro in Hungary in 1938.

Braille A system of writing or printing using raised dots on a page, allowing blind people to read by touch. Originally developed by Louis Braille, a blind French teacher (1809–52).

British Broadcasting Corporation (BBC) Established under royal charter in 1927, it transmitted the world's first open-circuit TV broadcasts. It runs two national television stations, five national radio stations, and a number of local radio stations, and provides external services in 38 languages.

computer A device for processing information at high speeds by electronic methods.

cuneiform A non-alphabetic system of writing used throughout the ancient world for over 2,000 years. It was probably invented by the Sumerians. A symbol was constructed out of sets of wedge-shaped strokes made in soft clay with pieces of reed.

Cyrillic A form of alphabet used in Russian, Bulgarian, and other eastern European languages which is derived from the Greek alphabet.

e-business Commercial transactions carried out on the Internet. Also called e-commerce.

e-mail Electronic mail, typed messages sent and received electronically via a computer network.

electrotype A copy of engravings and type made by an electroplating process.

engraving A plate engraved for printing, or a printed illustration.

etymology The study of the history of words, tracing them back to their earliest recorded forms.

fax Short for facsimile, a machine that enables people to send

Braille

a b c d

e f g h

i j k l

m n o p

copies of documents or pictures over telephone lines or radio links.

full color printing A process by which all colors can be reproduced from combinations of three primary colors—yellow, cyan (blue), and magenta (red)—and black.

heliograph A system of sending signals by flashing sunlight from a mirror, used in the 1800s.

hieroglyphics A writing system which uses picture-characters to represent words, ideas, or sounds. Different forms were developed by the ancient Egyptians and early American Indians, such as the Aztecs.

ideogram A pictorial system used in a writing system to represent an entity or an idea. Ideograms are also called ideographs.

International Phonetic Alphabet A system developed during the late 19th century to symbolize every sound used in human language accurately. Used in the scientific study of pronunciation.

Internet A worldwide system of interconnected computer networks that may be accessed via a computer and a modem.

ISDN International Subscriber Digital Network, a digital system of telephone connections.

Italic type A slanting style of letterforms developed for printing in Italy by Francesco Griffo in 1501.

kinesics The study of the way in which facial expressions and body movements are used for the purposes of communication. This is also known as body language, as is proxemics.

linguistics The scientific study of language. It has produced many specialized fields of study such as phonetics, grammar, and semantics.

linotype A typesetting machine invented in 1884. It speeded up the hitherto manual process by allowing a whole line of individual letters to be set at once, using a keyboard.

lithography A form of planographic printing invented in 1798.

logogram A symbol used to represent a complete word or phrase. For example, the sign $, for dollar, is a logogram.

mail server A central computer that forwards e-mail messages.

modem Modulator / demodulator, a device that converts computer signals into a form that can be transmitted down telephone lines.

Morse Code Code invented by Samuel Morse for transmitting telegraph messages in 1791–1872. He erected the first telegraph line between Washington and Baltimore in 1844.

newsgroup An area on the World Wide Web where people who have a particular interest in common communicate with one

Morse code

A •■
B ■•••
C ■•■•
D ■••
E •
F ••■•
G ■■•
H ••••
I ••
J •■■■
K ■•■
L •■••
M ■■
N ■•
O ■■■
P •■■•
Q ■■•■
R •■•
S •••
T ■
U ••■
V •••■
W •■■■
X ■••■
Y ■•■■
Z ■■••

another, often with links to other websites.

papyrus A reedlike plant cultivated in Egypt and used by the ancient Egyptians to make paper.

photocopier A device that prints copies of documents and drawings from an optical image.

phototypesetting Typesetting using machines that superseded the old system of casting type from hot metal. Instead they create images of characters on photographic paper or film, which is then used for platemaking. The fastest can set 20,000 or more characters per second.

pictograms Pictures used to represent objects in hieroglyphic script, used widely in the ancient Middle East and by the Aztec and Maya of Central America.

printing The production of multiple copies of text or pictures, normally on paper. Printing has advanced rapidly and today complete pages can be produced by computers, transferred to paper by laser, and then photographed onto a printing plate.

radio The transmission of sound or other information by radio-frequency electromagnetic waves, pioneered by Marconi. Like television, radio plays an important part in people's lives broadcasting news, drama, entertainment, the arts, and educational programs.

radio telephone A type of radio tansmitter/receiver used for communicating with ships at sea from 1903 onward, before permanent cables were laid.

rebus A system using a mixture of words and pictures, the pictures representing syllables or words.

semaphore

A & 1   B & 2

runes Letters of an alphabet used by the Teutonic peoples of northern Europe before AD 1000.

satellite A spacecraft launched into orbit around the Earth or entering an orbit around some other body in the solar system. Satellites are used for gathering information, intelligence, and for communication. They transmit radio, telephone, and television signals. Constant radio links became possible in 1963.

C & 3   D & 4

satellite TV Television broadcasting using a space satellite to rebroadcast programs to home receivers rather than terrestrial transmitters or cable.

E & 5   F & 6

semaphore Signalling by means of two flags or mechanical arms, held in various positions to represent letters.

semiotics The study of signs and/or symbols; sometimes known as semiology.

spam Unwanted messages, such as advertising material, received via e-mail.

G & 7   H & 8

syllabary A set of symbols used for representing syllables, for example in Japanese writing.

telecommunications The transfer of information by any electromagnetic means such as wire or radio waves. It includes telephones, telegraphy, radio, and television. It relies on a transmitter, a transmission channel, and a receiver.

telegram A message transmitted by telegraph.

telegraphy The invention of the electric telegraph, perfected in 1838 by Morse, saw the beginning of modern electronic communications. In simple terms, it is the transmission of written or printed messages by electrical signals.

telephone Invented in 1876, the telephone has become a vital means of communication between people in business and everyday life. It carries sounds in the form of electrical signals along a wire. Mobile telephones are a more recent invention, allowing people to be contacted and to communicate while traveling in a car, train, and even aircraft.

teletext A fast form of telex that links word processors through a telephone line. Developed in Europe in the 1980s as a fast information service.

television The broadcasting of pictures and sound by radio waves or electric cable was invented by John Logie Baird in 1926.

telex A quick form of communication and an advance on simple telegraph systems. It transmits a message from one machine to a similar one anywhere in the world at about 100 words per minute.

typesetting The process by which type is assembled for printing.

typewriter A machine that prints individual letters onto paper, using a keyboard. The first machine was invented in the US in 1867, but the commercial success of the typewriter began in 1874, when the Remington company produced its own machines.

videotape recorders Machines that record pictures as well as sound on magnetic tape.

viewdata A system by which information can be stored at a central point and retrieved by the use of a telephone line linked to word processors. It enables the user to call up thousands of pages of information.

World Wide Web The mass of text and multimedia material that can be accessed via the Internet.

computing

ALU (Arithmetic and Logic Unit) The circuits in a CPU where calculations and comparisons are carried out.

analog computer A machine that works on data represented by some physical quantity which varies continuously.

application A program designed to perform a range of useful tasks, such as word processing.

ASCII (American Standard Code for Information Interchange). An eight-bit binary representation of letters and numbers.

backing store Programs or data saved outside a computer on tape or disk.

backup A copy made of important data and kept in case something goes wrong with the original.

BASIC Beginners' All Purpose Symbolic Instruction Code.

baud rate The speed at which a bit goes from one part of a computer to another. One baud is one bit per second.

binary A numeration system based on digits 0 and 1.

bit Short for binary digit, either 1 or 0.

booting The process of setting up all of the operating programs of a computer, section by section until complete and ready to operate.

browser A piece of software that allows a user to move around and look at pages in the World Wide Web.

bug A mistake in a program.

bus Tracks along which data is moved about the computer.

byte A unit of eight bits. Computer memories are measured in terms of thousands of bytes.

cache A temporary storage area in a computer's memory.

CAD Computer-aided design.

character A number, letter, or symbol.

chip A tiny bit of silicon on which electronic circuits are printed.

chip

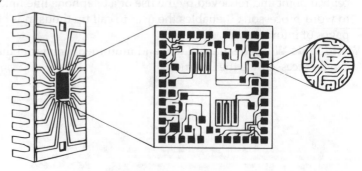

COBOL Common Business Oriented Language.

command An instruction to a computer, usually typed at a keyboard, that the computer obeys immediately.

computer A versatile electronic data-processing device with at least three components. Input and output is digital or analog, and processing involves storage, control, and arithmetical operations.

computer language A language in which the operator "talks" to a computer.

cookie A data file that a web server stores on a user's computer to identify the user and allow quick access the next time the user visits the server.

CPU (Central Processing Unit). Circuits controlling all parts of a computer where calculations occur.

crash When an irrecoverable failure occurs in hardware or software.

data Information for a computer to work on. Also, information and results from a computer.

database A collection of related data specially organized to be retrieved quickly.

dialect Any of several versions of BASIC using slightly different commands.

digital computer A computer working with data represented in digital form, usually binary 0s and 1s.

directory Another name for **folder**.

disk A flat plate, covered in magnetic material, which stores data on concentric tracks. Hard disks are internal and have greater storage capacity than floppy disks, which are external.

disk drive A machine that puts data on to, or reads it from, a floppy disk.

download To take data into a computer from an outside source, such as the Internet or a floppy disk.

emoticon An arrangement of typed characters used, when read sideways, to represent an emotion or state of mind, such as :-) symbolizing a smiling face.

file An amount of data handled as a unit and stored under a single name.

folder A collection of files stored under one heading.

Fortran A high-level programming language used mainly by scientists and mathematicians.

gate Arrangement of transistors that works on pulses travelling through a computer's circuits.

graphics Pictures made with a computer.

graphics tablet An input device which, by sensing pressure, translates the position of a pen or pointer on a special pad into a digital signal for a computer, allowing the user to draw shapes onto the screen and into the memory.

hard copy Programs or data printed out by a computer using a printer.

hardware A computer and its internal mechanism, or a piece of related equipment, such as a disk drive or printer.

hexadecimal system A counting system, based on 16 digits (0 to 9 and A to F), useful for low-level programming.

HTML Hypertext Markup Language; the format that all web pages are set up in.

icon A symbol or picture that represents an item of software or hardware.

input Any information or instructions that are fed into a computer.

input device A machine with which to give information to a computer.

integrated circuit A minute electrical circuit containing thousands of electronic components on a tiny chip of silicon.

interface Circuits converting computer signals into a form that other electronic equipment can read.

Internet A worldwide system of interconnected computer networks that may be accessed via a computer and modem.

interpreter A program checking, translating, and carrying out a written program one statement at a time.

joysticks Sticks for moving lights or shapes around screens.

JPEG A high-compression format for graphics files used widely on the Internet.

kilobyte (k) 1 kilobyte =1,024 bytes.

light pen A light-sensitive input device with which one can "draw" on a VDU.

joysticks

list A program written, typed, or printed out on paper.

load To put a program into a computer's memory from disk.

local area network A network of linked computers on one site, such as in an office.

LOGO A simple computer language useful for drawing shapes.

machine code A pattern of electronic pulse signals which a computer uses to do all its work.

mainframe computer Large computer with many terminals.

memory A store for data or program instructions, made up of a main store and its backing store.

microcomputer A computer that uses a microprocessor chip for its central processor.

microprocessor A computer held on a single chip.

minicomputer A small-sized computer with limited memory and a few peripheral devices.

mnemonics A code consisting of abbreviated instructions.

modem Short for modulator/demodulator. Converts computer signals into a form that can be transmitted down telephone lines.

monitor (1) The part of a ROM which holds instructions telling a CPU how to operate. (2) The computer screen.

motherboard A circuit board into which other PCBs can be slotted.

mouse A moveable desktop device with a ball underneath which relays speed and direction, guiding a cursor across a screen.

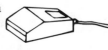
mouse

network A system of computers, sometimes with other peripherals, linked together to share information.

output Any information that a computer displays or prints.

output device A machine showing information processed by a computer.

PASCAL A high-level, general-purpose programming language.

patch A piece of software designed to be added to a program to correct errors.

PCB (Printed Circuit Board). A board inside a computer holding all chips and other components.

peripherals Equipment, such as extra screens, printers, or plotters, that can be attached to a computer.

pixels Tiny areas (dots) making up a computer graphic picture.

plotter A device for drawing a two-dimensional graphic output from a computer on paper.

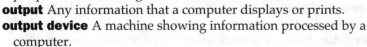

plug-in An additional piece of software added to an application.

port A socket on a micro where a lead is plugged in linking it to another device.

peripherals
printer

program A list of instructions telling a computer what to do.

programming language A language, such as BASIC, in which a program is written so that a computer will understand it.

prompt A message that a computer gives to its operator, such as a symbol, sentence, or colored light.

protocol A standardized method used to transfer data.

RAM (Random Access Memory). Temporary memory holding material lost if a computer is switched off.

ROM (Read Only Memory). A permanent store of data and programs.

run A command to tell a computer to carry out a program. Can also imply loading, execution and output of a whole package.

save To store a program or document either internally on the computer's hard disk or externally, usually on tape or disk.

scanner An input device collecting data by recording brightness values for small areas as it moves across a surface.

screen resolution The number of pixel groups on screen which a computer can control. Determines the sharpness of an image.

search engine A device used to find material on the World Wide Web by looking for combinations of words.

sensor A device for sensing and measuring light, pressure, or temperature, and sending information back to a computer.

server A computer that holds web pages and supplies them to browsers.

software computer programs

string A set of characters.

supercomputer A fast computer with a large memory, as used in research laboratories.

syntax error A mistake in a programming language.

terminal A device connected to a computer allowing input and output of data.

transistor A semiconductor used as an amplifier or a switching device.

upload To transfer data from a computer to a larger storage device or onto a network.

URL Uniform Resource Locator. A form of address that identifies the location on the World Wide Web of a page or file.

VDU (Visual Display Unit). A screen, similar to a TV screen, designed specially for a computer.

virtual Using computers to simulate realistic environments, objects, or activity.

virus An unauthorized program that inserts itself into a computer's data and interferes, often destructively, with the computer's functioning.

word processor A computer system designed to handle text. Faster and more flexible than a typewriter.

World Wide Web The mass of text and multimedia material that can be accessed via the Internet.

WYSIWYG "Wizziwig," or "what you see is what you get," the principle that what is shown on a computer's screen is what will be printed out, especially in word processing.

zip files Computer files that have been compressed to save space and speed up their transfer.

Neologisms and technical terms

above the fold The part of a webpage visible to a visitor without scrolling down.

administrivia A collective term for the administrative details such as copyright, licensing, and privacy information that appear on websites.

advermation Online advertisements that appear to offer information to the user but in fact offer marketing material.

advertainment Online advertisements that entertain the viewer at the same time as displaying marketing material. Advertainment is usually interactive.

affiliate marketing A form of shared marketing in which a company selling through a website pays a commission to the owners of other websites that send customers to them via links.

aggregation A service that allows a customer to view related information from a wide range of online sources on one website. For example, providing information about airfares from a range of different companies over the same route .

aggregator An application that collects input from numerous RSS feeds and displays them in one place.

aliasing The distortion of graphic elements on a computer screen. *See also* **jaggies**.

all your base are belong to us A grammatically nonsensical piece of subtitled dialog from a Japanese computer game of the late 1980s that became an internet phenomenon when it was adopted as a humorous phrase by the online community.

alpha geek The person with the greatest knowledge of a particular technology within a group of people with generally good knowledge of that technology.

alt text Text that appears describing an image on a website when the cursor hovers over it.

anacronym An acronym that is no longer in common usage.

angry garden salad A poorly constructed graphic user interface that fails to perform the actions chosen by the user or that performs actions different from the ones chosen.

anime A style of Japanese animation.

arrow shooter An individual who proposes a radical new idea and describes its potential future development.

astroturf campaign An attempt by a special interest group or lobbing organization to influence the opinion of lawmakers by sending a them a large number of emails.

attention economy The theory that the attention span of online users is a limited commodity that is subject to market forces. The economic model supposes the existence of a market place in which consumers agree to give their attention in exchange for services such as email or personalized news.

avatar A digital construct (often an image file) that represents the online user in a virtual world.

back end The part of a program that carries out the tasks the program is designed to perform as opposed to the front end of the program that allows the user to instruct and interact with the back end.

back hack The process of discovering who has hacked into a system by tracing information left by the hacker back to its source.

backhoe day A day on which no work can be done in an information industry company because of damage to the physical infrastructure that facilitates the transfer of information. The term implies that construction workers have severed buried fiber optic cables using mechanical digging equipment.

backronym The result of taking an existing word (which is not an acronym) or an existing acronym and using each letter of that word or acronym as the initial letter of the words in a new phrase or sentence. In other words changing the meaning of an existing acronym by making it stand for something else or treating a real word as if it were an acronym.

banana problem A problem or project that requires little expertise to carry out. A "one banana problem" is an easily solved problem.

bandwidth hog A large file that takes a long time to download and at the same time makes it impossible to access anything else online. Also a person who is online for long periods.

banner blindness The tendency of website visitors to ignore advertising banners and elements of the website that resemble advertising banners.

barfogenesis The sensation of nausea experienced by users of virtual reality headsets caused by a mismatch between movement perceived by the eye and movement perceived by the organs of balance.

Barney page A website or web page designed to take advantage of a short-lived popular trend.

bear paw A keyboard command that requires five keys to be pressed simultaneously.

below the fold The part of a web page that is only visible to a visitor by scrolling down.

beta A test period for new software or hardware.

big iron A large and powerful mainframe computer. Also known as big brass.

biobreak A visit to the bathroom.

bit bucket An imaginary place in cyberspace where all lost electronic files are said to end up.

bit flip A complete reversal of opinion or personality.

bitslag Large amounts of useless, erroneous, or repetitive information on the internet that has to be sifted through in search of useful or relevant information.

black box model A software or hardware development method in which the developer is able to input to and receive output from the product but has no access to its internal workings.

Black hat A general term for hackers or online users who have malicious or illegal intentions.

bleeding edge Technologies that are so advanced or innovative that there is no known application for them at present.

bloatware A piece of software that takes up a disproportionately large amount of disk space and processing power for its functionality.

blogosphere The collective online space occupied by bloggers.

blow a buffer To forget what one was about to say either through absent mindedness or surprise.

blue screen of death A blank blue screen on a computer monitor that results from a serious error in the Windows operating systems.

boat anchor A piece of obsolete hardware.

boiling the ocean Undertaking a project that is far too ambitious.

booth bunny An attractive woman hired to staff a technology company's booth at a trade show.

box A computer.

bozon The imaginary quantum unit of stupidity.

brain dump Writing down or explaining all the information one has on a particular technical topic.

brain fart To speak or act without considering the consequences or to forget important information.

brandalism The placement of corporate slogans or adverts in public buildings such as schools.

code 18 An error made by a computer user; the person sitting 18 inches in front of the screen.

concatenated speech Synthesized or recorded words that are spliced together by a software program to provide a spoken response to a human user of the system.

cookie A small text file that contains information about a computer that has been used to visit a website. Some web servers send cookies to all computers that access them and these are stored on the computer's hard drive. The next time the same computer is used to access the same website the web server for that site reads the cookie enabling it to identify the user and implement any preferences that user may have decided on during their last visit.

copyleft A distribution agreement that allows everybody who receives a copy of the work in question to freely distribute or adapt it on the condition that they do not claim copyright on it for themselves.

cracker A hacker who specializes in circumventing security systems with malicious intent.

crash test dummies Customers who pay for software that has not been properly tested.

crog A blog written by a person with expert knowledge. An acronym for Carefully Researched blOG.

cybersquat To register a domain name that contains the name of a large corporation or well-known brand with the intention of later selling it to the owners of that corporation or brand for a profit.

dancing baloney Unnecessary animated graphics on a web page intended to impress potential customers.

dark fiber Fiber-optic data transfer cable that has been installed but is carrying far less traffic than it has the capacity for.

darknet A network or internet service that allows users to transfer data anonymously.

data shadow Digital information that is left on a network every time a user sends an email, uses a cell phone, browses the web, or pays using a credit card.

debbie A user who is even less experienced than a newbie.

deep Web The large amount of information on web pages that search engines do not have access to.

designosaurs Designers who do not use computers.

destination page The web page a user intends to visit when clicking on a particular link.

destination site A website that serves as a starting point for other activities or that brings together frequently accessed online applications such as email, shopping, and newsfeeds in one place. Also known as a portal.

digital divide The division between the sections of the world's population who have computers and internet access and those who do not.

digital fingerprint A unique piece of information attached to a digital document that indicates if the document is changed in any way and also aids in the protection of intellectual property rights.

disruptive technology Any technology that causes a revolution in traditional business models.

dittoheads Individuals who are in complete agreement on a particular issue.

domainism Prejudice against individuals who use email addresses under domain names that are considered to be unfashionable.

doorway domain A domain name that is intended to attract to a website because it includes key words often used in internet searches.

dynamic content Content on a web page or website that depends on the input of a user (such as the content of a page showing search results) or that changes frequently.

easter egg A hidden element in a program or website that gives the user extra content when it is found.

eating their own dog food When a software development company uses its own software for internal projects.

e-bomb An unusually damaging computer virus.

echo chamber A group of bloggers that repeat and reinforce each others opinions.

ego-surfing Searching the internet for references to one's own name.

ejectrode A makeshift tool (usually a bent paperclip) used to manually eject a disk stuck in a disk drive.

emoticon A group of typed characters that resemble a facial expression. The most common is ":-)" – which resembles a smiling face tipped on its side.

Engrish Unintentionally ungrammatical or misspelled English words or phrases often seen in instructions for electronic products produced in Asia.

ethical hacker A hacker employed by a company to simulate hacking attempts on its systems in order to highlight potential security problems.

everyware An imagined state of technological development in which information processing has been integrated into almost all everyday items from clothing to food packaging to building materials. Also known as ubiquitous computing or ubicomp.

face time The time spent in the physical presence of somebody as opposed to time spent communicating via email, instant messaging, or videoconferencing.

fat pipe A high bandwidth connection.

favicon A small graphic icon that appears before the URL of a website in the address bar of most web browsers.

firefighter An internet user who tries to prevent or extinguish flame wars.

fisk To bring attention to errors, usually in a blog post, point-by-point and in great detail.

flame An insulting or impolite message sent via email, or as a post on a newsgroup or forum, or as a comment on a blog.

flame bait A statement likely to provoke a flame war.

flame war An online discussion on a newsgroup, forum, or thread of blog comments in which debate about a subject degenerates into an exchange of personal insults.

forelash A lack of enthusiasm for potential future products or technologies caused by excessive promotion before their release.

forestware Printed instruction manuals or user manuals for electronic hardware.

front end The part of a program that handles interaction with the user.

fuzzy logic A system of rules governing a decision making process in which propositions may be assigned degrees of truthfulness rather than a simple true or false value.

generation D People of any age who are familiar with digital technology.

generation X Americans and Western Europeans born between about 1963 and 1979.

generation Y People born into technologically advanced societies since 1980.

generica Regions of the urban landscape of the United States that are indistinguishable from one another because they have the same retail outlets, motels, and housing.

ghost site A website that is no longer maintained or updated but remains accessible online.

Googleganger A person with the same name as oneself who is discovered when ego-surfing on Google.

Googlewhack A two-term search on Google that returns just one result.

grrl A female who spends a lot of time online and is knowledgeable about technology.

IM *See* **instant messaging**

incubator An investment and support program in which entrepreneurs starting internet businesses are provided with management advice, access to finance, and technical assistance by a network of investors.

indigenous content Content created by an online community for their own use. Also known as user-generated content.

information age A description of the modern period in which the manipulation of information has become a major global industry.

instant messaging A program that allows users to communicate with each other instantaneously using typed messages.

Internet backbone The network of very high capacity data cables that connect the major population centers of the world and carry much of the world's Internet traffic.

Internet The totality of the world's interconnected communications networks.

interstitial advertising Advertisements that appear as a user is moving from one web page to another.

jaggies Images or graphics that have distorted by aliasing.

jump page A web page that used to redirect visitors when a website's URL has changed.

kewl A common deliberate misspelling of "cool."

key pal A correspondent who is communicated with primarily via a keyboard using email, instant messaging, or any other digital medium.

keyboard plaque Dirt, dust, and fragments of food that collect under and around the keys of a computer keyboard.

keylogger A program or piece of hardware that records every keystroke made on a computer keyboard.

keyword Any word typed into a search engine by a user in order to initiate an online search. Website developers strive to include as many potential keywords in their content as possible in order to maximize their potential visitors.

l33t *See* **leetspeak**.

lag A period of time during which a computer is apparently not responding to input.

landing page The web page on a website that a visitor sees first after clicking an online advertisement or a link from another website.

lasagna syndrome A piece of software that presents the user with too many overlapping dialogue boxes or windows.

latency The time period between a request for a network to perform an action and the action being carried out.

leaky reply A copy of an email sent to an unintended recipient.

leetspeak A form of online jargon in which alphabetical characters are habitually replaced by numerical or non-alphanumerical characters (such as hyphens, underscores, and punctuation symbols) For example the word "leet" may be spelled "l33t." Deliberate misspellings are also common. For example "cool" is commonly spelled "kewl."

legacy system An outmoded computer system that is still in use.

link farm A website that consists almost exclusively of links to other websites.

link rot Links on a website that is not regularly maintained may become obsolete over time. They are said to be subject to link rot.

long domain name A domain name that exceeds 26 characters in length. Originally domain names could not exceed 26 characters, but this was later changed to 67 characters.

lurker A person who regularly visits a chat room, forum, or blog but never contributes comments.

macrosite A website consisting of more than one web page that is subsidiary to a parent website. Macrosites often include interactive content such as surveys or polls. *See also* **microsite**.

mail bomb An email with a very large file attached to it that is intended to interrupt the functioning of the recipient's mail server.

malware Software that is intended to damage computer systems.

mash-up A website or application that combines content (such as video or music) from more than one source into an integrated product.

meatbot A human being.

meatjail The human brain.

meatloaf Unsolicited email sent between friends and usually containing jokes, surprising trivia, or links to entertaining web pages.

meatspace The physical world inhabited by people.

meh A common expression of indifference.

microsite A one page website that is subsidiary to a parent website. Microsites often include interactive content such as surveys or polls. *See also* **macrosite**.

nerd bird Any passenger aircraft on a regular direct flight between US cities with large concentrations of high technology companies such as San Jose (Silicon Valley) and Seattle.

nerd wrangler A person in the human resources department of a high technology company who has the job of hiring programmers.

netiquette The accepted standards of behavior in online communication.

netizen A person who spends a lot of time on the Internet. Also used to apply to any person who uses the Internet.

newbie An inexperienced user of the Internet or of computers in general.

noob A derogatory term for a newbie. Often written as "n00b" in leetspeak.

nooksurfer An Internet user who rarely or never explores the online world beyond their email account or one or two specialized websites.

nym A false name or a nickname used online. A contraction of "pseudonym."

nym-rod A person or online community that makes excessive use of contractions or acronyms.

official site A website owned by a company or celebrity rather than a website about a company or celebrity owned and run by somebody else.

open your kimono To reveal secret business plans.

organ donor An obsolete piece of hardware used as a source of spare parts.

organic search results Websites that appear in search results because they are considered by the search engine to be relevant to the keywords used in the search rather than because the owners of those websites have paid to have their websites appear in the results of searches using those keywords.

overshare Revealing excessive amounts of personal information on a blog or social networking site.

peer-to-peer (P2P) A relationship between two computers on the same network such that they are able to share information without a third computer having to act as a server. Peer-to-peer networking is often used on the Internet to facilitate the sharing of music and video files (often illegally) between users.

pharming A method of committing fraud by redirecting the customers of a legitimate online business, such as a bank, to a website where details such as account numbers and passwords may be recorded. The website to which customers are redirected is often designed to resemble the legitimate company's website. Unlike phishing, pharming is aimed at every person who accesses the target website.

phishing A method of committing fraud by sending emails to the customers of a legitimate online business, such as a bank, that pretend to be from that business and ask for information such as account numbers or passwords.

pin bender An unprofessional technician.

ping To contact a person with a short message, usually to ask for their agreement or disagreement on an issue or to remind them of something.

podcast An audio file that can be downloaded for free; usually part or all of a radio program.

radio button A selectable button on a web page. A radio button is small and round and, once clicked, has a black dot in the center.

scooby snacks Non-monetary compensation for overtime work or for temporary casual work at a media or high technology company.

semantic search A method of searching the Internet that takes account of the meaning and use of key words in a website rather than just their frequency.

sig file A short piece of text appended to the end of an email massage that gives basic contact information about the sender of the email. Sig files are also used in newgroups and forums where they often contain a humorous saying or a quote. "Sig file" is an abbreviation of "signature file."

silver surfer A person over the age of 50 who regularly uses the Internet.

slivercast A video program or series of programs sent directly to a small special-interest audience over the Internet.

social ad An advertisement that targets users of social networking websites by selectively attaching itself to messages that mention particular products or activities.

social networking The use of websites that allow the

establishment and development of networks of online friendships and associations. All social networking websites have three characteristic features in common; the user creates a "profile" which has an image and some information about him and is visible to all other users, the user can associate himself with other users through mutual agreement, and associated users can communicate publicly and privately and exchange text, images, video, and audio files.

spam Any email message sent to a large number of people without their consent. Also known as unsolicited commercial email (UCE) or junk email.

spam filter A piece of software designed to delete spam or to redirect it into a folder separate from the user's main email inbox.

spambot A program that searches the Internet for valid email addresses to be used as the targets for spam.

spider A program that searches the Internet for previously unknown web pages or other publicly accessible documents so that they can be included in the databases of Internet search engines. Also known as a crawler or webcrawler.

splog A blog set up purely for the purpose of collecting revenue from the advertisements it carries. "Splog" is a contraction of "spurious blog."

spyware Any software that gathers information about a user as they navigate around the Internet. Spyware is typically installed on a computer without the user's knowledge or consent.

sticky content Information or other features on a website that are very popular with users or that consume a large amount of the time spent by the average visitor to a website.

superstitial ad An advertisement that is launched in a new browser window while a visitor is waiting for a website to load.

sysadmin The person responsible for maintaining the operation of a computer system. A contraction of "system administrator."

tag A descriptive label attached to a website or web page that provides information about its content.

tchotchkes Promotional items such as baseball caps or mouse pads distributed at high technology trade fairs and exhibitions.

technobabble The excessive use of Internet jargon and high technology terminology, especially when used to intimidate inexperienced computer users.

telco An abbreviation for "telecommunications company."

the edge A collective term for wireless enabled devices such as WAP enabled cell phones and palmtop computers.

throttle To restrict the amount of data that may be transferred across a network or to restrict the flow of certain kinds of data. Throttling is often performed by telecommunication companies to ensure that certain kinds of data, such as peer-to-peer data traffic, do not take up an excessive amount of their available bandwidth.

top-level domain (TLD) The final portion of a Uniform Resource Locator (URL), commonly known as a website address. Top-level domains include country code top-level domains (ccTLDs), for example ".uk" (United Kingdom), and ".jp" (Japan), as well as international suffixes such as ".com" and ".net."

treeware *See* **forestware**.

troll A person who posts deliberately inflammatory messages on newsgroups, forums, or blog comment threads with the intention of provoking angry responses.

turklebaum Any deliberately misleading story or piece of false information disseminated primarily via the Internet. Named for a widely known hoax story about a man named Turklebaum who died at his desk without his co-workers noticing for several days.

twitch game Any computer game that requires rapid hand-eye coordination.

twitter Short but frequent status reports about a person's ordinary day-to-day activities made available to that person's online network of friends and associates.

typosquat To register a domain name that is a common misspelling of a popular domain name (or the domain name of a well-known brand) in order to capture Internet traffic from users who mistype domain names.

Uniform Resource Locator (URL) The location and access method for a web page or any other resource on the Internet. A URL describes the access protocol being used (commonly "http"), and the address of the resource (for example "www.site.com").

vaporware Software that has been promoted for a long period but never becomes available for use.

viral A piece of information, such as a short video, that is rapidly and broadly disseminated via the Internet.

vulcan nerve pinch A keyboard command that involves pressing three or more key simultaneously. *See also* **bear paw**.

weasel text A message on a web page explaining why a popular or controversial piece of content has been removed.

Web 2.0 The perceived evolution of the Web from a first generation, or original, incarnation into a second generation incarnation. The second-generation Web may be broadly characterized by its greater emphasis on user-generated content, the proliferation of social networking, the widespread adoption of services such as free blogging, and a resurgence in economic activity conducted over the Internet.

whack A forward slash (/) character.

whittling The surgical alteration of the thumbs or fingers to enable more efficient use of handheld electronic devices such as cell phones.

World Wide Web The totality of the interconnected web pages that can be read and interacted with via a computer connected to the Internet. The Web and the Internet are not synonymous. The Internet makes worldwide access to the Web possible, but the Web itself is characterized by the use links from one page to another.

zerg To conspire against somebody in an online network.

zot To censor or ban material on the Web.

Common Internet message acronyms

AAK Asleep at the keyboard

AAR8 At any rate

ADAD Another day, another dollar

AFAIC As far as I'm concerned

AFK Away from keyboard

ASAP As soon as possible

ATM At the moment

B4N Bye for now

BBS Be back soon

BC Because

BCNU Be seeing you

BFN Boyfriend

BFN/B4N Bye for now

BG Big grin

BIL Boss is listening

BITD Back in the day

BMG Be my guest

BOTOH But on the other hand

BRB Be right back

BTDT Been there, done that

BTW By the way

BYKT But you knew that

CID Consider it done

COZ Because

CSL Can't stop laughing

CU See you

CUL / CUL8R See you later

DQMOT Don't quote me on this

EG Evil grin

EOM End of message

EZ Easy

F2F Face to face

F2T Free to talk
FAQ Frequently asked questions
FWIW For what it's worth
FYI For your information
G2G Got to go
GAL Get a life
GF Girlfriend
GGN Got to go now
GJ Good job
GL Good luck
GOL Giggle out loud
GR8 / GRT Great
GTG Got to go
GW Good work
H8 Hate
HAK Hugs and kisses
HAND Have a nice day
IAC In any case
IAE In any event
IC I see
IDC I don't care
IDK I don't know
ILY I love you
IM Instant Message
IMHO In my humble opinion
IMNSHO In my not so humble opinion
IMO In my opinion
IMPOV In my point of view
IOW In other words
IRL In real life
JIC Just in case
JK Just kidding
JTLYK Just to let you know
K Okay
KIS Keep it simple
KIT Keep in touch
L8 Late
L8R Later
LBH Let's be honest
LOL Laughing out loud
MIRL Meet in real life
MorF Male or Female
MOS Mom over shoulder
MTFBWU May the force be with you
NBD No big deal

NE Any
NMU Not much, you?
NP No problem
NRN No response necessary
OIC Oh, I see
OMG Oh my god
OTP On the phone
OWTTE Or words to that effect
P911 Parent emergency
PAW Parents are watching
PCM Please call me
PIR Parent in room
PLS / PLZ Please
POC Point of contact
POS Parent over shoulder
POV Point of view
PRW Parents are watching
Q Question
RL Real life
ROTFL Rolling on the floor laughing
RSN Real soon now
RUOK? Are you okay?
S2R Send to receive
SFETE Smiling from ear to ear
SIT Stay in touch
SOZ Sorry
SYS See you soon
TAFN That's all for now
TBH To be honest
THX Thanks
TIA Thanks in advance
TMB Text me back
TOY Thinking of you
TTYL Talk to you later
TY Thank you
W/E Whatever
WB Welcome back
WFM Works for me
WTG Way to go
WTH What the hell?
WU What's up?
XOXO Hugs and kisses
YT You there?
YW You are welcome
ZZZ Bored (or tired)

Sports & Leisure

8

sports

American football

blitz Rush by additional defenders to tackle the opposing quarterback before he can get rid of the ball.

clipping Violation by an offensive player who blocks a defensive player from behind beyond the line of scrimmage.

conversion Score (one point) immediately after a touchdown by place-kicking the ball over the crossbar and between the goalposts. Two points scored after a touchdown by ball-carrying or passing play.

dead ball Ball kicked beyond the end zone, or one caught by the kick returner in the end zone while touching the ground with his knee.

defensive team Team without the ball defending against the offensive team.

down Any of four attempts by the offense (three in Canadian football) to advance the ball at least 10 yards by passing or running.

draw Play in which the quarterback drops back to feign pass then hands the ball to a running back.

fair catch Catch of a kicked ball by a player who signals by raising a hand at arm's length above his head. He may not advance the ball and may not be tackled.

field goal Score (three points) made by place-kicking or drop-kicking the ball over the crossbar during ordinary play.

field position Location of the ball on the field.

flag Yellow cloth thrown in the air by an official to signal a violation.

forward pass Thrown ball from behind the line of scrimmage to any one of five possible receivers.

fumble This occurs when a runner loses the ball before being tackled; results in a free ball.

gridiron The football field, marked with white lines.

I-formation Offensive formation in which the running backs line up directly behind the quarterback.

interference This occurs when the pass receiver or pass defender is tackled, blocked or pushed while the ball is still in the air.

kick-off Kick that puts the ball into play. The ball must travel at least 10 yds after a kick off. Either team may then recover it.

line of scrimmage Imaginary line passing through the end of the ball nearest a team's own goal line. Each team has its own line. It marks the position of the ball at the start of each down.

National Football League (NFL) The only major professional outdoor football league in the US, made up of 32 teams.

neutral zone Area between the two lines of scrimmage.

offensive team Team with the ball.

offside This occurs when a player crosses the line of scrimmage before the ball is snapped.

onside kick Short kick-off that travels just far enough to be recoverable by the kicking team.

option Offensive maneuver in which a back may choose to pass the ball or run with it.

rollout Maneuver in which a passer retreats behind the line of scrimmage and runs to the left or right before passing the ball.

rouge or single point In Canadian football, one point scored when the ball is played into the opposition goal area and becomes dead in the opponents' possession, touches or crosses the boundary lines, or touches the ground or a player beyond those lines.

roughing Foul committed against a passer or kicker.

running back Halfback or fullback who carries the ball.

sack The tackle of a quarterback before he can pass the ball.

safety Score (two points) made by the defense when it tackles the ball carrier in his own end zone.

screen pass Occurs when the quarterback behind the line of scrimmage passes the ball to a receiver behind several blockers.

scrimmage Period from the moment the ball goes into play until the moment it is declared dead.

snap This occurs when a center quickly puts the ball in play from its position on the ground by passing it through his legs to a teammate behind.

Super Bowl Game played each season for the National Football League title.

T-formation Offensive formation with two running backs lined up side by side behind the quarterback.

time out A period of 90 seconds during which play is suspended. Each team is allowed up to three time outs in each half. In Canadian football, can be requested only during the last three

kick off

snap

minutes of a half and the last minute of extra time, and last 30 seconds.

touchback Play in which a ball is put down by a player behind his own goal line after an opposing player has put it across the goal line. The ball is then put in play on the receiving team's 20-yard line.

touchdown Score (six points) by running the ball or catching a pass over the opposing team's goal line.

trap Play in which a player is allowed to cross the line of scrimmage and then is blocked from the side; the ball carrier then runs through the resulting gap.

yard lines White lines marked across the field every 5 yds.

zone coverage System of defense in which each back is responsible for a certain area.

touchdown

Athletics

baton Short bar carried by runners in a relay race.

cage A net cage within which discus and hammer events are undertaken.

cat jump An early style of high jumping.

eastern cut-off An old style of high jumping in which a jumper twists the top part of the body to face the bar as he or she goes over it.

final Last round of any event.

Fosbury flop The modern style of high jumping in which an athlete jumps head first over a bar, with their back to the bar.

heats Preliminary races to eliminate slower runners in crowded events.

lap One circuit of the track.

leg The distance run by each competitor in relay.

mile Th only non-metric race still featured in many major athletics meets.

no-jump A disallowed trial in the jumping events.

octathlon Indoor contest for men, consisting of eight events.

"spikes" Popular name for spiked athletic shoes used to improve grip. The number and size of spikes is strictly controlled.

split times Times taken at different stages of a race to determine whether the winning athlete will be fast or slow.

staggered start For races run around bends, starts are staggered so that all runners cover the same distance.

starting blocks Rigid blocks positioned at the start of each race in each lane from which competitors must begin running.

steeplechase A men's 3000 m race in which runners must clear hurdles and water jumps.

straddle An old style of high jumping in which a jumper takes off from the foot nearest to the bar, crossing it stomach downward in a draped position.

take-over zone An area in relay racing in which the baton must change hands.

trial An attempt to jump or throw; also qualifying rounds for inclusion in, for example, an Olympic team.

western roll A high jumping style in which the jumper crosses the bar, facing it, with the side of the body.

Badminton

faults Infringements that end a rally. If the server commits a fault, the serve passes to the opponent. If the non-server does so, the server wins a point.

let Allows a rally and resulting score to be disregarded. Lets are declared by the umpire without appeals from the players.

Badminton server

match Generally consists of the best of three games.

receiver Player who receives the service.

server Player who opens the rally.

setting If both players or sides reach the same score during the last stages of a game, play may be extended by "setting" a new deciding score. The player or side entitled to "set" the game must decide to do so before the next service is taken when the score first reaches the "setting" score. The score reverts to 0–0 and proceeds to 2, 3 or 5 as appropriate. The final score is the total number of points scored in the game.

Baseball

balk An illegal act by the pitcher while one or more runners are on base. Any runner may then walk on to the next base.

ball A pitch outside the strike zone that is not struck at by the batter.

bases Located at the home plate and the other three corners of the infield, where they are canvas bags pegged to the ground.

batter's box Area to left and right of the home plate in which the batter stands.

bunt A batted ball hit softly within the infield.

diamond Nickname for the infield.

double A hit for two bases.

bunt

double play Two players put out on the same pitch.

fair territory The area formed by the 90° angle between home plate and first and third bases.

force play When a runner is forced to move on to the next base because the batter has become a runner.

home plate Slab of whitened rubber sunk into the ground in front of the catcher.

home run A hit that allows the batter to get around all the bases in one turn.

infield A square area with a base at each corner.

outfield Grass-covered area between the infield and the fences or walls farthest from home plate.

pinch-hitter Substitute batter.

pitcher's mound Mound near the center of the infield from which the pitcher throws the ball.

run Scored by a batter who progressively reaches first, second, third, and home bases without being put out.

single A hit for first base.

squeeze play The batter bunts the ball so that a runner on third base can get home.

steal The advance by a runner from one base to another when no hit has been made, usually while the pitcher is pitching.

strike Called by the umpire when the batter misses a legal pitch or does not swing at a pitch in the strike zone.

strike out Three strikes on the batter, which is an out.

strike zone Area over the home plate between the batter's armpits and knees.

tagging Putting out a runner who is off a base by a fielder touching the base with a foot while holding the ball, or by touching the runner with the ball.

triple A hit for three bases.

umpire One of four officials stationed round the bases. The home plate umpire stands behind the catcher and calls balls and strikes.

strike zone

tagging

Basketball

assist A pass that leads directly to a basket being scored.

backboard Rectangular board of clear fiberglass or metal to which the basket is attached.

backcourt A team's defensive half of the court.

basket The target for shooting the ball, consisting of a metal hoop with a loose, open string net hanging down. The basket is fixed to a backboard.

center Usually the tallest and most important player of a team, playing between the two forwards; must be good on the rebound.

center jump Method of starting a game. An official tosses the ball into the air between opposing centers standing in the center circle; they jump up and try to tap it to a teammate.

delay Offensive strategy to use up time by denying the ball to the opponents and thus preserve a lead.

double-team Defensive maneuver in which two players converge on the player with the ball, hoping to force the player into an error.

dribble To move the ball by repeatedly tapping it with the hand.

dunk A field goal made by jumping very high and stuffing the ball through the basket from above the rim.

center jump

fake to feign

fast break An attempt to score quickly after the offensive team gains possession of the ball.

field goal A successful shot by any offensive player from anywhere on the floor during normal play. Counts three points if taken from behind a 3-point line, otherwise two points.

free throw Uncontested shot from behind the free throw line, as a penalty after certain fouls; scores one point.

dribbling the ball

front court The offensive team's half of the court.

goaltending Illegal interference with a field goal attempt when the ball is above the basket.

guards Two good dribblers and passers who direct the offense.

Harlem Globetrotters A dazzling all-black professional team that dominated the game in the 1930s and later switched to exhibition matches.

held ball Ball held and claimed by two opposing players simultaneously; possession is determined by a jump ball between the two players.

free throw

lay-up A shot attempted close to the basket.

National Basketball Association (NBA) US professional body formed in 1949 by the merger of the National Basketball League (NBL) and the Basketball Association of America (BAA).

personal foul Committed by a player who pushes, holds, or charges into an opponent or hits an opponent when in the act of shooting.

pick The legal blocking of a defensive player in order to free a teammate for a shot.

post The position played by the center on offense.

rebound Ball that bounces back into play off the backboard or rim of the basket after an unsuccessful shot.

screen *See* **pick.**

steal Interception of a pass, or other legal means of gaining possession of the ball from the offense.

technical foul Usually called for unsportsmanlike conduct toward an official.

three-point play Takes place when a player is fouled while making a successful shot and then goes on to score from the free throw.

three-point shot A basket scored from behind the 3-point line.

time out Legal stoppage of play, usually to discuss tactics. Seven "time outs" of 90 sec each are allowed during a game. Each team is also allowed one 20-sec "time out" in each half.

tip-in A field goal scored by tipping a rebound into the basket.

trap *See* **double-team.**

turnover Loss of possession by the offensive team without taking a shot.

violations Minor offenses, such as ball-handling errors, usually by the offensive team; penalty is usually loss of possession.

Billiards

balk line Line at the top of the table.

break Opening shot.

bridge Position of the hand on which the cue rests.

cannon Hitting both object balls.

cue Long tapered stick with a leather tip used for striking the cue ball.

cue ball White ball struck by the cue and propelled on to an object ball.

D A semicircle centered on the balk line from within which the cue ball is struck at the start of a game.

in-off Scoring stroke in billiards when the cue ball goes into a pocket after striking the object ball.

mechanical bridge Rod with a metal bridge on which the cue slides.

object ball Ball aimed at.

Billiard Table
1 Cushion
2 Bottom pocket
3 The balk area
4 The "D"
5 Balk line
6 Balk line spot
7 Center pocket
8 Center spot
9 Pyramid spot
10 The spot
11 Top pocket

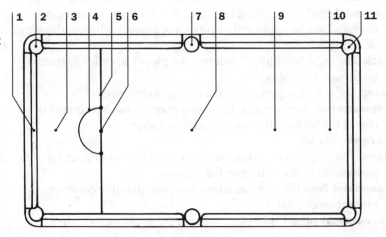

pot Scoring stroke in which the object ball is hit into a pocket.

rest *See* **mechanical bridge**.

snooker A layout of balls in which the path from the cue ball to the object ball is blocked by one or more other balls.

winning hazard a pot

Boxing

below the belt Foul punch below the waistline, especially in the groin area.

break Come out of a clinch.

canvas The floor of the ring.

clinch Holding on to an opponent.

cross Counter-punch crossing over the opponent's head.

decision Official verdict to determine the winner.

distance The full number of rounds.

hook Bent-arm punch thrown from the side at close range.

infighting Close-range fighting.

jab Light, straight punch by the leading arm.

knockout (KO) End of the fight, when one boxer is knocked unconscious or is floored for at least 10 sec.

neutral corner One of two corners not used for resting between rounds. When one boxer is floored, his opponent must retire to a neutral corner while the referee counts.

points win Victory by scoring more points (more punches landing on the target area).

purse Prize money for the boxers.

rabbit punch Foul punch landing on the back of the neck.

reach Length of a boxer's arms.

ring Three-roped square platform with a post at each corner.

round One of several periods of boxing during a bout.

southpaw Left-handed boxer who leads with his right hand and right foot forward.

spar To practice boxing, or threaten punches.

target area Any part of the front or sides of the head or body above the belt line.

technical knockout (TKO) Referee's decision to stop the fight because one boxer can no longer defend himself.

throw in the towel A boxer's seconds throw a towel into the ring to signal that they want to stop the fight and save him further punishment.

uppercut Bent-arm punch delivered upward to the chin.

weigh-in Weighing of boxers before a fight to check that they are within the correct limits.

hook

jab

rabbit punch

uppercut

Cricket

Ashes, the Trophy competed for by England and Australia in test matches, comprising the remains of a burnt cricket stump in a small urn.

bails Two small pieces of wood that rest horizontally in grooves on top of the stumps.

bouncer Ball bowled short so that it bounces high and fast at the batsman as it pitches.

boundary When a batsman strikes the ball over the boundary of the field, scoring four runs. If the ball clears the boundary without bouncing, the score is six runs.

bowler Team member who delivers the ball. Must have straight arm and deliver the ball with the back foot between the return creases.

bowling crease White line, 8 ft 8 in long, drawn through the stumps.

bye A run not struck by the bat and allotted to extras.

declaration Voluntary closure of an innings announced by the batting team's captain before all ten wickets have fallen.

duck A score of zero by a batsman who has lost a wicket.

extras Runs scored not by the bat but by errors in the fielding side.

follow-on Immediate second innings forced on a team that has failed to score a prescribed total of runs in the first innings.

full toss Ball that does not bounce before reaching the batsman.

hat-trick Three wickets taken with three successive balls.

howzat! ("How's that!") A shouted appeal to the umpire by the fielders, meaning "Is the batsman out?"

innings The batting turn of a team or player, ended when ten batsmen are dismissed or the captain makes a declaration. Matches may be of one or two innings per team.

leg before wicket (lbw)

leg Side of the field to the left of and behind a right-handed batsman facing the bowler.

leg before wicket (lbw) A way in which a batsman may be out if any part of the body except the hands prevents the ball from hitting the wicket, provided the ball has not first touched the bat or a hand.

legbreak Ball that breaks from leg to off when it hits the ground.

leg bye Run scored when the ball misses the bat but touches any other part of the batsman's body except the hands.

leg bye

long hop Short-pitched ball that is easy to hit.

Lord's A major cricket ground in London, headquarters of the Marylebone Cricket Club (MCC).

maiden over An over in which no runs are scored.

national championships Series held to determine the best national teams. They include the County Championships (England); Sheffield Shield (Australia); Plunket Shield (New Zealand); Currie Cup (South Africa); Shell Series (West Indies), and the Ranji Trophy (India).

no-ball A ball judged illegal because of some infringement by the bowler. The batting side scores one run unless the batsman hits it.

nonstriker Batsman at the wicket opposite that of the striker.

off Part of the field to which the batsman presents the bat when taking strike; i.e., the right-hand side for a right-hander.

off-break Ball that breaks from off to leg when it hits the ground.

no-ball

over Series of six or sometimes eight balls bowled from one end by the same bowler.

over the wicket Bowling with the bowler's arm nearest the wicket.

popping crease White line drawn 4 ft in front of the bowling crease. The bowler must deliver the ball with some part of the front foot behind the popping crease. A batsman cannot be stumped or run out if a foot or the bat is touching the ground behind the popping crease.

return creases Lines drawn from each end of the bowling crease, extending forward to the popping crease and back at least 4 ft behind the bowling crease.

round the wicket Bowling with the bowler's arm farthest from the wicket.

run Score usually achieved after one batsman has hit the ball and each batsman has run safely to reach the opposite wicket.

seamer Medium pace bowler who moves the ball by angling the seam of the ball.

striker Batsman standing at the far end from the bowler and receiving the ball from him.

stump Any of the three upright wooden sticks that form a wicket.

test matches International competitions at the highest level between seven nations.

wicket Three wooden stumps and two bails that rest on top of the stumps, 9 in wide, 2 ft 4 in high.

wicket keeper Member of the fielding side who stands behind the batsman and the wicket to catch or stop the ball from the bowler.

wide A ball bowled so wide or high that the batsman cannot reach it. A run is added to the score and an extra ball added to the over.

yorker Ball that pitches just under or just behind the bat.

Cycle racing

box Tactic by which a rider rides just behind and to one side of another, and thus prevents a third rider from overtaking without swinging right out.

break-away Getting clear of the field.

circuit races (criteria) Road races consisting of several laps over a circuit of roads. Races vary in length up to 62.14 miles.

control points (pits) Set up on long road-race events for feeding and repairs.

Course des primes A race with intermediate prizes (primes) at specified laps, or other points along the course.

demi-fond A middle-distance, paced track event.

domestique A team rider in road racing, whose job it is to help the team leader to win.

King of the mountains The title given to the winner of most points in hill climbs as part of a road, circuit, or stage race.

lanterne rouge (red lantern) A booby prize for the last rider in a stage race.

maillot jaune (yellow jersey) Worn by the current leader of the Tour de France and some other major events.

musette Cotton bag in which food is handed up to a rider in a road race.

omnium A track event in which the competitors ride in several races of different types.

peleton The main bunch of riders in a road race.

repêchage A kind of "second chance" race to allow losers from the heats an additional opportunity to qualify for the next round of the series in a progressive race.

sag wagon One of the last following vehicles in road events used to pick up riders who have dropped out.

stayer A track rider in a motor-paced race.

Darts

bull's-eye Small disk in the center of the board; scores 50 points.

bust To score more points than needed to win. The player forfeits the rest of his or her turn and the points thus scored.

check out to finish

double ring Outer ring on the board; scores double the value of its respective segment.

double top Double 20, the number located at the top of the board.

dartboard

flights Three pieces of plastic or polyester that balance the dart in flight.

oche (toe line) Line from behind which the player throws. It is 7ft 9in from the board.

semicenter (outer bull) Small ring that encircles the bull's-eye; scores 25 points.

toe the oche to begin play

triple ring Inner ring on the board; scores triple the value of its respective segment.

wire dart Dart that hits the board and bounces back; does not score.

Golf

address A player's stance before hitting the ball.

albatross Three under par for a hole.

approach shot Iron shot or long putt to the hole.

birdie One under par for a hole.

bogey One over par for a hole.

borrow Slope on a putting green.

bunker (sand trap) A type of hazard, usually a sand-filled hollow.

caddie Person who carries a player's clubs and gives advice.

chip Short, lofted approach shot.

divot Piece of turf dug out by a properly played iron shot; it should be replaced.

dogleg Hole with a sharp bend in it between tee and green.

draw A hook executed deliberately.

drive A golfer's first stroke from the tee.

driver Wooden club with which the player drives the ball.

eagle Two under par for a hole.

fade A slice executed deliberately.

fairway Smooth turf between tee and green.

fore! Warning shout by a player about to play a shot.

green Area around the hole closely mown for putting.

halved hole A hole in which opponents make the same score.

handicap A way of equalizing competition by allowing a certain

drive

number of strokes to a golfer playing against a better opponent.

hazard Obstacle on the course, usually a bunker or an area of water.

hole-in-one Occurs when a player's tee shot goes straight into the hole; a rare feat.

hook A badly executed drive where in the ball curls to the left (in a right handed shot) or to the right (in a left-handed shot).

iron Club with a metal head.

lie The position in which the ball lies on the course after a stroke.

nineteenth hole Slang name for the bar in the clubhouse.

par Estimated standard score for a hole or course based on the ability of a first-class player.

pin Flagpole marking the hole on a green.

play through Pass slower players in front by playing a hole before they do.

putter Club used for putting.

putting Strokes played on the green to try to roll the ball into the hole.

rough Untrimmed grass bordering the fairway.

slice A badly executed drive where the ball curves to the right (in a right-handed shot) or to the left (in a left-handed shot).

tee Slightly elevated area from which a player drives the ball; also the peg on which the ball is placed.

wedge Wedge-shaped club used for lofting the ball.

wood Wooden club used for longer shots.

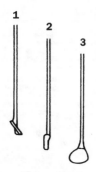

Types of golf club
1 Iron
2 Putter
3 Wood

Gymnastics

balance routine Routine consisting of elements without flight phase: pyramids, handstands, balances, individual elements, choreographic, and combination movements.

pirouettes Turns around longitudinal axis of body.

saltos Turns around short axis of body.

tempo routine Routine consisting of elements with flight phase: turns, somersaults (including at least two elements where partner is caught), individual elements, choreographic element, and a tumbling series.

tsukahara Men's vault exercise, named after Japanese gymnast who first performed it.

tsukahara

yamashita Women's vault exercise.

bully Played on the spot where an incident or accident occurred to restart the game. A player taps the stick first on the ground on his/her own side of the ball, then against his/her opponent's stick above the ball. This is done three times after which one player must strike the ball.

charging A player deliberately pushing an opposition player out of the way when playing the ball.

corner Awarded to the non-offending side when a defender sends the ball unintentionally over his or her own goal line. The ball must be hit along the ground from a spot on the goal line within 3 yd (or 5 yd for women) of the corner flag.

charging

dangerous play When the ball or stick rises above shoulder level when hit.

offside A player is offside when within his or her opponents' half when the ball is played by a teammate further from the goal-line, and when there are fewer than two opponents nearer the goal line.

free hit Awarded to the non-offending side for infringements committed outside the shooting circle.

hit in When the ball is hit out of play over a side line a player of the opposing team may push or hit the ball from the side.

dangerous play

passback A player from one team knocks the ball back to a teammate; this is used to start the game and re-start after a goal.

penalty corner Awarded to the non-offending side when an opponent deliberately plays the ball over the goal line, or for offenses within the shooting circle. Taken from anywhere on the goal line at least 10 yd from the goal post.

penalty stroke Awarded against defenders in the circle for an intentional foul, an unintentional foul preventing a goal, or deliberate positioning infringement at penalty corners. Taken by an attacker from a spot 7 yd in front of the center of the goal.

push-in Awarded to the opposition when a player hits the ball over the sideline.

reverse stick Turning the stick over in order to play the ball on the other side of the body.

roll-in *See* push-in.

short corner *See* penalty corner.

shooting circle (striking circle) A wide arc extending from the goal line in front of each goal.

Ice hockey

assist The passing of the puck by another player to the goal-scorer.

back-checking Defensive tackling to break up an attack.

blockers The goalie's leather gloves with a large pad on the back.

boarding Forcing an opponent into the boards at the edge of the rink.

body-checking A hip or shoulder charge against an opponent to try to block his progress or unbalance him.

butt-ending Striking an opponent with the end of a stick; a major penalty.

drop pass Leaving the puck behind for a teammate.

face-off An official drops the puck between two opponents in order to start play at any time.

flip pass A pass to a teammate that rises off the ice.

fore-checking Tackling an opponent who has the puck in his own defending zone.

high-sticking Carrying the stick above shoulder level.

hooking A minor penalty is imposed on a player who impedes or tries to impede an opponent by hooking with the stick.

icing the puck Illegal defensive move called when a player shoots the puck from his own half across the opponents' goal line; or when the player attempted to pass the puck to a teammate who failed to touch it .

interference A minor penalty is imposed if a player interferes with or impedes the progress of an opponent not in possession of the puck.

offside An illegal move that occurs when a player enters his team's attacking zone ahead of the puck; or when the puck is passed from the defending zone to a teammate beyond the centerline.

penalty box Area by the side of the rink to which players who break the rules are temporarily banished.

penalty killers Substitutes sent on to keep opponents away from the danger zone in front of goal by forming a square.

penalty shots Awarded for infringements, these are free shots at a goal defended only by the goalie.

power play This occurs when a team sends all its players except the goalie in a drive against the opponents' goal.

screening Blocking the goalie's view.

shut-out Achieved by a goalie who survives a match or period without allowing a goal.

stick checking Using the stick to hook the puck away from an opponent's stick.

Judo

atemiwaza Technique of striking or kicking to disable the opponent.

belt Color of belts show proficiency of contestants.

chui One of four penalties awarded for infringements.

dan One of 12 top grades for proficiency.

dojo practice hall.

hajime Refereee's call to start the match.

hansokomake Disqualification.

judogi costume

judoka learners

kanstsuwaza joint lock

kata Two fighters displaying routines of attack and defense in formal competition.

katamewaza Holding technique.

keioku One of four penalties for infringements.

matte Referee's call for a temporary halt.

nagewaza throwing technique

ne-waza ground technique

randori free fighting

shai a contest

shiaijo contest area

shido Minor penalty for infringement.

sono-mama Referee's command to "freeze."

tachiwaza Standing or throwing techniques.

yame Referee's call for temporary halt.

tsurikomishi-ashi footsweep maneuver

utsuri-goshi A maneuver known as countering.

ne-wasa

Motor Racing

drag racing High speed events to record the fastest time over a given distance. Cars compete in pairs on a straight paved track called a drag strip at speeds that may top 260 mph.

endurance racing Sports car events such as Le Mans lasting 3 to 24 hours. First to complete the distance or cover the most laps in the time wins.

Fédération International de l'Automobile (FIA) Organization established in 1904 to supervise international automobile racing.

fuel cell Safety petrol container in a leak-resistant metal or plastic tank.

Grand Prix "Large Prize" events for Formula One cars, which compete for the World Drivers' Championship.

Indianapolis 500 Race for Indy (Indianapolis) cars, which resemble Formula One cars. It takes place on the 2-mile Indianapolis Motor Speedway.

monocoque Racing car design whose central structure is a shell of strong, lightweight material such as aluminum or carbon fiber, with no separate chassis and body.

off-road racing Long distance events over rough, desert courses, usually for small trucks.

oval tracks Racing tracks, usually from about 0.25 mile to more than 2 miles long, with straightways and banked curves.

pits Special areas along racing tracks for refueling and servicing the cars.

power-to-weight formula Formula that allows cars of inferior horsepower to weigh less than competing cars with more powerful engines.

rallies Long-distance events for production models with driver and navigator, usually held on public roads.

road-racing courses Courses that resemble country roads, with hills, straightways, and unbanked curves.

roll bar Protective metal bar that arches over the driver in an open cockpit.

roll cage Structure of steel tubes in an enclosed car that supports the roof should the car overturn.

round-the-houses Events, such as in Monaco, held on temporarily cleared city streets.

sprint cars Cars, slightly bigger than midget cars, with a tall, narrow body, front engine, and open wheels, which race on oval tracks.

superspeedways Tracks with wide corners and high banking for speeds of up to 200 mph.

super Vee Cars with a Volkswagen engine, which resemble small Formula One cars. Raced usually by aspiring young drivers.

Trans-Am Championship Series of road races in US and Canada for top production sports cars.

turbocharging Increasing the power of a small engine by means of a turbine driven by the engine's exhaust gases.

Formula One

Indianapolis 500

Polo

penalty goal Awarded if the umpire considers that a goal would have been scored but for a foul by the defending side.

penalty hit Awarded at an appropriate distance by the umpire, according to the gravity of an offense. Failure to carry out penalty hits corrrectly may result in: a penalty goal, allowing members of the team that did not commit the fault to position themselves where they wish, retaking the hit, unless a goal was scored or awarded. Unnecessary delay in taking a free hit may result in the umpire bowling the ball from the same spot.

riding off Bumping between players riding in the same direction is permitted, though not at angles which may be dangerous to other players or their ponies.

right of way Held by the player(s) following the ball on its exact line, or at the smallest angle to it, and taking it on the offside. It is a foul for another player to cross or pull up in the right of way.

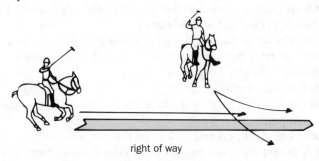

right of way

Pool

block Segment of a match played to an agreed point requirement—usually 150 in title matches.

break shot Opening shot.

bridge Position of the hand on which the cue rests.

cue Tapered stick with a leather tip used for striking the cue ball.

cue ball White ball struck by the cue and propelled onto an object ball.

foot spot Position on the table marking the apex of the racked 15-ball triangle.

head string (scratch line) Line at the top of the table behind which the cue ball is placed to start the game.

jump shot Shot where a player causes the cue ball to rise from the bed of the table.

mechanical bridge (rest) Rod with a metal bridge on which the cue slides, used when taking awkward shots.

racked Fifteen balls arranged in a triangle at the foot spot.

safety play A safety shot allows a player to end his or her turn without penalty. The cue ball must contact a cushion after sriking an object ball, or drive an object ball into a cushion.

strings Imaginary lines through the spots on a table and parallel to the ends of the table.

Rugby

All Blacks Members of New Zealand's international team, so-called because of their black team uniform.

backs The seven players who are not forwards. Made up of scrum halfback, stand-off or outside halfback, four three-quarter halfbacks, and fullback.

blind side The side of the scrum nearest to touch.

British Lions International touring team made up of the best players from England, Scotland, Wales and Ireland.

Calcutta Cup Prize awarded to the winner of the international match between England and Scotland.

conversion

conversion The act of kicking a goal following the scoring of a try; worth an extra two points in addition to the four points (three points in Rugby League) for the try.

dead ball Ball out of play.

drop goal Goal scored by drop-kicking the ball over the crossbar; worth three points.

drop-kick A ball dropped and kicked on the bounce.

drop-out A drop-kick taken from between the posts or from the center of the 24 yd line to bring the ball back into play.

dummy The pretense of passing the ball while still holding on to it.

drop kick

fair catch *See* mark.

Five Nations Championship The traditional competition, played between England, Scotland, Wales, Ireland and France.

forward pass A throw toward the opponents' goal line; an illegal move. All passes must be made laterally or backward.

forwards The eight large, strong players who force the play. In a scrum they are made up of a front row of a hooker flanked by two props, backed by a second row of two lock forwards flanked by two wing forwards, and a solitary No 8 forward at the rear.

five meters scrum A scrum formed 5 m (5.5 yd) from the goal line opposite the place where an infringement has occurred.

free kick An unimpeded kick awarded for a mark.

goal Scored when the ball is kicked over the crossbar.

hand-off Method used by a player carrying the ball to push away a tackling opponent with the palm of his hand.

hooker The central forward in the front row of the scrum whose main job it is to hook the ball with his heel to a teammate.

in-goal Area behind the posts that lies between the goal line and the dead ball line.

knock-on An infringement of playing the ball forward with hand or arm, earning the opponents a scrum (penalty in Rugby Union if deliberate).

line-out A set piece in Union play, for re-starting play after the ball has gone into touch. Some or all of the opposing forwards form two parallel lines at right angles to the touchline and jump for the ball when it is thrown in.

loose scrum *See* ruck.

mark (fair catch) In Union play, the act of a player, standing with both feet on the ground within his 24-yd line, who catches the ball cleanly from an opponent's kick and simultaneously shouts "Mark!", for which he is awarded a free kick.

maul In Union play, a crowd of opposing players pushing against each other and closing around a player who is carrying the ball. The ball must not touch the ground.

no side The end of the game.

offside A player is offside when he is in front of a teammate who has played the ball.

pack Collective name for the forwards.

penalty goal Goal scored direct from a penalty kick; worth three points.

penalty kick Awarded to the non-offending side for an infringement; the opponents must retire at least 10 yds.

penalty try Awarded when a player is illegally stopped from scoring a certain try; worth four points in Rugby Union, three in Rugby League.

place kick

place kick Made by kicking the ball after it has been placed on the ground for that purpose.

punt A ball dropped from the hands and kicked before it touches the ground.

Ranfurly Shield Trophy competed for by the top teams in New Zealand.

ruck (loose scrum) Similar to a maul but with the ball being kicked on the ground; it must not be handled.

scrum Formation in which the forwards link themselves together tightly, lower their heads, and push against the opposing pack. The non-offending side tosses the ball into the tunnel between the packs and the respective hookers try to heel it back to a teammate.

scrum

strike Act of hooking the ball in the front row of the scrum.

strike against the head Describes the opponents' winning of the ball from the opposition in the scrum.

touch Area out of play beyond a touchline.

Triple Crown Imaginary prize, part of the Five Nations Championship, awarded to the home international side of England, Scotland, Wales or Ireland that wins all three of its matches against the other home teams.

try Scored when a player runs through the defense to touch a ball down in the opponents' in-goal area; worth four points in Rugby Union, three in Rugby League.

try

up-and-under A ball kicked toward the opponents' goal line high enough to allow the kicking side to rush after it and be underneath it when it comes down.

Sailing

aback When the wind blows on the wrong side of the sail, preventing forward motion.

abeam At right angles to the length and center of a boat.

aft Toward or at the rear of stern.

America's Cup World's oldest international sailing competition, first won in 1851 by the schooner *America*.

athwart Across the width of a boat.

berth Place reserved for a boat at mooring.

buoys Shaped and colored floats, anchored to the seabed, to indicate channels, obstructions, or moorings.

helmsman Person at the wheel or tiller.

knot One nautical mile (1.2 mi) per hour.

leeward Facing the direction toward which the wind is blowing.

marina Docking facility for sailboats and other pleasure craft.

Olympic classes Seven classes of sailboat eligible for competition in the Olympic games: Finn, Flying Dutchman, 470, Soling, Star, Tornado, Windglider.

twelve-meter formula Complex formula governing a yacht's eligibility for entry into the America's Cup competition.

waterline Line where a boat's hull meets the surface of the water.

windsurfing Sailing across the water while standing on a surfboard equipped with mast and sail.

windward Side of a boat against which the wind blows.

Skiing

Alpine skiing Type of skiing that includes downhill, slalom and giant slalom races.

cross-country skiing

cross-country skiing Form of Nordic skiing, usually over long distances up and down hills and on flat ground.

fall line Most direct route to the bottom of a slope.

gates Two solid uniform flagpoles, alternately blue or red with flags of the same color; used to define twisting slalom courses.

giant slalom A longer kind of slalom with gates farther apart and competitors free to choose their own line between the gates.

jumping Form of Nordic skiing in which competitors take off from a specially constructed hill; each jumps twice to try for the greatest distance.

mogul Snow mound usually formed by many skiers turning in the same place.

Nordic skiing Type of skiing made up of cross-country skiing and ski jumping.

piste Prepared downhill trail.

sitzmark Impression left in the snow by a fallen skier.

slalom Form of alpine skiing made up of two different downhill runs over a winding course marked by gates.

waxing Wax applied to ski bottoms for greater control.

Snooker

balk line A line drawn across the width of the table marking the top quarter. The "D" is marked on this line.

break Sequence of scoring shots.

bridge Position of the hand on which the cue rests.

cue Tapered stick with a leather tip used for striking the cue ball.

cue ball White ball struck by the cue and propeled on to an object ball.

D Semicircle, centered on the balk line, from within which the cue ball is struck at the start of a frame.

frame A complete game.

in-off Foul stroke where the cue ball goes into a pocket after striking the object ball.

mechanical bridge Rod with a metal bridge on which the cue slides.

on ball (object ball) Ball that is next to be struck in a sequence.
pot Scoring stroke in which the object ball is knocked into a
  pocket.

Soccer

corner kick Awarded to the attacking team after the defending
  team has played the ball over its own goal line. A player from
  the attacking team kicks the ball from the quarter circle at a
  corner of the pitch.
cross (center) Ball kicked into the penalty area from near the
  touchline.
dead ball Ball kicked from a stationary position, such as a corner
  or free kick.
defenders Defensive players who try to stop goals being scored
  by the opposing team.
dribbling Trying to beat opponents by running with the ball at
  the feet.
far post Goal post farthest away from the player in possession.
free kick Kick awarded to a team for a foul committed by the
  opponents. A direct free kick is awarded for any of nine specific
  offenses. A goal cannot be scored from an indirect free kick
  without first being touched by a second player.
forwards Offensive players whose job is to score goals
full backs Defenders who patrol the side areas of the field
goal kick Kick taken by the defending team after the attackers
  have kicked the ball over the goal line but not into the goal.
handball Foul committed by a player who deliberately touches
  the ball with a hand or arm.
heading Striking the ball with the head.
kicking (shooting) Striking the ball with the foot.
killing the ball Rendering the ball stationary.

killing the ball

linesman Two linesmen patrol the side of the perimeter field.
  Their job is to indicate with a flag when the ball goes outside
  the perimeter. They also give offside decisions.
marking Staying within playing distance of an opponent.
midfield player Player staying mostly in the central areas of the
  field, linking defense and offense.

near post Goal post nearest to the player in possession.

offside An offensive player is offside if, when the ball is played, he is nearer the opposing goal than, or level with, an opponent, unless he is in his own half of the field or an opponent was the last player to touch the ball.

overhead kick Also known as the bicycle kick due to the cycling movement involved. As the body falls back into a horizontal position, the ball is hooked over the head.

overhead kick

over the top Foul play involving running over the top of the ball and kicking the opponent.

penalty kick Kick awarded for one of nine specific fouls within the penalty area, taken from the penalty spot. All players except the kicker and the goalkeeper must stand outside the penalty area.

red card Displayed by the referee to a player for violent conduct or for a serious foul after having already been cautioned by a yellow card; the player is then sent off the field and no substitute allowed.

referee Arbiter who officiates the game and is also the time keeper.

save Made by the goalkeeper or another player to stop the ball from entering the goal.

set piece Corner, free kick, throw-in , or similar, in which predetermined tactical moves can be carried out.

shoulder charges Legal charges, shoulder to shoulder.

sliding tackle A tackle performed by sliding in feet first to rob the opponent of the ball.

stopper One of two centerbacks.

striker An offensive player who normally stays forward in an attempt to score goals.

sweeper A player operating behind the defensive line of four, sweeping up loose balls.

throw-in Return of the ball to play after it has crossed the touchline to go out of play. The throw must be taken with both hands from behind and over the head by a member of the opposing team to the one which sent it out of play.

volleying Kicking a ball when it is in the air.

wall Line-up of defending players between the ball and the goal to block a free kick at goal. All opponents must be at least 29.5 ft from the ball.

winger Offensive player who attacks down the side areas of the field.

yellow card Displayed by the referee to a player guilty of a serious foul or persistent lesser fouling; constitutes a caution.

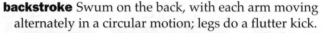
Swimming

backstroke Swum on the back, with each arm moving alternately in a circular motion; legs do a flutter kick.

backstroke

breaststroke Arms are extended in front of the head and swept back on either side; legs do a breaststroke kick.

butterfly Arms plunge forward together in large circular movements; legs make two dolphin kicks with each stroke.

dog paddle Cupped hands rotate in a circular motion under water; legs do a flutter kick.

dolphin kick Both legs move up and down together.

flip turn Underwater somersault to reverse direction after touching the end of the pool.

breaststroke

flutter kick Legs move up and down alternately with a bend at the knees.

freestyle race Race in which swimmers may use any strokes they choose.

front crawl Arms reach forward alternately and pull back through the water; legs use the flutter kick.

butterfly

medley events Races in which individual competitors swim an equal distance for each of four strokes—butterfly, backstroke, breaststroke and freestyle. In medley relays, each swimmer swims one stroke for the set distance—backstroke, breaststroke, butterfly or freestyle.

scissors kick One leg moves forward as the other bends back; they then come together in a scissors-like action.

sidestroke Swum on the side with arms thrusting downward and backward alternately; legs do a scissors kick.

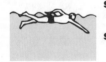
front crawl

spearhead principle In each event, the competitor with the fastest entry time swims in the center lane, with other competitors placed left and right in descending order of speed.

survival bobbing Method of indefinite survival by means of floating on one's front while bobbing up and down on the water's surface.

synchronized swimming Graceful, rhythmic water sport in which swimmers match rhythm and mood to music. A women-only sport.

Table tennis

game Won by the player or pair first scoring 21 points, unless both have scored 20 points, when the winner is the first to score two points more than the opposition.

let When no point is scored, for example, when the ball touches the net in service.

match Best of three or five games.

rally Period when the ball is in play.

receiver Player who strikes the ball second in a rally.

server Player who strikes the ball first in a rally.

Tennis

ace A service winner that the receiver is unable to touch.

advantage The first point served after deuce.

deuce The score after each player has scored three points (40–all). Deuce is also the score of any tied result after 40–all in the same game. If both players score advantage, the score is deuce once more until one player wins two consecutive points to win a game.

fault A service that lands in the net or outside the receiver's service court.

foot fault An illegal move. The server is on or over the base line, or walks or runs while serving.

grand slam The winning of the four major championships in one year (Wimbledon, US Open, French Open and Australian Open).

ground stroke Any stroke played after the ball has bounced once on the court.

let A service that touches the net before dropping into the proper service court. It does not count and has to be replayed.

love A score of zero.

receiver The player receiving service.

seeding The placing of the best players in separate sections of a draw so that they do not meet until the later rounds.

service

service The stroke that starts each point, played from behind the base line into the service court diagonally opposite.

tie-breaker A method of deciding the winner of a set that is tied (usually at 6–all) by playing a certain number of extra points.

cookery

Cooking methods and processes

à la paysanne

acidulate To make food slightly acid (e.g. by adding lemon juice or vinegar).

agitate To gently shake the contents of a pan.

à la paysanne To cut into thin, even pieces that are round, square or triangular.

al dente Pasta which has been cooked so that it is just firm to the bite.

amandine To cook or coat with almonds.

arroser To sprinkle with a liquid, or to baste.

assaisonner to season

bain-marie A form of poaching in which food is placed in a container which is in turn placed into another container (the bain-marie) half full with heated water.

bake To cook in an oven or oven-like appliance.

bake blind To line a pie tin with pastry and bake it before adding the filling.

barbecue To roast slowly over burning coals or under a heat source on a rack or spit.

bard To tie slices of fatty bacon over the breast of poultry or game.

baste

baste To moisten food with the fatty liquid in which it is cooking.

bat out To flatten raw meat slices with a cutlet bat.

beat To make a mixture smooth and aerated by rapidly turning it using a hand beater, electric mixer, wire whisk or spoon.

bind (1) To add eggs, melted fat or cream to a mixture to stick dry ingredients together. (2) To add starch to a liquid to solidify or thicken it.

beat

blanch To plunge food briefly into boiling water and then immediately into cold water.

blend To combine ingredients with a spoon, beater or electric blender until a uniform mixture is achieved.

boil To cook in water at 212 °F. At this temperature water bubbles rapidly.

bone To remove the bones from fish, meat or poultry.

braise To cook meat and/or vegetables by first lightly browning in fat, and then cooking slowly in a tightly covered container with a small quantity of water.

braise

bread To coat food with breadcrumbs, biscuit crumbs or cereal crumbs.

broil To cook food uncovered directly under heat or over an open fire.

brown To make food turn brown on the surface, usually by cooking at a high temperature in a little fat.

brush To spread fat, milk or beaten egg onto the surface of food, using a pastry brush.

caramelize To heat sugar or foods containing sugar until the sugar melts and turns brown.

casserole To cook meat, seafood or poultry with vegetables in the oven in a casserole dish.

chine To separate the backbone from the ribs in a joint of meat.

chop To cut into small pieces.

chop

clarify To make fats clear and free of impurities by heating and draining through a fine filter.

coat a spoon To test the thickness of a sauce: if a spoon dipped into a sauce emerges with a thick, even coating, the consistency is right.

coddle To simmer food in water just below boiling point.

cool (1) To leave food to stand at room temperature until it is no longer warm to the touch. (2) To refrigerate.

cream To beat a mixture with a spoon or mixer until it is the consistency of cream.

cream

crimp (1) To gash or score meat with a knife. (2) To make a decorative border on a pie crust.

curdle To cause a sauce or fresh milk to separate into liquid and solids by overheating.

cure To preserve meat or fish by salting, drying or smoking.

cut in To combine flour and fat or other dry ingredients with a cutting motion, using two knives, until the fat is broken up and coated with flour.

decant (1) To gently pour off a liquid without stirring up any sediment at the bottom. (2) To pour a liquid from one bottle to another.

crimp

deep-fry To fry food by immersing it completely in hot oil.

déglacer To make a sauce or gravy from the juices and food fragments remaining in the bottom of a pan.

dégraisser To skim fat off a liquid.

devil To coat food with a mixture of highly seasoned ingredients (e.g. mustard or hot spices).

dice To cut into small cubes.

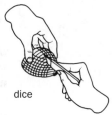

dilute (1) To mix a powder, e.g. flour, with a liquid. (2) To add water to a concentrated liquid.

dice

dot To sprinkle with small pieces of an ingredient, usually fat.

dredge To cover with a sprinkling of flour or sugar.

dress (1) To mix a salad with a sauce or dressing. (2) To remove the head, tail, fins, scales and insides of a fish before cooking. (3) To pluck, draw and truss poultry or game.

dust To sprinkle lightly with flour or sugar.

en papillotte To cook food in tightly sealed, oiled grease-proof paper or foil so that no steam escapes.

fillet To remove the bones and fat from meat, poultry or fish.

flake To break into natural segments.

flambé *See* **flame**.

flame To ignite spirits poured over a dish (as with Christmas pudding).

flour To coat with seasoned flour, usually before frying.

flute To make a decorative indented edging, e.g. around a pie crust.

fold To combine one ingredient or mixture with another by turning them gently with a spatula or metal spoon.

frost To cover a cake with a thin layer of icing sugar.

fry To cook food in fat or oil over direct heat.

garnish To enhance a dish with edible decorations.

glaze To coat food with a shiny liquid finish, e.g. a sauce or syrup.

grate To shred food by rubbing it against a grater.

grease To coat the inside of a pan or dish with fat.

grill The British and Canadian term for cooking uncovered food directly under heat or over an open fire (broil).

hang To suspend game in a dry, cool place to allow time for enzymes to tenderize and improve the flavor of the flesh.

hull To remove the leaves and stems from soft fruit.

infuse To flavor a liquid by soaking herbs, leaves or other ingredients in it.

joint To divide game, meat or poultry into pieces.

julienne To cut vegetables into fine strips.

julienne

knead To stretch, press and fold dough or a similar mixture until it has a smooth texture.

knock up To encourage flaky pastry layers to separate during cooking by making small cuts in the edges.

lard To thread thin strips of fat through meat which is too lean.

leaven To use an ingredient such as yeast, baking powder or eggs to make other ingredients rise in cooking.

line To place greaseproof or wax paper inside a cooking tin.

knead

macerate To soak food in a liquid.

marinate To tenderize and flavor food before cooking by soaking it in a seasoned liquid.

microwave To cook or reheat food in a microwave oven.

mix To combine ingredients by continuous stirring.

mouler To grind dry food into a powder or soft food into a purée.

oil a mould To brush oil over the insides of a container to prevent food from sticking to it.

parblanch To remove salt or strong tastes from food by boiling it for a short time and then plunging it into cold water.

parboil To boil until partially cooked.

pare To peel the skin from a food.

pass To pass ingredients through a strainer or sieve.

pasteurize To kill microorganisms in milk by heating.

peel To take the skin off something, usually a fruit or vegetable.

pickle To preserve meat or vegetables in a vinegar or salt solution.

pipe To decorate by applying icing, purée, butter, etc., through a forcing bag and nozzle.

pipe

pluck To remove the feathers from poultry or a game bird.

poach To cook food very gently in a simmering liquid, just below boiling point.

pot roast (pôelé) To cook large cuts of meat by browning in fat and then cooking slowly in a covered pot.

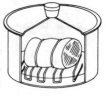
pot roast

preheat To set an oven at the desired cooking temperature some time before it is needed so that the food to be cooked is placed into an oven that is already hot.

preserve To treat food so that it keeps in good condition.

pressure cook To cook food using steam under pressure in a special sealable pot.

prove To allow a yeast dough to rise and expand by leaving it to rest in a warm place.

pulp To reduce food to a soft mass by boiling or crushing.

purée To sieve, mash or liquidize food into a smooth, thick paste.

raise To use an ingredient such as yeast, baking powder or eggs to make other ingredients rise in cooking.

réchauffer to reheat

reconstitute To restore concentrated food to its original state by adding water.

reduce To concentrate a liquid by boiling it without a cover, causing water to evaporate.

rehydrate To soak dried foods so that they reabsorb water.

relax To let pastry stand, especially after rolling out, so that it is not stretched.

rest To let batter stand for half an hour to allow starch grains to swell before cooking.

rissoler To fry to a golden brown.

roast To cook food in heated air, usually in an oven.

rub To rub fat and flour together with the fingers until the mixture resembles breadcrumbs.

rub

sauté To cook food rapidly in a frying pan using a small amount of fat, until it turns golden-brown.

scald (1) To pour boiling water over something. (2) To heat milk

sa*u*té

until it begins to bubble and rise.

scallop To alternate solid food with layers of creamy sauce.

score To make a series of shallow cuts on the surface of food.

seal To seal the outside surface of meat by heating it quickly in an oven or pan so that color and juices are retained.

sear To brown the surface of food by cooking over direct heat or in the oven at high temperature.

season To improve the flavor of something by adding salt, pepper, spices or herbs.

shallow-fry To fry food using just enough preheated fat to stop the food sticking to the pan.

shell To remove nuts from their shells, or peas from their pods.

shred To cut food into slivers.

sift To remove lumps from or thoroughly mix ingredients by passing them through a sieve.

simmer To cook food gently just below boiling point, at around 185–200 °F.

singe To brown or color by applying heat to the surface.

skewer To fasten food onto a pointed wooden or metal stick.

skim

skim To remove fat or scum from the surface of a liquid.

skin To remove the skin from food.

slake To mix cornflour or a similar ingredient with a cold liquid to make a thin paste before adding a hot liquid to cook the starch.

souse To pickle food in vinegar or salt water.

steam To cook food in steam (moist heat).

sterilize To destroy dangerous organisms by heat.

stew To simmer food gently, usually in the oven.

skin

stir To mix something gently, using circular motions with a spoon.

stir-fry To cook small pieces of food in a wok over high heat.

strain To separate solids from liquids using a sieve or muslin.

sweat To cook vegetables very slowly in butter or oil.

tenderize To make meat more tender by beating with a meat mallet or by adding certain herbs, spices and juices.

toast To brown food in a dry heat.

toss (1) To turn over the contents of a pan by throwing the food lightly upwards. (2) To use utensils to lift and turn a salad, mixing it with a dressing in the process.

truss To secure poultry with string and/or skewers so that it will hold its shape during cooking.

strain

whip To beat very rapidly, using a hand or electric whisk, until the liquid becomes foamy.

whisk To beat air into eggs, cream or batter using a looped wire utensil (a whisk).

Cooking ingredients

agar-agar A vegetarian gelatine, made from seaweed.

alfalfa A plant with tiny seeds which are sprouted and used in salads or casseroles.

allumettes Vegetables cut into thin strips.

anaheim A mild-tasting chilli with bright green pod, 5–7 in long. Used in Mexican cooking.

arrowroot A fine-grained starch prepared from the rhizomes of a tropical plant. Excellent for thickening sauces.

arugula *See* **rocket**.

asafetida A pungent brown resin used in Indian cooking.

balsamic vinegar Vinegar flavored with plant extracts. Has a sweet flavor and relatively low acidity.

bamboo shoots The young shoots of a tall tropical grass. Used in Oriental cooking.

basmati rice A fine-grained, aromatic rice from North India and Pakistan.

bean curd Milky, white, custard-like squares made from soaked, mashed and strained soya beans. Used in Asian cooking.

bean sauce A fine or coarse purée of fermented soya beans. Used in Oriental cooking.

benne oil The Malaysian term for sesame oil.

bhindi Oblong sticky green vegetable pod used in Indian cooking.

bitter gourd A courgette-shaped vegetable of the marrow family. Used in Asian cooking.

black salt Dark, pungent salt used in Indian cooking.

blini A Russian pancake made of buckwheat and yeast.

bottarga The dried and salted roe (eggs) of mullet and tuna. Used in Italian cooking.

bhindi

bouillon The unclarified stock or broth from fish, meat or vegetables.

bouquet garni A bunch of herbs, including marjoram, thyme, and parsley. Used to flavor stews and soups.

brioche A slightly sweet, soft bread roll made from a light yeast dough.

bulgar wheat Cracked kernels of boiled and dried wheat. Used in Middle Eastern cooking.

Californian green chilli *See* **anaheim**.

cantaloupe A variety of melon with a ribbed rind and orange flesh.

capers The buds of a Mediterranean shrub. Used pickled in sauces and garnishes.

carambola A yellow fruit from an Indonesian tree. Used to

carambola

decorate fruit salads and ice cream.

carob flour A chocolate-like powder prepared by grinding the ripe dried pod of the carob tree. Used in cakes and biscuits or to make drinks, desserts and candy.

cassava A root vegetable resembling a large, brown sweet potato.

caviar The salted roe (eggs) of sturgeon.

cayenne pepper A hot condiment, made from the dried red seeds and pods of a tropical plant.

celeriac A type of celery with a large turnip-like root.

chantilly Slightly sweetened whipped cream, sometimes flavored with vanilla.

chapati flour Finely ground wholewheat flour, usually made from wheat that is low in gluten. Used to make many kinds of Indian breads.

chard A variety of leaf vegetable with succulent leaves and thick stalks.

chiffonade A garnish of shredded lettuce, spinach and sorrel.

Chinese peas *See* **snow peas.**

celeriac

chorizo A highly seasoned, smoked pork sausage used in Spanish and Mexican cooking.

choux pastry Light pastry made by beating eggs into a cooked paste of flour, fat and water.

clotted cream A very thick cream which can be spread.

coquille The French term for scallop.

corn flour The British term for cornstarch.

cotechino A variety of Italian spiced pork sausage.

coulis A concentrated liquid, usually from fish or meat, obtained by long slow cooking.

crème fraîche Matured, lightly fermented cream which has not been allowed to go sour.

crêpe A thin pancake.

croûtons Small cubes or other shapes of bread, deep-fried until golden and used as a garnish.

curd A semi-solid substance formed by the coagulation of milk.

dashi A clear stock made from tuna and seaweed. Used in Japanese cooking.

doong gwooh A Chinese dried mushroom, brownish-black in color, with a stronger and more distinctive flavor than fresh mushrooms.

dripping The fat that exudes from meat, poultry or game during roasting.

dumpling A small ball of dough, usually cooked and served with stew, or in a soup.

duxelle A purée of finely chopped mushrooms, cooked in butter with chopped shallots. Used for stuffing meat or as a basis for sauces.

eggplant The large, egg-shaped dark purple fruit of the eggplant.

endive A lettuce-like vegetable, the frilly leaves of which are used in salads.

escalopes Thin slices of meat, usually veal, which are beaten flat and shallow fried.

aubergine

farina Fine flour made from wheat, potatoes and nuts.

felafel Ground chickpeas shaped into balls and deep fried. Used in eastern Mediterranean dishes.

filo pastry Made from paper-thin sheets of pastry dough. Used in Greek cooking.

fines herbes A mixture of finely chopped chervil, chives, parsley and tarragon.

endive

foie gras The preserved livers of specially fattened ducks or geese.

fumet The concentrated liquid in which fish, meat or vegetables has been cooked.

galanga root A root of the ginger family. Used in Southeast Asian cooking.

garam masala A mixture of spices, including cinnamon, cardamom, and cloves. Hot to the taste and used in Indian cooking.

garbanzos The Spanish and Mexican term for chickpeas.

gelatine A solid protein made by boiling animal bones and hides. Used to make jellies and other gelatinous foods.

ghee Butter which has been clarified by boiling and is totally free of milk solids. It has a nutty flavor and is used in Indian dishes.

giblets The edible internal organs and trimmings of poultry and game, including the gizzard, liver, heart, and neck.

ginseng A Korean root used in salads, for flavoring, and to make ginseng tea.

glace de viande A concentrated meat stock.

gnocchi Dumplings made from semolina paste, potatoes or choux pastry.

golden syrup The uncrystalizable liquid which remains after cane sugar is finally crystalized; similiar to a light molasses or heavy corn syrup.

grappa An Italian spirit made from the remains of grapes after they have been used for wine making.

gravlax A dry-cured salmon, marinated in sugar, salt and spices. Used in Scandinavian cuisine.

grissini breadsticks

guava

guava A tropical edible fruit, which turns from green to yellow when ripe. The fruit is best stewed or made into jam or jelly.

hoisin sauce A thick red sauce that is sweet in flavor. Used in Chinese cooking with shellfish, spareribs, duck and vegetables.

icing A sweet coating used to decorate cakes, etc.

jalapeño A very hot, dark green chilli, about 2 in long. Used in Mexican cooking.

jus The French term for the juice from roasting meat.

lady's finger *See* bhindi.

lard Natural or refined fat from a pig.

leaven A raising agent, such as yeast, that causes dough or batter to rise.

legumes Vegetables, especially beans or peas.

lemon grass A tall, greyish-green grass used for its aroma and flavor in Southeast Asian cooking. Gives a lemon-peel-like flavor.

luganega A lightly spiced variety of Italian pork sausage.

lychee A tropical fruit with a translucent flesh in a papery skin.

mangetout A variety of pea in which the vegetable pod is also edible.

mango An Asian fruit with sweet orange flesh.

maple syrup The concentrated sweet sap of the sugar maple and black maple, used to make candy and puddings, and as a sweetener on pancakes.

marinade A seasoned blend of oil, wine or vinegar in which food

lychee

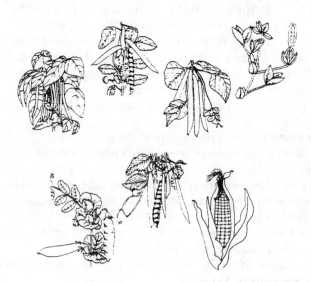

legumes

is soaked before cooking.

marsala A fortified wine used in Italian cooking.

mascarpone A thick Italian cream cheese made from cow's milk, and used in sweet and savory dishes.

medallions Small circular cuts of fish, meat or pâté.

mirabelle A small yellow plum, used as a pie filling.

mirin A thick sweet Japanese wine used for cooking.

miso A variety of pastes made from fermented soya beans and grains. Used as a flavoring in Japanese cooking.

molasses A by-product of sugar refining that can be used as a spread or in a similar way to golden syrup in recipes.

moules The French term for mussels.

noodles Flat ribbons of pasta.

nori The Japanese term for seaweed.

okra *See* **bhindi**.

panada A mixture of flour and water, or of bread soaked in milk, used to bind ingredients and as a thickening agent. Used in Spanish and South American cooking.

pancetta A mild, unsmoked Italian bacon.

papaya (pawpaw) A Caribbean fruit with sweet yellow flesh and small black seeds.

pearl barley Barley which has been ground into small round grains. Used in soups and stews.

papaya

pectin A substance extracted from ripe fruit and vegetables which is used to set jams and jellies.

pesto A pasta sauce made with oil, parmesan cheese, garlic, nuts, and basil leaves.

petit pois Tiny sweet green peas.

pignoli The Italian term for pine nuts.

pimiento A small, red, mild, Spanish pepper, used in salads or as a stuffing for green olives.

pine nuts Seeds from Mediterranean pine cones, with a delicate nutty flavor. Used in Italian, Spanish, and Middle Eastern dishes. Also known as pine kernels.

petit pois

pith In citrus fruit, the soft fibrous tissue lining the inside of the rind.

poblano A hot, dark green chilli of triangular shape and about 4 in long. Used in Mexican dishes.

porcini A fungus used in Italian cooking. It is usually dried.

prosciutto The Italian term for ham. There are several regional varieties (e.g. Prosciutto di Parma, which is known in English as Parma Ham).

pulp The fleshy tissue of fruits and vegetables.

purée Raw or cooked food forced through a sieve or processed in an electric liquidizer.

ratafia A flavoring made from bitter almonds.

relish A spicy sauce made with fruit or vegetables.

rennet A substance containing the enzyme renin, extracted from the stomach lining of calves and used to coagulate milk for making cheese.

rocket A peppery salad leaf plant widely used in Italian cooking.

roux A mixture of equal parts of flour and melted butter. Used as a base for savory sauces.

sake Japanese rice wine.

salami A highly seasoned Italian pork sausage.

sauerkraut Shredded and pickled cabbage. Used in German cuisine.

scallion A collective term for salad vegetables with small root bulbs and long leaves, e.g. green onion.

scaloppine Small escalopes of veal, about 3 in square and weighing 1–1½ oz.

seasoned flour Flour flavored with salt and pepper.

seasoning Salt, pepper, herbs or spices added to food to enhance flavor.

shallot

sesame oil An aromatic oil, particularly the unrefined, thick brownish version, made from sesame seeds. Used more as a flavoring than as a cooking oil.

shallot A vegetable similar to the onion.

shiitake A Japanese mushroom.

snow peas Very small peas in flat pea pods, eaten pod and all (known as mangetout peas).

soya beans Round, dull-yellow beans, used to make soya milk and bean curd, and which may be boiled or fried. Available in dried form.

soy sauce Sauces made from fermented soya beans, ranging in flavor from light to salty to syrupy-sweet.

squash

squash The American and Canadian term for a family of marrow-like vegetables.

starch Carbohydrate from cereals and potatoes.

star fruit *See* **carambola.**

suet The fat around beef and lamb kidneys and loins.

sugar snap peas Similar to snow peas but plumper. Eaten whole (known as mangetout peas).

Swiss chard *See* **chard.**

taco A filled tortilla, usually fried.

tahini A paste made from sesame seeds. Used in Middle Eastern sauces and dips.

tapioca *See* **cassava.**

tofu Unfermented soya bean curd, made from soya bean milk.

tortilla A form of flat unleavened bread, originating in Mexico.

truffle A rare European mushroom-like fungus, black or white in color. Regarded as a delicacy.

tutti-frutti Small pieces of candied mixed fruits, fresh or dried, added to ice-cream.

unleavened bread Bread which is made without a raising agent.

vanilla sugar Sugar flavored with vanilla.

vinaigrette A salad dressing made from oil, vinegar, salt and pepper, and sometimes flavored with herbs.

vinegar A clear, sour-tasting liquid, consisting of impure dilute acetic acid, made by the fermentation of wine, cider or malt beer.

water chestnut A dark, chestnut-sized bulb, grown in water. Used in Oriental cooking.

whey The liquid that separates from the curd when milk is coagulated for cheese-making.

yam A root of tropical climbing plants and a staple food in parts of Africa.

yeast Fungus cells used in raising dough for bread and for fermenting alcohol.

yogurt A thick custard-like food, prepared by curdling milk using bacteria; often sweetened and flavored with fruit or used plain in savory dishes.

zest The grated rind of citrus fruits.

zucchini A long, smooth-skinned green variety of squash.

zucchini

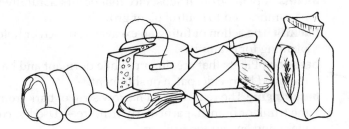

gardening

accent plant A design term for a plant that contrasts with its neighbors and so catches the eye.

adventitious Growth produced where it does not normally occur. For example, roots or buds produced along stems.

aeration Mechanical loosening of the soil surface to allow air to penetrate deeply. Spiking of lawns to achieve the same result.

aerial root A root produced above soil level.

acid soil A soil that contains little lime (calcium) and has a pH of less than 7. The soil needed to grow acid-loving (lime-hating) plants, such as azaleas and rhododendron.

air-layering A method of propagation where the stem of a plant is wounded and packed with sphagnum moss which is kept moist by wrapping in polythene. After rooting, the stem can be severed and potted up.

air-layering

alkaline soil A soil that contains a lot of lime (calcium) and has a pH of more than 7.

alpine Any herbaceous plant or small shrub that grows above the tree line in mountainous regions. Term often loosely applied to other plants grown for growing in a rock garden.

amendment An ingredient such as peat or sand that is used to improve the soil.

annual Any plant that completes its lifecycle in a single growing season.

anti-transpirant A chemical that is sprayed onto foliage to prevent water loss through transpiration. Often used on transplanted evergreens.

aquatic A plant that grows with its base in water, including marginal, submerged and floating.

auxins A plant growth substance that occurs naturally and can be synthesized to control plant growth.

backfill The action of filling an excavated trench or hole, while planting for example.

bare-root Plants that are dug up while dormant and have the soil removed before despatch or shipment.

bark-ringing The removal of a narrow strip of bark from around the trunk or branch, particularly fruit trees. Used to control vigor and encourage fruiting.

bark-ringing

base dressing An application of fertilizer or manure to the soil before planting or sowing.

bed system A method of growing vegetables intensively in blocks separated by narrow paths.

biennial A plant that dies after its second growing season, usually not flowering until the second year.

biennial bearing When a fruiting plant produces heavy and
light crops in alternate years.

blanching A method of excluding light from growing stems or
leaves to keep them succulent.

bleed The loss of sap by a plant through a cut or wound.

blind A flowering plant that fails to produce flowering shoots.

blown The overdevelopment of a flower or heart-producing
vegetable, such as cabbage or cauliflower.

bog plant A plant that grows in permanently moist soil, such as
that found by streams and ponds.

bolting The premature opening of flowers and production of
seed, sometimes brought on by stress due to heat or drought.

bracts Modified leaves produced to protect embryo flowers.
Usually inconspicuous but can also be brightly colored and
collectively have the appearance of a flower.

broadcast A method of spreading seed (or fertilizer) evenly over
a wide area by scattering.

bulb fiber A special compost made from a mixture of peat,
charcoal and oystershell for growing bulbs in containers
without drainage holes.

callus The healing tissue produced by plants to cover a wound
resulting from a cut or other physical damage.

capillary matting An water-absorbent mat that draws water by
capillary action from a reservoir. Container-grown plants
placed on the mat can draw water as required.

capping A solid crust-like layer that forms on the surface of
compacted soil, often caused by heavy rain.

certified stock Plants certified by government bodies
(Department of Agriculture in the USA and the Ministry of
Agriculture, Fisheries and Food in the UK) as being healthy and
free of disease.

chilling The dormant period that some plants need to experience
to initiate flowering.

chlorosis The yellowing of leaves usually caused by a deficiency
of iron.

clamp A traditional method of storing rootcrop vegetables
outdoors with a layer of straw and soil for insulation and a
central chimney for ventilation.

cloche A portable protective structure usually made from
polythene, plastic or glass. They can usually be placed in a line
to warm prepared soil before sowing or to protect a row of
early sowings from frost.

clone A group of genetically identical plants produced by
vegetative propagation, such as by cutting, grafting or division.

blanching

cloche

coldframe A small, unheated, glazed garden structure with hinged or removable top, used to protect plants from the cold.

companion planting A method of discouraging pest attack by positioning plants that are thought to deter pests alongside susceptible crops.

compost (1) A material either based on loam, peat or a peat substitute, such as coir, used for potting up plants in containers. (2) An organic material that results from the decomposition by bacteria and fungi of waste matter, such as grass clippings, prunings and leaves. It can be incorporated into the soil to act as a soil improver or used as a mulch.

contact action The method by which certain weedkillers and pesticides affect only what they come in direct contact with.

coppice The pruning back to ground level each spring of decorative shrubs or trees to produce colorful stems or more attractive foliage.

coppice

cordon The pruning and training method that results in a single stemmed plant. Used for dwarf fruiting trees, tomatoes and related plants.

corm A swollen stem that has a bulb-like appearance, but without the scales of true bulbs. Corms usually have a papery outer skin. Unlike tubers, a new corm is produced annually.

crop rotation A growing method which helps prevent the buildup of soilborne pests and diseases. The vegetable plot is divided into three or four areas each of which is used to grow a specific family of related crops (e.g. the cabbage family). These areas are rotated annually.

crown (1) The upper part of a tree where the branches form the canopy. (2) The base of a herbaceous plant where the stems join and new shoots are produced each year.

cultivar ("cultivated variety") A cultivated plant that has one or more distinctive characteristics which make it different from other plants, characteristics which are preserved when the plant is propagated.

cutting A method of propagating a plant vegetatively by cutting off a leaf, shoot, root or bud, and encouraging the development of new roots.

cuttings

damping down A method of increasing humidity and reducing the temperature of a greenhouse in hot weather by wetting the floors and staging with water.

dead-heading A technique of removing old flowers once they start to fade. This prevents them looking unsightly and encourages the plant to produce further flushes of flowers.

dibber A tool used to make small planting holes for seedlings, rooted cuttings, and young plants.

dieback Dead shoot tips of plants caused by cold, wind chill, or disease.

dioecious A term that indicates that male and female flowers are produced on separate plants.

disbudding The selective removal of some immature buds to encourage those that remain to produce better quality flowers or fruit.

division (1) A method of propagating a herbaceous plant vegetatively by lifting the crown and cutting it into small sections each with roots and shoots. (2) A useful technique for reinvigorating an old herbaceous plant using the same method.

division of plants

dormancy A period of no growth when deciduous hardy plants loose their leaves and herbaceous plants die back to a crown beneath the ground.

double digging A method of deep cultivation where the soil is worked to twice the depth of a spade by first digging a trench and then digging the bottom of the trench.

drill A method of sowing seed in rows in well prepared soil by creating a narrow furrow using the corner of a hoe or other tool and sowing seed thinly in the bottom of the furrow.

drip line The point where the canopy of a tree or shrub sheds water, forming a wet ring around the plant after rain.

earthing up (1) A technique where soil is drawn up around the base of a plant to keep it stable in windy weather. (2) A technique of drawing soil up around stems to encourage blanching. (3) A technique where soil is drawn up around the stems to encourage stem rooting.

epiphyte A plant which does not root in the soil, but grows on another plant without being parasitic. It draws moisture and nourishment from the atmosphere. Examples include many orchids, bromeliads and ferns.

espalier A pruning and training method of fruit trees where the main stem is trained vertically with branches either side trained horizontally to form evenly spaced layers in a single plane.

espalier

fastigiate A form of growth where the branches grow up vertically almost parallel to the main stem.

floating cloche A sheet of translucent and porous fabric which is laid on top of a crop to keep out pests and trap the warmth of the sun.

force A technique of inducing a plant to flower, fruit, or grow out of season by controlling the environment.

formative pruning A method of pruning during the early years of a tree to establish a framework of branches.

friable Soil with a breadcrumb-like appearance which is easily worked.

graft

frost pocket An area, such as behind a solid barrier on a slope or in a hollow, that traps dense cold air and so is prone to frosts.

girdling (**1**) The removal of bark from right around the trunk or branch of a tree or shrub caused by pests, such as rabbits and deer. (**2**) *See* **bark-ringing**.

graft A propagation method which joins the top-growth of one plant (scion) to the root system of another (rootstock) to form a single plant.

green manure A leafy crop, such as lupins or mustard, that is grown to dig back into the soil to enrich it.

ground cover Low-growing plants that are grown to smother the ground and suppress weeds.

hardening off A technique of acclimatizing tender plants raised under cover to the prevailing conditions outside.

heeling in A method of planting temporarily until the specimen can be planted out in its final position.

humus The organic content of soil produced as a result of the decomposition of plants and animals.

hydroculture A technique where plants are grown in nutrient enriched water rather than soil or compost.

hydroponics A method of growing plants in inert granules irrigated by a solution of nutrients.

intercropping A method of growing quick-maturing vegetables between widely spaced, longer-term crops to make efficient use of the growing area.

knot garden

knot garden A garden design based on an intricate pattern of beds, often geometric and symmetrical, edged by low-growing clipped hedges.

layering A method of propagation where a wounded stem is encouraged to root in soil or compost while still attached to the parent plant.

leaching The loss of soluble nutrients from soil or compost.

leaf mold The pleasant-smelling, flaky material that results from the decomposition of leaves.

lime Compounds of calcium (mainly calcium carbonate and calcium hydroxide) added to a soil to make it more alkaline.

loam A medium-texture soil that is rich in humus and contains roughly equal parts of sand, silt and clay particles. It is usually well drained and easy to work.

maincrop Varieties of vegetables that grow during the main part of the growing season.

marginal A plant that grows with its roots submerged in the shallows at the edge of a pond or stream.

marginal plants

monoecious A term that indicates that male and female flowers are produced separately, but on the same plant.

mulch A technique of adding a layer to the surface of the soil to suppress weeds and prevent water loss through evaporation. There are three main types: fabric sheet mulches; organic loose mulches, such as chipped bark; and inorganic loose mulches, such as gravel or pebbles.

naturalized (1) Bulbs planted to appear as if they were natural, either in grass or under the canopy of trees and shrubs. (2) An introduced plant behaving like a native by growing freely in the wild.

naturalized bulbs

node The joint on a stem where a leaf, stem, shoot, or flower are produced.

nutrients The soluble minerals required by plants to grow. Nitrogen, phosphorus and potassium are required in large amounts, while minor nutrients include boron, calcium, iron, manganese, magnesium and molybdenum.

organic (1) Chemical compounds containing carbon resulting from the decomposition of plants and animals. (2) Term applied to some composts and mulches derived from plants. (3) Method of growing plants without using man-made chemicals.

peat There are two types: sphagnum peat is produced partially decayed sphagnum moss, and sedge peat from partially decayed sedges and heathers.

perennial Any plant that lives for three or more years. There are two types: woody perennials, such as trees and shrubs; and herbaceous perennials, which do not have any woody stems above ground.

pH scale A 1 to 14 scale that measures alkalinity or acidity: pH7 is neutral, below 7 is acid and above 7 is alkaline.

pinching out A technique where the growing point of a stem is removed to encourage a plant to produce bushy growth and flowers.

pleaching A training method where the branches of a hedge are intertwined to form a wall of foliage.

plunge A method of protecting the roots of container plants over winter by sinking the pot rim-deep in sand or peat.

pinching out

pollarding A pruning method where the new growth of a tree is cut back to the main stem or a framework of stubby branches.

potting on A technique of moving a container plant into a larger pot.

potting up A method of moving young plants or rooted cuttings individually into containers.

pricking out A technique of moving seedlings from where they germinated and spacing them in pots or trays.

renewal pruning A method of pruning new growth to replace exhausted old branches, particularly on trained fruit trees.

revert Where stems of a variegated plant change to produce plain green leaves.

rootball (1) The roots and compost of a container-grown plant. (2) A technique for digging up a plant growing in soil so that the soil remains intact around its roots. Usually used for fibrous rooted conifers and other evergreens.

rootbound Encircling roots at the bottom the rootball of a container-grown plant that indicate it has been left too long in too small a pot.

root crop A vegetable, such as beetroot, carrot, parsnip and potato, that is grown for its edible roots.

rooting hormone A chemical preparation in either liquid or powder form that is used to encourage root production.

rootstock (1) The bottom portion (root system) of a grafted plant. (2) The crown of a herbaceous plant.

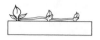

runner

runner A stem that grows horizontally on the soil surface and roots at the nodes (leaf joints) as it spreads.

scarifying (1) A technique of removing thatch (moss and dead grass that builds up in grassed areas) using a rake or powered scarifier. (2) A seed treatment where the seed coat is abraded to promote speedy water absorption and, thus, quicker germination.

scion The bud or stem of a desired variety that is grafted on to the rootstock (root system) of another plant.

seedhead

seedhead (1) A term used to describe the inflorescence that contains developing seed of some plants, particularly grasses. (2) A generic term used to describe the inedible fruit that contains ripe seed.

self-sow (or self-seeding) A term that describes a plant that, without assistance, sheds viable seed which germinate around the parent plant.

sheet mulch *See* **mulch**

snag A short stub left behind after incorrect pruning which is prone to disease infection.

spit The depth of a spade's blade, usually about 10 inches.

sport A spontaneous mutation, or genetic change, where a plant is distinctly different from its parent (e.g. has variegated foliage).

spray A group of flowers produced from one branching stem.

spur A short stubby branch on fruit trees that produces flowers and subsequently fruit.

standard (1) A tree or shrub pruned and trained with a clean stem. (2) The upright petal at the back of pea or bean flower.

station sow A method of sowing seed at set intervals in small groups along a row.

stratify A seed treatment where seed is stored in hot or cold conditions to overcome dormancy and promote germination.

subsoil The layer of soil below topsoil which has a poorer structure and is usually less fertile.

sucker Any shoot that is produced from underground buds on the roots or stem. On grafted plants, any shoot produced from below the graft.

systemic action The method by which certain weedkillers and pesticides are absorbed into and distributed around the whole plant.

sucker

taproot The thick and strong downward-growing root produced by some plants, shrubs, and trees.

tender Describes plants damaged by freezing temperatures.

terminal bud The bud at the end of each stem.

terrestrial Describes plants that grow in the soil.

thatch The build-up of dead organic matter and moss at soil level.

thinning (1) Reducing the number of seedlings in a row so that they are spaced correctly. (2) The pruning out of selected stems to improve air circulation and vigor. (3) The removal of excessive developing fruits to improve the quality of those that remain.

thinning fruit

tilth Soil with a breadcrumb-like appearance that is easily worked.

top-dress An application of fertilizer or manure to the soil surface after planting.

topiary A method of pruning trees and shrubs to produce formal geometric or decorative shapes.

topsoil The layer of soil that lies on the surface that is normally well-structured and fertile.

trace elements Chemical elements needed by plants in very small amounts (also known at micronutrients).

transplanting A method of moving established garden plants to a new position.

variegated Plants with foliage marked striped or blotched with white, cream or other color to produce an irregular pattern.

water shoots Upright growing vigorous shoots that sometime arise around pruning cuts on trees.

windbreak A fence, hedge or mixed border of trees and shrubs that filter the wind and provide shelter.

windrock The buffeting effect of wind that results in distablized plants with loosened root systems.

wound paint A chemical preparation applied to large pruning wounds to help prevent infection by fungal spores.

Notes

NOTES

word	definition

word | **definition**